# Discretionary Land Use Controls
### Avoiding Invitations to Abuse of Discretion

## by Brian W. Blaesser

## Robinson & Cole LLP
*Boston • Hartford • Stamford • Greenwich • New York*

## WEST GROUP

A THOMSON COMPANY

ISBN 0–8366–1469–0

Bancroft-Whitney • Clark Boardman Callaghan • Lawyers Cooperative Publishing • WESTLAW® • West Publishing

To Grażyna, Brandon, Alan,
and my parents

# Foreword

Brian Blaesser's timely book is important and unique because it explains to those people moving through the American land use system the practical ways of successfully dealing with government's discretionary land use controls. This book is necessary because the author has seen it all. So, too, I suspect, has the reader. We all have, though we may not always wish to admit it. We've seen the planning commission staffer who bends the application of an environmental guideline to the breaking point, even though it drives up the cost of middle-class housing in a proposal that comports with all aspects of the master plan, zoning ordinance, and subdivision regulations. We've encountered the developer who seeks a commercial rezoning by promising to abide by a master plan's buffer area height limit and then, once the site is rezoned, returns a few years later and convinces a pliant local council that only by quadrupling the allowed height on his site will commercial development be desirable. And we've come across the elected or appointed officials who render a land use decision based not on the facts and law before them but on the volume of the voters in the hearing room.

Land use is political because it's all about where and how people will live, work, and play. Therefore, we need land use controls to set out the rules of the game. Problems arise, however, when the rules are either so vague as to mean virtually anything, opening the door wide to arbitrariness and lack of predictability, or so strict as to become a substitute for thought and judgment. Land use becomes land abuse when vagueness or strictness of the rules leads to absurd or unfair results.

## Discretionary Land Use Controls

Brian Blaesser's step-by-step critique on how to avoid abuse by government is a welcome antidote to the too-frequent tendency of planning and zoning officials to let the discretionary nature of certain land use controls get the best of them. By explaining in plain terms the proper and improper ways of applying such standard legal techniques as special uses, floating zones, site plan reviews, and the like, the author conveys not only the rules through real world examples but also the sense of the law.

Everyone in the land use game's iron triangle-property owner (or developer), neighbor (or community group), and government (local, state, or federal)-needs to be reminded that we need written law for a reason: to provide sufficient certainty and consistency in the relations among the triangle's members. Think of the iron triangle as the engine driving the land use machine. Discretion is the oil necessary to keep the engine, fueled by the law, running smoothly. Too little discretion, and the engine grinds to a halt; too much, and it becomes a slippery mess. Only through accountability of each member of the triangle to the other two can discretionary land use controls be kept in good running order.

In the end, it is the Constitution that ensures accountability. Unlike guidelines, regulations, ordinances, and statutes, Constitutions (federal and state) are not easily amended. And unlike most other rules and laws, Constitutions not only establish balance among governmental branches but also, most importantly, make clear that individual rights are not subservient to the state or the majority will. The Due Process and Takings Clauses, like the rest of the Bill of Rights, have one overarching aim-to protect the individual from abuse by government. As Justice Brennan reminded us in a land use case in 1981, if a policeman must know the Constitution, then why not a planner?

The government may dislike the Takings Clause, the developer may dislike the government, and the neighbor may dislike the developer, but each member of land use's iron triangle has at least one thing in common-they must abide by the Constitution. After all, the Constitution was never meant to make things easy; it was meant to make things right.

In Brian Blaesser's book, developers and planners are provided a clear guide through the discretionary thicket. He explains how discretionary land use techniques, case examples, and the law intersect in the work-a-day world of planning and zoning. There is much to be learned here about how to make things, if not easier, at least more right.

Washington, D.C.
January 12, 1997

**Gus Bauman**
*Former Litigation Counsel,*
*National Association of Home Builders (NAHB)*
*and Former Chairman, Maryland National*
*Capital Park & Planning Commission*

# Preface to the First Edition

Most fields of human endeavor involve some degree of judgment, or the exercise of discretion, in making decisions. The field of land use and real estate development is no exception, particularly in the 1990s. We are at a time in this country when many local governments are attempting to address increasingly complex, sometimes subjective issues—preservation of "community character," urban design, "cumulative impacts" of land uses, growth control, environmental protection, affordable housing, and infrastructure needs—through regulation.

Unfortunately, these regulatory decisions often reflect judgment gone awry—the exercise of judgment outside the legal bounds of the authority that was given to the decision maker. Why? Certainly this circumstance can be explained in many instances by poorly drafted, overly broad regulations whose purpose, standards, and procedures fail to give proper guidance to the decision maker. Sadly, it may also result from the timid actions of some government officials when faced with a roomful of opposition to a development proposal that complies with the regulations. In other cases, such overreaching decisions may be explained by the unabashed arrogance of staff and officials who may feel emboldened by a strict regulatory scheme or who believe that their view of the public interest should override established land use policies relied upon by the applicant. Whatever the reasons, and certainly others may offer more, abuse of discretion abounds in the implementation of land use and development regulations.

Over the years, as a practitioner in land use and development law matters around the country, I have been frustrated, yet fascinated, by the behavior of planning and zoning officials and government bodies when presented with opportunities to abuse the discretion given them under their particular regulatory schemes. This book is about that experience, written from the perspective of the landowner and developer who may have little recourse, even through litigation, in the face of such abuses of discretion.

Of course, landowners and developers are not without fault when the land use decision-making system goes awry. When they are overtly self-interested, or inconsiderate of public objectives, their behavior may induce the very abuses of discretion of which they complain. But it is the local government, in the first instance, that sets the regulatory stage upon which all the players must perform. Therefore, it has the first opportunity and responsibility to construct a stage on which, ideally, all the players are able to perform to the best of their abilities so as to produce discretionary decisions that balance public objectives with the practical constraints and uncertainties of land development in a market economy.

The typical regulatory stage is constructed from two basic building blocks: *rules and standards.* Supporters of the current movement in this country to roll back the layers of government regulation, to literally "reinvent government," lambast the use of detailed rules. They see reliance upon rules as a misguided attempt to make regulation certain, uniform, complete, self-executing, and dispassionate, a naive attempt to eliminate the potential for arbitrariness and abuse. In fact, they argue, rules create loopholes by opening up a world of angles and advantages that can be exploited. Because a rule cannot be written to cover every possible situation, it has a tendency to be under-inclusive, opening up the opportunities for exploitation.

Unlike rules, which dictate a result no matter what, standards, it is argued, allow the decision maker to take into account all relevant factors, permitting the exercise of judgment to fit the particular circumstances or facts. They allow us to think, to be pragmatic. In other words, standards allow for a balancing of factors or considerations in light of the policies or objectives at stake. Standards and procedures are the principal components of discretionary decision-making systems for land use and development in this country. From the developer's perspective, a discretionary decision-making system may be preferable when pragmatic judgment is needed in the review of a development project that is subject to a complex array of land use, growth control, and environmental regulations. But when that judgment is exercised arbitrarily, the developer's traditional preference for predictability surfaces, and the straightforwardness of rules becomes more attractive. This tension between developers' preference in the regulatory scheme for certainty, but equal need for flexibility, emerges as a theme throughout the pages of this book.

Although I take pains to explain what the current law is as applied to discretionary land use controls, I have chosen to write this book in more subjective prose, giving vent, where appropriate, to the personal experience that necessarily underlies the law. I have endeavored to do so with a measure of humor, explaining not only what the law is, but what I think it should be if we are to be successful in limiting the invitations to abuse discretion that currently exist at the local government level in the implementation of land use and development regulations in this country. I leave it to the reader to judge whether I have been successful in that endeavor.

**Brian W. Blaesser**
*Boston, Massachusetts*
*January 2, 1997*

# Preface to the Second Edition

In the Preface to the First Edition, I explained the essential purpose of this book—to address judgment gone awry in the exercise of discretionary land use controls. Less than two years later, my ongoing experience and that of other practitioners confirm that there remains ample subject matter for this book as well as the need to identify abuses of discretion and to suggest ways in which local government can improve the exercise of discretion in deciding land use matters.

One of the salutary developments in the law that has given local governments pause is the courts' increasing willingness to shift the burden of justifying discretionary decisions to the local government. Traditionally, courts handled local land use decisions gingerly, giving them great deference unless there was clear evidence of a taking or a violation of a landowner's constitutional right to equal protection. This deference stemmed from the Jeffersonian faith in local institutions and the view that planners could supply the rigor necessary to curb arbitrary thinking by local legislators. Alas, as commentators have long observed, the politics of zoning and development controls often override factual findings and sensible solutions to land use issues. Particularly in the area of discretionary exactions, as explained in the following pages, the U.S. Supreme Court has imposed the two-prong standard of requiring an "essential nexus" between the exaction imposed and the public purpose identified as being served and "rough proportionality" between the exaction and the projected impact of the proposed development. Most important, the Supreme Court has instructed local governments that, when the discretionary exaction is imposed by an administrative body, the burden of justification shifts to the local government to justify its decision. These new developments in the law will certainly give local governments the incentive to improve discretionary decision making.

The increasing judicial skepticism toward *ad hoc* discretionary exactions and the court's refusal to apply the traditional presumption of validity, while encouraging more rigor and exactitude in discretionary decisions, may also put a halt to what has been described in other arenas as "mission creep"—that is, the gradual, unauthorized broadening of a decision-making body's original jurisdiction or mission. One of the best examples of this "mission creep" is the way in which planning commissions use site plan review to address "off site" impacts that should have been decided at the initial zoning stage.

Another example that involves "legislative" abuse of discretion is one I recently discovered, known as "call up" authority, a practice exercised by the local legislative bodies of some jurisdictions. This authority allows the local legislative body to "call up" for further review and decision an already final decision made by an administrative body. Whether a particular project ends up on the "call up" list may be a function of mere curiosity by a particular local legislator or constituent pressure that was not successful at the administrative level; as a result, the important objectives of providing certainty and predictability in the development process are lost. This type of mission creep allows local decision-makers to introduce new requirements and considerations that go beyond the original purpose and scope of the particular type of discretionary decision.

As before, I leave it to the reader to judge whether in this edition I have been successful in both explaining what the law is regarding discretionary land use controls and what I think the law should be if we are to be successful in enabling all the players on the regulatory stage to perform to the best of their abilities so as to produce discretionary decisions that balance public objectives with the practical constraints and uncertainties of land development in a market economy.

**Brian W. Blaesser**
*Boston, Massachusetts*
*August 1, 1998*

# Preface to the Third Edition

This third edition contains one principal organizational change and a number of substantive additions, along with an overall update of case law. The organizational change is the creation of an Appendix into which have been placed all of the state statutes authorizing development agreements and determinations of vested property rights—material that was previously found at the end of Chapter 7. Readers will, hopefully, find that this change improves their ease of access to these statutes. The principal substantive additions are found in Chapters 1, 3, and 8, and are intended to address current relevant topics and issues.

In Chapter 1, I have added a new section on Discretionary Decisions and Substantive Due Process. In the face of irrational or wrongful land use regulatory decisions that may *not* amount to a taking, landowners and developers generally have relied on substantive due process claims in federal court as an important means to remedy such actions. To their dismay, however, landowners and developers are learning from a series of federal court decisions in some of the circuits, that as the *degree of discretion* that can be exercised by a government decision-making body increases, the less likely it is that they will be deemed to have any "property interest" to protect, regardless of how arbitrarily that discretion is exercised in a particular case. This unfortunate development in many of the federal circuits is discussed in Section 1.11. In Chapter 8, I have added a discussion of two topics that reflect the escalating national debate over the issue of "sprawl" and the efforts of communities to "manage" growth and preserve "community character" and promote "quality of life"—design review of signs, and neo-traditional design codes.

"Sprawl" is generally described as unlimited, poorly planned, noncontiguous, low-density residential and commercial development extending outward from urban areas into rural areas. This pattern of land use is viewed as wasteful of both land and natural resources and costly to serve with public facilities. For some people it may also be physically unattractive, but for others, the face of sprawl is not so bad. Sprawl in many respects is the product of American affluence, enabling people to have a low-density residential environment that allows property owners to "borrow" and enjoy the open space that surrounds them. Sprawl also includes work places located within reasonable distances of affordable housing. As the saying goes, "You drive until you qualify." The relative ease of commuting and shopping makes suburban sprawl attractive to many families.

The antidote to sprawl is growth management—a set of planning and regulatory initiatives directed at controlling the rate, amount, type, location and quality of growth that began in the 1960s. The current form of growth management that has captured national attention is "smart growth," a concept that originated with the state of Maryland's growth management initiative in 1997. The term "smart growth," generally defined, means a planning and regulatory approach that attempts to promote economic prosperity and enhance the quality of life in communities by implementing policies that prioritize and/or limit growth areas based on certain criteria—particularly the location of existing or planned infrastructure and the preservation of natural and agricultural resources. Unfortunately, "smart growth" is the kind of term that enables all sides in the growth management debate to say they do not support "sprawl" and to give an attractive label to their particular prescriptions.

In their efforts to implement "smart growth" initiatives directed at the location and quality of development and the preservation of "community character," communities are embracing concepts and techniques that involve a high degree of discretionary decision making. Some of these are not new, for example, the special use permit, which communities can utilize in their growth management efforts as a "wait and see" weapon. As discussed in Chapter 3, this permit enables communities to require developers to address a wide range of development "impact" issues before deciding if the "location" of the proposed use is appropriate in light of various factors, including infrastructure capacity. Other techniques include design review of signs, view protection regulations and tree preservation ordinances.

The problem with the use of some of these techniques to preserve community character is that communities are more inclined to assert that they are "special" rather than define what their "character" is—leaving the answer to that question to case by case determinations by local aesthetically oriented advisory boards and committees who make ad hoc determinations without sufficient principles and standards that define what is "special" about their community. Part of the problem also is that preservation of a community's character is about more than just preserving or enhancing the aesthetics of the physical environment. Aesthetics-based regulatory techniques don't address economic and social factors that determine the viability, and ultimately the character of a community. Nor should they.

One movement that at least recognizes the various physical, social, and economic elements that give meaning to "community" is the New Urbanism. In its "Charter of the New Urbanism," the Congress for the New Urbanism states that it "views the disinvestment in central cities, the spread of placeless sprawl, the increasing separation by race and income, environmental deterioration, loss of agricultural lands and wilderness, and the erosion of society's built heritage as one interrelated community-building challenge." The main thrust of New Urbanism is the physical—to provide a "coherent and supportive physical framework" that the New Urbanists believe will, in turn, sustain economic vitality, community stability and environmental health. New Urbanists are committed to "reestablishing the relationship between the art of building and the making of community, through citizen-based participatory planning and design." Design—architecture and landscape design—is the principal planning and implementation tool of the New Urbanism.

The main objective of New Urbanism planning and design is to recreate neo-traditional villages of the sort that predated zoning in this country. The principal mechanism for creating neo-traditional patterns of development is the "design code." Unlike traditional zoning regulations, the neo-traditional design code emphasizes visual design archetypes rather than textual standards. Because these design codes emphasize flexibility over precision, the same vagueness and other due process problems arise when these design codes replace communities' zoning codes. This is the subject of a new section in Chapter 8.

The perspectives and vision that the New Urbanism has brought to the debate over sprawl and growth management are extremely important. Unfortunately, the New Urbanists convey the view, with uncompromising zeal, that neo-traditional development is the only responsible pattern of development. In 1973, a Rockefeller Brothers Fund Task Force concluded that no ideal pattern of development exists. The most important goal, in the view of the task force, was quality of development. Quality development, in my view, is best assured by land use decision-making processes that encourage a synthesis of view points regarding appropriate or ideal development patterns and that, at the implementation level, provide certainty, consistency, and finality in the review of development proposals. At a time in this a country when local governments are increasingly targeting "sprawl" with regulations based upon "smart growth" principles and New Urbanism—approaches that rely heavily upon discretionary land use controls—it is all the more important to ensure that invitations to abuse discretion in the name of preserving "community character" and "quality of life" are avoided. As with the prior editions of this book, this third edition continues the endeavor to identify such abuses in local government decisions and to explain how they can be avoided.

**Brian W. Blaesser**
*Boston, Massachusetts*
*July 1, 2000*

# Preface to Fourth Edition

The fervor over "smart growth"—aka growth management—discussed in the Preface to the third edition of this book continues. However, in the aftermath of the attack on the World Trade Center, many firms are consciously seeking to decentralize their functions, where possible. Employees will follow, reinforcing the *outward* movement of development—contrary to "Smart Growth" efforts to encourage or mandate more compact urban forms. There will also be increased demand for a *horizontal* built environment that can accommodate the automobile needs of workers. This market demand for a different built environment may conflict with the growth management policies of many communities. Local governments will be tempted to utilize their discretionary land use controls to justify denial of development proposals that address the need for different living and working environments caused by the events of September 11.

The discretionary component of government regulatory programs is seen as necessary to achieve many of the qualitative objectives of smart growth, namely, preservation of community character, better site design and better building design—objectives that are viewed as unachievable under the traditional zoning scheme. That is because traditional zoning, as described in Sections 1.03 and 7.03 of this book, relies upon a use classification system that segregates "incompatible" uses from one another and applies the uniformity rule to require that regulations for each class or kind of buildings within a use district be uniform.

Ironically, this discretionary approach to land use decision making means that the landowner or developer may find it hard to secure a *final* decision—a necessary procedural step if she intends to seek judicial review of an unfavorable decision. A discretionary approval process is particularly susceptible to extraordinary delay, during which time the owner may have no economically viable use of the property. Alternatively, because a discretionary approval process may allow for the standardless imposition of conditions, those conditions may place severe limitations on the use of the property.

In the case of extraordinary delay in reaching a decision, a "temporary" regulatory taking may have occurred. In the case of a harsh regulatory decision, a "permanent" regulatory taking may have occurred. In both cases, the U.S. Supreme Court's pronouncements on the so-called *ripeness doctrine* mean that the landowner or developer has little likelihood of proving a taking unless she can demonstrate that she did, in fact, obtain a final decision. As the Supreme Court explained in the *Suitum* case, this "final decision" requirement is viewed by the U.S. Supreme Court as the means to address "the high degree of discretion characteristically possessed by land-use boards in softening the strictures of the general land use regulations they administer."

Because the ripeness doctrine has become increasingly important in determining the likelihood of a landowner's success in challenging discretionary decisions alleged to amount to "taking," I have added a new Section 1.10 in Chapter 1 that explains the doctrine and its pitfalls for property owners who seek to challenge regulatory decisions that flow from a discretionary decision making process. The U.S. Supreme Court's recent decision in *Palazzolo v. Rhode Island*, refined the doctrine and is also discussed in this new section.

In addition to updating the case law in each chapter, I have also added two other new sections to this fourth edition. Section 1.08 addresses temporary takings and includes an analysis of the recent federal court decision involving a challenge by property owners to a series of moratoria instituted by the Tahoe Regional Planning Agency (TRPA). This case, *Tahoe-Sierra Preservation*

*Council v. Tahoe Regional Planning Agency*, has been taken by the U.S. Supreme Court on a grant of *certiorari* and will hopefully clarify when a moratorium constitutes a temporary taking. Section 1.09 examines more closely the question of whether the *Nollan/Dolan* test for discretionary exactions applies to *legislatively* adopted development exactions.

My endeavor throughout this fourth edition continues to be to explain what the law is regarding discretionary land use controls, and what I think the law should be. In that way, I hope this book will continue to provide a practical resource for practitioners while also provoking thought on how to prevent abuses of discretion when the "strictures" of land use regulations are "softened."

**Brian W. Blaesser**
*Boston, Massachusetts*
*November 1, 2001*

# Acknowledgments

This book was made possible through the encouragement of my family, and the technical assistance, insights, and thoughtful suggestions of friends and colleagues. In particular, I thank Dan Mandelker for his foresight in seeing the need for this type of book and for his rigorous critique of draft chapters for the first edition. My review of relevant statutes and case law was made possible through the skillful research of Jennifer Wolz. I am grateful to Mark Dennison for using his considerable writing and editing talents to suggest ways to improve the overall quality of the original manuscript. Keane Callahan provided very helpful suggestions for the chapter on site plan review. I am indebted to Bob Brown and Mark Keener for contributing their urban design expertise to the chapter on design review. Denise Sekelsky, Principal Attorney Editor, at West Group was very helpful throughout the writing of this third edition of the book, and Alan Forrest, West Group Editorial Director, has been supportive of the book from its inception. I thank Denise and the West Group design staff, for their flexibility and creativity in solving formatting issues as they arose during the preparation of the publication. Most important, I thank my wife, Grażyna, for her love and patience during the many hours I spent writing this book, and our sons Brandon and Alan who, though too young to be patient, are always an inspiration for my efforts.

# About the Author

**BRIAN W. BLAESSER** is a partner in the law firm of Robinson & Cole LLP. He heads the Land Use and Development Group in the firm's Boston office where he practices in the areas of commercial real estate development and leasing, multifamily residential development, land use and environmental law, planning law, condemnation law and litigation. Mr. Blaesser represents real estate owners, investors, and developers in analyzing and securing requisite land use and development approvals from local governments, negotiating and drafting development agreements, and handling development projects which involve a wide range of environmental transactional and regulatory permitting matters with the U.S. EPA and the U.S. Army Corps of Engineers.

Mr. Blaesser formerly served as Special Assistant Attorney General for eminent domain actions brought by the Illinois Departments of Transportation and Conservation and has extensive experience in state and federal trial and appellate courts in real estate and land use litigation, including the taking issue, vested rights, condemnation, U.S. EPA enforcement actions and violations of Section 1983 of the Civil Rights Act.

In 1999, Mr. Blaesser chaired a National Task Force on Growth Management for the National Association of Industrial Office Properties (NAIOP), which produced a report entitled *Growing to Greatness* (1999). He is the principal author of the book, *Condemnation of Property: Practice and Strategies for Winning Just Compensation* (Wiley Law Publications: 1994) and the author of numerous publications on land use and real estate development, including "Growth Management: A Developer's Perspective," in XXIX Development No. 3 (1998); "New Federal Wetlands Policy: The Landowner's Perspective," in 46 Land Use Law & Zoning Digest No. 1 (Jan. 1994); "Negotiating Entitlements," in Urban Land (Dec. 1991); "Impact Fees: The Second Generation," 38 Journal of Urban & Contemporary Law 401 (1990); Chapter 2: "The Problem in the 1980s and 1990s: The Meaning and Scope of Wipeouts" in Wipeouts and Their Mitigation: The Changing Context for Land Use and Environmental Law (Lincoln Institute of Land Policy, 1990); "Closing the Federal Courthouse Door on Property Owners: The Ripeness and Abstention Doctrines in Section 1983 Land Use Cases," 2 Hofstra Property Law Journal 73 (Spring 1989).

Mr. Blaesser received his B.A. from Brown University and his J.D. from Boston College where he served as an editor of the Law Review. He also holds a masters in city planning (M.C.P.) from the Massachusetts Institute of Technology (M.I.T.) and was a Fulbright Scholar. He is frequent speaker at national, state, and local programs on land use, real estate development and litigation issues, and is the appointed chair of NAIOP's National Growth Issues Subcommittee. He is an elected member of Lambda Alpha International, the honorary land economics society.

# Table of Contents

**CHAPTER 2**
**Variances**

**CHAPTER 3**
**Special Use Permits**

# Discretionary Land Use Controls

**CHAPTER 5**
**Site Plan Review**

**CHAPTER 8**
**Design Review**

**CHAPTER 1**

# The Nature of Discretionary Controls

## Scope of Chapter

## § 1.01   Introduction

We seem to have achieved the worst of both worlds: a system of regulation that goes too far while it also does too little.

This paradox is explained by the absence of the one indispensable ingredient of any successful human en-

deavor: use of judgment. In the decades since World
War II, we have constructed a system of regulatory
law that basically outlaws common sense. Modern
law, in an effort to be "self-executing," has shut out
our humanity.

—Philip K. Howard in
*The Death of Common Sense*

[T]here is ample reason to fear and distrust government, to probe it, make it come clean, demand
access.. . . We can stand some inefficiency when it is
the necessary concomitant of accountability. To get
neither is the curse of a government machinery that
protects itself more than the people it is meant to
serve.

—Gary Wills
*A Necessary Evil: A History of American Distrust of
Government*

The plain sentiment in this country against overregula-
tion is certainly echoed in the land development industry
as it struggles with the ever more complex array of land
use and development controls that are imposed to preserve
the "quality of life," to manage growth, protect natural resources, preserve community "character," provide for
infrastructure needs, and secure public amenities. However, if one probes below the uniform layer of resentment
against government intrusion, one finds a more complicated set of emotions over the land use control system as
it has evolved since the genesis of zoning in the 1920s.
The complication arises from what Philip K. Howard
describes above as the one key ingredient of successful human endeavor—the exercise of judgment. Generally, landowners and developers welcome the exercise of judgment
in the implementation of land use and development
controls, provided the addition of this human ingredient
generally improves the efficiency and predictability and
accountability of the decision-making process, and promotes pragmatic government flexibility that allows the
developer to respond to the physical constraints of development sites and changes in the market.

However, if a photo essay on "One Day in the Life of
Developers" were done simultaneously around the country,

it would tell a tale of extreme frustration with the way "judgment" is frequently exercised in the administration of land use controls—a preference for predictability over flexibility, almost a yearning for the "self-executing" system of land use controls envisioned by creators of zoning in the 1920s. But not quite. Realistically, the developer knows that the review of a development project in light of today's more complex land use, growth, and environmental considerations, in many cases, requires the ingredient of human judgment in order to provide pragmatic resolution of these issues. It is when judgment is exercised arbitrarily—and the invitations to do so abound—that there is abuse of discretion.

This chapter outlines some of the ways this exercise of discretion in land use decision making is abused and explores the tension between the developer's preference for certainty but equal need for pragmatic solutions that only the exercise of judgment can provide.

Reprinted by permission of William Costello.

## § 1.02 Meaning of Discretion

Discretion is nothing more than the exercise of judgment. In the context of land use and development approvals, discretion means the substantive and procedural choices made by a legislative or an administrative body

3

for the purpose for which the power was delegated.[1] Generally speaking, when the decision-making body exercises judgment that exceeds the bounds of its delegated authority, we have a case of *abuse* of discretion.

## § 1.03 Limited Discretion Under Traditional Zoning

As originally conceived, zoning was supposed to require very little exercise of discretion. Rather, it was intended to be a self-administering land use allocation system—that is, a system of prestated land use classifications and rules under which only cases of particular hardship would require administrative (variance) or legislative (zone amendment) action to resolve. This original premise was driven by a desire to avoid legislative or administrative interference with the land market.[2] In other words, concern for property rights and the goal of maximizing the productivity of private actors in the land market led the founders of zoning to design a "zoning by rules" system of land use control.

Although designed as a rules-based system for allocating land uses and providing for development approvals, few people, I think, would argue today that zoning has remained faithful to that original concept. Perhaps it is because of the traditional zoning system's inability to anticipate the timing of land development, to address the complexity of land development proposals, or to handle the conflicting and often-changing demands placed upon it

---

[1] *See generally* Davis, Kenneth C.,*Discretionary Justice*, Louisiana State University Press Reprint, Urbana, Ill.: University of Illinois Press, 1979.

[2] *See* Krasnowiecki, "The Basic System of Land Use Control: Legislative Preregulation v. Administrative Discretion," in *The New Zoning: Legal, Administrative, and Economic Concepts and Techniques* 3 (N. Marcus and M. Groves eds. 1970); Kmiec, "Deregulating Land Use: An Alternative Free Enterprise Development System," 130 U. Pa. L. Rev. 28, 50 (1982).

by the players in the zoning game.[3] Wherever one wants to place the cause, there is no doubt that the use of discretionary techniques and procedures in land use and development controls has grown far beyond the original limited concept of the variance procedure. However, the fact that the rules approach of traditional zoning has been inadequate does not mean that rules are ill-suited for the objectives of land use. Indeed, I think the pendulum has now swung far toward the use of discretion in ways that invite abuses of discretion by local government.

## § 1.04   Abuses of Discretion

The regulatory circumstances that most easily invite abuses of discretion in land use decision making may be defined in five categories: (1) regulations that allow as-of-right uses to be converted to special or conditional uses and subjected to discretionary review; (2) vague regulatory statements of purpose and accompanying standards; (3) "advisory" citizen-based commissions or committees whose recommendations are guided by few standards but given great weight by the legislative body; (4) approval procedures that give those "advisory" commissions or committees virtual veto power over development requests; and (5) staff use of the application review process to impose arbitrary substantive changes and delay processing. The following discussion details the regulatory scenarios that give rise to such opportunities for discretionary abuse.

## [1]   "Automatic" Conversions to Conditional Use

An example of local government administrative actions that attempt to "convert" a permitted use to a "conditional use" and impose conditions through design review after an applicant has demonstrated compliance with all zoning

---

[3] *See generally* Babcock, Richard F., *The Zoning Game*, Madison, Wis.: The University of Wisconsin Press, 1966.

code requirements for a permitted use permit is found in a Minnesota case.[4] In that case, the applicant sought approval for a convenience food restaurant, which was listed as a permitted use in the zoning district, subject to specific performance standards. His application complied with all site-plan requirements for curb cuts, safety signage, lighting, landscaping, parking, screening of view, and architectural appearance. However, at the public hearing, neighborhood residents expressed the desire that the property be used for residential use rather than commercial use, and argued that the restaurant was inconsistent with the area's pro-residential comprehensive plan. Following a discussion of how the proposal was "inappropriately" commercial and inconsistent with the comprehensive plan, the planning commission voted to deny the building permit on the basis of noncompliance with the following provision of the Minneapolis Zoning Code:

> The architectural appearance and functional plan of the building shall not be so dissimilar to existing buildings as to cause impairment in property values within reasonable distance of applicant's zoning lot.

However, no facts regarding dissimilar architectural design or impairment of property values were presented at the hearing to rebut the applicant's evidence on these issues. In the subsequent mandamus proceeding brought by the developer, the city argued that the conditions placed on the approval of the permit under the ordinance "recharacterized" the requested use as conditional, which gave the city discretion to consider it in light of the general welfare and city's planning goals. The court, however, ruled that the city could not arbitrarily convert the permitted use to a conditional use in such a manner. Because the application complied with the zoning code in all respects, approval was required as a matter of right.[5]

Another flagrant example of a legislative attempt to automatically convert permitted uses to conditional uses

---

[4] Chase v. Minneapolis, 401 N.W.2d 408 (Minn. Ct. App. 1987).
[5] *Id.* at 413.

in wholesale fashion was the proposed "Model Traffic Management Ordinance" prepared for the DuPage Mayors and Managers Conference of Illinois. The ordinance's controlling concept was "traffic impact." It stated:

> All other development of lots of record which are not otherwise classified as Planned Unit Development, Special or Conditional Uses, Zoning Variations, or Zoning Amendments, but which create a traffic impact as defined and determined by this Ordinance, shall be considered and reviewed procedurally as a Special or Conditional Use. . . .[6]

If implemented in the municipal jurisdictions of DuPage County, such a provision would surely be challengeable as a violation of due process and the uniformity[7] and special use provisions of the zoning enabling legislation, consistent with the holdings in other jurisdictions.[8]

### [2]  Vague Statements and Standards

Vague statements of purpose and vague performance standards as applied to development requests are also open invitations to abuse of discretion. In a Washington

---

[6] Section 3.0–6 of the Draft Model Traffic Management Ordinance for DuPage County Municipalities (August 8, 1990). Section 3.0–5 of the Ordinance also automatically converted any subdivision that creates a traffic impact to a planned unit development, subject to the standards and procedures for processing PUDs.

[7] The *uniformity provision* found in most zoning enabling statutes requires the regulations within each zoning district to be uniform, while regulations in distinct zoning districts may differ from one another.

[8] *See, e.g.,* SCIT, Inc. v. Planning Bd. of Braintree, 19 Mass. App. Ct. 101, 472 N.E.2d 269 (1984) (invalidating a zoning provision requiring all permitted uses in a business district to be submitted to the special permit granting authority for approval). *See also* Waterville Hotel Corp. v. Board of Zoning Appeals, 241 A.2d 50 (Me. 1968) (invalidating a standardless provision that required "all major changes of uses of land, buildings or structures" in a commercial zone to be approved by the board of zoning appeals).

case,[9] the following statement of purpose for a commercial zone was held to be impermissibly vague as applied to a "beauty bark" retailer and wholesaler whose operations became the subject of neighborhood complaints:

> [T]o provide for the location of . . . enterprises which may involve some on-premises retail service but with the outside activities and display or fabrication, assembling and service features, *including manufacturing and processing in limited degree,* and which uses, if permitted to locate in strictly on-premises retail and service areas, would introduce factors of heavy trucking and handling of materials that destroy the maximum service and attraction of strictly retail areas. (Emphasis added).

Finding no explanation in the zoning code for how a procedure was to be deemed "limited,"[10] the court held that the code unconstitutionally left the county officials with the task of determining what activities were prohibited.[11] Nor was this vague language cured by the accompanying performance standards that described, in general terms, the characteristics of uses considered appropriate for the zoning district.[12]

---

[9] Burien Bark Supply v. King County, 106 Wash. 2d 868, 725 P.2d 994 (1986).

[10] To illustrate, the court noted that one could consider the number of steps in the process, the percentage of business time devoted to the process, the extent to which the process is necessary for the overall business, or the physical size of the process.

[11] Burien Bark Supply v. King County, 725 P.2d at 996 (Wash. 1986). *Compare* Burien Bark Supply v. King County, 106 Wash. 2d 868, 725 P.2d 994 (1986) *with* Mitchell v. City of Issaquah, 97 Wash. App. 1017, 1999 WL 675326 (Div. 1 1999), review denied, 140 Wash. 2d 1018, 5 P.3d 9 (2000) (holding rezoning ordinance not unconstitutionally vague because unlike the ordinance in *Burien Bark Supply*, the ordinance did not leave important determinations to the discretion of city officials).

[12] These performance standards provided in part: The uses enumerated in this classification are considered as having common or similar performance standards in that:

> A. They are heavier in type than those uses permitted in the strictly business classifications and yet are measurably

Similarly, in an Illinois case,[13] the court found that the use of the phrase "but not limited to" in both the permitted and prohibited use lists, when read in combination with the standard for granting a special use permit by the village board—that the use be "[s]imilar and compatible" to those uses already allowed as permitted uses—was nonsensical: No person could tell what is similar and compatible to an incomplete list of permitted uses. The court therefore held that the ordinance constituted an unconstitutional delegation of legislative power to the village board of trustees.

Not surprisingly, a court found the following statement of sign criteria held in a New Jersey case[14] to be impermissibly vague, inviting mischievous results:

> Signs that demand public attention rather than invite attention should be discouraged. Color should be selected to harmonize with the overall building or scheme to create a mood and reinforce symbolically the sign's primary communication message. . . . Care must be taken not to introduce too many colors into a sign. A restricted use of color will maintain the communication function of the sign and create a visually pleasing element as an integral part of the texture of the street.[15]

The potential for abuse in decision making is particularly high when the review body does not even attempt to relate

---

lighter uses than those first permitted in the industrial classifications; . . . .

D. They involve a greater handling of materials and commodities and more trucking than uses permitted in a strictly retail area, but do not require large sites nor involve as much handling of materials and commodities or heavy trucking as uses first permitted in strictly industrial areas. *See Burien,* 725 P.2d at 995 n.1

[13] Union Nat. Bank & Trust Co. of Joliet v. Village of New Lenox, 152 Ill. App. 3d 919, 105 Ill. Dec. 875, 505 N.E.2d 1 (3d Dist. 1987).

[14] Diller and Fisher Co., Inc. v. Architectural Review Bd. of Borough of Stone Harbor, 246 N.J. Super. 362, 587 A.2d 674 (Law Div. 1990).

[15] *Id.*

its decision to a standard or meaningful evidence, revealing the utter subjectiveness of its decision. When this happened in a New York case involving the denial of a subdivision application based solely on aesthetic grounds,[16] the court reversed the decision and ordered that the permit be granted. The court explained:

> [A permit denial must] . . . be based upon a showing that "the offense to the eye . . . [is] substantial and . . . [has a] material effect on the community or district pattern." In a word, the planning board's denial must be based on evidence more substantial than a generalized feeling that neighbors should have the aesthetic pleasure of viewing a mansion on the central portion of a lot some four times the size of their own. Since the record before us fails to disclose anything more than such a generalized feeling, i.e., fails to contain any evidence that the subdivision petitioners contemplate would result in a substantial offense to the eye or have a material effect on the area involved, we reverse for lack of substantial evidence and direct the planning board to approve the application for subdivision.[17]

Architectural design review ordinances provide some of the worst examples of vague statements of purpose and overbroad standards that invite abuse. Such ordinances frequently lack sufficiently clear standards and vest too much subjective decision making in the architectural review board officials.[18] However, in some instances, vaguely worded standards have been upheld when the

---

[16] The meanings of *aesthetic* and *aesthetic controls* in the land use context are discussed in Ch. 8, Sec. 8.02, *infra*

[17] Sackson v. Zimmerman, 103 A.D.2d 843, 478 N.Y.S.2d 354, 356 (2d Dep't 1984), quoting from Cromwell v. Ferrier, 19 N.Y.2d 263, 279 N.Y.S.2d 22, 225 N.E.2d 749, 21 A.L.R.3d 1212 (1967), reargument denied, 19 N.Y.2d 862, 280 N.Y.S.2d 1025, 227 N.E.2d 408 (1967).

[18] *See* Pacesetter Homes, Inc. v. Village of Olympia Fields, 104 Ill. App. 2d 218, 244 N.E.2d 369 (1st Dist. 1968); Waterfront Estates Development, Inc. v. City of Palos Hills, 232 Ill. App. 3d 367, 173 Ill. Dec. 667, 597 N.E.2d 641 (1st Dist. 1992). For a more complete discussion of this problem, *see* Ch. 8, Secs. 8.03 and 8.04, *infra*.

board makes specific findings that indicate how the design standards are to be applied.[19]

Performance standards, although potentially more objective in substance, do not necessarily cure the vagueness problem. In fact, performance zoning provisions sometimes can *appear* to provide clearer standards when, in fact, they only perpetuate the vagueness problem. The courts do not necessarily scrutinize such provisions with the rigor needed to evaluate the meaningfulness of weighted performance criteria. For example, in a recent Missouri case,[20] the county had adopted a unified development code (UDC) to replace its traditional zoning scheme. According to the introduction in the UDC, the county commission had determined that "traditional zoning, which divides land into broad categories of use, would not adequately meet the needs and desires of [the] County's citizens, nor would it be able to adequately respond to varied and unique development issues in different areas of the County." Therefore, the UDC was adopted as a means to provide for "a more flexible and dynamic approach to land use regulation." The UDC established a "Permit System" under which all development is evaluated on the basis of the established performance criteria that are referred to in the UDC as either "absolute" or "relative" policies. The "absolute" policies address the topics of wastewater control, on-site sewage disposal, soil and erosion control, storm drainage, utilities, access to existing roads, and other topics deemed essential to real estate development. Failure to comply with any relevant "absolute" policy results in a denial of a permit.[21]

The provision on "relative" policies states that these policies "encourage or discourage certain kinds of performance by developments. A development must receive a cumulative score, on all relative policies, of 'zero' (0) or

---

[19] *See, e.g.*, State ex rel. Stoyanoff v. Berkeley, 458 S.W.2d 305, 41 A.L.R.3d 1386 (Mo. 1970).

[20] Animal Shelter League of Ozarks, Inc. v. Christian County Bd. of Adjustment, 995 S.W.2d 533 (Mo. Ct. App. S.D. 1999).

[21] *Id.* at 535-36.

better to receive approval."[22] The provision governing scoring standards for "relative" policies states:

> Each relative policy has been assigned an importance factor ranging from the numbers "one" (1) through "five" (5), as explained in Table 9-1. A development's performance on each relative policy is rated on a scale that ranges from "minus two" (-2) to "plus two" (+2), as explained in Table 9-2. The score on each relative policy is determined by multiplying its importance factor by its performance rating.

Table 9-1 reads:

> Assignment of Importance Factors
>
> (1) is assigned to the least important relative policies
>
> (2) is assigned to relative policies of minor importance
>
> (3) is assigned to relative policies of average or normal importance
>
> (4) is assigned to important relative policies
>
> (5) is assigned to the most important relative policies[.]

The second table referred to above (Table 9-2) is "Assignment of Performance Ratings". It provides the following scheme:

> (+2) is awarded for creating a significant public benefit with no substantial public detriment or for an excellent job of implementing the policy.
>
> (+1) is awarded for crating some public benefit, mitigating a public detriment, or for doing a good job of implementing the policy.
>
> (0) is awarded when the policy is irrelevant to the proposed development, if there is not public benefit or detriment, if there is a public detriment which is fully mitigated, or for a marginal job of implementing the policy.

---

[22] *Id.* at 536.

(-1) is awarded for an inadequate job of implementing the policy or when some public detriment is created.

(-2) is awarded when there is essentially no effort at policy implementation or a significant public detriment is created.

The landowner in this case, a nonprofit corporation, challenged the decision by the board of zoning adjustment denying a permit to build an animal shelter on a 4.42 acre site in a rural area. The permit was denied because the landowner had failed to satisfy the "relative" policies under the UDC. Both sides agreed that the landowner had satisfied the "absolute" policies. The court therefore was asked to review the board's decision with respect to the relative policies only. The county planning commission scored the landowner's application on thirty-nine "relative" policies using the scoring standards described above, which involved multiplying each "relative" policy by an "importance factor" for each "relative" policy. On this basis, the landowner was determined to have amassed a "minus" total of twenty. This minus twenty against a positive score of fifteen on other policies resulted in a total score of minus five, which was fatal to the landowner's application.

The court's reasoning in upholding the county's denial of the permit appears to reflect more of a deference to a point system then a reasoned examination of the evidence. For example, the landowner pointed out that it had satisfied the UDC's "absolute" policy regarding on-site sewage disposal when the county health department approved its proposed septic system. Therefore, the landowner argued, a finding that the discharge of treated wastewater from the septic system would create a potential off-site nuisance under the UDC was "arbitrary." The court, however, disagreed. It reasoned that a score of minus one, as given to the landowner's project, was authorized under the UDC where a proposed development creates a potential off-site nuisance. While acknowledging that "the evidence as to noise from abandoned animals (and other annoyances by them) might not alone have supported a score of minus one, that evidence combined with the evidence as to storm-water run off and discharge of treated wastewater was sufficient to support such a [minus one] score."[23]

On another point, the landowner argued that there was no competent and substantial evidence that the animal shelter would limit the viability of existing agriculture uses. Again, while acknowledging that the UDC's scoring standards "require a somewhat subjective assessment of the potential impact of the proposed shelter on existing agriculture uses in this prime agriculture area," the court found that it is precisely that feature of the UDC that enabled it to find there was sufficient evidence to support a finding that the land use change proposed by the land-owner would create some public detriment by limiting the viability of existing agriculture uses. Without devoting further space here to the court's reasoning in this "perfor-mance zoning" case, I suggest that this particular type of performance scheme, which determines the important of self described "relative" policies by "weighting" each such policy with an "importance factor," merely layers subjectiv-ity on top of a seemingly objective numerical system—compounding the vagueness problem.

### [3] Undue Legislative Weight Given to Advisory Recommendations

Traffic safety committees, or commissions, are increas-ingly prevalent in the development approval processes of suburban communities facing population growth. Typi-cally, they are citizen-based and are given a simple charge under the ordinance that bestows upon them formal status and duties. For example, one such ordinance merely states that powers and duties of the traffic safety commission with respect to development proposals are:

> 2. To review and make comments and recommenda-tions on all proposed developments brought before the

---

[23] *Id.* at 540.

Plan Commission or before the Building Department as provided in the Procedural Control Ordinance of the Village.

3. To review traffic studies and reports and make recommendations regarding the same to the President and Board of Trustees.[24]

The following dialogue is from the proceedings of a traffic safety commission:

Attorney: We would welcome some discussion from the Commission as to what evidence indicates lack of safety on the turn into the shopping center. You have been presented a study by petitioner's traffic consultant that indicates just the opposite. I'm not aware of anything in the record that supports the conclusion that ingress and egress from Linden Street to the shopping center would create a traffic hazard. In fairness we carried our burden in trying to demonstrate with facts, and in fairness we should certainly hear some evidence that suggests the study and your own staff engineer's recommendation are somehow not sufficient for you to make a favorable decision.

Commissioner: Are you suggesting we're not entitled to use our own discretion as an arm of local government?

Attorney: I'm suggesting that you have evidence that you should weigh and I'm only asking for you to identify what the other evidence is that you are weighing relative to the study and the recommendation of your own engineer.

Commissioner: Perhaps it's our own experience, from living in the village, our common sense as drivers and not necessarily the opinions of a "hired gun."

Attorneys will appreciate the fact that the "hired gun" label was directed at the petitioner's traffic consultant. Ironically, as this dialogue reveals, a developer of a

---

[24] Traffic Safety Commission Ordinance of municipality in suburban Illinois.

"permitted" use may often fair more poorly on the traffic issue when subjected to the undocumented perceptions of a citizen traffic commission than a developer of a "conditional" use listed as such in the ordinance. In the latter case, in the context of specific standards for the granting of a conditional use, such nonspecific citizen testimony regarding possible traffic hazards is not sufficient to overcome the city engineer's favorable testimony.[25]

However, where the citizen traffic safety committee is advisory only, but the legislative body has an understood policy of rarely overriding the committee's recommendations, the applicant's burden of proving arbitrary denial of a request is compounded, particularly where any traffic-related restriction recommended by the committee is adopted by ordinance as a legislative act, unconstrained by any predefined standards, and subject to review only under the fairly debatable standard.[26] However, even that relaxed standard of review can be overcome where the legislative body's denial of a proposed use based on alleged traffic hazard problems is without factual foundation and primarily reflective of neighborhood opposition. Such general neighborhood objections are not enough to support such a denial.[27]

### [4]  Is the Administrative Body Truly "Advisory"?

Because a local government often characterizes its traffic safety, appearance, or other type of committee as "advisory" only, it is more difficult to address the extent to which specific standards must be established to guide the decisions of such a committee. However, there are recognized principles of administrative law that distinguish between decisions that are "declaratory" in nature and those

---

[25] *See* Chanhassen Estates Residents Ass'n v. City of Chanhassen, 342 N.W.2d 335, 340 (Minn. 1984).

[26] *See, e.g.,* Southland Corporation-7 Eleven Stores v. Mayor & City Council of Laurel, 75 Md. App. 375, 541 A.2d 653 (1988).

[27] *See* Minnetonka Congregation of Jehovah's Witnesses, Inc. v. Svee, 303 Minn. 79, 226 N.W.2d 306, 308 (1975).

that are "advisory" only. Advisory decisions generally are not reviewable and have no binding effect, except where estoppel can be demonstrated. By contrast, declaratory decisions are binding upon applicants and are also appealable.[28]

Ordinance language, however, does not always clearly establish the "advisory" or "declaratory" role that the particular committee plays in the decision-making process. For example, in an Illinois case,[29] the developer's application to construct a single-family residence was referred to the Architectural Advisory Committee which determined that because the residence was "architecturally similar" to other buildings in the area, the application should be disallowed. The committee's action was authorized under an ordinance which provided that (1) if the committee determined that the permit should be issued, then the village board had no authority in the matter; and (2) if the committee determined that the permit should be disapproved, then the building permit could not be issued unless expressly authorized by the village board on appeal. The court held that the Architectural Advisory Committee's function under those procedures was declaratory rather than advisory, and therefore the principles governing the delegation of legislative powers to administrative bodies were applicable.[30]

### [5] Tyranny by Review Staff

Another level at which municipalities and government agencies allow abuses of discretion to occur on a daily basis is the staff level. One Illinois practitioner, while sympathetic to the municipal perspective and the use of "advisory" committees, was nevertheless quite candid. He wrote:

---

[28] *See* Davis, *Administrative Law Treatise*, Vol. I, Sec. 4.09.

[29] Pacesetter Homes, Inc. v. Village of Olympia Fields, 104 Ill. App. 2d 218, 244 N.E.2d 369 (1st Dist. 1968).

[30] *Id.* at 372; *see also* Waterfront Estates Development, Inc. v. City of Palos Hills, 232 Ill. App. 3d 367, 173 Ill. Dec. 667, 597 N.E.2d 641 (1st Dist. 1992).

> Where many municipalities *are* failing, in my opinion, is in allowing the "tyranny of the staff" to go unchecked. I represent an oil company which has been attempting to get two gas stations rebuilt in one of the northwest suburbs. Our plans have been altered a half-dozen times based on the often conflicting recommendations of staffers who seem to be working at cross purposes. We have lost months because one staffer has left, somebody else comes on board, and that person has new ideas. . . . To be sure, the advisory bodies were duplicative and might be considered amateurish. On the other hand, at least they dealt in the open. It was the staff reports, phone calls, suggested changes, etc. which cost us so much time and money.[31]

This practitioner's story corroborates what other landowners, developers, and their attorneys know well: The land use permitting process is fraught with delays and uncertainties resulting from the arbitrary decisions at the staff level, and unfortunately, in some cases, unevenness in staff competency to review, analyze, and resolve issues as they arise. The same practitioner added: "I believe municipalities owe developers a straight and expeditious shot before the matter goes to public hearing. Developers and municipal staffs and attorneys should work together to resolve as many of our issues at the front end and give a clear path to the advisory bodies to do their job."[32]

## § 1.05 The Debate over Rules Versus Standards in Regulation

If these examples of abuses of discretion are evidence that the pendulum has indeed swung too far toward discretionary decision making, then how much discretion should operate in zoning and other land use decisions? We

---

[31] Letter from attorney John. B. Murphey to author, dated December 12, 1990.
[32] *Id.*

can't really answer that question without discussing the difference between two basic forms of government regulation: rules and standards. A rule prescribes specific, detailed legal consequences to a specific set of "triggering" facts. A standard, on the other hand, defines a policy or principle that is applied to the particular facts of a case.[33] An example of a rule in land use regulation that is designed to control noise pollution would be: "The emission of noise above 70 decibels shall be punished by a fine of $300.00 per day for each day of violation." The same type of regulation written in the form of a standard might read: "Excessive noise shall be enjoinable upon a showing of irreparable harm."[34]

---

[33] These definitions of rules and standards are borrowed from Schlag, "Rules and Standards," 33 UCLA L. Rev. 379, 382 n.16 (1985), who in turn drew upon the works of Hart and Sacks and Kennedy. *See* Hart, H. and Sacks, A., *The Legal Process: Basic Problems in the Making and Application of Law* (Tentative ed.), Cambridge, Mass.: [s.n.], 1958, and Kennedy, "Form and Substance in Private Law Adjudication," 89 Harv. L. Rev. 1685 (1976).

[34] Standards can be further categorized into prescriptive standards and performance standards. In the land use regulatory context, a *prescriptive standard* is usually a dimensional standard that establishes a numerical maximum or minimum condition which governs the development of a site, such as maximum height or minimum front-yard setback. This type of standard is intended to promote uniformity of development in terms of the dimensions controlled. A *performance standard* establishes certain criteria that must be met, or an outcome that must be achieved on a site, but allows considerable flexibility as to how the criteria can be met, or the outcome achieved. For example, a performance standard to control stormwater runoff might state: "The rate of stormwater runoff after the development is completed shall not exceed the rate prior to development for a 50-year storm." This performance standard allows the developer to decide how to satisfy the standard, whether through use of a buffer, reduced pavement, a detention basin, or some other method. Because the performance standard provides the most flexibility, it is usually preferred by the landowner or developer, provided the standard is accompanied by the guarantee that compliance will allow the project to receive approval or at least proceed to the next stage in the approval process.

Reprinted by permission of Ruth Sofair Ketler.

Rules, it is argued, confine the decision maker to facts and so ensure certainty and uniformity in the decision-making process. However, supporters of the current movement in this country to roll back the layers of government regulation—to literally "reinvent government"—harshly criticize the use of detailed rules as a misguided attempt to make regulation certain, uniform, complete, self-executing, dispassionate, and consequently devoid of the potential for arbitrariness and abuse. In reality, argues one critic,[35] the detailed rules of modern law have shut out our humanity—that is, our capacity to use judgment.[36] In fact, instead of closing all loopholes for mischievious-ness, precise rules actually create loopholes by opening up a world of angles and advantages that can be exploited.[37] This occurs, in part, because in order for a precise rule to function efficiently, a categorical set of facts must exist to trigger the rule, and the facts of a case can always be characterized or distorted so that the rule does not apply

[35] Howard, Philip K., *The Death of Common Sense*, New York: Random House, 1994.
[36] *Id.* at 11.
[37] *Id.* at 43.

or applies in some manner that was not anticipated.[38] In other words, because a rule cannot be written to cover every possible situation, it has a tendency to be under-inclusive, opening up opportunities for exploitation.

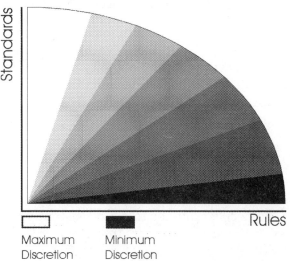

Proponents of allowing more discretion in regulation argue that standards are a more useful regulatory form because they reflect the reality that "there is a limit inherent in the nature of language to the guidance" that words can give.[39] Unlike rules, which always dictate a result, standards, by allowing the decision maker to take into account all relevant factors, permit the exercise of judgment to fit the particular circumstances or facts. They allow us to think, to be pragmatic. In other words, standards allow for a balancing of factors or considerations in light of the policies or objectives at stake.

In this current antiregulation climate, how do we sort through the arguments for and against the choice of rules over standards or standards over rules? As with many such matters, the truth lies somewhere in between. Here's a brief attempt to make sense of it all and to suggest some

---

[38] Schlag, "Rules and Standards," 33 UCLA L. Rev. 379, 416 (1985).
[39] Hart, H.L.A., *The Concept of Law*, London: Oxford University Press, 1961.

basic questions that should be asked by local governments when they design land use regulations.

## [1] Arguments for and Against Rules and Standards

Most arguments in the debate for and against rules and standards fall into four basic valuation categories or criteria: (1) fairness; (2) predictability/productivity; (3) political freedom; and (4) accountability/democracy. Some of these criteria echo the considerations that underlay the design of the original zoning system.

### [a] Fairness

Because a rule is triggered by a categorical set of facts, it forces the decision maker to act consistently by treating like cases in the same manner. In other words, fairness is equated with formal equality of treatment.[40] For example, a rule-based development approvals system prevents the decision maker from taking into account the distinguishing attributes of different applicants, and thereby reduces the danger of arbitrariness and bias. However, hard and fast rules can also be arbitrary at the edge, forcing the decision maker to treat two cases differently despite the fact that they are *substantively* the same in terms of underlying policy objectives. Why must they be treated differently?

The reason is that their respective facts are different in specific, but insignificant, respects and the rules cannot take that into account. In other words, rule-based decision making suppresses relevant similarities and differences. By contrast, standards allow the decision maker to treat like cases that are substantively alike, without being bound in one direction of review by the dictates of a rule.

---

[40] *See generally* Weber, Max, *Economy and Society*, edited by Guenther Roth and Claus Wittich, Berkeley: University of California Press, 1978.

## [b] Predictability/Productivity

Property owners, developers, and other private actors in the market economy feel most keenly about the need for certainty and predictability in order to organize their affairs and make productive business decisions. Standards can produce a climate of uncertainty and consequently inhibit the risk taking necessary for productive actions in the marketplace, while rules afford the certainty and predictability necessary to maximize productivity. However, those who hold a pessimistic view of human nature argue that the bright lines provided by rules also give incentives to individuals to take advantage of situations that rules may not adequately cover, or to exploit situations where knowledge or access to information is distributed unequally, fostering a syndrome of "fools" and "sharp dealers." Rules tend toward obsolescence because unanticipated situations always arise. Standards, being more flexible, allow decision makers to adapt to changing circumstances over time.

## [c] Political Freedom

There are those who argue that rules are essential to political freedom.[41] Equating liberty with laissez-faire capitalism, these advocates of the rule of law view rules as ensuring that "government in all its actions is bound by rules fixed and announced beforehand—rules which make it possible to foresee with fair certainty how the authority will use its coercive powers in given circumstances, and to plan one's individual affairs on the basis of this knowledge."[42] Further, these advocates argue that standards which "qualify legal provisions increasingly by ref-

---

[41] *See generally* Hayek, Frederich A., *The Constitution of Liberty*, Chicago: The University Press, 1960.

[42] Hayek, Frederich A.,*The Road to Serfdom* at 72–73, Chicago: University of Chicago Press, 1944; *See also* Hayek, Frederich A., *The Political Ideal of the Rule of Law* at 43–49, 58–60, Cairo, 1955.

erence to what is 'fair' or 'reasonable'" destroy the rule of law and open the way for official "arbitrariness."[43]

Drawing by Gross © 1996 The New Yorker Magazine, Inc.

### [d] Accountability/Democratic Process

Where there is more than one decision maker, rules have the benefit of helping to allocate roles (jurisdiction) and corresponding power among these decision makers. In effect, rules establish and constrain the jurisdiction of each decision maker. Rules in this context work when there is a theory, such as separation of powers, that defines the relevant role of each decision maker. On the other hand, rules allow the decision maker to avoid responsibility on the ground that the particular rules dictate the results. By contrast, because standards require a balancing of considerations, they make the decision maker more accountable to the weighing process that was done to arrive at a particular decision.

### [2] Summary of Benefits and Drawbacks to Rules and Standards

As is apparent from the preceding discussion, there are merits to both sides of the argument over the use of rules versus standards in regulation. As summarized in the

---

[43] Hayek, Frederich A., *The Road to Serfdom* at 78.

chart below, rules and standards each have benefits and drawbacks.

| RULES | | STANDARDS | |
|---|---|---|---|
| **Benefits** | **Drawbacks** | **Benefits** | **Drawbacks** |
| Certainty | Rigidity | Flexibility | Arbitrariness |
| Uniformity | Overly Detailed | Pragmatism | Favoritism |
| Self-executing | | Simplicity | |

But these benefits and drawbacks do not lead to clear conclusions as to the proper approaches to take in land use regulation. Certainly the "benefits" of rules and the "benefits" of standards serve purposes that are desirable in land use and development regulations. How do we guard against the potential "drawbacks" of each approach?

## § 1.06 Considerations in Utilizing Rules and Standards

When should rules be used instead of standards? When should standards be given priority over rules? I suggest that answers to the following questions should help determine the proper approach.

*Questions*

    (1)   Is the land use/development matter of a substantive or procedural nature?

    (2)   How much information on the land use matter is available to the decision maker?

    (3)   How important is it to the parties concerned that there be dialogue on the issue presented?

    (4)   What is the size/complexity of the project for which approval is sought?

    (5)   Does more than one decision maker have a role to play in deciding the application for approval?

    (6)   Given the type of land use/development issue, is there a significant risk that official arbitrariness

or bias will be reflected in a decision based on standards?

(7) Given the type of land use/development issue, is there a significant risk that the landowner or developer will exploit the rule to produce a result unintended by policy behind the rule?

Addressing these questions before devising a regulatory approach, if it is necessary, will help ensure a better balance in the use of standards and rules to achieve legitimate public purposes.

## § 1.07 Constitutional Limitations on the Exercise of Discretion by Administrative Bodies

At issue in these two governmental approaches to discretionary review is fundamental fairness—the heart of due process. This central principle of the Fifth and Fourteenth Amendments to the Constitution requires that citizens be protected from the fluctuations of legislative policy.[44] Because the right to develop property is a valuable property right,[45] the failure to articulate clear, workable standards reduces the property owner to a state of uncertainty and effectively deprives the owner of that right. Failure to establish standards to guide the exercise of discretion at the administrative level also risks uneven treatment, a denial of equal protection. At worse, as expressed by the Supreme Court of Maine,[46] standardless administration of a zoning ordinance can encourage roving discrimination:

> Without definite standards an ordinance becomes an open door to favoritism and discrimination, a ready

---

[44] West Main Associates v. City of Bellevue, 106 Wash. 2d 47, 720 P.2d 782 (1986), citing The Federalist No. 44 at 301 (J. Madison) (J. Cooke ed. 1961).

[45] Louthan v. King County, 94 Wash. 2d 422, 617 P.2d 977 (1980).

[46] Waterville Hotel Corp. v. Board of Zoning Appeals, 241 A.2d 50, 53 (Me. 1968).

tool for the suppression of competition through the granting of authority to one and the withholding from another. . . . A zoning ordinance cannot permit administrative officers or boards to pick and choose the recipients of their favors.[47]

The two key doctrines that limit the exercise of discretion, and hence its abuse, in the imposition of land use controls are the doctrines of nondelegation of legislative power and void for vagueness.[48] But first a word about the role of "process" in decision making and the constitutional requirement of "due process."

### [1] Due Process

Just as "rules" are viewed as a regulatory method to avoid the potential for abuse, "process" is also touted as a device to avoid "the untidiness of human judgment."[49] Just as "certainty" is the promise of detailed rules, so "responsibility" was the original promise of process. The concept, as championed during the era of the Johnson War on Poverty, was "maximum feasible participation" in decision making, turning process into an end unto itself; the idea being that process contributes to rationality which in turn contributes to effectiveness.[50] In many respects, this concept was a reaction to the New Deal view that purpose was all important and that the power to exercise discretion should be placed in the hands of neutral experts who should be liberated from procedural red tape to accomplish the objectives of the administration.[51] After World War II, perceived abuses during this era led to the

---

[47] *Id.* at 53, quoting Osius v. City of St. Clair Shores, 344 Mich. 693, 75 N.W.2d 25, 58 A.L.R.2d 1079 (1956).

[48] For a general discussion of these principles, *see* Blaesser and Weinstein, eds., *Land Use and the Constitution*, Chicago, Ill.: Planners Press, 1989.

[49] Howard, Philip K., *The Death of Common Sense* at 60, New York: Random House, 1994.

[50] *Id.* at 80.

[51] *Id.* at 77.

adoption of the Administrative Procedures Act (APA), which was designed as a "bill of rights for all who deal with government."[52]

In essence, process in governmental matters has become a rule by itself. The problem is not with procedures established to get something done—a management device—but rather procedures established to protect citizens against government coercion—known as *due process*. Its purpose is to place procedural conditions on government before it may coerce. To effectively protect our freedoms granted under the Constitution, due process must necessarily be inefficient.

### [2]  Nondelegation Doctrine

Legislative power is the power of the legislative branch to make laws—that is, to establish public policy. The making of legislative decisions is generally not subject to the requirements of the due process clause. This means that legislative decision making is relatively informal. In making *legislative* decisions, the legislative body, whether it is the county board of commissioners or a city council, is not required to recite the facts it considered in reaching its decision. The requirement to make findings of fact is imposed on administrative bodies whose decision-making concerns are to carry out the policies or purposes previously declared by the legislative body. These bodies are subject to procedural due process requirements, such as holding formal hearings on matters for decision, avoiding *ex parte* contacts[53] outside of hearings, providing the opportunity for cross-examination on the evidence presented,

---

[52] *See generally* Administrative Procedure Act: Legislative History, Washington, D.C.: Government Printing Office, 1946.

[53] The term *ex parte* in this context refers to a contact done for the benefit of one party only.

and, as mentioned, preparing written findings of fact and conclusions.[54]

Local legislative bodies may not delegate their legislative or policy-making power to administrative boards, commissions, or committees. Legislative bodies may, however, delegate to administrative bodies the authority to exercise discretion provided that the delegation is accompanied by standards and specific procedural guidelines.[55] The delegation issue also implicates the ability of a local legislative body to act as an administrative body. The courts in many states hold that a village board or city council acts in a legislative capacity when it is authorized to approve special uses or planned unit developments. Therefore, no precise standards are necessary.[56] Nor is the village board or city council bound by the recommendations of its staff or experts on such matters.[57]

What if an ordinance provides that an administrative body's ruling is submitted to the city council and the mayor — an executive official — for final approval? Is there a delegation problem? In an Illinois case,[58] an "Appearance Regulation Ordinance," enacted to regulate the external appearance of property, provided for just such a

---

[54] Because administrative bodies must review and draw conclusions from facts presented with respect to a specific parcel of property under these procedural due process requirements, similar to those followed in a court of law, their actions are sometimes referred to as *quasi-judicial* or *adjudicative*—that is, judicial-type or adjudicating actions performed by individuals who are not judges. In some jurisdictions, notably Oregon, the courts have held that a decision by a local legislative body concerning the zoning of an individual parcel is a quasi-judicial rather than a legislative decision. *See* Fasano v. Board of County Com'rs of Washington County, 264 Or. 574, 507 P.2d 23 (1973) (superseded by statute as noted in Menges v. Board of County Com'rs of Jackson County, 44 Or. App. 603, 606 P.2d 681 (1980)).

[55] Montgomery County v. Woodward & Lothrop, Inc., 280 Md. 686, 376 A.2d 483, 500 (1977), citing 8 McQuillin, *Municipal Corporations,* § 25.35 et seq. (3d ed. rev. 1976).

[56] *See, e.g.,* LaSalle Nat. Bank v. Lake County, 27 Ill. App. 3d 10, 325 N.E.2d 105, 110 (2d Dist. 1975).

[57] Minnetonka Congregation of Jehovah's Witnesses, Inc. v. Svee, 303 Minn. 79, 226 N.W.2d 306 (1975).

[58] Waterfront Estates Development, Inc. v. City of Palos Hills, 232 Ill. App. 3d 367, 173 Ill. Dec. 667, 597 N.E.2d 641 (1st Dist. 1992).

procedure for the approval of a certificate of appropriateness. The ordinance stated that the Commission's decisions "shall be submitted to the Mayor and City Council for final decision." The city argued that there was no delegation problem so long as the Commission was required to submit its decisions to the legislative body for final decision. The court found this reasoning defective for two reasons. First, noted the court, because the mayor, as was acknowledged by city, is an executive official, that means that the final decision was not just left to the legislative body. Second, because the ordinance provided no standards to govern the mayor's vote, that may constitute an unconstitutional delegation of legislative power to an executive official.[59]

### [3]  Void for Vagueness

The void for vagueness doctrine is derived from the due process clause of the Fourteenth Amendment, specifically, the procedural due process requirement of notice. The doctrine concerns the lack of clarity or certainty in the language of regulation. Its purpose is to place a limit upon arbitrary and discretionary enforcement of the law.[60] Local courts, when presented with a void for vagueness challenge to a regulation, most frequently echo the U.S. Supreme Court's language,[61] namely, that "[a]n ordinance is unconstitutionally vague when men of common intelligence must necessarily guess at its meaning."[62] In other words, due process of law in legislation requires definiteness or certainty.

The void for vagueness doctrine remains viable in most jurisdictions—except in California. Its state and federal

---

[59] *Id.* at 648.

[60] Burien Bark Supply v. King County, 106 Wash. 2d 868, 725 P.2d 994, 996 (1986) (vagueness found), citing State v. White, 97 Wash. 2d 92, 640 P.2d 1061 (1982).

[61] Broadrick v. Oklahoma, 413 U.S. 601, 93 S. Ct. 2908, 37 L. Ed. 2d 830 (1973).

[62] Union Nat. Bank & Trust Co. of Joliet v. Village of New Lenox, 152 Ill. App. 3d 919, 105 Ill. Dec. 875, 505 N.E.2d 1, 3 (3d Dist. 1987).

court decisions reveal a strong presumption in favor of local governmental controls, including discretionary review provisions. Perhaps the most notorious of such provisions authorizing broad discretionary review powers to an administrative body is exemplified by Section 26 (Part III, Art. I, Permit Procedure) of the Municipal Code of the City of San Francisco. It states:

> In the granting or denying of any permit, or the revoking or the refusing to revoke any permit, the granting or revoking power may take into consideration the effect of the proposed business or calling upon surrounding property and upon its residents, and inhabitants thereof, and in granting or denying said permit, or revoking or refusing to revoke a permit, may exercise its sound discretion as to whether said permit should be granted, transferred, denied or revoked.

In a handful of decisions since 1943, California courts have been consistent in holding that this provision vests the city planning commission with "sound discretion" to deny, approve, or approve with conditions any building permit over which it chooses to exercise "discretionary review."[63] In the name of "sound discretion," the planning commission has used the sparse language of Section 26 to impose a wide range of conditions on requests for building permits for uses otherwise allowed as of right in the zoning district. For example, in one case, the owner of a building with shops and apartments in a business district applied for a permit to renovate the building by replacing some of the rental units with commercial uses. But the planning commission invoked its power of discretionary review in response to the tenants' protest over the planned conversion of their units to commercial space. As conditions for its approval of the requested building permit, the

---

[63] *See* Guinnane v. San Francisco City Planning Com., 209 Cal. App. 3d 732, 257 Cal. Rptr. 742 (1st Dist. 1989); City and County of San Francisco v. Superior Court of City and County of San Francisco, 53 Cal. 2d 236, 1 Cal. Rptr. 158, 347 P.2d 294 (1959); Lindell Co. v. Board of Permit Appeals of City and County of San Francisco, 23 Cal. 2d 303, 144 P.2d 4 (1943).

commission required that the owner not only "cause" replacement units to be developed within a three-quarter-mile radius of the building, but provide relocation assistance to boot![64]

Remarkably, the California courts have upheld the planning commission's expansive interpretation of its discretionary review powers on the basis of a 1954 city attorney opinion stating that "[s]uch long-standing administrative interpretation of a statute by an agency charged with its enforcement and interpretation is entitled to great weight."[65]

Not surprisingly, a management audit of the Department of City Planning prepared for the San Francisco Board of Supervisors observed the following about discretionary review:

> In discharging its responsibilities with respect to prescribing conditions of approval in discretionary review and conditional use cases, the Planning Commission sometimes includes provisions, in excess of those necessary to insure that a particular proposed project is beneficial to its neighborhood and to the City, that have been agreed to by community groups and project sponsors. Reportedly, project sponsors will agree to such additional conditions in order to avoid the litigation that would be brought by community groups in the absence of additional conditions.

* * *

> We believe that the practice of the Planning Commission requiring cash contributions and being party to agreements which go beyond the purposes of the Planning Code, with respect to a particular project, and which are constructed to bring a benefit to a com-

---

[64] See Pearl Inv. Co. v. City and County of San Francisco, No. 878–347, San Francisco Superior Court; Pearl Inv. Co. v. City and County of San Francisco, 774 F.2d 1460 (9th Cir. 1985).

[65] See Guinnane v. San Francisco City Planning Com., 209 Cal. App. 3d 732, 257 Cal. Rptr. 742, 746 (1st Dist. 1989).

munity and to allow a project sponsor to avoid litigation, is questionable.[66]

Unfortunately, these critical findings from the management audit do not appear to have led to any lessening of the abuses of discretion that occur under Section 26 of the San Francisco Municipal Code.

## § 1.08   The "Takings Clause" and Discretionary Exactions

U.S. Supreme Court Justice Stevens once remarked that "even the wisest of lawyers would have to acknowledge great uncertainty about the scope of this Court's taking jurisprudence."[67] Nevertheless, it is necessary to understand some generally accepted background principles about the so-called "Takings Clause" of the Fifth Amendment to the U.S. Constitution before explaining how that clause acts as a check on discretionary decision making in land use decisions.[68] What is a taking? Government appropriation of private land, either directly pursuant to a statute (eminent domain) or indirectly through the restrictive effect of its regulations (inverse condemnation), is termed a *taking*. There is a critical distinction between these two kinds of taking. To exercise the power of eminent domain, the condemning authority must undertake statutorily prescribed procedures that will result in the formal transfer of title from the landowner to the condemning authority. By contrast, a regulatory taking is described as indirect, or an inverse condemnation, because it results from the restrictive impact of a land use planning or regulatory decision upon the landowner's property.

---

[66] Report to the San Francisco Board of Supervisors: Management Audit of the Department of City Planning at 53 (December 1988).

[67] Supreme Court Justice Stevens dissenting in Nollan v. California Coastal Com'n, 483 U.S. 825, 826, 107 S. Ct. 3141, 97 L. Ed. 2d 677, 26 Env't. Rep. Cas. (BNA) 1073, 17 Envtl. L. Rep. 20918 (1987).

[68] The Takings clause of the Fifth Amendment to the U.S. Constitution states in relevant part: "[N]or shall private property be taken for public use, without just compensation."

The United States Supreme Court has made clear that a property owner may be entitled to compensation for the time between the point at which a regulation is enacted and the point at which a court determines that the regulation is excessive.[69] Historically, a property owner's remedy was limited to an action to have the offending regulation declared unconstitutional, but pronouncements by the United States Supreme Court in 1987 have made it clear that invalidation of the offending regulation does not relieve government of its duty to pay damages for the period during which the taking was effective.[70]

## [1] Factors Considered in Determining Whether There Has Been a Regulatory Taking

The inquiry into whether or not a regulation is so excessive as to constitute a regulatory taking is multifaceted. With few exceptions, no single factor is dispositive. These factors, as derived from various U.S. Supreme Court cases,[71] are summarized below.

---

[69] First English Evangelical Lutheran Church of Glendale v. Los Angeles County, Cal., 482 U.S. 304, 107 S. Ct. 2378, 96 L. Ed. 2d 250, 26 Env't. Rep. Cas. (BNA) 1001, 17 Envtl. L. Rep. 20787 (1987); Lucas v. South Carolina Coastal Council, 505 U.S. 1003, 112 S. Ct. 2886, 120 L. Ed. 2d 798, 34 Env't. Rep. Cas. (BNA) 1897, 22 Envtl. L. Rep. 21104 (1992).

[70] Id.

[71] Penn Cent. Transp. Co. v. City of New York, 438 U.S. 104, 98 S. Ct. 2646, 57 L. Ed. 2d 631, 11 Env't. Rep. Cas. (BNA) 1801, 8 Envtl. L. Rep. 20528 (1978), reh'g denied, 439 U.S. 883, 99 S. Ct. 226, 58 L. Ed. 2d 198 (1978); First English Evangelical Lutheran Church of Glendale v. Los Angeles County, Cal., 482 U.S. 304, 107 S. Ct. 2378, 96 L. Ed. 2d 250, 26 Env't. Rep. Cas. (BNA) 1001, 17 Envtl. L. Rep. 20787 (1987); Hodel v. Irving, 481 U.S. 704, 107 S. Ct. 2076, 95 L. Ed. 2d 668 (1987); Keystone Bituminous Coal Ass'n v. DeBenedictis, 480 U.S. 470, 107 S. Ct. 1232, 94 L. Ed. 2d 472, 25 Env't. Rep. Cas. (BNA) 1649, 17 Envtl. L. Rep. 20440 (1987); Loretto v. Teleprompter Manhattan CATV Corp., 458 U.S. 419, 102 S. Ct. 3164, 73 L. Ed. 2d 868, 8 Media L. Rep. (BNA) 1849 (1982); San Diego Gas & Elec. Co. v. City of San Diego, 450 U.S. 621, 101 S. Ct. 1287, 67 L. Ed. 2d 551, 11 Envtl. L. Rep. 20345 (1981); Pennsylvania Coal Co. v. Mahon, 260 U.S. 393, 43 S. Ct. 158, 67 L. Ed.

---

## REGULATORY TAKINGS FACTORS

1. A land use regulation does not relate to a legitimate state interest; or

2. Assuming a legitimate state interest, the regulation does not substantially advance that interest; or

3. The advancement of a legitimate state interest places a disproportionate burden of securing a benefit upon a single landowner when it is more properly borne by the general community; or

4. The regulation entails a permanent physical occupation; or

5. Reasonable investments were made prior to the general notice of the regulatory program; or

6. The economic effect of the regulation deprives the landowner of all or substantially all beneficial use of the property and there are no offsetting reciprocal benefits; or

7. The regulation abrogates an essential element of private property.

---

These factors require factual inquiries and, except when a regulation has deprived a landowner of all economically beneficial use or entails a permanent physical occupation, must be weighed together in determining whether a regulation taking has occurred.[72] For this reason, it is unlikely that the mere enactment of a law or the promulgation of a regulation will result in a regulatory taking.

---

322, 28 A.L.R. 1321 (1922); Mugler v. Kansas, 123 U.S. 623, 8 S. Ct. 273, 31 L. Ed. 205 (1887).

[72] Lucas v. South Carolina Coastal Council, 505 U.S. 1003, 1019 n.8, 112 S. Ct. 2886, 120 L. Ed. 2d 798, 34 Env't. Rep. Cas. (BNA) 1897, 22 Envtl. L. Rep. 21104 (1992), citing Penn Cent. Transp. Co. v. City of New York, 438 U.S. 104, 124, 98 S. Ct. 2646, 57 L. Ed. 2d 631, 11 Env't. Rep. Cas. (BNA) 1801, 8 Envtl. L. Rep. 20528 (1978), reh'g denied, 439 U.S. 883, 99 S. Ct. 226, 58 L. Ed. 2d 198 (1978). See also Palazzolo v. Rhode Island, 121 S. Ct. 2448, 150 L. Ed. 2d 592 (U.S. 2001).

Reprinted by permission of Inman News Features.

## [2] Categorical Taking Rules

The U.S. Supreme Court has identified two clear instances of a regulatory taking:

(1) A regulation entailing the permanent physical occupation of property.

(2) A regulation depriving landowners of all productive use of the land.

### [a] Regulation That Results in Permanent Physical Occupation of Property

The first instance is when a regulation causes a property owner to suffer a physical invasion of property. This always constitutes a taking no matter how small the intrusion or how great the public purpose.[73] Thus, a regulation

---

[73] Loretto v. Teleprompter Manhattan CATV Corp., 458 U.S. 419, 102 S. Ct. 3164, 73 L. Ed. 2d 868, 8 Media L. Rep. (BNA) 1849 (1982); Lucas v. South Carolina Coastal Council, 505 U.S. 1003, 1017, 112 S.

compelling building owners to permit a cable television company to install cables on the property was deemed a taking, notwithstanding that the area required to be physically occupied was extremely small and the economic impact on the owner indiscernible.[74]

The application of this per se rule is illustrated in another U.S. Supreme Court case. In *Nollan*, a California case involving the actions of the California Coastal Commission,[75] the Commission granted a permit to the Nollans to replace a small bungalow on their beachfront property with a larger house. However, as a condition of its permission, the Commission required the Nollans to grant an easement to the public to pass across their private beach which was located between two public beaches. The Commission's stated purpose for this condition was the public's interest in being able to see the beach so as to avoid psychological barriers to its access and in preventing congestion on the beaches. The Nollans claimed that the easement requirement constituted a taking of property without just compensation.

In assessing the Nollans' taking claim, the Supreme Court held that the regulation must "substantially advance" the "legitimate state interest" sought to be achieved; that is, there must be a sufficient connection ("essential nexus") between the regulation and the state interest to justify the regulation imposed.[76] Even assuming that the state had a legitimate interest in the public's being able to see the beach so as to avoid psychological barriers to its access and in preventing congestion on the beaches, the Court concluded that the easement did not substantially advance those interests. Being able to walk

---

Ct. 2886, 120 L. Ed. 2d 798, 34 Env't. Rep. Cas. (BNA) 1897, 22 Envtl. L. Rep. 21104 (1992).

[74] *Loretto*, 458 U.S. at 420.

[75] Nollan v. California Coastal Com'n, 483 U.S. 825, 107 S. Ct. 3141, 97 L. Ed. 2d 677, 26 Env't. Rep. Cas. (BNA) 1073, 17 Envtl. L. Rep. 20918 (1987).

[76] *Id.* at 834, 841 (emphasis added) (quoting Agins v. City of Tiburon, 447 U.S. 255, 260, 100 S. Ct. 2138, 65 L. Ed. 2d 106, 14 Env't. Rep. Cas. (BNA) 1555, 10 Envtl. L. Rep. 20361 (1980)).

across the Nollans' property would not reduce the obstacle to seeing the beach created by the new house, lessen psychological barriers to use of the public beaches, or remedy congestion caused by the Nollans' activity.[77]

The Court illustrated its point another way, using the per se taking rule regarding permanent physical occupation. It analyzed the condition imposed by the California Coastal Commission independently of the permit approval, noting that if the Commission had required the easement from the Nollans without tying it to the permit approval, it would have had to pay just compensation. This is because the right to exclude others from one's property is a protected property interest under the Fifth Amendment. An easement giving the public the permanent and continuous right to traverse the Nollans' property would entail a permanent physical occupation, which is always a taking requiring compensation.[78]

One of the regulatory results under smart growth initiatives directed at the quality and character of communities is a new generation of tree preservation ordinances.[79] The underlying premise of these new tree preservation ordinances is that all trees are a public resource. The assumption is that government may control all public resources. If that assumption is true, then government may also control all trees. This is a tremendous shift from the concept of private ownership for trees growing on private property to the perception of community ownership of trees growing on private property.

Traditionally, tree preservation ordinances limited their scope to the protection of trees located in public rights-of-way, streets, avenues and public parks. Such ordinances also provided for the regulation of privately owned trees

---

[77] Id. at 837–39.

[78] Id. at 832, 836, and 841–42.

[79] See discussion of "smart growth" in the Preface to the third edition. The analysis presented here is based in large part on the article by Ruthmarie Shae in the State and Local Government Section publication of the American Bar Association. See Shae, "A Shorter Cut to Forestation: The Constitutionality of Local Tree Ordinances," State & Local News (Vol. 20, No. 4, Summer 1997).

when they are dead, diseased or constitute a threat to public safety. The legal authority for this type of tree ordinance is derived from the common law of nuisance[80] and the police power—the legislative power that resides in each state and is delegated to municipalities to establish laws and ordinances to preserve the public order and to promote the public health, safety and morals, and other aspects of the general welfare.

The new variety of tree preservation ordinances seeks to regulate privately owned trees for reasons that have nothing to do with abating nuisance, preventing disease, transmission or avoiding injury to the public. Typical language of a statement of purpose for a new tree ordinance is:

> To protect *public health* by absorbing air pollutants and contamination, by providing buffering to reduce excessive noise, wind and storm impacts, then by maintaining visual screening with its accompanying cooling effect during the summer months;
>
> To provide for *public safety* through the prevention of erosion, siltation and flooding;
>
> To contribute significantly to the *general welfare* of the City by providing natural beauty and recreational opportunities for existing and future residents.[81]

Based upon these statements of purpose, this new type of tree ordinance typically requires that for each tree removed from the landowner's property, another tree like

---

[80] The term "nuisance" refers to the use of one's property in a manner that seriously interferes with another's use or enjoyment of his or her property (a private nuisance) or is injurious to the community at large (a public nuisance). Unlike the concept of "trespass" to land, nuisance does not require a physical invasion of others' property. *See generally* Blaesser & Weinstein, eds., *Land Use and the Constitution* 9(Planners Press: 1989). *See also* the U.S. Supreme Court's discussion of the "nuisance exception" in the *Lucas* case in Section 1.08[2][b] *infra*.

[81] *See* City of Sterling Heights, Macomb County, Michigan, Ordinance No. 292, Article III, Tree Preservation (1991) (emphasis in original).

it be replanted elsewhere on the site.[82] If that is not feasible, the ordinance may also require payment of a fee in lieu to a community tree preservation fund. Some ordinances also provide that removing, cutting, "severely over pruning" a tree deemed protected under the ordinance constitutes a public nuisance, punishable by criminal penalties.[83] Another typical tree preservation ordinance provision is that which prohibits property owners from removing trees on their land prior to or "in anticipation of" development.

---

[82] *See* Georgetown County, South Carolina Tree Protection Regulations, Article IX, §§ 1102-1103 (Draft of Proposed Regulations dated June 14, 1999).

[83] *See, e.g.*, City of Jacksonville, Florida Landscape and Tree Protection Regulations, Part 12, Chapter 656, Section 656.1210 (proposed amendments to regulations dated July 7, 1999).

"I'll tell you what else in there deserves to be protected:
$744,000 of mine!"

Reprinted by permission of William Hamilton, the Rockefeller Brothers Fund, and *The Use of Land: A Citizen's Policy Guide to Urban Growth* (1973).

If a person owns property in fee simple absolute, that ownership means that the person possesses a full and unrestricted right to use the property, provided that he does not commit a nuisance against his neighbor. In fact, this fee simple ownership is generally recognized as broadly including the right to make any use of the land, including cutting timber.[84] It can be argued that the new tree ordinances, by authorizing the local government to monitor and impose penalties on property owners who remove trees on the site essentially are down grading the property owner's fee interest to that of a *life estate*. A life estate in property means that one has use of the property during one's lifetime subject to the rule that the holder of the life estate interest must not commit "waste" on the property— that is a duty owed to the owner of the balance of the fee interest: the remainderman. In effect, tree removal on private property is now waste for which the remainder persons must be compensated. The remainder persons are the people in the community—present and future. By the local government intervening on behalf of the community, effectively has created a constructive easement in trees over the private property owner's property.

It seems to me that this regulatory circumstance is no different than the circumstance presented in the *Nollan* case, where the California Coastal Commission imposed a constructive easement as a condition for granting a permit.[85] The Court in *Nollan* said that the Coastal Commission could require an easement, but it had to pay for it. The new generation of tree preservation ordinances that are sprouting up around this country do not provide for payment for the easements they create on private property. They merely assume that the control of privately owned trees is a public resource for which no compensation is required.

### [b] Regulation That Deprives Landowner of All Productive Use

The second per se taking rule is when *all* economically beneficial or productive use of land is eliminated by a regulation. This rule, already applied by most state courts,

---

[84] *See* H. Tiffanny, *A Treatise on the Modern Law of Real Property* § 29 (1940).

[85] *See* discussion of *Nollan* case in Section 1.08[2][a] *supra*.

was only recently clarified by the U.S. Supreme Court in the *Lucas* case.[86] This rule states that total economic deprivation by regulation is, by definition, a taking, subject only to the Supreme Court's "nuisance" exception discussed below.

The facts of the *Lucas* case are relatively simple. Lucas bought two residential lots on a South Carolina barrier island on which he intended to build single-family homes. Property on both sides of the lots were improved with single-family residences. In 1988, the state legislature enacted the Beachfront Management Act which prohibited Lucas from constructing any permanent habitable structures on his parcels. Lucas admitted that the Beachfront Management Act was a lawful exercise of the State's police power, but argued that it nonetheless deprived him of all economically viable use of his property—a taking requiring the payment of just compensation. The South Carolina Supreme Court held that no taking had occurred in light of Lucas's failure to attack the act's validity, accepting and deferring to the legislative findings that a valuable public resource, the state's coastal zone, was threatened. The South Carolina court engaged in one of the traditional inquiries of takings analysis—whether the regulation prevented a harmful or noxious use or conferred an uncompensated benefit on the public. The court found that the regulation was designed to prevent a harmful or noxious use of property.

The United States Supreme Court reversed and remanded the case to determine if a taking had in fact occurred. The significant points of the Court's majority opinion can be summarized as follows:

> (1) A regulation which renders property valueless must be compensated, irrespective of whether or not the police power is lawfully exercised, unless the deprivation of value as a result of the regula-

---

[86] Lucas v. South Carolina Coastal Council, 505 U.S. 1003, 112 S. Ct. 2886, 120 L. Ed. 2d 798, 34 Env't. Rep. Cas. (BNA) 1897, 22 Envtl. L. Rep. 21104 (1992).

tion inhered in the title itself as found in the state's law of property and nuisance, or the regulation could be promulgated by the state under its complementary power to abate nuisances that affect the public generally.

(2)   The traditional distinction between "harm preventing" and "benefit conferring" is a subjective distinction, all in the eye of the beholder. Such determinations depend primarily upon one's evaluation of the worth of competing uses of real estate. This distinction is difficult, if not impossible, to discern and cannot serve as the basis to distinguish regulatory "takings" requiring compensation from regulatory deprivations that do not require compensation. Instead, the courts must look to the nature of the property interest held by the property owner, and whether the proscribed use was part of the owner's title to begin with.[87]

Based on these principles, the Supreme Court reversed the South Carolina Supreme Court's decision and remanded the case, directing the State of South Carolina to identify the background principles of nuisance and property law that prohibit Lucas from constructing residences on the property.

As noted above, Justice Scalia, writing for the majority in *Lucas*, rejected the harm-benefit rule that a land use regulation is a taking if it confers a public benefit rather than prevents a harm.[88] This rule had, in fact, favored landowners for two reasons. First, it allowed a court to find that a regulation was a taking even though the economic deprivation was minimal. Second, the rule imposed a narrow scope to governmental purpose, namely, harm prevention. Unfortunately, without this rule, in cases where a regulation does not deprive a landowner of all economically beneficial use, courts may now be free to-

---

[87] *Id.* at 1024–29.
[88] *Id.*

review the regulation under the broader balancing of factors approach discussed above and find that there has been no taking.[89]

*"By God, for a minute there it suddenly all made sense!"*

### [3] Temporary Takings

Once upon a time—prior to 1987—a government found liable for a regulatory taking had the option of rescinding the offending regulation, without being required to pay compensation for the period of time that the regulation was in effect. The U.S. Supreme Court's 1987 decision in the *First English* case[90] recognized that government had this rescission option, but held that it may also be required to pay compensation for the period during which the taking was effective:

---

[89] *See* Mandelker, "Of Mice and Missiles: A True Account of Lucas v. South Carolina Coastal Council," 8 J. Land Use & Envtl. L. 285, 295 (Spring 1993).

[90] First English Evangelical Lutheran Church of Glendale v. Los Angeles County, Cal., 482 U.S. 304, 107 S. Ct. 2378, 96 L. Ed. 2d 250, 26 Env't. Rep. Cas. (BNA) 1001, 17 Envtl. L. Rep. 20787 (1987).

> Once a court determines that a taking has occurred, the government retains the whole range of functions already available — amendment of the regulation, withdrawal of the invalidated regulation, or exercise of eminent domain. . . [B]ut no subsequent action by the government can relieve it of the duty to provide compensation for the period during which the taking was effective.[91]

The Supreme Court also reiterated its prior statement in *Agins*[92] that unreasonable delay during the land use decision making process may amount to a temporary taking. This does not mean that the delays resulting from the "tyranny of staff" problem[93] previously discussed constitute a temporary taking. In fact, the Supreme Court was careful to state that its decision did not address the "quite different questions that would arise in the course of normal delays in obtaining building permits, changes in zoning ordinances, variances and the like."[94]

But an interim control[95], such as a moratorium, does raise a temporary taking issue. A moratorium either

---

[91] *Id.* at 321. See also Lucas v. South Carolina Coastal Council, 505 U.S. 1003, 112 S. Ct. 2886, 120 L. Ed. 2d 798, 34 Env't. Rep. Cas. (BNA) 1897, 22 Envtl. L. Rep. 21104 (1992) discussed in Section 1.08 [2] [b] in which the Supreme Court applying the compensation principle of *First English* held that the South Carolina statute that deprived Mr. Lucas of any viable economic use of his property constituted a taking. After he filed his lawsuit, South Carolina amended the statute to create a permitting procedure to counter takings claims such as that brought by Mr. Lucas. This amendment also precluded a finding by the Court that the statute effected a permanent taking of Mr. Lucas' property. Rather, it found that a taking had occurred from the date of passage of the statute until its amendment—a temporary taking.

[92] Agins v. City of Tiburon, 447 U.S. 255, 100 S. Ct. 2138, 65 L. Ed. 2d 106, 14 Env't. Rep. Cas. (BNA) 1555, 10 Envtl. L. Rep. 20361 (1980). The Court stated: "Mere fluctuations in value during the process of governmental decision making, absent extraordinary delay, are 'incidents of ownership.'" *Id.* at 263.

[93] See Section 1.04[5] *supra.*

[94] First English, 482 U.S. at 321.

[95] *Interim controls* is a term used to encompass a broad range of techniques having the same objective, namely, to slow or halt development activity. Interim control techniques may include administrative refusal to process, or delay in processing, building permit applications, moratoria on provision of public facilities and services and other interim ordinances and resolutions designed to interdict development activity.

prohibits all development, or certain types of development, for a defined period of time. The moratorium is one of the principal tools in the "toolbox" of local governments for implementing growth management objectives. It typically is adopted by ordinance and, if adopted in good faith, is intended to provide a community with the time to conduct and review studies necessary for adopting or revising a land use plan and related regulations to achieve growth management policies. Because planning activities are time consuming, the moratorium allows for a "planning pause" period during which period land development activity is frozen or limited until permanent regulations implementing the plan can be adopted.

Generally, the legal defensibility of a moratorium against a temporary taking claim depends on whether the interim controls were adopted in good faith and for a reasonably short period of time and whether the local government proceeded diligently in completing whatever study or analysis was deemed necessary in adopting permanent regulations.[96] It is also important that there be reasonable and beneficial economic uses possible during the period of the moratorium.[97]

However, if the temporary restriction is sufficiently onerous, it is a taking—"not different in kind from permanent takings, for the which the constitution clearly requires compensation."[98] Of course, this statement from the Supreme Court does not really tell us when a temporary restriction effects a taking. But the facts in some cases are instructive. For example, in one Florida case,[99] Mr. Corn, the property owner, proposed building a 900 unit mini-warehouse on a parcel zoned for such a use. The city rejected the proposal because of a change in zoning

---

[96] See, e.g., Q.C. Const. Co., Inc. v. Gallo, 649 F. Supp. 1331 (D.R.I. 1986), judgment aff'd, 836 F.2d 1340 (1st Cir. 1987); Lake Illyria Corp. v. Town of Gardiner, 43 A.D.2d 386, 352 N.Y.S.2d 54 (3d Dep't 1974).

[97] See, e.g., Merriam Gateway Associates v. Town of Newton, N.J., 91 F.3d 124 (3d Cir. 1996); Herrington v. City of Pearl, Miss., 908 F. Supp. 418 (S.D. Miss. 1995).

[98] First English, 482 at 318.

[99] Corn v. City of Lauderdale Lakes, 71 F. Supp. 1557 (S.D. Fla 1991).

and an enactment of a moratorium. It was apparent that the moratorium was consciously designed to stop the project and not truly in the public interest. The Court decided: "The moratorium seems nothing more than an attempt at *post hoc* rationalization. In short, the city council was motivated solely by an irrational desire to thwart Corn's plans."[100]

Municipalities frequently assert that the power to impose a moratorium is essential to its power to regulate land use—a legitimate governmental purpose. However, a recent decision by the Pennsylvania Supreme Court flatly rejected that position.[101] In that case, the township had enacted a moratorium on certain types of subdivision and land development approvals while it completed the process of revising its comprehensive plan. The township had no express statutory authority to enact such a moratorium, relying instead on the premise that such power was implicitly granted or incidental to the zoning powers expressed conferred on municipalities by statute.

The Pennsylvania Supreme Court concluded that the "power to *enact* a zoning ordinance, for whatever purpose, does not necessarily include the power to *suspend* a valid zoning ordinance to the prejudice of a land owner." The court went on to conclude that the "power to *suspend* land development" is a power "distinct from and not incidental to any power to *regulate* land development," and was not permissible without express legislative authorization.[102] The reasoning of this decision is significant in that it underscores the importance of establishing by express legislation the authority for local governments to adopt moratoria and defining what are deemed legitimate purposes for moratoria. This limits the potential for a municipality to use a moratorium under the guise of growth management as a *post hoc* rationalization for an arbitrary purpose such as occurred in Mr. Corn's case.

---

[100] *Id.* at 1569.
[101] Naylor v. Township of Hellam, 773 A.2d 770 (Pa. 2001).
[102] *Id.* at 774.

The U.S. Court of Appeals for the 9th Circuit has recently rendered a dicision that appears to ignore the U.S. Supreme Court's pronouncements on temparary takings. The case involved a challenge by property owners to a series of moratoria instituted by the Tahoe Regional Planning Agency (TRPA).[103] The 9th Circuit distinguished a development moratorium from the type of temporary taking in *First English.* The case involves approximately 450 owners of property in the Lake Tahoe Basin. The TRPA—the regional governmental body established by a Congressionally approved compact between California and Nevada—has the power to plan and control development within the 501 square mile bi-state region around the lake.

Beginning in 1981, the TRPA enacted a series of moratoria to halt development while a new regional plan was being prepared to protect the alpine lake from environmental impacts. These moratoria were put in place between 1981 and 1987, when the second of two plans was adopted. The case on appeal to the 9th Circuit concerned the federal district court's holding that for some of the property owners, the development moratoria constituted a categorical taking under *Lucas.* The property owners had not just argued that the moratoria constituted a temporary taking. Rather, as explained by the 9th Circuit:

> The plaintiffs contend that, for purposes of determining whether the regulations constitute a categorical taking under *Lucas,* we should not treat the plaintiffs' properties as the fee interests they are. Instead, they argue, we should define narrowly, as a separate property interest, the temporal "slice" of each fee that covers the time span during which Ordinance 81-5 and Resolution 83-21 were in effect. It is this carved-out

---

[103] Tahoe-Sierra Preservation Council, Inc. v. Tahoe Regional Planning Agency, 216 F.3d 764, 30 Envtl. L. Rep. 20638 (9th Cir. 2000), reh'g and reh'g en banc denied, 228 F.3d 998 (9th Cir. 2000) and cert. granted in part, 121 S. Ct. 2589, 150 L. Ed. 2d 749 (U.S. 2001). The case before the 9th Circuit was the culmination of prior court decisions, appeals, amendments and consolidations from the litigation that the property owners brought beginning in 1985.

piece of each plaintiff's property interest, the plaintiffs assert, that has been "taken" by the regulations.[104]

The "slices" referred to by the 9th Circuit referred to four periods of time as defined by the district court for analyzing the plaintiffs' claims: the first slice being the two-year period of the initial moratorium from 1981 to 1983 when Ordinance 81-5 was in effect; the second slice being the next eight months when Resolution 83-21 was in effect; the third slice being the three-year period running from the 1984 plan to the adoption of the 1987 plan; and the fourth slice being the period of the 1987 plan to the present.

Viewing each of these periods as separate, the trial court had found the TRPA liable for a temporary regulatory taking for the first two moratorium periods, but not liable for the last two.[105]

Instead of setting a valuation trial to address compensation, the district court certified the liability for an interlocutory appeal to the 9th Circuit, which reversed the district court's temporary regulatory taking finding.

The 9th Circuit rejected the plaintiffs argument (accepted by the trial court) that the U.S. Supreme Court's holding in *First English* requires severing or "slicing" the property owners' fee interests into temporal periods—in this case, the four time periods during which the property owners had no use of their property. That, said the court, is "flatly incorrect," stating:

> Contrary to the plaintiffs' suggestion, . . the Court's holding in *First English* was not that temporary moratoria are "temporary takings." In fact, the opposite is true. The *First English* Court very carefully defined "'temporary' regulatory takings [as] those

---

[104] *Id.* at 774.

[105] As for the last two time periods, the trial court found no injury due to the 1984 plan because it was enjoined as soon as it was adopted. It ruled the takings claim for the time period beginning with the 1987 plan was time barred because the statute of limitations ran out while the plaintiffs were before the 9th Circuit seeking reversal of the dismissal of their original complaints.

regulatory takings which are ultimately invalidated by the courts." [Citations omitted] What is "temporary," according to the Court's definition, is not the regulation; rather, what is "temporary" is the taking, which is rendered temporary only when an ordinance that effects a taking is struck down by a court. In other words, a *permanent* regulation leads to a *"temporary"* taking when a court invalidates the ordinance after the taking.[106]

In sum, the 9th Circuit held that the "temporary takings" doctrine of *First English* does not apply to temporary development moratoria.[107]

The 9th Circuit elaborated on this holding by explaining that, in its view, a temporary taking should not be considered a denial of all economically viable use under the holding in *Lucas.* According to the court, the "use" of plaintiffs' property "runs from the present to the future." The temporary moratorium instituted by the TRPA only "denied the plaintiffs only a small portion of this future stream". . . a small fraction of the useful life of the Tahoe properties."[108]

The 9th Circuit's rejection of the concept of temporal severance was based in large part on the *Agins* case in which the Supreme Court had stated that "[m]ere fluctuations in value during the process of governmental decisionmaking, absent extraordinary delay, are 'incidents of ownership.' They cannot be considered as a 'taking' in the constitutional sense."[109] It seems to me, however, that the 9th Circuit's holding that a temporary development moratorium should not ever be considered a taking under the holding in *Lucas* begs the question of when a moratorium extended over time incrementally, in fact, constitutes "extraordinary delay" in government decision making. The holding effectively precludes property owners denied economically viable use of their property during an

---

[106] *Id.* at 778 (Emphasis in original).
[107] *Id.*
[108] *Id.* at 782.
[109] Agins v. Tiburon, 447 U.S. 255, 263 (1980).

extended moratorium from pursing the compensation remedy under *First English*. The U.S. Supreme Court's decision to grant certiorari in this case will give the Court the opportunity to clarify temporary regulatory takings law in light of its decisions in *First English* and *Lucas*.

## § 1.09 The "Rough Proportionality" Test for Discretionary Exactions

In June of 1994, in the *Dolan* case,[110] the U.S. Supreme Court announced a new federal takings standard with respect to property exactions. This new standard answered a question that was left unanswered by the Supreme Court in a California case,[111] in which the Court held that there must be an "essential nexus" between a condition imposed and the "legitimate state interest."[112] The question the Court did not answer was "the required degree of connection between exactions and the projected impact of the proposed development."[113] This was because it concluded that the Coastal Commission's justification for requiring an easement over the Nollans' beach property did not even meet the essential nexus standard. In *Dolan*, the Supreme Court finally addressed this second question and, in the process, articulated a new constitutional standard that will require local governments to change the ways in which they impose conditions on development approval.

### [1]   Facts of *Dolan*

In *Dolan*, the landowner, Florence Dolan, owned and operated a plumbing and electrical supply store in an area

---

[110] Dolan v. City of Tigard, 512 U.S. 374, 114 S. Ct. 2309, 129 L. Ed. 2d 304, 38 Env't. Rep. Cas. (BNA) 1769, 24 Envtl. L. Rep. 21083 (1994).

[111] Nollan v. California Coastal Com'n, 483 U.S. 825, 107 S. Ct. 3141, 97 L. Ed. 2d 677, 26 Env't. Rep. Cas. (BNA) 1073, 17 Envtl. L. Rep. 20918 (1987).

[112] *Id.* at 837.

[113] *Dolan*, 512 U.S. at 386.

zoned as a central business district (CBD). The store covered approximately 9,700 square feet on the eastern side of a 1.67-acre parcel. A creek flowed through the lot's southwestern corner and along its western boundary. The portion of the property lying within the creek's 100-year floodplain was virtually unusable for commercial development. The City adopted a comprehensive plan and codified it in its community development code (CDC). Among the plan's requirements, property owners in the CBD needed to comply with a 15 percent open space and landscaping requirement. The City also adopted a plan for a pedestrian/bicycle pathway to encourage alternatives to automobile transportation in the CBD, as well as a master drainage plan to alleviate flooding problems along the creek, which included an area near the Dolan property.

Ms. Dolan applied to the City for a permit to increase her store's size to 17,600 square feet and to pave a 39-space parking lot. The City Planning Commission approved the permit application subject to conditions imposed by the CDC, which contains the following standard for site development review approval:

> Where landfill and/or development is allowed within and adjacent to the 100-year floodplain, the City shall require the dedication of sufficient open land area for greenway adjoining and within the floodplain. This area shall include portions at a suitable elevation for the construction of a pedestrian/bicycle pathway within the floodplain in accordance with the adopted pedestrian/bicycle plan.[114]

Consequently, the City Planning Commission required that Dolan (1) dedicate the portion of her property line within the 100-year floodplain for improvement of the storm drainage system along the creek; and (2) dedicate an additional 15-foot strip of land adjacent to the floodplain as a pedestrian/bicycle pathway. The dedication required by that condition encompassed approximately 7,000 square feet or roughly 10 percent of the property.

---

[114] *Id.* at 379.

In imposing the development conditions on the approval of the Dolan permit, the Commission made a series of findings regarding the project's anticipated impacts. First, it noted that "[i]t is reasonable to assume that customers and employees of the future uses of this site could utilize a pedestrian/bicycle pathway adjacent to this development for their transportation and recreational needs."[115] The Commission further found that creating a convenient, safe pedestrian/bicycle pathway system "could offset some of the traffic demand on [nearby] streets and lessen the increase in traffic congestion."[116] The Commission also concluded that the required floodplain dedication would be reasonably related to Dolan's request to intensify the use of the site given the increase in the impervious surface. Based on the anticipated increase in stormwater flow, the Commission concluded that "the requirement of dedication of the floodplain area on the site is related to the applicant's plan to intensify development on the site."[117]

### [2] Supreme Court's Holding

In an opinion written by Chief Justice Rehnquist, the Supreme Court held that the required floodplain dedication was unconstitutional because it did not merely prohibit the landowner from building in the floodplain but demanded that she grant a permanent easement for the public to use the dedicated strip of land as a public greenway along the river, thus constituting a taking of property without just compensation. With respect to the bicycle path condition, the Court also declared that the development exaction was unconstitutional. While it acknowledged that dedications for streets, sidewalks, and other public ways are reasonable exactions to control traffic congestion generated by a proposed property use, it stated that "the city has not met its burden of demonstrating

---

[115] *Id.*
[116] *Id.* at 382.
[117] *Id.*

that the additional number of vehicle and bicycle trips generated by the petitioner's development reasonably relate to the city's requirement for a dedication of the pedestrian/bicycle pathway easement." Rather, noted the Court, "[t]he city simply found that the creation of the pathway 'could affect some of the traffic demand . . . and lessen the increase in traffic congestion.' "[118] Although the city's findings need not be based on a precise mathematical calculation, "the city must make some effort to quantify its findings in support of the dedication . . . beyond the conclusory statement that it could affect some of the traffic demand generated."[119]

### [3]  The "Rough Proportionality" Test

After reviewing the standards that state courts have traditionally applied to assess the constitutionality of development exactions, the Court announced its own new test as follows:

> We think the "reasonable relationship" test adopted by a majority of the state courts is closer to the federal constitutional norm than either of those previously discussed. But we do not adopt it as such, partly because the term "reasonable relationship" seems confusingly similar to the term "rational basis" which describes the minimal level of scrutiny under the Equal Protection Clause of the Fourteenth Amendment. We think a term such as "rough proportionality" best encapsulates what we hold to be the requirement of the Fifth Amendment. No precise mathematical calculation is required, but the city must make some sort of individualized determination that the required dedication is related both in nature and extent to the impact of the proposed development.[120]

The Court did not impose a mathematical standard for judging development exactions. Nor was it clear as to how

---

[118] *Id.* at 395.
[119] *Id.*.
[120] *Id.* at 391.

precise the exaction must be to the individual use that is proposed. However, it did make clear that the local government must do more than simply find that proposed developments (e.g., the plumbing store) create a certain number of vehicle trips. Rather, the government must answer the question of how many vehicle trips will be *reduced* by the requirement that a bike path be provided as a condition of approval.

### [4] Burden of Proof in Administrative Decisions

A significant portion of the *Dolan* decision concerns the question of who has the burden of proof in development approvals involving exactions. Decisions on building permit applications are adjudicative in nature, calling for the local decision-making body to weigh specific findings to determine whether permit approval should be allowed under the applicable regulations and comprehensive land use plan. Local land use decisions have traditionally been accorded a strong presumption of constitutional validity because courts grant substantial deference to the expertise and findings of the local decision-making body. Decisions on variances, special uses, and building permit applications are generally upheld unless the challenger proves that the decision was arbitrary, capricious, or not supported by substantial evidence in the record. Courts have also applied this substantial evidence standard to conditional zoning approvals like those involved in *Dolan*. The burden has always been on the landowner to overcome the deferential presumption of validity. If the landowner can offer facts showing that the municipality's decision was not supported by the evidence (e.g., no findings were made), the burden would then shift to the municipality to justify its decision.

In *Dolan*, for the first time, the Supreme Court stated that when the local government imposes an exaction in an administrative or "adjudicative" decision, it is the local government which must bear the burden of proof. Specifically, the Court stated:

> [I]n evaluating most generally applicable zoning
> regulations, the burden properly rests on the party
> challenging the regulation to prove that it constitutes
> an arbitrary regulation of property rights. *See, e.g.,*
> *Village of Euclid, Ohio v. Ambler Realty Co.*, 272 U.S.
> 365, 47 S. Ct. 114, 71 L. Ed. 303, 4 Ohio L. Abs. 816,
> 54 A.L.R. 1016 (1926). Here, by contrast, the city
> made an adjudicative decision to condition petitioner's
> application for a building permit on an individual
> parcel. In this situation, the burden properly rests on
> the city. *See Nollan*, 483 U.S. 836.[121]

In stating this new standard regarding the burden of proof
in adjudicative exaction decisions, the Court explained
that it "[saw] no reason why the Takings clause of the
Fifth Amendment, as much as part of the Bill of Rights as
the First Amendment or Fourth Amendment, should be
relegated to the status of a poor relation" when applied to
the regulation of economic enterprise.[122]

## [5]  Application of the "Unconstitutional Conditions" Doctrine to Property Rights

As noted above, Justice Scalia, speaking for the majority in *Dolan*, pointedly stated that there was no reason to
relegate the Takings clause to the "status of a poor relation" to other amendments of the Bill of Rights, such as
speech, religion, and unreasonable search and seizure,
which are fundamental rights. Therefore, the Court
concluded that the "unconstitutional conditions" doctrine,
which previously applied only to these fundamental rights,
should be extended to protect a citizen's right to receive
just compensation under the Takings clause. As summarized by the Court in *Dolan*, the unconstitutional conditions doctrine says that "the government may not require
a person to give up a constitutional right . . . in exchange
for a discretionary benefit conferred by the government

---

[121] *Id.* at 391 n.8.
[122] *Id.* at 392.

where the property sought has little or no relationship to the benefit."[123] Under this doctrine a court may invoke the heightened scrutiny of the "essential nexus" (substantially advance the legitimate state interest) test because the exaction arguably triggers a constitutional right, namely, the right under the Fifth and Fourteenth Amendments to receive just compensation when property is taken for a public use.[124]

---

[123] *Id.* at 374. One commentator has defined the doctrine as follows: "The doctrine of unconstitutional conditions holds that government may not grant a benefit on the condition that the beneficiary surrender a constitutional right, even if the government may withhold that benefit altogether." Sullivan, Kathleen M., "Unconstitutional Conditions," 102 Harv. L. Rev. 1415 (May 1989).

[124] *Id.*

Reprinted with permission of Milan Trenc.

## [6]  Immediate Ramifications of the *Dolan* Decision

*Dolan*, like *Nollan* before it, involved the dedication of an interest in land (i.e., deeding an easement). It did not concern traditional land use controls such as a prohibition on development in the floodplain. Therefore, although it can be expected that the reasoning of *Dolan* may ultimately be extended to more innovative types of land use controls such as incentive systems requiring dedication of

59

land in exchange for a density bonus,[125] the immediate practical ramifications of the decision are in the area of development exactions.

For example, to the extent that traditional exactions such as dedications of right-of-way for perimeter streets or drainage facilities as conditions of plat approval are not quantified, they may now be subject to challenge under *Dolan*. Imposing such dedication requirements as part of thoroughfare or drainage plans may satisfy the "essential nexus" part of the constitutional test, but unless such plans also include the quantification necessary to satisfy the "rough proportionality" test, these dedication requirements will be subject to challenge under the authority of *Dolan*.[126]

---

[125] *Density bonus* refers to an increase in the density that would otherwise be allowed under the applicable zoning district. Residential density is usually defined to mean the number of dwelling units or housing structures. The term "density bonus" is sometimes used informally with reference to nonresidential development; such a density bonus actually refers to an increase in the "intensity" of use. "Intensity" of use is most frequently expressed in terms of "floor area ratio." Floor area ratio ("FAR") is the gross floor area of all buildings or structures on a lot divided by the total lot area. A "density bonus" expressed in terms of FAR would be, for example, an increase from an FAR of 2:1 to an FAR of 4:1, which would enable the developer to construct twice as much square feet of building area on the lot as under an FAR of 2:1.

[126] The Supreme Court did state that "[d]edications for streets, sidewalks and other public ways are generally reasonable exactions to avoid excessive congestion from a proposed property use." *Dolan*, 114 S. Ct. at 2321. But the Court also explained that such dedication requirements must nevertheless meet the burden of demonstrating in quantifiable terms that the expected impact of a development reasonably relates to the dedication required. *Id.* See also City of Annapolis v. Waterman, 357 Md. 484, 745 A.2d 1000 (2000), reconsideration denied, (Mar. 8, 2000) in which the court explains the difference between a subdivision exaction that is a *dedication,* and a *condition* imposed on subdivision approval. The subdivision dedication "requires a developer to give the public the right to use a portion of her property, or give one of the incidents of ownership (e.g., an 'in lieu' fee) to the public at large to use"; the condition on subdivision approval, according to the court, "merely limits the method in which a property owner may thereafter use the property." *Id.* at 1011-1012. In that case, the court considered a challenge to a condition of subdivision approval requiring that 2,375 square feet of recreational area required in phase one of the subdivi-

### [7] Application of *Nollan* and *Dolan* to *Ad Hoc* Exactions Other Than Land Dedications

Development exactions include more than mandatory land dedications. In addition to land dedications, development exactions include fees in lieu of mandatory dedications, water or sewer connection fees, and impact fees.[127] These types of development exactions, as well as *ad hoc* conditions attached to rezonings and plat approvals, may now be subject to heightened scrutiny under the "unconstitutional conditions doctrine" as articulated in *Dolan.*

In 1999, the U.S. Supreme Court held in *City of Monterey v. Del Monte Dunes,*[128] that it had not extended the "rough proportionality" test beyond the special context of exactions, which the Court defined as the "conditioning of land use approvals on the dedication of property."[129] Therefore, as a matter of federal constitutional law, a federal court presented with a challenge to a monetary exaction such as the exaction imposed in *Ehrlich,* coud be expected to rule that the "rough proportionality" test of *Dolan* does not apply.

However, because the imposition of development exactions is a matter of state law, the constitutional test may vary across state jurisdictions. The U. S. Supreme Court's pronouncements on the federal constitutional test for development exactions does not prevent state courts in reviewing the constitutionality of monetary development exactions from imposing a test that may afford property

---

sion be located in a particular lot in phase three of the subdivision. The court concluded that because the recreational space was intended only for the use of those residing within the development, and not for general public use, that the requirement was not a dedication and, hence, not subject to the *Nolan/Dolan* exactions taking test, but rather the "regulatory takings" test of whether the regulation deprives the owner of all viable economic use of the entire property. *Id.*

[127] For a discussion of development exactions, and impact fees in particular, see Blaesser and Kentopp, "Impact Fees: The Second Generation," 38 J. of Urb. & Contemp. L. 401 (1990).

[128] City of Monterey v. Del Monte Dunes at Monterey, Ltd., 526 U.S. 687, 119 S. Ct. 1624, 143 L. Ed. 2d 882, 48 Env't. Rep. Cas. (BNA) 1513, 29 Envtl. L. Rep. 21133 (1999).

[129] *Id.* at 702.

owners more constitutional protection. In other words, federal law only sets the "floor" of constitutional protection, and a state court could decide that the *Nollan/Dolan* test does apply to monetary exactions.

A California Supreme Court case provides some insight as to how at least one state jurisdiction will apply the *Nollan* and *Dolan* decisions to *ad hoc* exaction cases that do not involve dedication of land as a condition of approval. The *Ehrlich* case[130] had been remanded to the California courts after the U.S. Supreme Court issued a writ of certiorari and vacated the state court judgment with instructions that the California Court of Appeals reexamine its prior judgment in favor of Culver City, the defendant, in light of *Dolan*. The case involved the owner/operator of a private tennis club and recreation facility. He closed the facility as a result of financial losses and applied for a permit to develop a condominium complex on the property, which required a specific plan amendment and rezoning. Culver City issued a development permit conditional on payment of a $280,000 "recreation fee" to mitigate the loss of the facility and a $33,200 in-lieu art fee. The amount of the fee was based on the cost of partially replacing lost recreational facilities. Mr. Ehrlich had challenged these two conditions as an illegal taking. On remand, the California Court of Appeals did not change its decision. The California Supreme Court then agreed to hear the case.[131]

The California Supreme Court had never before examined whether a monetary fee, rather than a dedication of real property as a condition to development, triggers the application of the heightened scrutiny test defined in *Nollan* ("essential nexus") and *Dolan* ("rough proportionality"). It decided that the heightened scrutiny

---

[130] Ehrlich v. City of Culver City, 15 Cal. App. 4th 1737, 19 Cal. Rptr. 2d 468 (2d Dist. 1993), reh'g denied, (June 23, 1993) and cert. granted, judgment vacated, 512 U.S. 1231, 114 S. Ct. 2731, 129 L. Ed. 2d 854 (1994), appeal after remand, 12 Cal. 4th 854, 50 Cal. Rptr. 2d 242, 911 P.2d 429 (1996), reh'g denied, (Apr. 11, 1996).
[131] Ehrlich v. City of Culver City, 12 Cal. 4th 854, 50 Cal. Rptr. 2d 242, 911 P.2d 429 (1996), reh'g denied, (Apr. 11, 1996).

test applies to monetary exactions as well as dedications.[132] The court further explained that this test applies to monetary exactions when discretionary permit conditions are imposed on developments propsed by individual property owners, since that is the circumstance when there is an increased potential for abuse of discretion under the police power.[133] Applying this rule, the court held that the $280,000 recreation fee did not satisfy the "rough proportionality" test, finding that the city had failed to adequately tie the amount of the fee to the actual impact of the land use change. Under the city's formula, the court noted that:

> . . . the public would receive, ex gratia, $280,000 worth of recreational facilities, the cost of which it would otherwise have to finance through membership fees. . . . The city may not constitutionally measure the magnitude of its loss, or of the recreational exaction, by the value of facilities it had no right to appropriate without paying for.[134]

However, the court also held that in situations when exactions are imposed based on generally applicable legislative acts, local governments are within their traditional police powers and are only subject to review under the less stringent "reasonable relationship test." Because the in-lieu art fee was, in the court's judgment, more akin to traditional land use regulations, such as design and landscaping requirements, it held that the fee is not a development exaction subject to heightened scrutiny under *Nollan/Dolan*.[135]

### [8] Application of *Nollan* and *Dolan* to Legislatively Adopted Development Exactions

The California Supreme Court's analysis in *Ehrlich* does not adequately explain why "legislatively" adopted

---

[132] *Id.* at 257.

[133] *Id.*

[134] *Id.*

[135] *Id. See also* Arcadia Development Corp. v. City of Bloomington, 552 N.W.2d 281 (Minn. Ct. App. 1996).

development exactions need not satisfy the heightened scrutiny test of *Nollan/Dolan*. In other words, if the underlying analysis to support the generally applied exaction is faulty and does not satisfy the "rough proportionality" test, it should not escape the heightened scrutiny under the Takings clause. As Supreme Court Justice Thomas observed: "The distinction between sweeping legislative takings and particularized administrative takings appears to be a distinction without a constitutional difference."[136] Although Justice Thomas uttered those words in a dissenting opinion, not a Court holding, his observation has resonated with other courts. For example, an Illinois court stated that Justice Thomas' comments were consistent with the rationale underlying *Dolan* and similar cases, adding: "Certainly a municipality should not be able to insulate itself from a takings challenge merely by utilizing a different bureaucratic vehicle when expropriating a citizen's property."[137]

California appellate courts in their decisions since *Ehrlich* have sought to explain further why the *Nolan/Dolan* two prong test for exactions does not apply to generally applicable legislative enactments. There appear to be two rationales. First, as a general matter, these courts believe that it is inappropriate to require that "'a complex, generally applicable piece of economic legislation that will have many effects on many different persons and entities accomplish precisely the goals stated in a legislative preamble in order to preserve its constitutionality.' "[138] Second, they conclude that where development exactions are generally applicable through legislative enactments, "'the

---

[136] Parking Ass'n of Georgia, Inc. v. City of Atlanta, Ga., 515 U.S. 1116, 115 S. Ct. 2268, 2269, 132 L. Ed. 2d 273 (1995) (Thomas J., dissenting).

[137] Amoco Oil Co. v. Village of Schaumburg, 277 Ill. App. 3d 926, 214 Ill. Dec. 526, 661 N.E.2d 380 (1st Dist. 1995), reh'g denied, (Feb. 20, 1996). *See also* Schultz v. City of Grants Pass, 131 Or. App. 220, 884 P.2d 569 (1994) (invalidating a 20,000 square foot exaction imposed through a local ordinance).

[138] Home Builders Ass'n of Northern California v. City of Napa, 90 Cal. App. 4th 188, 197, 108 Cal. Rptr. 2d 60 (1st Dist. 2001) citing Santa Monica Beach, Ltd. v. Superior Court, 19 Cal. 4th 952, 81 Cal.

heightened risk of the 'extortionate' use of the police power to exact unconstitutional conditions is not present.' "[139]

But neither of these rationales is any more convincing than the California Supreme Court's rationale in *Ehrlich*. The first rationale equates ordinances imposing development fees with "complex, generally applicable economic legislation." But, for example, impact fee ordinances, if properly done, are quite specific in nature, based upon technical methodologies for determining impacts that are then expressed in a "schedule" of fees for categories of development. If the data analysis and methodologies are improperly done, the result can be that "as applied" to individual development proposals, new developments will be required to pay a disproportionate share of their impacts on capital facilities and services. Also, impact fee ordinances typically provide for a separate individualized determination in cases where a development believes the fee schedule is incorrect as applied to its development. If the outcome of that determination is also incorrect, the mere fact that such a determination is done under the auspices of a legislatively adopted procedure should not relieve the local government from satisfying *Dolan's* rough proportionality test.

The second rationale appears to suggest that in the case of unconstitutional exactions imposed on an *ad hoc* basis, the decision maker's intent is to "extort". However, whether or not there is intent to act unconstitutionally should be irrelevant in the same way that the government's intention in imposing a condition that amounts to a physical occupation is irrelevant. If a legislatively adopted scheme of development exactions is based upon faulty analysis that fails to properly define the relationship between the amount of a development impact fee or other exaction and the impacts of development, such evidence "as applied" to an individual property, should be

---

Rptr. 2d 93, 968 P.2d 993 (1999), cert. denied, 526 U.S. 1131, 119 S. Ct. 1804, 143 L. Ed. 2d 1008 (1999).
[139] *Id.*

challengeable under *Dolan* as an unconstitutional exaction, regardless of government intent.

Whether or not to apply the *Nollan/Dolan* test in a challenge to a legislatively adopted impact fee ordinance was recently addressed by the Supreme Court of Ohio in a case of first impression.[140] The court concluded that the heightened scrutiny of the federal test for development exactions should apply to impact fee ordinances, explaining:

> Although impact fees do not threaten property rights to the same degree as land use exactions or zoning laws, there are similarities. Just as forced easements or zoning reclassifications can inhibit the desired use of property, an unreasonable impact fee may affect the manner in which a parcel of land is developed. Further, impact fees are closer in form to land use exactions than to zoning laws. Both forced easements and impact fees, while imposing a condition on the use of land, do not necessarily deny a landowner his or her intended use of the land. Zoning laws, to the contrary, may alter the classification of the land and, therefore, could deny the owner's intended use of the property.

* * *

> [T]he dual rational nexus test, is based on the Nollan and Dolan cases, and Hollywood, Inc. . . . It is our opinion that [it] balances both the interests of local governments and real estate developers without unnecessary restrictions. The trial court applied this test, and it is also the test we adopt for evaluating the constitutionality of an impact fee ordinance when a Takings Clause challenge is raised.[141]

The Ohio court's reference to the *Hollywood Inc.* case reflects the reality that state court litigation over impact

---

[140] Home Builders Assn. of Dayton & the Miami Valley v. Beavercreek, 89 Ohio St. 3d 121, 729 N.E.2d 349 (2000), reconsideration denied, 89 Ohio St. 3d 1471, 732 N.E.2d 1002 (2000).
[141] *Id.* at 356.

fees generated a constitutional test long before *Nollan* and *Dolan* shaped American land use and takings jurisprudence. Much of this litigation was in Florida and resulted in what the Ohio court properly refers to as the *Dual Rational Nexus Test.*[142] There are two prongs to this test. The first prong requires that there be an identified "nexus" (connection) between the new development and the need for the improvements for which a fee is imposed. In order to satisfy the first prong, the nexus must be substantial, rationally linked and direct between the new development and the identified need for the improvements. The second prong requires that the development that has been assessed the cost (fee) must receive a substantial benefit from the improvements constructed with a fee. This is the constitutional test followed in the majority of the states in which impact fees are legally authorized. The Supreme Court's decision in the *Nollan* case reinforced the use of the Dual Rational Nexus Test by state courts in assessing the validity of impact fee programs.

As illustrated in the diagram below, the Supreme Court said in *Nollan* that a development condition or impact fee must have an essential nexus to some legitimate governmental purpose in order to satisfy the first prong or first nexus. If that stated purpose is not really a legitimate objective based on a court's review of the objective as stated, then the Supreme Court has said that lack of a substantial relationship between the exaction and a legitimate state interest may constitute a taking of property.

The second prong, or the second nexus, as illustrated in the diagram, is that there must be a "rough proportionality" between the exaction or impact fee and the impact of, or need created by, the proposed development. As that second prong was articulated in the Supreme Court's decision in the *Dolan* case, it means that local government, not the developer, has the burden of substantiating the purpose and the amount of the impact fee. The connection

---

[142] *See, e.g.,* Hollywood, Inc. v. Broward County, 431 So. 2d 606 (Fla. Dist. Ct. App. 4th Dist. 1983), petition for review denied, 440 So. 2d 352 (Fla. 1983).

between development impact and fee amount need not be mathematically precise. But a court must be able to determine whether there is a methodology and if that methodology supports the condition imposed upon the development. *(See Diagram)*

## The *Nollan/Dolan* Dual Nexus Test

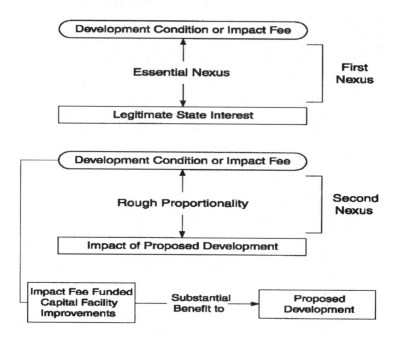

As indicated at the bottom of the diagram, the capital facility improvements funded with the impact fee must substantially benefit the proposed development. This concept has always been embedded in modern impact fee systems and is consistent with the impact fee case law as it developed at the state level before *Nollan,* now called the rough proportionality test. In other words, it is not enough to demonstrate some connection between a fee and the kind of need that a development is creating. It is also necessary to show that the fee payer, the developer, will receive the benefit of that improvement. The discipline of making sure that the fee payer actually receives the benefit of the fee is critically important in an impact fee program. This is typically done by establishing zones and requiring that fees paid for development within a zone are spent for improvements in the same zone.

### § 1.10 Ripeness to Bring Takings Claim

Bringing a challenge to a discretionary decision that effects a taking of property is no easy matter. The claimant must first overcome a doctrinal bar to takings claims known as the ripeness doctrine. As developed by the U.S. Supreme Court in response to regulatory takings claims, the ripeness doctrine requires a court to inquire whether a local government's decision regarding the application of its regulations to a particular property was sufficiently "final" to enable the court to properly assess whether the regulation has gone "too far" and constitutes a taking under the Fifth Amendment.[143] In order for this constitutional determination to be made, the decision must be definitive enough so that a court knows "the extent of permitted development."[144]

---

[143] Williamson County Regional Planning Com'n v. Hamilton Bank of Johnson City, 473 U.S. 172, 105 S. Ct. 3108, 87 L. Ed. 2d 126 (1985).

[144] MacDonald, Sommer & Frates v. Yolo County, 477 U.S. 340, 106 S. Ct. 2561, 91 L. Ed. 2d 285, 16 Envtl. L. Rep. 20807 (1986), reh'g denied, 478 U.S. 1035, 107 S. Ct. 22, 92 L. Ed. 2d 773 (1986).

The finality requirement consists of three thresholds: (1) an application threshold; (2) an administrative relief threshold; and (3) a reapplication threshold. Each must be satisfied in order to avoid dismissal of an "as applied" taking claim on the ground of prematurity. The application threshold requires that a property owner have applied for and received a decision on a particular development plan before her claim is mature for a court to make a takings determination under the Fifth Amendment. In order to satisfy the second threshold, the requirement that administrative relief be sought before coming to court, the applicant must have sought such variances or other modifications as would possibly overcome the local government's objections to the project. The third threshold requires that a plaintiff have sought reapplication of the proposed development, unless the plaintiff can demonstrate that such reapplication would be futile—known as the "futility exception."

Reprinted with permission of Doug Lloyd

Because the second and third thresholds were imprecisely and, to many practitioners, unrealistically, defined by the U.S. Supreme Court in the *Hamilton Bank* and *MacDonald* cases, the finality requirement of the ripeness doctrine has become virtually insurmountable by plaintiffs seeking to bring taking claims under the Fifth Amendment to the U.S. Constitution.

In the *Suitum* case,[145] the U.S. Supreme clarified the finality requirement somewhat. In that case, the plaintiff owned a lot located in an area classified as a Stream Environment Zone, through which runoff was carried into the lake's watershed. The Tahoe Regional Planning Agency's denied Mrs. Suitum's application to build a home on the lot. She appealed to the agency's governing board which affirmed the denial. But the agency also had a program of transferable development rights (TDR), intended to give property owners such as Mrs. Suitum the opportunity to reduce the impact of the restrictive regulations. Under the program, a property owner could sell her development rights to the owner of an eligible "receiver" parcel, upon approval of the agency. Mrs. Suitum sued without first applying to the agency to use her development rights.

The Court held that despite the fact that Mrs. Suitum had not applied to transfer her development rights, she had satisfied the finality requirement, for the basic reason that the agency had already determined that her land was not developable by virtue of its location in the zone that did not permit development. It also held that an action by the agency to allow her to transfer her development rights was not the kind of "final" action required under the ripeness doctrine because the number of development rights assigned to Mrs. Suitum's parcel had already been determined. A discretionary action by the agency was not necessary for her to obtain them or to offer them for sale.

---

[145] Suitum v. Tahoe Regional Planning Agency, 520 U.S. 725, 117 S. Ct. 1659, 137 L. Ed. 2d 980, 44 Env't. Rep. Cas. (BNA) 1673, 27 Envtl. L. Rep. 21064 (1997), on remand to, 123 F.3d 1322 (9th Cir. 1997).

The latest land use decision by the U.S. Supreme Court in the *Palazzolo* case[146] has added a dose of practicality to deciding the futility exception under the finality requirement. The 5-4 decision written by Justice Kennedy addressed two key points of contention in the ongoing takings debate: (1) when a land use regulatory decision is sufficiently "final" to satisfy the ripeness doctrine; and (2) whether a regulatory taking claim is automatically barred when the enactment of a restrictive regulation predates the owner's acquisition of the property.

It seems that by the time these takings cases reach the Supreme Court, often the plaintiff has become an octogenarian. As was Mrs. Suitum in her case before the Court, the Petitioner, Mr. Palazzolo, is now an 80 year old, retired from the auto wrecking business. In 1959, he and some associates formed Shore Gardens, Inc (SGI) for the purpose of investing in three undeveloped, adjoining parcels consisting of approximately 22 acres along the coastline in the Rhode Island town of Westerly.

Eighteen acres of this coastal land are a salt marsh, subject to tidal flooding—i.e., a classic wetland—requiring fill up to 6 feet in some places before significant structures could be built. SGI subdivided the entire property into 80 lots. In 1960, Palazzolo became the sole shareholder of SGI. By 1969, following various lot transactions, SGI had 74 lots remaining, totaling about 20 acres.

Beginning in 1962, Palazzolo sought to develop the property and submitted an application to the Rhode Island Division of Harbors and Rivers (DHR) to dredge from the adjacent Winnapaug Pond and to fill the entire property. The application was denied for lack of essential information, and in 1963 Palazzolo submitted a second application. While the second application was still pending, Palazzolo submitted, in 1966, a third application to do a more limited fill to allow the construction of a private beach club. In 1971, DHR approved the second and third applications,

---

[146] Palazzolo v. Rhode Island, 121 S. Ct. 2448, 150 L. Ed. 2d 592 (U.S. 2001).

giving Palazzolo the option of either constructing a bulkhead and filling the marsh or constructing a beach facility. However, 7 months later, the DHR revoked its assent, which Palazzolo did not appeal.

In the meantime, two important events occurred. First, in 1971, Rhode Island established the Coastal Resources Management Council (CRMC), with authority to regulate coastal wetlands. In 1977, the CRMC promulgated regulations that prohibited the filling of coast wetlands without approval of a special exception by the CRMC. Second, in 1978, SGI's corporate charter was revoked for failure to pay corporate income taxes, and title to the property passed to Palazzolo by operation of law.

In 1983, Palazzolo, now the fee owner, filed an application with the CRMC similar to the 1962 application, requesting permission to construct a bulkhead and to fill the entire salt marsh. It was rejected, and Palazzolo did not appeal. In 1985, with an application similar to the 1966 application to build a private beach club, he again applied to the CRMC—specifically to fill 11 acres with gravel to accommodate "'50 cars with boat trailers, a dumpster, port-a-johns, picnic tables, barbecue pits of concrete, and other trash receptacles.'" Palazzolo at 2456. This application was also denied by CRMC for failure to meet the special exception "compelling public purpose" standard under the regulations.

This time Palazzolo appealed, bringing an inverse condemnation action, and seeking damages in the amount of $3,150,000, based on the estimated value of a 74-lot subdivision. He lost at trial, and the Rhode Island Supreme Court affirmed on the grounds that Palazzolo (1) had not satisfied the "finality" requirement of the ripeness doctrine and hence his the takings claim was not ripe; (2) had no right to challenge regulations predating 1978 when he became the owner by operation of law; and (3) had not been denied all economically viable use because of the undisputed fact that he had $200,000 in development value on the upland portion of the property.[147]

The U.S. Supreme Court disagreed with the Rhode Island Supreme Court's conclusions that Palazzolo's takings claim was not ripe and that he was barred from bringing a takings claim because the 1978 restrictive regulations predated his succession to ownership of the property. The Court did agree with the Rhode Island Court's conclusion that Palazzolo was not deprived of all economic use of his property because the upland portions of the property still had development value, but remanded the case for consideration of Palazzolo's claims under the multifactor takings test of *Penn Central*[148] which had not been examined fully by the Rhode Island Court because it had found Palazzolo's takings claim under *Penn Central* barred.[149]

The Court concluded from CRMC's interpretations of its regulations to deny Palazzolo's various applications, the briefs, and the candid statements of counsel for both sides, that it was clear that the state had no intention of allowing any fill in the wetlands nor any use involving substantial structures or improvements: "[N]o fill for any ordinary use. . . [N]o fill for its own sake; no fill for a beach club, either rustic or upscale; no fill for a subdivision; no fill for any likely or foreseeable use. And with no fill there can be no structures and no development on the wetlands. Further permit applications were not necessary to establish this point."[150]

The Respondents pressed two other ripeness issues. First, they pointed out that the Rhode Island Supreme Court had also found Palazzolo's claim unripe because he

---

[147] Palazzolo v. Rhode Island, 121 S. Ct. 2448, 2457, 150 L. Ed. 2d 592 (U.S. 2001).

[148] Penn Cent. Transp. Co. v. City of New York, 438 U.S. 104, 123-25, 98 S. Ct. 2646, 57 L. Ed. 2d 631, 11 Env't. Rep. Cas. (BNA) 1801, 8 Envtl. L. Rep. 20528 (1978), reh'g denied, 439 U.S. 883, 99 S. Ct. 226, 58 L. Ed. 2d 198 (1978).

[149] Palazzolo v. Rhode Island, 121 S. Ct. 2448, 2457, 2465, 150 L. Ed. 2d 592 (U.S. 2001).

[150] *Id.* at 2459.

had not sought permission to develop the upland portion of the property and that it had found that "it would be possible to build at least one single-family home" on that area—the phrase "at least" meaning that additional development beyond the single-family dwelling was possible. The Supreme Court rejected this argument stating: "Ripeness doctrine does not require a landowner to submit applications for their own sake. Petitioner is required to explore development opportunities on his upland parcel only if there is uncertainty as to the land's permitted use." Here there was no uncertainty. Moreover, the "attempt to interject ambiguity as to the value or use of the uplands . . . comes too late in the day," said the Court, noting that the $200,000 figure for the uplands was not only uncontested, but cited in the state's brief in opposition.[151]

Second, Respondents argued that Palazzolo based its claim for damages of $3,150,000 on a 74 unit subdivision proposal for which it had never sought permission to develop. At a minimum such a proposal would have required zoning approval from the town of Westerly and a sewage permit from the Rhode Island Department of Environmental Management. The Court rejected the relevance of this argument, reasoning that since the CRMC had denied permission to fill the wetlands, and filling was necessary to build the 74 dwellings, "submission of this proposal would not have clarified the extent of development permitted by the wetlands regulations, which is the inquiry required under our ripeness decisions."[152]

Justice Ginsburg, in her dissent, joined by Justices Souter and Breyer, complained that, before the Rhode Island courts, Palazzolo's claim had been solely a *Lucas*-based takings claim, namely, that the state had refused to allow any development, and that therefore he had been denied "all economically beneficial or productive use of

---

[151] *Id.* at 2460.
[152] *Id.*

land."[153] In response to this Lucas claim, the state argued in defense that it "'would [have been] happy to have [Palazzolo] situate a home' on the uplands, 'thus allowing [him] to realize $200,000 dollars.' "[154] Hence, in Justice Ginsburg's view, the Rhode Island Supreme Court properly held his case unripe because he had never sought permission to develop the upland portion of the property, and the U.S. Supreme Court would not have granted certiorari to review the application of MacDonald and Lucas to the facts of Palazzolo's case. [155]

But then with the aid of new counsel (the Pacific Legal Foundation), Palazzolo asserted new takings theories not advanced below, namely, a takings claim based upon the multifactor inquiry set out in *Penn Central Transp. Co. v New York City,*[156] and that the claim that even if the one house was permissible on the uplands, the regulations amount to a taking because the landowner is left with property having only a "'few crumbs of value.' "[157] Justice Ginsburg acknowledged that the state had failed to appreciate that Palazzolo "had moved the pea to different shell," but argued it was unfair for the majority to conclude that the state's belated effort to argue that the uplands had more than $200,000 in value came too late in the day. With unusual bluntness, Justice Ginsburg observed: "Change your theory and misrepresent the record in your petition for certiorari; if the respondent fails to note your machinations, you have created a different record on which this Court will review the case."[158]

---

[153] Lucas v. South Carolina Coastal Council, 505 U.S. 1003, 1015, 112 S. Ct. 2886, 120 L. Ed. 2d 798, 34 Env't. Rep. Cas. (BNA) 1897, 22 Envtl. L. Rep. 21104 (1992).

[154] Palazzolo v. Rhode Island, 121 S. Ct. 2448, 2474, 150 L. Ed. 2d 592 (U.S. 2001).

[155] *Id.* at 2475.

[156] Penn Cent. Transp. Co. v. City of New York, 438 U.S. 104, 123-25, 98 S. Ct. 2646, 57 L. Ed. 2d 631, 11 Env't. Rep. Cas. (BNA) 1801, 8 Envtl. L. Rep. 20528 (1978), reh'g denied, 439 U.S. 883, 99 S. Ct. 226, 58 L. Ed. 2d 198 (1978)

[157] *Id.* (quoting Petition for Certiorari at 20-22).

[158] *Id.* at 2476.

It may very well be true that Palazzolo "hid the ball" on the state in framing the question of the true nature of the development upon which he was basing his petition for certiorari. But from the development practitioner's viewpoint, local governments at times also use the "finality" requirement of the ripeness doctrine to "hide the ball" on applicant landowners. Unscrupulous government officials can and frequently do assert, after the fact, as the state sought to do in *Palazzolo*, that they "would have been willing" to consider an intensity of use or an alternative type of use that a landowner never proposed. This assertion before a court considering a takings claim can be sufficient to cause the court to dismiss the takings claim on ripeness grounds. In *Palazzolo*, ironically, the state tried to defeat Palazzolo's takings claim by asserting belatedly that it "'would [have been] happy to have [Palazzolo] situate a home' on the uplands," but this time to no avail.

The second issue addressed by the Court was whether a regulatory taking claim is automatically barred when the enactment of a stringent regulation predates the owner's acquisition of the property. The argument in favor of this result is that since property rights are created by the State, new legislation shapes and defines property rights and reasonable investment-backed expectations. So owners of property subsequent to the enactment of such legislation take title with notice of the limitation and cannot claim injury for lost property value.

At the time Palazzolo became the owner by operation of law, the wetlands regulations were already in place. Hence, the Rhode Island Supreme Court had held that Palazzolo's post regulation acquisition was fatal to both his *Lucas* and *Penn Central* takings claims. The U.S. Supreme Court rejected this result, reasoning that such a "single, sweeping, rule," would "absolve the State of its obligation to defend any action restricting land use, no matter how extreme or unreasonable." Such a rule would, in effect, allow the State "to put an expiration date on the

Takings Clause."[159] Instead the Court looked to its prior decision in *Nollan*[160] striking down as unconstitutional a California Coastal Commission requirement that ocean-front landowners provide lateral beach access to the public as a condition of development approval. In that case, the majority held that "[s]o long as the Commission could not have deprived the prior owners of the easement without compensating them, the prior owners must be understood to have transferred their full property rights in conveying the lot."[161]

The dissent in *Palazzolo* argued that *Nollan* had been limited by the decision in *Lucas*[162] in which the Court had cautioned that the landowner's ability to recover for government deprivation of all economically viable use was limited by "those restrictions that background principles of the State's law of property and nuisance already place upon land ownership."[163] But the *Palazzolo* Court rejected the proposition that any new regulation, once enacted, becomes a background principle of property law, which cannot be challenged by those subsequently acquiring title to property.

Without attempting to define the "precise circumstances when a legislative enactment can be deemed a background principle of state law or whether those circumstances are present here," the Court held that *Lucas* did not overrule its holding in *Nollan* and that "the determination whether an existing, general law can limit all economic use of prop-

---

[159] *Id.* at 2463-2464.

[160] Nollan v. California Coastal Com'n, 483 U.S. 825, 107 S. Ct. 3141, 97 L. Ed. 2d 677, 26 Env't. Rep. Cas. (BNA) 1073, 17 Envtl. L. Rep. 20918 (1987).

[161] *Id.* at 834, n. 2.

[162] Lucas v. South Carolina Coastal Council, 505 U.S. 1003, 112 S. Ct. 2886, 120 L. Ed. 2d 798, 34 Env't. Rep. Cas. (BNA) 1897, 22 Envtl. L. Rep. 21104 (1992), on remand to, 309 S.C. 424, 424 S.E.2d 484, 23 Envtl. L. Rep. 20297 (1992).

[163] *Id.* at 1029.

erty must turn on objective factors, such as the nature of the land use proscribed."[164]

The Court's decision leaves clarification of some of its opinion for a later day—particularly the "objective factors" relevant to a determination of whether a legislative enactment becomes a background principle of property law. But it has finally added a degree of practical focus to determining when "enough is enough" under the ripeness "finality" requirement by holding that an applicant need not make meaningless permit applications when the government's interpretation of its regulations make clear the extent to which it will permit development on a site. Also, *Palazzolo* does away with the notice defense to takings claims. Property owners will now be able to bring takings claims despite having purchased property with notice of restrictive regulations.

## § 1.11 Limitation on Legislative Discretion

Although the delegation and vagueness doctrines are most frequently discussed with emphasis on the exercise of discretion by local administrative bodies, it is the local legislative body, in the first instance, that creates the constitutional issue by either improperly delegating its policy-making powers or adopting an ordinance containing vague regulations.

### [1] Local Legislative Body's Initial Exercise of Discretion

In its enthusiasm for discretionary review procedures that lend themselves to analyses of development "impact," a local government often overlooks the well-established legal principle that the *adopting* by a local legislative body of zoning classifications with related terms, standards,

---

[164] Palazzolo v. Rhode Island, 121 S. Ct. 2448, 2464, 150 L. Ed. 2d 592 (U.S. 2001)

and requirements applicable to all persons is, in fact, its fundamental exercise of discretion: "The acts of administering a zoning ordinance do not go back to the questions of policy and discretion which were settled at the time of the adoption of the ordinance."[165]

## [2]  Abuse of Discretion by the Local Legislative Body

A Monterey, California case provides a palpable example of the abuse of discretion by the local legislative body.[166] The case involved 37.6 oceanfront acres known as the

---

[165] Valley View Indus. Park v. City of Redmond, 107 Wash. 2d 621, 733 P.2d 182, 192 (1987), quoting State ex rel. Ogden v. City of Bellevue, 45 Wash. 2d 492, 275 P.2d 899 (1954).

[166] Del Monte Dunes at Monterey, Ltd. v. City of Monterey, 920 F.2d 1496 (9th Cir. 1990), appeal after remand, 95 F.3d 1422, 27 Envtl. L. Rep. 20139 (9th Cir. 1996), reh'g granted, 118 F.3d 660 (9th Cir. 1997)

"Dunes." Adjacent to the Dunes are a multifamily residential development, other private property, a railroad right-of-way, and a state beach park. Seven tank pads and an industrial complex remain on the property from its prior use as a petroleum tank farm. The developer's predecessor had sought permission to develop the Dunes into 344 residential units. The city rejected that application; the developer then submitted three more applications for 264, 224, and 190 residential units, respectively. The Ninth Circuit Court of Appeals later noted that the type and density of these proposals "could potentially have conformed to the City's general land use plan and zoning ordinances."[167] Nevertheless, the city rejected each of these applications. After having submitted a fifth plan—a modified development plan for 190 units—the developer transferred the Dunes to Del Monte Dunes, which continued with the application and, ultimately, the litigation that resulted.

Under California law, the city first had to grant approval of a "tentative map" for the modified 190-unit plan—a drawing detailing precisely the design of the project and the conditions on and around the development project that must be met before a final map is approved. The local planning commission typically reviews the application and recommends to the legislative body acceptance or rejection. In this instance, the planning commission recommended denial of the tentative map. Del Monte appealed to the city council. The city council overruled the planning commission and approved a site plan for the Dunes with the 190 residential units subject to an eighteen-month conditional use permit with sixteen conditions attached. Del Monte worked with the professional planning staff in revising the plan to comply with the sixteen conditions, and the subsequent staff report

---

and reh'g en banc denied, 127 F.3d 1149 (9th Cir. 1997) and cert. granted, 523 U.S. 1045, 118 S. Ct. 1359, 140 L. Ed. 2d 509 (1998) and aff'd, 526 U.S. 687, 119 S. Ct. 1624, 143 L. Ed. 2d 882, 48 Env't. Rep. Cas. (BNA) 1513, 29 Envtl. L. Rep. 21133 (1999).

[167] 920 F.2d at 1499.

concluded that the conditions had been substantially met and recommended findings that acknowledged consistency with the city's objectives, policies, and general land uses. Even so, the planning commission denied the tentative map. Incredibly, on appeal to the city council, the same city council members who had previously approved the 190 unit plan subject to the conditions, now, by the same vote, denied the 190 unit tentative map!

As a result, Del Monte brought a civil rights action against the city alleging, among other things, a taking and a violation of equal protection. In a jury trial before the federal district court, the jury found that the city's actions denied Del Monte equal protection and resulted in an unconstitutional taking and awarded Del Monte $1,450,000 in damages. The Ninth Circuit upheld the jury award; it also made clear that the jury was correctly instructed to find a taking if (1) all economically viable use of the Dunes had been denied or (2) the city's decision to reject Del Monte's development application did not substantially advance a legitimate public purpose. The second test, explained the court, requires that "[e]ven if the City had a legitimate interest in denying Del Monte's development application, its action must be 'roughly proportional' to furthering that interest."[168] The court concluded that Del Monte had presented evidence that none of the city's stated reasons for denying Del Monte's application was sufficiently related to the city's legitimate interests.

The City appealed the judgment to the U.S. Supreme Court. The Supreme Court affirmed, but held that the rough proportionality test of *Dolan* should not be extended "beyond the special context of exactions—land use decisions conditioning approval of development on the dedication of property to public use".[169] The Ninth Circuit's discussion of rough proportionality, said the Court, was

---

[168] 95 F.3d at 1430.

[169] City of Monterey v. Del Monte Dunes at Monterey, Ltd., 526 U.S. 687, 702, 119 S. Ct. 1624, 143 L. Ed. 2d 882, 48 Env't. Rep. Cas. (BNA) 1513, 29 Envtl. L. Rep. 21133 (1999).

unnecessary to its decision to sustain the jury's verdict finding that the City's denial of the 190-unit proposal was not substantially related to legitimate public interests.[170]

The *Del Monte Dunes* case points to the severe consequences that may result when the local legislative body disregards its own land use policies and standards and denies a development application that is consistent with those policies and standards.

## § 1.12 Substantive Due Process Protection Against Abuse of Discretion

When discretionary decision making goes awry, and judgment is exercised arbitrarily, there is abuse of discretion that may amount to a constitutional violation in the form of substantive due process—actionable under federal law. Substantive due process refers to the fact that the Fourteenth Amendment to the U.S. Constitution imposes both substantive and procedural requirements when it prohibits any government action that deprives "any person of . . . liberty or property without due process of law."[171]

### [1] Discretionary Decisions and the Substantive Due Process Clause

The substantive component of the Due Process Clause bars "certain arbitrary, wrongful government actions 'regardless of the fairness of the procedures used to implement them.'"[172] It has been referred to by some, notably Judge Posner of the U.S. Court of Appeals for the Seventh

---

[170] *Id.*

[171] This section is based upon an article by the author entitled "Substantive Due Process Protection at the Outer Margins of Municipal Behavior," 3 Wash. U. J. L. & Pol'y 583 (2000).

[172] Zinermon v. Burch, 494 U.S. 113, 125, 110 S. Ct. 975, 108 L. Ed. 2d 100 (1990)(quoting Daniels v. Williams, 474 U.S. 327, 331, 106 S. Ct. 677, 88 L. Ed. 2d 662 (1986)).

Circuit, as a "diluted constitutional clause,"[173] but that view would appear to be accurate only in the context of a facial attack on a land use regulation. When a land use regulation is attacked as it is "applied" to a particular development proposal, however, substantive due process works at full strength, or at least it should.

### [2] The Search for a Protected Property Interest—Another Threshold Barrier to Judicial Relief

The right not to be subject to arbitrary or capricious action by a government legislative or administrative action is a substantive due process right In the face of irrational or wrongful land use regulatory decisions that may *not* amount to a taking, landowners and developers have relied on substantive due process claims in federal court as an important means to remedy such actions. To their dismay, however, landowners and developers are learning from federal court decisions in some of the circuits, that as the *degree of discretion* that can be exercised by a government decision making body increases, the less likely it is that they will be deemed to have any "property interest" to protect, regardless of how arbitrarily that discretion is exercised in a particular case.

This approach is particularly evident in the Second, Fourth, and Sixth Circuits, which require, as a threshold step before even reaching the alleged substantive due process violation, that the plaintiff landowner or develop first prove a legitimate claim of entitlement to a desired land use or approval so as to establish a protected property interest in the benefit sought from the decision making authority.[174] Other circuits, notably, the First and Seventh Circuits, regard land use disputes as political disputes

---

[173] Coniston Corp. v. Village of Hoffman Estates, 844 F.2d 461, 10 Fed. R. Serv. 3d 1294 (7th Cir. 1988).

[174] *See, e.g.,*Triomphe Investors v. City of Northwood, 49 F.3d 198, 202, 1995 FED App. 81P (6th Cir. 1995); Gardner v. City of Baltimore Mayor and City Council, 969 F.2d 63 (4th Cir. 1992).

rarely containing facts sufficient to state a substantive due process claim.[175] Only one circuit, the Third Circuit, has concluded that ownership of property, in and of itself, is a property interest that deserves substantive due process protection.[176] This divergence among the federal circuits can be attributed in large part to the fact that the U.S. Supreme Court has never given the lower federal courts adequate guidance for how to deal with land use cases involving substantive due process claims of arbitrary and capricious action by local governments. With local governments increasingly employing discretionary land use control systems, the decisions of those circuits that require proof that a protected property interest exist before proceeding to the alleged substantive due process violation are the most troubling. This is because the prevailing standard of proof—the *degree of discretion* that can be exercised by the decision maker—is subject to manipulation to defeat legitimate claims of entitlement to a desired use or a permit approval. Whether such manipulation is merely the changing of "shall" to "may" in describing the regulator's approval authority, or creating broad standards under special use or conditional use procedures, or subjecting all proposed projects to development "impact" determinations as a condition of approval, the point has not been lost on municipal attorneys.[177]

---

[175] *See, e.g.*, Nestor Colon Medina & Sucesores, Inc. v. Custodio, 964 F.2d 32, 45, 23 Fed. R. Serv. 3d 1054 (1st Cir. 1992); Coniston Corp. v. Village of Hoffman Estates, 844 F.2d 461, 467, 10 Fed. R. Serv. 3d 1294 (7th Cir. 1988).

[176] *See* DeBlasio v. Zoning Bd. of Adjustment for Tp. of West Amwell, 53 F.3d 592, 25 Envtl. L. Rep. 21227 (3d Cir. 1995), relying upon the analysis in Bello v. Walker, 840 F.2d 1124 (3d Cir. 1988). See also Acierno v. New Castle County, 2000 WL 718346 (D.Del.)

[177] *See, e.g.*, Hollister & Abare-Brown, Protected Property Interest Analysis: The First Line of Defense in Due Process Litigation (Address to the NIMLO 1990 Annual Conference (Sept. 23, 1990).

*"God's country? Well, I suppose it is.
But I own it."*

Reprinted by permission of William Hamilton, the Rockefeller Brothers Fund, and *The Use of Land: A Citizen's Policy Guide to Urban Growth* (1973).

The preoccupation of certain federal circuits with finding a property interest in substantive due process challenges to land use regulatory decisions stems from the U.S. Supreme Court's two 1972 nonland use decisions—*Regents v. Roth*[178] and *Perry v. Sindermann*.[179] Both of these cases addressed the question of whether there was an interest in employment and the degree of *procedural* protection—not substantive due process—that should be accorded under the Fourteenth Amendment to the U.S.

---

[178] Board of Regents of State Colleges v. Roth, 408 U.S. 564, 92 S. Ct. 2701, 33 L. Ed. 2d 548, 1 I.E.R. Cas. (BNA) 23 (1972).

[179] Perry v. Sindermann, 408 U.S. 593, 92 S. Ct. 2694, 33 L. Ed. 2d 570, 1 I.E.R. Cas. (BNA) 33 (1972).

Constitution. *Roth* has had the most influence on federal court review of substantive due process challenges to land use decisions.

### [a] Procedural Due Process Protection

In *Roth*, the Court considered whether a university's refusal to renew a untenured professor's employment contract was a deprivation of liberty or property under the Fourteenth Amendment. Before reaching that question, the Court asked whether the professor had a constitutionally protected interest in his continued employment. In its analysis, the Court recognized that in addition to property interests arising from ownership of real estate, chattels or money, there exists a class of property interests that includes "the security of interests that a person has already acquired in specific benefits."[180] However, said the Court, a person's property interest in a benefit or entitlement must be based upon more than an abstract need or desire, or unilateral expectation for such an entitlement. It must be based upon "a legitimate claim of entitlement."[181] Hence, the untenured professor whose contract was not renewed had only a unilateral expectation of continued employment and no legitimate claim of entitlement. Because professor Roth did not have a property interest in his continued employment, he could not claim a violation of procedural due process.[182]

### [b] Substantive Due Process Protection

Since *Roth*, when asked to consider a substantive due process challenge to land use regulation, some federal

---

[180] *Roth*, at 576. This expanded definition of property interests had been articulated by the Court two years earlier, in Goldberg v. Kelly, 397 U.S. 254, 90 S. Ct. 1011, 25 L. Ed. 2d 287 (1970), for dissenting opinion, see, 397 U.S. 280, 90 S. Ct. 1028, 25 L. Ed. 2d 307 (1970), in which the Court extended procedural due process protection to persons whose welfare benefits are terminated. *See also* Reich, "The New Property," 73 Yale L.J. 733 (1964).

[181] *Id.* at 577.

[182] *Id.* at 576–77.

circuits that have been the most reluctant to become involved in what they consider to be "local" land use matters, have incorporated *Roth*'s property interest inquiry into their analysis in order not to reach the substantive due process question. If they must reach that question because the facts demonstrate the plaintiff has a protected property interest, they apply a strict, narrow test for substantive due process.

The Second Circuit has become the most emphatic example of this approach to substantive due process claims. Its formulation of *Roth* entitlement analysis in substantive due process challenges to land use decisions, or one similar to it, appears to be shared by a number of the federal circuits.[183] The Second Circuit's most significant entitlement decision is *RRI Realty Corp. Inc. v. Village of Southampton*[184] for what it reveals about the reasoning and attitude of many federal courts when presented with substantive due process challenges to land use decisions. The court in that case commenced its analysis by noting that its prior decision in a licensing case, *Yale Auto Parts, Inc. v. Johnson*,[185] had committed the circuit to an entitlement test that focused on whether "absent the alleged denial of due process, there is either a certainty or a very strong likelihood that the application would have been granted."[186] Because in that case the court had found that the licensing authorities had discretion in the issuance of the requested permit, there was no protected property interest.[187] The court then expressed the sentiment that is frequently uttered by federal judges who are presented with land use cases that land in their courts:

---

[183] *See, e.g.*, Triomphe Investors v. City of Northwood, 49 F.3d 198, 202, 1995 FED App. 81P (6th Cir. 1995); Gardner v. City of Baltimore Mayor and City Council, 969 F.2d 63 (4th Cir. 1992); RRI Realty Corp. v. Incorporated Village of Southampton, 870 F.2d 911 (2d Cir. 1989).

[184] RRI Realty Corp. v. Incorporated Village of Southampton, 870 F.2d 911 (2d Cir. 1989).

[185] Yale Auto Parts, Inc. v. Johnson, 758 F.2d 54 (2d Cir. 1985).

[186] RRI Realty Corp., 870 F.2d at 917, quoting Yale Auto Parts, Inc. v. Johnson, 758 F.2d 54, 59 (2d Cir. 1985).

[187] *Id.*

If federal courts are not to become zoning boards of appeals (and not to substitute for state courts in their state law review of local land use regulatory decisions), the entitlement test of Yale Auto Parts—"certainty or a very strong likelihood" of issuance—must be applied with considerable rigor.[188]

At least as defined, the *Yale Auto Parts* entitlement test would appear to focus upon the likelihood that an application will be granted. The court in *RRI Realty* stated that its proper application means that it "must focus primarily on the degree of discretion enjoyed by the issuing authority, not the estimated probability that the authority will act favorably in a particular case."[189] If we summarize the standard as applied by the Second Circuit in *RRI Realty Corp.*, we have the following.

| PERMIT ENTITLEMENT STANDARD *(Second Circuit)* | | |
|---|---|---|
| **FACTORS** | | **DEGREE OF OFFICIAL DISCRETION** |
| | | **High** |
| **PROBABILITY OF PERMIT ISSUING** | **High** | No Protected Property Interest |
| | **Low** | No Protected Property Interest |

As the chart above illustrates, so long as the degree of official discretion is high, or deemed by the court to be significant, it always trumps whatever probability of permit issuance there is, whether high or low. The court's formulation would not appear even to depend upon whether the degree of discretion is "high"—only that there is an "opportunity" to deny:

Even if in a particular case, objective observers would

---

[188] *Id.*
[189] *Id.* (emphasis added)

> estimate that the probability of issuance was ex-
> tremely high, the opportunity of the local agency to
> deny issuance suffices to defeat the existence of a
> federally protected property interest.[190]

Because the Second Circuit applies this entitlement test independent of the probability of permit approval, it is virtually impossible to establish a protected property interest so long as the government decision maker retains discretion or the "opportunity" to deny the approval sought. In an era of land use controls that rely upon discretionary review and decision making mechanisms, the extent to which other circuits embrace this harsh entitlement test has serious implications for property owners and developers who seek to challenge arbitrary decisions by local government.

The acknowledged motivation of the Second Circuit and other federal circuits—not to become federal zoning boards of appeals—is the same motivation that has led the federal courts increasingly to employ the ripeness and abstention doctrines to either dismiss or stay constitutional challenges to land use decisions—in effect, leaving the federal courthouse door only slightly ajar for land use cases that involve only the most egregious examples of arbitrary action by local governments.[191] The irony in the case of the Second Circuit's entitlement test is that while the Second Circuit professes deference to state law as interpreted by state courts in zoning and land use matters—the Second Circuit applied the test in *RRI Realty Corp.* without regard for the very state and municipal law upon which the state

---

[190] *Id.*

[191] *See generally* Delaney & Desiderio, "Who Will Clean Up the 'Ripeness Mess'? A Call for Reform so Takings Plaintiffs Can Enter the Federal Courthouse," 31 Urb. Law. 195 (1999); Overstreet, "The Ripeness Doctrine of the Takings Clause: A Survey of Decisions Showing Just How Far Federal Courts Will Go to Avoid Adjudicating Land Use Cases," 10 J. Land Use & Envtl. L. 37 (1995); Blaesser, "Closing the Federal Courthouse Door on Property Owners: The Ripeness and Abstention Doctrines in Section 1983 Land Use Cases," 2 Hofstra Prop. L.J. 73 (Spring 1989). See also discussion of ripeness doctrine in sec. 1.10 *supra.*

court had relied for its decision and which defined the degree of discretion the local agency had to deny the permit. After all, as the U.S. Supreme Court has explained, property interests are "created and their dimensions defined by existing rules or understandings that stem from an independent source such as state law."[192]

In *RRI Realty Corp.*, the plaintiff, RRI, purchased a sixty-three-room mansion on waterfront property and sought a building permit for extensive renovations to the mansion. The Building Inspector advised RRI to make one omnibus building permit application when its plans were finalized. In the meantime, he issued a limited building permit to cover minor structural renovations, and construction began in early 1981. RRI also applied for an received a height variance from the Zoning Board of Appeals (ZBA). In 1983, RRI submitted its final overall design plan to the Architectural Review Board (ARB), whose approval was required before the Building Inspector could issue the permit. The ARB approved the final overall design plan and RRI then submitted the comprehensive building permit application, and applied for another height variance from the ZBA to allow a portion of the structure to exceed the height limitations of the previously granted variance. While the variance application was pending, the Building Inspector divided the building permit application into three stages, with stage one being for the structural work covered by the initial building permit that had already been issued, stage two covering the balance of the construction allowed under the zoning and first variance granted. Stage three was for the portion of the structure for which the pending height variance was required.

At the Building Inspector's request, RRI submitted a new set of more detailed plans for everything but the state three work. These plans also were referred to the ARB for its approval as a prerequisite to the issuance of a building permit. In spring 1984, the Building Inspector notified

---

[192] Webb's Fabulous Pharmacies, Inc. v. Beckwith, 449 U.S. 155, 161, 101 S. Ct. 446, 66 L. Ed. 2d 358 (1980).

RRI that a building permit was forthcoming, but by then the mansion renovation had become controversial among residents. Without informing RRI, the ARB decided to take no action, allowing a mandatory thirty-day time period under the Zoning Code for the village to act, to expire. Then the mayor, reacting to the residents' pressure, ordered the Building Inspector to issue a stop work order because RRI did not have the building permit for work past the stage one permit. The ZBA denied the stage three variance request.

RRI then secured a state court decision holding that the ARB had arbitrarily refused to approve the stage two building permit for RRI's project because it knew that the stage three permit (requiring the height variance that had been denied) would violate the existing regulations. This action, the court held, exceeded the ARB's jurisdiction, which was limited to matters of aesthetic judgment. The state court also held that the village had failed to act within the requisite time frame of thirty days following receipt of RRI's application, and therefore RRI was entitled to the stage-two permit as a matter of law.

Subsequently, RRI brought a Section 1983 action[193] in federal district court seeking damages for the delay in the issuance of the stage two building permit and for attorneys fees and costs. The jury awarded RRI $1.9 million in damages and attorney fees and costs. However, the Second Circuit reversed, finding that, as a matter of law, there was no property interest in the stage-two permit. The court's reasoning is difficult to fathom. Most importantly, if the court's approach to determining the existence of a protected property interest is followed in other circuits, the substantive due process question will rarely be reached in challenges to land use decisions.

Because the Second Circuit focused upon the *degree of discretion* within the power of the regulator, the facts of the case evidencing probability of permit issuance were virtually irrelevant. These facts were that (1) ARB had

---

[193] 42 U.S.C.A. § 1983.

approved RRI's initial overall design, (2) the two-stage construction was in full compliance with the zoning law, (3) there was correspondence between the Building Inspector and RRI and other discussions to support RRI's assertion that approval of the application could be expected and, most importantly that (4) ARB's time limits within which to act on the application had expired caused, causing it to forfeit any discretion it may have had in approving the permit.

The court's reasoning on the expiration of the thirty-day time period to act is particularly baffling. The court essentially dismissed the significance of the thirty day "deemed approved" provision of the Village Code concluding that RRI's claim to the permit could not be "fragmented" into two claims—one subject to the ARB's discretion within thirty days and one subject to a mandatory duty to issue a permit after thirty days. That, however, is precisely what the Village's own regulations provided. Incredibly, the court held that despite the fact that the Village's regulatory provisions divested the ARB of all discretion after the thirty-day period had expired without action, somehow the ARB's discretion remained.

The Second Circuit's disregard for the state court determinations of state law that were relevant to the entitlement analysis is perhaps not surprising in view of that Circuit's entitlement test that, by definition, disregards the probability of permit issuance. Its approach ignores the U.S. Supreme Court's admonition in *Schad v. Borough of Mount Ephraim*, that the standard of review in constitutional challenges to land use regulations should be determined by the "nature of the right assertedly threatened or violated rather than by power being exercised or the specific limitation being imposed."[194] The Second Circuit's entitlement test is so rigorous that it invariably results in the court focusing exclusively on the power (degree of discretion) being exercised as a matter of

---

[194] Schad v. Borough of Mount Ephraim, 452 U.S. 61, 68, 101 S. Ct. 2176, 68 L. Ed. 2d 671, 7 Media L. Rep. (BNA) 1426 (1981).

law, obviating the need for the court to consider the nature of the right (substantive due process) being asserted.

### [3] Courts' Varying Definitions of "Arbitrary"

The Second Circuit, like other federal circuits that apply the *Roth* entitlement test rigorously to determine if a protected property interest exists, views the substantive due process right as a narrowly defined right that is rarely triggered by local government action, which is given great deference whenever some rational basis for the action can be identified. This means that for these circuits only arbitrary action that is extreme in some form merits consideration under substantive due process For example, the Sixth Circuit has adopted the "shocks the conscience" standard for determining when a local zoning decision violates substantive due process.[195] While one Sixth Circuit panel acknowledged that the terminology is "more apt for cases involving physical force"[196] another panel observed that it is "useful in zoning context too, to emphasize the degree of arbitrariness required to set aside a zoning decision by a local authority. . .."[197] The Seventh Circuit defines the level of arbitrariness required to sustain a substantive due process claim as "invidious or irrational" government action.[198] The Eighth Circuit has indicated that the government action must be "truly irrational," meaning the standard is more stringent than "arbitrary, capricious, or in violation of state law."[199]

Other circuits, notably the First and Ninth, by announcing their great deference toward local land use decisions

---

[195] Pearson v. City of Grand Blanc, 961 F.2d 1211, 1222 (6th Cir. 1992).

[196] Cassady v. Tackett, 938 F.2d 693, 698 (6th Cir. 1991).

[197] Pearson v. City of Grand Blanc, 961 F.2d at 1222.

[198] Coniston Corp. v. Village of Hoffman Estates, 844 F.2d 461, 467, 10 Fed. R. Serv. 3d 1294 (7th Cir. 1988).

[199] Anderson v. Douglas County, 4 F.3d 574, 577, 24 Envtl. L. Rep. 20624 (8th Cir. 1993); Chesterfield Development Corp. v. City of Chesterfield, 963 F.2d 1102, 1105 (8th Cir. 1992). See also, Carpenter Outdoor Advertising Co. v. City of Fenton, 251 F.3d 686 (8th Cir. 2001).

whenever there is any conceivable rational basis, signal by implication, that for government land use decisions to be actionable under substantive due process, the decision must be extremely irrational.[200] For example, the First Circuit has been reluctant to find a substantive due process violation in a zoning decision even when it involved claims of malicious obstruction of a landowner's rights.[201] The Ninth Circuit, although it will apply substantive due process analysis to a local zoning decision involving an individual property owner's claim, it reviews such decisions under the highly deferential standard used for legislation.[202]

### [a] Parcel Specific Zoning Decisions—Legislative or Administrative?

One principal reason for the lack of harmony among the federal circuits on substantive due process is the divergence among the states themselves on the question of treating a parcel specific zoning decision as a *legislative* versus a *quasi-judicial* decision. The courts in many states hold that a village board or city council acts in a legislative capacity when it approves a special use or a planned unit development—typical discretionary review mechanisms. Consequently, no precise standards are necessary.[203] Nor is the village board or city council bound by the recommendations of its staff or experts on such matters.[204] Unlike legislative decision makers, administra-

---

[200] *See, e.g.*, Dodd v. Hood River County, 59 F.3d 852, 864 (9th Cir. 1995); Nestor Colon Medina & Sucesores, Inc. v. Custodio, 964 F.2d 32, 45, 23 Fed. R. Serv. 3d 1054 (1st Cir. 1992).

[201] Cloutier v. Town of Epping, 714 F.2d 1184, 1189 (1st Cir. 1983); Creative Environments, Inc. v. Estabrook, 680 F.2d 822, 17 Env't. Rep. Cas. (BNA) 2180 (1st Cir. 1982).

[202] Southern Pacific Transp. Co. v. City of Los Angeles, 922 F.2d 498, 507 (9th Cir. 1990).

[203] *See, e.g.*, LaSalle Nat. Bank v. Lake County, 27 Ill. App. 3d 10, 325 N.E.2d 105, 110 (2d Dist. 1975).

[204] Minnetonka Congregation of Jehovah's Witnesses, Inc. v. Svee, 303 Minn. 79, 226 N.W.2d 306 (1975).

tive bodies must review and draw conclusions from facts presented with respect to a specific parcel of property under these procedural due process requirements, similar to those followed in a court of law, their actions are sometimes referred to as *quasi-judicial* or *adjudicative*, that is, judicial-type or adjudicating actions performed by individuals who are not judges. In some jurisdictions, most notable, Oregon, the courts have held that a decision by a local legislative body concerning the zoning of a individual parcel is a quasi-judicial rather than a legislative decision.[205] Courts in several other states have embraced this view.[206] However, the majority of the states continue to view parcel specific zoning decisions made by a legislative body as "legislative." Consequently, the majority of the federal circuits mirror this view. Some, such as the Seventh Circuit, go even as far as characterizing a site plan decision for a single parcel as "legislative," which frees the decision maker of making any findings of fact, and makes it's decision, however driven by protectionist or parochial motives, immune from challenge on substantive due process grounds so long as there is some relation to land use.[207] The First Circuit also views zoning as a legislative act, such that due process is satisfied where the decision bears a "conceivable rational relationship" to "legitimate governmental ends."[208]

From a review of the circuits' discussion of what is meant by "arbitrary" for purposes of substantive due process claims, it appears that there are three basic categories. These are:

---

[205] *See* Fasano v. Board of County Com'rs of Washington County, 264 Or. 574, 507 P.2d 23 (1973) (superseded by statute as noted in Menges v. Board of County Com'rs of Jackson County, 44 Or. App. 603, 606 P.2d 681 (1980)).

[206] *See, e.g.*, Board of County Com'rs of Brevard County v. Snyder, 627 So. 2d 469 (Fla. 1993); New Castle County Council v. BC Development Associates, 567 A.2d 1271 (Del. 1989); Golden v. City of Overland Park, 224 Kan. 591, 584 P.2d 130 (1978).

[207] New Burnham Prairie Homes, Inc. v. Village of Burnham, 910 F.2d 1474, 1479, R.I.C.O. Bus. Disp. Guide (CCH) P 7540, 30 Fed. R. Evid. Serv. 1052 (7th Cir. 1990).

[208] Gilbert v. City of Cambridge, 932 F.2d 51 (1st Cir. 1991).

- Decision is inadequately supported by the record

- Decision is irrational—no reasonable basis in law

- Decision is outside substantive limits of delegated authority (abuse of discretion)

The following briefly illustrates each of these categories of arbitrariness.

### [b]   Decision Inadequately Supported by Record

This form of arbitrariness, which occurs primarily as a result of quasi-judicial decisions, may not rise to the level of a substantive due process violation, provided there is truly a rational basis for the decision. For example, in *Sylvia Development Corporation v. Calvert County, Maryland*,[209] the plaintiff brought a civil rights action against the board of county commissioners after a state court had reversed the board's denial of the developer's application for designation of its property as a "Transfer Zone District" (TZD). That designation would allow the increase in density on a parcel through transfer of development rights from participating agricultural property owners under the county's transferable development rights (TDR) program. The state court had found that the board's decision was "arbitrary"—made without the support of any evidence in the record, and ordered the board to approve the application. In its subsequent civil rights action in federal court, the developer argued that the state court's decision that the board had acted arbitrarily and ordering the TZD application approved, created an entitlement to the TZD zone. The Fourth Circuit rejected this reasoning, stating "a court order requiring the Board to approve the application does not mean that the applicant had a preexisting legal right to that approval."[210] In support of this conclu-

---

[209] Sylvia Development Corp. v. Calvert County, Md., 48 F.3d 810 (4th Cir. 1995).
[210] *Id.* at 827.

sion, the court quoted from *RRI Realty Corp*: "The fact that the permit could have been denied on nonarbitrary grounds defeats the federal due process claim."[211] However, this statement begs the question, since a violation of substantive due process occurs if the decision is not, in fact, rational, not that it could have been rational. The better reasoning, stated elsewhere in the court's opinion, is that the decision was, in fact, rational—based on inadequate road access to accommodate the increase density—but not supported by sufficient evidence in the record.[212]

### [c] Irrational Decision—No Reasonable Basis in Law

Even though the Second Circuit's entitlement test means that it rarely reaches the step of analyzing the substantive due process claim, it has found that a decision is arbitrary where it is based upon improper motive—in one case involving revocation of a permit because of "impermissible political animus"[213] and in another case where a town official acted with wrongful motive in imposing unreasonable conditions upon a permit.[214] The Eleventh Circuit has also found that deprivation of a property interest rises to the level of a substantive due process violation when done for improper motives. In one case, for example, the court held that a town's "reinterpretation" of a ten-year termination date for a residential planned unit development, contrary to prior written representations upon which the developer had relied, violated substantive due process.[215]

---

[211] *Id.* (citing to its decision in Gardner v. City of Baltimore Mayor and City Council, 969 F.2d 63, 71 (4th Cir. 1992) in which it had quoted RRI Realty Corp. v. Incorporated Village of Southampton, 870 F.2d 911, 918 (2d Cir. 1989)).

[212] *Id.* at 825.

[213] Brady v. Town of Colchester, 863 F.2d 205, 212–13 (2d Cir. 1988).

[214] Walz v. Town of Smithtown, 46 F.3d 162, 167–69, 25 Envtl. L. Rep. 20770 (2d Cir. 1995).

[215] Resolution Trust Corp. v. Town of Highland Beach, 18 F.3d 1536, 1549 (11th Cir. 1994), reh'g en banc granted, opinion vacated and rehearing en banc granted, 42 F.3d 626 (11th Cir. 1994).

## [d]   Decision Outside Substantive Limits of Delegated Authority

The best example of this category of arbitrary decision making that rises to the level of a substantive due process violation is the Second Circuit's decision in *RRI Realty Corp.*, discussed above. There, the Architectural Review Board (ARB) had refused to approve the stage two building permit for RRI's project because it knew that the stage three permit (requiring the height variance that had been denied) would violate the existing regulations. This action, the state court had held, exceeded the ARB's jurisdiction, which was limited to matters of aesthetic judgment. In other words, the ARB had abused its discretion by acting outside the substantive authority delegated to it.[216] However, because of the Second Circuit's peculiar entitlement formulation, it was able to make a "threshold rejection" of the substantive due process claim—despite the clear abuse of discretion committed by ARB.

If we examine the circuits' decisions involving these three categories of arbitrary government behavior, in my view, as summarized in the table below, at least two of these categories are sufficiently wrongful to always constitute a violation of substantive due process. When the courts have not found these two categories of government action to violate substantive due process, it is principally because either they never get past the threshold inquiry of whether there is a protected property interest, or apply the extremely deferential rational relationship test appropriate only for truly "legislative" decisions, which individual zoning decisions arguably are not. The only category of arbitrariness that, on its face, may appear not to rise to the level of a

---

[216] *See* discussion *supra* at note 2.

| ARBITRARY GOVERNMENT ACTION | |
| :---: | :---: |
| CATEGORIES OF ARBITRARINESS | SUFFICIENT TO CONSTITUTE SUBSTANTIVE DUE PROCESS VIOLATION |
| Decision Inadequately Supported by Record | Sometimes |
| Irrational Decision No Reasonable Basis in Law | Always |
| Decision Outside Delegated Authority (Abuse of Discretion) | Always |

substantive due process claim is when the decision maker fails to support an otherwise rational decision with adequate evidence in the record. According to the Second Circuit, that is a matter of state law for the state court to resolve. If a developer who is denied the requisite approval based on a facially reasonable rationale that is unsupported by the record, loses its financing and ultimately the property as a result, certainly it has incurred damages as a result of the violation of due process, which is actionable under 42 U.S.C.A. § 1983. This would seem particularly so when the purported rationale for a denial, such as adequate road access, however legitimate as a land use matter generally, is not be adequately supported in the record precisely because it is not really an issue—regardless of how significant neighboring property owners may think it is. In such instances, a federal circuit such as the First Circuit, that looks for any "conceivable rational relationship" to "legitimate government ends," is unlikely to find a substantive due process violation.

### [4] Issue Needing Clarification

When land use regulatory decisions are the result of improper motive such as personal animus, political bias and conflicts of interest, or are the result of judgment being exercised outside the legal bounds of the authority that was given to the decision maker, such wrongful government action is barred by the substantive component of the Due Process Clause. Because we are at a time in this country when many local governments are attempting to address increasingly complex, sometimes subjective issues—preservation of "community character," urban design, "cumulative impacts" of land uses, growth control, environmental protection, affordable housing and infrastructure needs—through discretionary regulations, there is significant risk of arbitrary decision making.

Landowners and developers who seek a substantive due process remedy for injury resulting from such arbitrary decision making face an almost insurmountable barrier in those federal circuits that have erected the protected property interest threshold test in order to avoid becoming zoning boards of appeal. As recognized by the Third Circuit, ownership of property should be sufficient to invoke substantive due process protection from arbitrary government action. Landowners and developers face an equally difficult hurdle in those circuits that look for any conceivable rational relationship between a parcel specific zoning decision and a legitimate governmental objective—perpetuating the fiction that such decisions are "legislative" in nature.

As with the confusion among the federal circuits over the application of the ripeness doctrine in land use disputes, landowners and developers await clarification from the U.S. Supreme to resolve the confusion among the federal circuits in addressing substantive due process claims for arbitrary government actions.

# CHAPTER 2

# Variances

## Scope of Chapter

## § 2.01   Introduction

Although the variance remains in most of our zoning ordinances, its crude use to grant and deny favors was subjected to substantial criticism, not only from the courts but from the professional writers as well. The indictment has been that, far from being a safety valve, the variance is a handy gimmick to permit "leakage" from the certainty provided by the concept

> of districting. Today the variance has become a
> rather small bore weapon in the arsenal of the
> municipality, not because of the criticism directed
> against it but because of its inadequacy as a device
> for meeting the pressures placed upon our munici-
> palities by the developers and by the outsiders who
> wish to come into the municipality.
> —Richard Babcock in *The Zoning Game*

If, as suggested earlier, the "self-administering" premise of zoning was faulty, it is not surprising that the variance, too, has also proved to be inadequate. Just as the "certainty" of the zoning district system could not meet the demands of the marketplace, the variance has not been an effective flexibility mechanism. Perhaps this is in part because the variance was conceived as a device necessary to protect the zoning ordinance from constitutional objection.[1] Adjustments to avoid constitutional infirmity are not always sufficient to address the practical realities and economic constraints that affect land use and development decisions.

## § 2.02  Function of Variance

The original language in the Standard State Zoning Enabling Act (SSZEA) describing the role of the zoning variance authorizes the Board of Adjustment:

> [T]o authorize upon appeal in specific cases such vari-
> ance from the terms of the ordinance as will not be
> contrary to the public interest, where, owing to special
> conditions, a literal enforcement of the provisions of
> the ordinance will result in unnecessary hardship,

---

[1] *See* Freeman v. Board of Adjustment of City of Great Falls, 97 Mont. 342, 34 P.2d 534, 538 (1934); Thomas v. Board of Standards and Appeals of City of New York, 263 A.D. 352, 33 N.Y.S.2d 219, 230 (2d Dep't 1942), order rev'd on other grounds, 290 N.Y. 109, 48 N.E.2d 284 (1943).

and so that the spirit of the ordinance shall be observed and substantial justice done.[2]

The language in Section 7 of the SSZEA provides an administrative procedure for allowing property to be used in a manner inconsistent with the literal requirements of the zoning ordinance. In effect, a variance is a license to violate the zoning ordinance—a license originally dictated by a concern to shield the ordinance from constitutional objection, but gradually used primarily to address the broader purpose of assuring that property can be put to productive use.[3] In other words, the variance was originally conceived as a "safety valve" to give relief to a landowner while protecting the ordinance from invalidation on the constitutional ground that the particular landowner's property is burdened to a greater extent than other land in the vicinity, in violation of the due process clause.[4]

### § 2.03 Board of Adjustment—Authority and Procedure

The zoning board of adjustment or, in some states, the zoning board of appeals, is the "quasi-judicial" administrative body[5] that decides variances. This body was first created in the original New York City zoning ordinance of 1916,[6] and subsequently replicated in the zoning enabling acts of most states. Typically, the developer will determine up front, what, if any, variances are needed in connection

---

[2] U.S. Dep't of Commerce, A Standard State Zoning Enabling Act § 7 (rev. ed. 1926).

[3] *See* Green, "The Power of Zoning Board of Adjustment to Grant Variances from the Zoning Ordinance," 29 N.C. L. Rev. 245, 250–261 (1951).

[4] Nectow v. City of Cambridge, 277 U.S. 183, 48 S. Ct. 447, 72 L. Ed. 842 (1928) (invalidating a zoning ordinance on constitutional grounds as applied to a particular parcel, and articulating a balancing test weighing the public interest against the private interest).

[5] The meaning of the term "quasi-judicial" is discussed in Ch. 1, Sec. 1.07[2], *supra*.

[6] The actual name given to the board in the 1916 ordinance was the Board of Appeals. *See* Bassett, *Zoning*, 133–141 (2d ed. 1940).

with the development project. Failure to analyze the zoning ordinance standards in advance to make this determination can lead to a zoning administrator or other local government official making a belated determination that the developer's application requires application for a variance. Typical variance procedures allow presentation of evidence in support of the petition for a variance, present expert witness testimony under oath, and examination and cross-examination. The board must then make written findings to support its grant of a variance, which must be included in the record of the case (usually the board's minutes). If done properly, these findings should include both the board's conclusions and the factual reasons for those conclusions. Unfortunately, as noted below, this step is performed poorly, or not at all, by many boards. The board's decision is considered a "final order" which means that the developer or other individual adversely affected by the decision may appeal the decision to a court. The court's review of the case is confined to the transcript of the record before the board, unless the board did not make proper findings. In some states, for example, the board's failure to file written findings means that the court may hear additional evidence.[7]

---

[7] *See* Ohio Revised Code (ORC) § 2506.03; Talbut v. Perrysburg, 72 Ohio App. 3d 475, 594 N.E.2d 1046, 1049 (6th Dist. Wood County 1991).

© 1970 *Look* magazine

*"We who serve as your Zoning Board of Appeals ask neither thanks nor compensation, but would greatly appreciate not being addressed as, "You swine up there!"*

## § 2.04  Specter of Abuse

Perhaps no other zoning flexibility technique has received as much criticism as the variance.[8] The principal reason for regarding the variance process as a vehicle for public and private abuse, according to the dissenting judge in one case, is that the standards are "so spongy and flexible" that the risk of arbitrary decision making is extremely high.[9] The two principal standards that have been applied to the granted variances are the "unnecessary hardship" standard found in the Standard State Zoning Enabling Act and the "practical difficulties" standard,

---

[8] *See, e.g.*, Dukeminier and Stapleton, "The Zoning Board of Adjustment: A Case Study in Misrule," 50 Ky. L.J. 273 (1962); Note, "Zoning Variances and Exceptions: The Philadelphia Experience," 103 U. Pa. L. Rev. 516 (1955).
[9] *See* Duncan v. Village of Middlefield, 23 Ohio St. 3d 83, 491 N.E.2d 692, 698 (1986) (dissenting opinion).

which some states have added by statute. Imbedded in the language of the SSZEA is the requirement that the "spirit" of the ordinance be observed and that "substantial justice" be served. These ephemeral concepts receive little attention in the variance decisions, and understandable so. Whether the abuses are the result of a misunderstanding of these standards or just plain corrupt decision making, there is no doubt that in actual practice, the granting of variances departs significantly from the original theory of variance law.

## § 2.05  Use Variance and Area Variance—The Difference

The courts generally distinguish between a use variance and an area variance. The area variance, arguably, fits the notion that was originally intended in the SSZEA. It authorizes departures from ordinance restrictions on the construction or placement of buildings and other structures. In other words, the area variance allows adjustments to the requirements for yards, height, frontage, setbacks, and similar dimensional aspects, and a use variance permits a use that is otherwise prohibited in the particular zoning district.[10] Most state statutes require a showing of "unnecessary hardship" for entitlement to a use variance, whereas a lesser showing of "practical difficulty" is required for a nonuse or area variance.[11] These two standards are discussed below.

---

[10] For a discussion of the difference between the use variance and the area variance, *see* City of Merriam v. Board of Zoning Appeals of City of Merriam, 242 Kan. 532, 748 P.2d 883 (1988).

[11] Colo. Rev. Stat. § 30–28–118(c); Ill. Ann. Stat. ch. 24, §§ 11–13–4, 11–13–5; Md. Local Gov't Code Ann. Art. 66B, §§ 1.00, 4.07; Mo. Rev. Stat. § 89.090.1(3); N.J. Stat. Ann. §§ 40:55D-70(c), 40:55D-70(d); N.Y. Town Law § 267-b; Ohio Rev. Code Ann. § 303.14(B); Wash. Rev. Code Ann. § 36.70.810. Legislation of some states fails to differentiate between the two and imposes the "unnecessary hardship" standard for the granting of either type of variance. *See* Mass. Gen. Laws ch. 40A, § 10; Mich. Comp. Laws Ann. § 125.1515; 53 Pa. Stat. Ann. § 10910.2.

Reprinted by permission of Sam Molloy.

## § 2.06   Use Variance Prohibited

Some states, either by judicial decree or statute, prohibit the granting of use variances.[12] But other courts
have held that their respective state zoning statutes, based

---

[12] Livingston v. Peterson, 59 N.D. 104, 228 N.W. 816 (1930); Board
of Adjustment of City of San Antonio v. Levinson, 244 S.W.2d 281 (Tex.
Civ. App. San Antonio 1951); Arrow Transp. Co. v. Planning and Zoning Com'n of City of Paducah and Municipal Area, McCracken County,
299 S.W.2d 95 (Ky. 1956); Cook v. Howard, 134 Ga. App. 721, 215
S.E.2d 690 (1975); Walton v. Tracy Loan & Trust Co., 97 Utah 249, 92
P.2d 724 (1939). For an example of a statutory prohibition, see § 65906
of the California Government Code which states:

> A variance shall not be granted for a parcel of property
> which authorizes a use or activity which is not otherwise
> expressly authorized by the zone regulation governing the
> parcel of property. The provisions of this SS shall not apply
> to conditional use permits. See also Ariz. Rev. Stat. Ann.
> § 9-462.06; Ind. Code Ann. § 36-7-4-918(d); Minn. Stat.
> Ann. § 394.27(7); Va. Code Ann. § 15:1–431(p).

on the SSZEA, authorize a use variance.[13] Not surprisingly, those decisions which hold that a use variance is prohibited reason that such a change requires a formal amendment to the zoning ordinance, and using any other means to accomplish this end undermines the amendment power. Some courts straddle the issue by approving use variances on a case-by-case basis, provided the size of the parcel affected by the variance is not large. In one New Jersey case, for example, the court held that "[t]he basic inquiry in each such case must be whether the impact of the requested variance would be to substantially alter the character of the district as that character has been prescribed by the zoning ordinance."[14]

## § 2.07    The "Unnecessary Hardship" Standard

Although "unnecessary hardship" constitutes only one portion of the SSZEA standard, it has become the prime focus of attention for applicants and boards of adjustment. The most frequently cited statement of what is meant by "unnecessary hardship" is in an oft-quoted New York case,[15] in which the court identified three key elements:

> Before the Board may . . . grant a variance upon the ground of unnecessary hardship, the record must show that (1) the land in question cannot yield a reasonable return if used only for purpose allowed in that zone; (2) that the plight of the owner is due to unique circumstances and not to the general conditions of the neighborhood which may reflect the unreasonableness of the zoning ordinance itself; and

---

[13] Strange v. Board of Zoning Appeals of Shelby County, 428 N.E.2d 1328 (Ind. Ct. App. 1st Dist. 1981); Appeal of Kenney, 374 N.W.2d 271 (Minn. 1985); Clarke v. Morgan, 327 So. 2d 769 (Fla. 1975).

[14] Dover Tp. v. Board of Adjustment of Dover Tp., 158 N.J. Super. 401, 386 A.2d 421 (App. Div. 1978).

[15] Otto v. Steinhilber, 282 N.Y. 71, 24 N.E.2d 851 (1939), reargument denied, 282 N.Y. 681, 26 N.E.2d 811 (1940).

(3) the use to be authorized by the variance will not alter the essential character of the locality.[16]

These three elements are discussed below.

### [1] No Reasonable Return

The strictness of this test is reflected by one court's description of it as requiring that land must be virtually zoned into oblivion—"zoned into inutility."[17] Under this standard, it must be proven that the ordinance deprives the owner of all beneficial use of the property, or that the restrictions make the use of the property nonproductive.[18] Courts have held that to satisfy this standard, the applicant must demonstrate that of all the uses permitted under the zoning ordinance on that property, none can be conducted.[19] However, the proper focus for this test should be the economic feasibility of devoting the property to a permitted use, not the absolute impossibility of using the property at all.[20] Merely making a case for variance upon showing that one's property could be devoted to a more profitable use if the variance were granted does not satisfy the hardship test. Normally, a court will look for evidence that the owner cannot sell the property as indicative of a lack of reasonable return under the existing zoning ordinance. Except in New York, where the courts have required the applicant to show actual efforts to sell the

---

[16] *Id.* at 853.

[17] Davis Enterprises v. Karpf, 105 N.J. 476, 523 A.2d 137, 139 (1987).

[18] Perrin v. Town of Kittery, 591 A.2d 861 (Me. 1991); Goldreyer v. Board of Zoning Appeals of City of Bridgeport, 144 Conn. 641, 136 A.2d 789 (1957); Packer v. Hornsby, 221 Va. 117, 267 S.E.2d 140 (1980).

[19] Power v. Town of Shapleigh, 606 A.2d 1048 (Me. 1992) (proof of hardship required evidence that the land could not produce a reasonable return without the variance); Richard v. Mullen, 181 A.D.2d 679, 580 N.Y.S.2d 787 (2d Dep't 1992) (owner failed to prove deprivation of any reasonable use of the land and/or that the land had not already yielded a reasonable return under any of the permissible uses).

[20] Valley View Civic Ass'n v. Zoning Bd. of Adjustment, 501 Pa. 550, 462 A.2d 637, 642 (1983).

property, without success,[21] most courts will accept evidence outside the applicant's personal efforts as probative of the applicant's inability to sell the property.[22] This latter approach is more fair and more realistic, since it focuses on the property itself, not the current owner, and recognizes the impact of the general real estate market upon salability.

Of course, the concept of "reasonable return" suffers from vagueness. In 1973, when a group of lawyers gathered to examine the zoning variance, the following questions were raised regarding the standard: Reasonable return on what? The cost of the land? The present value of the land? Is the cost or value of existing buildings and other improvements to be considered?[23] Their questions underscored the difficulty of applying this concept in variance law.

---

[21] Forrest v. Evershed, 7 N.Y.2d 256, 196 N.Y.S.2d 958, 164 N.E.2d 841 (1959). Effective July 1, 1992, New York supposedly codified its variance case law and established the following standards for granting use variances, which, compared with other states, are now among the most stringent for granting use variances:

> No such use variance shall be granted by a board of appeals without a showing by the applicant that applicable zoning regulations and restrictions have caused unnecessary hardship. In order to prove such unnecessary hardship the applicant shall demonstrate to the board of appeals that (1) under applicable zoning regulations the applicant is deprived of all economic use or benefit from the property in question, which deprivation must be established by competent financial evidence; (2) that the alleged hardship relating to the property in question is unique, and does not apply to a substantial portion of the district or neighborhood; (3) that the requested use variance, if granted, will not alter the essential character of the neighborhood; and (4) that the alleged hardship has not been self-created. N.Y. Town Law Section 267-b(2)(b) (McKinney 1992).

[22] See, e.g., Valley View Civic Ass'n v. Zoning Bd. of Adjustment, 501 Pa. 550, 462 A.2d 637 (1983); Guenther v. Zoning Bd. of Review of City of Warwick, 85 R.I. 37, 125 A.2d 214 (1956).

[23] Report of ABA Committee on Planning and Zoning of Section of Local Government Law and Committee on Public Regulation of Land Use of Section of Real Property, Probate and Trust Law (Spring 1973).

## [2]  Unique Circumstances

If the property does not suffer from some unique or unusual problem, then presumably the same hardship is shared by other properties in the vicinity, making a zoning amendment the more appropriate form of relief. For this reason, the test focuses upon *unique* hardship to the property in order not to undermine the amendment power. This means that the mere fact that a property has topographical characteristics which make it difficult for development does not, by itself, satisfy the uniqueness test. The key determinant is the topography of surrounding properties.[24]

Topography, however, need not be the only indicator of uniqueness. It is also possible that the owner is surrounded by properties whose uses are incompatible with the owner's use of the property. If, as a result, the owner cannot earn a reasonable return, if limited to the permitted use, and there is no evidence that the public interest is promoted by maintaining the restriction, the variance may be granted.[25]

What about personal hardship? Normally this is not a legitimate basis for asserting uniqueness under the hardship standard, unless there is some meaningful connection to the property itself.[26] In other words, where the types of personal hardship are unrelated to the land itself, such as health problems[27] or personal losses,[28] the courts are not sympathetic.

---

[24] Hanson v. Manning, 115 N.H. 367, 341 A.2d 764 (1975); Topanga Assn. for a Scenic Community v. County of Los Angeles, 11 Cal. 3d 506, 113 Cal. Rptr. 836, 522 P.2d 12 (1974).

[25] Hammond v. Board of Appeal of Bldg. Dept. of Springfield, 257 Mass. 446, 154 N.E. 82 (1926); School Committee of City of Pawtucket v. Zoning Bd. of Review of City of Pawtucket, 86 R.I. 131, 133 A.2d 734 (1957).

[26] Fuhst v. Foley, 45 N.Y.2d 441, 410 N.Y.S.2d 56, 382 N.E.2d 756 (1978).

[27] Ex parte Chapman, 485 So. 2d 1161 (Ala. 1986).

[28] Vassallo v. Penn Rose Civic Ass'n, 429 A.2d 168, 171 (Del. 1981).

### [3] Impact on the Surrounding Area

This third element of the unnecessary hardship test, namely, that the variance must not alter the essential character of the neighborhood,[29] has been referred to as the "negative" criterion.[30] For example, a request for an area variance in order to shoehorn a house on an undersized lot could be denied on the ground that the bulk of the house would adversely impact the character of the neighborhood.[31] A use variance to allow gasoline storage tanks in a predominantly residential area could be denied on the ground that it would create a potential safety hazard in the residential area.[32]

### [4] Variations on the Hardship Test

However a particular state has chosen to enunciate the hardship test, these three elements or factors from the New York court's decision have provided a guiding thread in the development of the hardship doctrine in other states. The cases and statutes reveal that the majority of states use some form of hardship test including or expanding upon these criteria.

For example, in New Hampshire, to obtain a variance, the applicant must demonstrate that: (1) denying the variance would impose an unnecessary hardship; (2) surrounding properties would not suffer a diminution in value; (3) the proposed use would not be contrary to the spirit of the ordinance; (4) allowing the variance would be in the

---

[29] Otto v. Steinhilber, 282 N.Y. 71, 24 N.E.2d 851 (1939), reargument denied, 282 N.Y. 681, 26 N.E.2d 811 (1940).

[30] Amberley Swim & Country Club, Inc. v. Zoning Bd. of Appeals of Amberley Village, 117 Ohio App. 466, 24 Ohio Op. 2d 260, 191 N.E.2d 364 (1st Dist. Hamilton County 1963); Culinary Institute of America v. Board of Zoning Appeals of City of New Haven, 143 Conn. 257, 121 A.2d 637 (1956).

[31] Commons v. Westwood Zoning Bd. of Adjustment, 81 N.J. 597, 410 A.2d 1138 (1980).

[32] Glaser v. Larkin, 21 Misc. 2d 379, 198 N.Y.S.2d 257 (Sup 1960).

public's interest; and (5) granting the variance would accomplish substantial justice.[33]

Under the Pennsylvania Municipalities Planning Code, the board may grant a variance, provided that all of the following findings are made where relevant to a given case:

(1) That there are unique physical circumstances or conditions, including irregularity, narrowness, or shallowness of lot size or shape, or exceptional topographical or their physical conditions peculiar to the particular property and that the unnecessary hardship is due to such conditions and not the circumstances or conditions generally created by the provisions of the zoning ordinance in the neighborhood or district in which the property is located.

(2) That because of such physical circumstances or conditions, there is no possibility that the property can be developed in strict conformity with the provisions of the zoning ordinance and that the authorization of a variance is therefore necessary to enable the reasonable use of the property.

(3) That such unnecessary hardship has not been created by the appellant.

(4) That the variance, if authorized, will not alter the essential character of the neighborhood or district in which the property is located, nor substantially or permanently impair the appropriate use or development of adjacent property, nor be detrimental to the public welfare.

(5) That the variance, if authorized, will represent the minimum variance that will afford relief and

---

[33] Goslin v. Town of Farmington, 132 N.H. 48, 561 A.2d 507 (1989); Rowe v. Town of North Hampton, 131 N.H. 424, 553 A.2d 1331 (1989); Biggs v. Town of Sandwich, 124 N.H. 421, 470 A.2d 928 (1984).

will represent the least modification possible of the regulation in issue.[34]

Connecticut employs a two-prong approach that in essence embodies the requirements laid out in the three- or five-part tests from other jurisdictions. For a variance to be granted under the Connecticut General Statutes, two conditions must be fulfilled: (1) the variance must be shown not to affect substantially the comprehensive zoning plan; and (2) adherence to the strict letter of the zoning ordinance must be shown to cause unusual hardship that is unnecessary to the carrying out of the general purpose of the zoning plan.[35]

## § 2.08  The "Practical Difficulties" Standard

From the developer's perspective, if given a choice, the "practical difficulties" test is preferable to the "unnecessary hardship" test. The practical difficulties test is applied to area variances in those states where the zoning statute separates "practical difficulties" from "unnecessary hardship." In one Alaskan case,[36] however, because the zoning ordinance stated these two tests conjunctively, the court refused to apply the separate practical difficulties test for area variances.[37] When a court such as the Alaskan

---

[34] 53 Pa. Stat. § 10910.2. *See also* Vanguard Cellular System, Inc. v. Zoning Hearing Bd. of Smithfield Tp., 130 Pa. Commw. 371, 568 A.2d 703 (1989); Goodman v. Zoning Bd. of Adjustment of City of Philadelphia, 132 Pa. Commw. 298, 572 A.2d 848 (1990), relying on Jacquelin v. Zoning Hearing Bd. of Hatboro Borough, 126 Pa. Commw. 20, 558 A.2d 189 (1989).

[35] Connecticut General Statutes § 8-6 (3). *See also* Kelly v. Zoning Bd. of Appeals of Town of Hamden, 21 Conn. App. 594, 575 A.2d 249 (1990); Smith v. Zoning Bd. of Appeals of Town of Norwalk, 174 Conn. 323, 387 A.2d 542 (1978). *See also* Grillo v. Zoning Bd. of Appeals of City of West Haven, 206 Conn. 362, 537 A.2d 1030 (1988).

[36] City and Borough of Juneau v. Thibodeau, 595 P.2d 626 (Alaska 1979).

[37] Property owners should also be careful before seeking an area variance that they have reviewed whether the state court views their type of local government as has having the authority to apply the

court refuses to apply the practical difficulties test to an area variance, the landowner is almost certainly doomed. In that particular case, the landowner had received a zoning amendment to expand a store, and then sought an area variance to reduce the number of parking spaces that would otherwise be required. The court was not persuaded that this was an appropriate grant of an area variance because the physical conditions of the land did not distinguish it from land in the surrounding area. The fact that the "ordinance merely deprives the landowner of a more profitable operation" was not sufficient reason to grant the area variance.[38]

Depending upon the state, the court can apply different factors to determine whether practical difficulties justify an area variance. Some of the more common factors applied by the courts include the following: (1) the significance of economic injury; (2) the magnitude of the variance being sought; (3) whether the difficulty was self-created; and (4) whether other means exist that could avoid the difficulty.[39] The "significant economic injury" factor is usually applied less rigorously under the practical difficulties test than the unnecessary hardship test, and is

---

practical difficulties standard to area variances. In Ohio, for example, there is a split among the courts as to whether both "townships" and "municipalities" have that authority. Because the zoning authority of townships is derived from the state statute only (which applies the hardship standard to variances of any type), while the zoning authority of municipal corporations derives from the Ohio Constitution, the minority view is that townships can grant area variances only under the traditional hardship standard. In Dsuban v. Union Twp. Bd. of Zoning Appeals, 140 Ohio App. 3d 602, 748 N.E.2d 597 (12th Dist. Butler County 2000), the appeals court adopted this minority view and invalidated the township's variance standards as exceeding the authority granted by the Ohio legislature. It probably didn't help the township's position that the township's standards were "an amalgamation of the unnecessary hardship and practical-difficulties standards." Id. at 610.

[38] Id. See also Marchi v. Town of Scarborough, 511 A.2d 1071 (Me. 1986) (denial of setback variance).

[39] Human Development Services of Port Chester, Inc. v. Zoning Bd. of Appeals of Village of Port Chester, 110 A.D.2d 135, 493 N.Y.S.2d 481 (2d Dep't 1985), order aff'd, 67 N.Y.2d 702, 499 N.Y.S.2d 927, 490 N.E.2d 846 (1986).

interpreted to mean that the use permitted by the zoning ordinance will not produce a reasonable return under the existing zoning restrictions.[40]

## § 2.09    Self-Created Hardship

Perhaps the most misunderstood criterion in deliberations over use and area variances is the notion that the mere purchase of property by a purchaser who is aware of severe zoning restrictions is sufficient to prove self-created hardship. The proper question is not whether the purchaser knew of the restriction, but whether the restriction is so severe that the original landowner would have been entitled to a variance had that owner sought one. The fundamental principle here is that the right to use property does not change merely because of the transfer of title between two individuals. The purpose of zoning controls is to control the use of land, not ownership. Where evidence exists as to the hardship created by the application of the zoning ordinance to the particular parcel of land, regardless of ownership, the variance should be granted. In other words, it is the actual *condition* of the land, not the owner, that should decide the question. Unfortunately, many courts fail to make this distinction.[41] Certainly, knowledge of existing zoning restrictions upon the property prior to purchase is a factor,[42] but it should

---

[40] Doyle v. Amster, 79 N.Y.2d 592, 584 N.Y.S.2d 417, 594 N.E.2d 911 (1992). *But see* Sasso v. Osgood, 86 N.Y.2d 374, 633 N.Y.S.2d 259, 657 N.E.2d 254, 265 (1995) (holding that the new Town Law, effective July 1, 1992, does not require the applicant for an area variance to make a showing of "practical difficulties." *See id.* at 259.

[41] Association For Preservation of 1700 Block of N St., N.W., and Vicinity v. District of Columbia Bd. of Zoning Adjustment, 384 A.2d 674 (D.C. 1978); Josephson v. Autrey, 96 So. 2d 784 (Fla. 1957); Sanchez v. Board of Zoning Adjustments of City of New Orleans, 488 So. 2d 1277 (La. Ct. App. 4th Cir. 1986), writ denied, 491 So. 2d 24 (La. 1986); Alleghany Enterprises, Inc. v. Board of Zoning Appeals of City of Covington, 217 Va. 64, 225 S.E.2d 383 (1976).

[42] In re Zoning Variance Application of Ray Reilly Tire Mart, Inc., 141 Vt. 330, 449 A.2d 910 (1982).

not be the controlling factor. Obviously, if a prior owner created a hardship through some action that relates to the land, the subsequent purchaser should not be able to overcome that created hardship merely by virtue of purchase. Otherwise, the better rule is that so long as the reasons for a variance can be said to arise from the condition of the land, not the actions of the prior owner, the variance, if merited, should be granted.

A common situation that may be considered a self-created hardship is when a landowner purchases property with knowledge of the zoning restrictions and then claims unnecessary hardship on the grounds that the property cannot yield a reasonable return.[43] Sometimes, financial hardship is alleged because the owner paid an excessive price for the property in anticipation of a variance. At one time, the majority view was that one who purchased property with knowledge of the zoning restrictions was absolutely barred from securing a variance because any hardship was considered self-created.[44] However, states are beginning to abandon the automatic application of this rigid view[45] for two reasons. First, since hardship for a variance is not measured solely by financial detriment to

---

[43] *See, e.g.,* Appeal of Gro, 440 Pa. 552, 269 A.2d 876 (1970) (court holding that it was the buyer's act of paying an inflated purchase price that made it impossible to put the property as zoned to any economically profitable use).

[44] *See, e.g.,* Clark v. Board of Zoning Appeals of Town of Hempstead, 301 N.Y. 86, 92 N.E.2d 903 (1950), motion denied, 301 N.Y. 681, 95 N.E.2d 44 (1950).

[45] *See, e.g.,* Twigg v. Town of Kennebunk, 662 A.2d 914 (Me. 1995) (rejecting broad proposition previously held in Bishop v. Town of Eliot, 529 A.2d 798 (Me. 1987) that actual or constructive knowledge of the restrictions of a zoning ordinance prior to purchase of property is tantamount to self-created hardship, and adopting the position that actual or constructive knowledge of such restrictions "may be considered by the Board as a factor , but is not determinative in evaluating self-created hardship)." *But see* Howes v. Langendorfer, 137 A.D.2d 960, 525 N.Y.S.2d 382 (3d Dep't 1988) (purchaser who bought property for use as parking lot was denied use variance because he was fully aware of residential zoning); Tuckner v. May Tp., 419 N.W.2d 836 (Minn. Ct. App. 1988); Chambers v. Smithfield City, 714 P.2d 1133 (Utah 1986); In re Zoning Variance Application of Ray Reilly Tire Mart, Inc., 141 Vt. 330, 449 A.2d 910 (1982) (when purchaser bought a small

the owner, nor solely by a comparison of value with and without the zoning restriction, it makes no sense to prohibit granting of a variance solely because the purchaser paid an excessive price for the property with knowledge of the zoning restrictions. It would be unfair to prevent the owner of the property from securing a variance merely because he or she paid more than the property's worth. Evidence of the price paid alone provides an especially weak justification for denying a variance because a low purchase price could just as easily be considered a reason to deny the variance on grounds that to allow a variance when the purchaser paid a low price would produce a windfall to the present owner.[46]

The second reason behind the gradual demise of the traditional rule is that the courts have realized that the rule fails to recognize that if the prior owner would have been entitled to a variance, the subsequent purchaser should not be precluded from asserting this same right just because he or she purchased with knowledge of the zoning restrictions.[47] As discussed below, a variance "runs with the land." Therefore, the better logic would be that

---

parcel, knowing that he would need a variance to develop, hardship was found to be self-created).

[46] *See, e.g.,* Cowan v. Kern, 41 N.Y.2d 591, 394 N.Y.S.2d 579, 363 N.E.2d 305 (1977), reargument denied, 42 N.Y.2d 910, 397 N.Y.S.2d 1029, 366 N.E.2d 1365 (1977) (court holding that price paid reflected value with zoning restriction and to grant a variance would cause a windfall to the purchaser); *but see* Searles v. Zoning Hearing Bd. of City of Easton, 118 Pa. Commw. 453, 545 A.2d 476 (1988) (evidence that purchaser paid an unduly high price for the property in anticipation of receiving a variance is required); Marlowe v. Zoning Hearing Bd. of Haverford Tp., 52 Pa. Commw. 224, 415 A.2d 946 (1980). In 1992, the New York legislature amended the Town Law to provide that the fact that the applicant's difficulty was self-created, does not necessarily preclude the granting of an area variance. *See* New York Town Law § 267-b[3][b][5] (1992) and Sasso v. Osgood, 86 N.Y.2d 374, 633 N.Y.S.2d 259, 657 N.E.2d 254, 265 (1995). The holding in Cowan v. Kern, supra, is now questionable in light of the new statutory language governing self-created hardship.

[47] *See, e.g.,* A.L.W., Inc. v. District of Columbia Bd. of Zoning Adjustment, 338 A.2d 428 (D.C. 1975); Schaaf v. Zoning Hearing Bd. of Borough of Edinboro, 22 Pa. Commw. 50, 347 A.2d 740 (1975); Jacquelin v. Horsham Tp., 10 Pa. Commw. 473, 312 A.2d 124 (1973).

the subsequent owner would take title to all rights in the land to which the prior owner was entitled.[48]

The current trend is to give the board of adjustment discretion to consider the variance applicant's purchase with knowledge along with all other factors when deciding whether to grant or deny the variance.[49] In this way, evidence of the price paid or knowledge of the zoning restrictions will not be considered in a vacuum, but rather in the context of all circumstances surrounding the purchase of the property.[50]

### § 2.10 Who Is Entitled to Apply for a Variance?

Typically, a prospective purchaser will hold an option to buy, conditioned on the obtaining of a variance. Unfortunately, some courts have held that holders of options cannot apply for a variance. The argument is that option holders have nothing to lose if the variance is denied. Therefore, they fail to meet the unnecessary hardship test.[51] However, if we remember the principle that the variance, and therefore the hardship, is based on the characteristics of the land rather than the person, it makes no sense to deny an option holder standing to seek a variance. The real question, as some commentators have observed, is whether the applicant has a legally enforceable right to use the land. Clearly, an option is a legally enforceable right to have ultimate use of the land. By hold-

---

[48] *See, e.g.,* Nuckles v. Allen, 250 S.C. 123, 156 S.E.2d 633 (1967).

[49] *See, e.g.,* National Merritt, Inc. v. Weist, 41 N.Y.2d 438, 393 N.Y.S.2d 379, 361 N.E.2d 1028 (1977).

[50] *See, e.g.,* De Sena v. Board of Zoning Appeals of Inc. Village of Hempstead, 45 N.Y.2d 105, 408 N.Y.S.2d 14, 379 N.E.2d 1144 (1978) (calling for a more flexible approach rather than mechanical application of self-created hardship to purchase with knowledge situations).

[51] Conery v. City of Nashua, 103 N.H. 16, 164 A.2d 247 (1960); Lee v. Board of Adjustment of City of Rocky Mount, 226 N.C. 107, 37 S.E.2d 128, 168 A.L.R. 1 (1946); Tripp v. Zoning Bd. of Review of City of Pawtucket, 84 R.I. 262, 123 A.2d 144 (1956).

ing that an option holder has no right to seek the variance, the courts personalize the variance process.[52]

## § 2.11  A Variance Runs with the Land

If a variance is appropriate for a particular parcel because of the peculiarities of that parcel, then the variance should apply to the land regardless of ownership. In other words, it "runs with the land."[53] Therefore, it is improper for a board of zoning adjustment to condition a variance upon the land being owned or used by a particular owner or type of owner. The true hardship occurs when such an improper condition is attached to a variance that ultimately is found improper, forcing the purchaser to reapply for the variance.[54] If the variance "runs with land," does this mean that the owner of the land which is subject to a variance has a "vested right"[55] to that variance? Probably not. Since the variance remains subject to the continuing regulatory power of the government, if the variance is not acted upon, the original grant of the variance confers no vested right on a subsequent purchaser.[56]

---

[52] *See* Arant v. Board of Adjustment of City of Montgomery, 271 Ala. 600, 126 So. 2d 100, 89 A.L.R.2d 652 (1960).

[53] New Jersey rejects the rule that a variance runs with the land. *See, e.g.,* Smith v. Paquin, 77 N.J. Super. 138, 185 A.2d 673 (App. Div. 1962).

[54] McClurkan v. Board of Zoning Appeals for Metropolitan Government of Nashville and Davidson County, 565 S.W.2d 495 (Tenn. Ct. App. 1977); St. Onge v. Donovan, 127 A.D.2d 880, 511 N.Y.S.2d 700 (3d Dep't 1987), appeal granted, 70 N.Y.2d 603, 518 N.Y.S.2d 1025, 512 N.E.2d 551 (1987) and order rev'd, 71 N.Y.2d 507, 527 N.Y.S.2d 721, 522 N.E.2d 1019 (1988).

[55] A *vested right* is a right secured under existing regulations that cannot legally be changed or taken away by a subsequent change in regulations. *See* discussion of vested rights in Ch. 7, Sec. 7.06, *infra*.

[56] *See* Goldberg v. City of Milwaukee Bd. of Zoning Appeals, 115 Wis. 2d 517, 340 N.W.2d 558, 561 n.4 (Ct. App. 1983).

## § 2.12 Variances and Nonconforming Uses

The owner of a nonconforming use[57] often wonders whether it is possible to obtain a variance in connection with a zoning ordinance provision that allows the nonconforming use to be altered or expanded. Even if the zoning policy of the community is to allow the expansion or alteration of a nonconforming use, it is unlikely that a variance in connection with such an expansion or alteration will be granted unless it can be shown that a reasonable return cannot be realized from any permitted use or from the existing nonconforming use.[58] When a use variance is being sought by a nonconforming user and the result will be a less intensive use than the existing nonconforming use, some courts have upheld a variance.[59] Interestingly, in Pennsylvania, the Pennsylvania Supreme Court has held that outright prohibitions on the natural expansion of nonconforming uses are unconstitutional.[60] Indeed, in Pennsylvania the amortization of a nonconforming use has been held to constitute a taking.[61] Nevertheless, the court has indicated that when seeking a variance, the nonconforming user must still satisfy the requisite elements of hardship.[62]

---

[57] A *nonconforming use* is defined in most zoning ordinances as a use or activity that was lawful prior to the adoption or amendment of the zoning ordinance, but is no longer permitted under the new regulations.

[58] *See* Goodman v. Zoning Bd. of Review of City of Cranston, 105 R.I. 680, 254 A.2d 743 (1969). *See also* Crossroads Recreation, Inc. v. Broz, 4 N.Y.2d 39, 172 N.Y.S.2d 129, 149 N.E.2d 65 (1958).

[59] O'Neill v. Philadelphia Zoning Bd. of Adjustment, 384 Pa. 379, 120 A.2d 901 (1956).

[60] Silver v. Zoning Bd. of Adjustment, 435 Pa. 99, 255 A.2d 506 (1969).

[61] PA Northwestern Distributors, Inc. v. Zoning Hearing Bd. of Tp. of Moon, 526 Pa. 186, 584 A.2d 1372, 8 A.L.R.5th 970 (1991).

[62] Walter v. Zoning Bd. of Adjustment, 437 Pa. 277, 263 A.2d 123, 126 (1970).

## § 2.13 Conditions on Variances

The Standard State Zoning Enabling Act does not expressly authorize the Board of Adjustment to attach conditions to variances. Most state zoning enabling acts do not provide for this power either. However, the courts generally have recognized that the power to impose conditions is inherent to the power to grant variances. The reason is that if the variance allows what amounts to a violation of the ordinance under unique circumstances, then conditions are appropriate to alleviate the harm that might otherwise result.[63] The essential point, from the applicant's standpoint, however, is that these conditions must relate to the use of the land. However much of a "deadbeat" the applicant may appear to be to the board of adjustment, the conditions cannot be tailored to that individual.[64]

The critical question with respect to a condition imposed through the variance procedures is whether an "essential nexus" exists between the condition of the land for which the variance is being sought and the impacts it may have.[65] The importance of this has been reinforced by the U.S. Supreme Court's decisions in the *Nollan* and *Dolan* cases.[66] If the necessary nexus is absent, the condition is invalid.[67]

---

[63] Everson on Behalf of Everson Elec. Co. v. Zoning Bd. of Adjustment of City of Allentown, 395 Pa. 168, 149 A.2d 63 (1959); Town of Warren v. Frost, 111 R.I. 217, 301 A.2d 572 (1973).

[64] National Black Child Development Institute, Inc. v. District of Columbia Bd. of Zoning Adjustment, 483 A.2d 687 (D.C. 1984); DeFelice v. Zoning Bd. of Adjustment of Borough of Point Pleasant Beach, 216 N.J. Super. 377, 523 A.2d 1086 (App. Div. 1987); Fox v. Shriver-Allison Co., 28 Ohio App. 2d 175, 57 Ohio Op. 2d 234, 275 N.E.2d 637 (7th Dist. Mahoning County 1971).

[65] National Black Child Development Institute, Inc. v. District of Columbia Bd. of Zoning Adjustment, 483 A.2d 687, 691–92 (D.C. 1984).

[66] *See* discussion of these cases in Ch. 1, Sec. 1.09, *supra*.

[67] Allen v. Hattrick, 87 A.D.2d 575, 447 N.Y.S.2d 741 (2d Dep't 1982).

## [1]   Violation of Conditions

If the applicant who receives a variance violates conditions imposed as part of the approval, the municipality
may immediately bring an action for injunctive relief.[68]

## [2]   Modification of Conditions

Landowners should be aware that, if justified by
changed circumstances, the board of adjustment may
modify the conditions imposed in the original grant of the
variance.[69] However, notice must be given to the affected
owner.[70] If the landowner wishes to dispute the original
condition rather than modify a condition due to a change
of circumstances, he or she must take an appeal from the
board's original order.[71]

## § 2.14   Time Limits on Variances

Courts have approved variances that are issued for
limited periods of time.[72] It is also possible to condition a
variance upon the happening of a future event.[73] The argument in favor of time limits on variances is that the hardship must be balanced against the public's interest. Where
an indefinite time period could unnecessarily impede the
government from addressing changed circumstances,

---

[68] *See, e.g.,* Build-A-Rama, Inc. v. Peck, 475 N.W.2d 225 (Iowa Ct.
App. 1991); City of Santa Clara v. Paris, 76 Cal. App. 3d 338, 142 Cal.
Rptr. 818 (1st Dist. 1977).

[69] Cohen v. Borough of Fair Lawn, 85 N.J. Super. 234, 204 A.2d 375
(App. Div. 1964).

[70] Huntington v. Zoning Bd. of Appeals of Hadley, 12 Mass. App. Ct.
710, 428 N.E.2d 826, 829 n.4 (1981).

[71] Atlantic Richfield Co. v. Marshall Tp. Bd. of Sup'rs, 74 Pa.
Commw. 100, 459 A.2d 860 (1983).

[72] Guenther v. Zoning Bd. of Review of City of Warwick, 85 R.I. 37,
125 A.2d 214 (1956) (two-year variance); New York Life Ins. Co. v.
Foley, 13 A.D.2d 768, 216 N.Y.S.2d 267 (1st Dep't 1961) (five-year
variance).

[73] People ex rel. St. Albans-Springfield Corporationv. Connell, 257
N.Y. 73, 177 N.E. 313 (1931).

providing for temporary relief from the restriction is the better approach. It is also argued that without such a time limit, vested rights could be acquired that would make it difficult to apply subsequent regulations to the landowner, even in the face of change. However, it seems to me that without careful fact finding to support such a time-limited variance, this approach can easily lead to abuses of discretion. It is always easier to make a temporary decision and avoid a permanent decision.

Variances are also typically conditioned upon the applicant initiating the variance within a specified period of time. If the applicant does not exercise the variance within the set time period, then the variance expires and the applicant must reapply.[74] If, however, a request to extend the period for the exercise of the variance is timely, it is improper, absent a showing of changed circumstances, to deny the extension of the variance.[75]

## § 2.15 Variance Made Subject to Neighbors' Consent

It is certainly an abuse of discretion for a board to require the applicant seeking a variance to obtain the consent of neighboring landowners.[76] Such a condition is an improper delegation of legislative authority.[77]

## § 2.16 Practice Tips

### [1] Know the Physical Site Thoroughly

The landowner or developer presumably has a thorough knowledge of the development site. But the attorney and

---

[74] Hunters Brook Realty Corp. v. Zoning Bd. of Appeals of Bourne, 14 Mass. App. Ct. 76, 436 N.E.2d 978 (1982).

[75] Dil-Hill Realty Corp. v. Schultz, 53 A.D.2d 263, 385 N.Y.S.2d 324 (2d Dep't 1976).

[76] Luger v. City of Burnsville, 295 N.W.2d 609 (Minn. 1980); Appeal of Lindquist, 364 Pa. 561, 73 A.2d 378 (1950); Parker v. Zoning Bd. of Review of City of East Providence, 90 R.I. 166, 156 A.2d 210 (1959).

[77] Lakin v. City of Peoria, 129 Ill. App. 3d 651, 84 Ill. Dec. 837, 472 N.E.2d 1233 (3d Dist. 1984). *See* discussion of delegation of authority in Ch. 1, Sec. 1.07[2], *supra*.

any consultants who may become expert witnesses must also visit the site. The attorney and potential expert witnesses may possibly identify new on-site information that the landowner overlooked, and should be able to take existing information and determine its usefulness and weight in supporting the variance petition.

### [2] Determine the Factual Basis for the Variance

From knowledge of the site and related documents, the developer's attorney, in consultation with the other members of the development team, should determine the factual basis that would appear to justify the zoning variance and weigh the evidence in support of the application in relation to the variance standards (use or area variance) and the relevant state law on variances.

### [3] Confirm the Procedural Steps and Deadlines

The developer or his or her attorney must ascertain all filing deadlines and submission and notice requirements for the variance application in advance and make a checklist to guide the application process.

### [4] Obtain and Review the Rules and Procedures of the Board

Often a board of adjustment is authorized to establish its own procedural rules for hearings on variance applications. It is wise for the developer's attorney to request a copy of the rules and regulations governing variance proceedings before the Board and become very familiar with the Board's procedures.

### [5] Meet with Those Who May Oppose the Variance

If neighbors and others who might be expected to oppose the variance understand the purpose and limits of the variance requested, it may be possible to eliminate, or at least mute, the extent of opposition voiced at the hearing. The simple courtesy of meeting with these individuals may not only pay off at the hearing, but also help the landowner/developer anticipate and prepare to answer the objections in advance.

### [6]   Check Everything an Expert Witness Prepares

In addition to exercising care in selecting an expert to testify on the landowner's behalf, it is essential that the landowner's attorney check the expert's work carefully. Whether that person is an appraiser, an architect, a planner, or some other expert whose testimony is needed to support the variance application, that expert generally cannot commit the amount of time to the case as does the landowner and the attorney. Checking the expert's work will help avoid embarrassing and potentially decisive mistakes at the hearing.

### [7]   Use Simple Exhibits

The simpler the exhibit, the better.

### [8]   Remember to Make a Complete Record at the Hearing

At the hearing itself, the most important thing to keep in mind is the record. The landowner's attorney must strive to assure that all testimony and documents in support of the petition are formally made part of the record, and that a complete transcript of the hearing is recorded in case the Board's decision is later challenged or the client needs to appeal an adverse determination. Judicial review of the Board's decision will normally only constitute a review of the record below to determine whether the Board's decision was supported by substantial evidence.

The typical format at the hearing calls for the applicant to present his or her witnesses for direct examination. The attorney may choose to deliver an opening statement before testimony is given. After each witness testifies, the board's counsel cross-examines the witnesses. Then, the members of the Board cross-examine, and finally, members of the public attending the hearing may ask questions of the witnesses. This procedure is followed for each witness. It is crucial that the attorney for the applicant pay close attention to the questions asked on cross-examination because questions relating to direct testimony may not accurately depict the prior testimony, or the witness may not fully understand the questions being posed. If this occurs, the attorney should preserve an objection on the record. The informal nature of the hearing also allows the attorney to help the witness in such a situation.

### [9]  Avoid Emphasis upon Legal Pronouncements at the Hearing

The key to the successful presentation of a variance petition is a persuasive set of facts. Facts, not the law, are most easily grasped by lay persons who sit on administrative bodies. Because many lay persons believe that the law and lawyers inject unnecessary complexity in proceedings that only hinders the process, overemphasis upon what the law says the Board must do will be counterproductive.

# CHAPTER 3

# Special Use Permits

## Scope of Chapter

## § 3.01   Introduction

The extreme of the special permit device is a case-by-case licensing of virtually all new development. This extreme may be illustrated by Rhode Island's enabling legislation, which permits local boards of adjustment to "make special exceptions to the terms of the ordinance in harmony with its general purpose and intent and in accordance with general or specific rules therein contained, or where such exception is reasonably necessary for the convenience or welfare of the public." The requirement has been interpreted to mean that the terms of the permits need not be re-

131

lated to district regulations. This provision permits
the board to grant permission for any use in any zone
so long as prescribed "conditions and safeguards" are
met. This is perhaps the ultimate form of "wait-and-
see" zoning, a total departure from any recognizable
zoning process, and a violation of the usual principles
of rationality, predictability, uniformity and equality.
—Michael J. Meshenberg, *The Administration of
Flexible Zoning Techniques*

I doubt that Edward M. Bassett, the principal architect
of the original zoning system, anticipated that the special
permit, which he labeled the "special exception" in the
Standard State Zoning Enabling Act,[1] would be pressed
into service as the ultimate "wait-and-see" weapon for
communities. As I have discussed elsewhere,[2] the original
zoning system was designed to be rigid and self-
administering. Under such a system, the special exception
was a necessary tool to handle the gasoline stations,
churches, hospitals, and other such uses that could not be
grouped into districts of their own and that had the
potential for creating negative impacts if allowed to mix in
with other uses as of right. But that limited function
reflected the thinking of practitioners in built-up urban
areas. As one noted commentator has said, Bassett and
the others who devised the zoning scheme were a bunch of
New Yorkers, concerned primarily with the encroachments
by the garment industry on the upscale residential and
shopping character of Fifth Avenue.[3] Their rigid concept of
land use control perhaps was appropriate within the urban
context that formed their experience, but:

For suburban communities in the path of develop-

---

[1] *See* Advisory Committee on Zoning, U.S. Department of Commerce,
Standard State Enabling Act, § 7 (authorizing a Board of Adjustment
to grant "special exceptions to the terms of the ordinance in harmony
with its general purpose and intent and in accordance with general or
specific rules therein contained") (rev'd ed. 1926).

[2] *See* discussion in Ch. 1, Sec. 1.03, *supra.*

[3] For an insightful discussion of Edward M. Bassett and the original
zoning scheme, *see generally* Krasnowiecki, "Abolish Zoning," 31 Syracuse L. Rev. 719 (1980).

ment, Bassett's program made no sense at all. The Standard Zoning Enabling Act was saying to them: describe what you want your community to look like in the end (end state), promulgate the regulations that will permit all of the described development to occur as of right, sit back, and let it rip.[4]

It is not surprising, then, that the one mechanism in this rigid land use control system that was seized upon by developing communities to add some zoning administration flexibility for responding to growth pressures was the special exception.

## § 3.02  Definition and Purpose

The term "special exception" has now given way in most zoning ordinances to the terms conditional use and special use; most courts now consider all three terms to be interchangeable. In this chapter, I use the term "special use," or "special use permit," because I think it best captures the purpose of this device. A special use has been defined as a "species of administrative permission which allows a property owner to put his property to a use which the regulations permit under conditions specified in the zoning regulations."[5] In other words, a special use involves an "administrative" proceeding. In view of the potential, described by Michael Meshenberg, for the special permit to facilitate *ad hoc* decision making, it is important to emphasize that the courts in most jurisdictions do not support that level of unfettered discretion, with its potential for abuse. Rather, they take the view that because a special use is listed in a zoning ordinance, it means that the local government has, in effect, found that the particular special use is in harmony with the comprehensive zoning ordinance and will not adversely affect the community.

---

[4] *Id.* at 726.
[5] Nunamaker v. Board of Zoning Appeals of Jerusalem Tp., 2 Ohio St. 3d 115, 443 N.E.2d 172, 173 (1982).

This "presumption" is important to the developer, in particular, since the popular view held in some communities is that a special use is a sort of second-class citizen when compared with uses permitted by right in a particular zoning district. The presumption means that a local government cannot arbitrarily deny an application for a special use.[6] Although most courts adhere to this general rule, some jurisdictions, Illinois being one, do not afford this presumption of validity to a special use listed in the zoning ordinance. One Illinois court stated:

> [W]e note that compliance with all of the standards required for a special-use permit does not necessarily mean that the denial of the permit is arbitrary and unreasonable. The nature of a special use does not make the issuance of a permit mandatory upon compliance with the county standards. [citation omitted]. The granting of a special-use permit is not merely a ministerial function of a legislative body. Rather, whenever a special use is proposed a legislative body must make an independent determination that the particular use and the proposed location is designed in such a way as to be compatible with the surrounding area.[7]

The Illinois court's reasoning appears to be based upon the premise that a special use decision is a "legislative" function, and hence completely discretionary, despite the developer's compliance with the special use standards. As a practical matter, in jurisdictions that hold to the Illinois view, the legislative body's "independent determination" is more likely to be susceptible to considerations beyond the special use standards found in the zoning ordinance. In other words, the potential for abuse of discretion is greater when the special use is treated as a "legislative" rather than an "administrative" function.

---

[6] Cove Pizza, Inc. v. Hirshon, 61 A.D.2d 210, 401 N.Y.S.2d 838 (2d Dep't 1978); South Woodbury Taxpayers Ass'n, Inc. v. American Institute of Physics, Inc., 104 Misc. 2d 254, 428 N.Y.S.2d 158 (Sup 1980).

[7] LaSalle Nat. Bank v. Lake County, 27 Ill. App. 3d 10, 325 N.E.2d 105, 111 (2d Dist. 1975).

## § 3.03 Purpose

A report prepared in 1976 by the American Society of Planning Officials (ASPO) identified the various purposes of special uses, stating that they essentially fell into four classes. The report defined these four classes, with some candid commentary, as follows:

(1) *To control use types.* This is the most common application of the device.

(2) *To establish preconditions for particular uses.* Preconditions should be attached to the granting of special permits; when they are not, officials are left with virtually complete discretion.

(3) *To limit or time growth.* This is a significant and rarely used departure from traditional purposes. It is used—and some say abused—to accomplish growth control in the absence of specific authorizing legislation.

(4) *To accomplish unspecified objectives.* By keeping conditions vague, the device can be used to seek higher levels of amenity during the negotiation process.[8]

As the ASPO report indicates, the control of certain types of uses is the most frequent application of the special use technique. Typically, uses subject to a conditional use fall into two broad categories: (1) commercial uses, such as gasoline service stations, perceived by communities to have special impacts upon residential neighborhoods in particular; and (2) institutional uses, such as schools, places of worship, hospitals, social clubs, nursing homes, and the like, which also, because of their "institutional" character, are deemed to have unusual impacts upon surrounding neighborhoods. Both categories of uses are considered desirable by communities and generally com-

---

[8] Meshenberg, Michael J., *The Administration of Flexible Zoning Techniques* at 26 (Planning Advisory Service (PAS) Report No. 318: 1976).

patible with the basic use classification of a particular zone, but they are not permitted by right at any location within the particular zoning district because of considerations, such as traffic congestion, population density, noise, or other considerations, which may pertain to a particular location.

The second purpose, establishing "preconditions" for particular uses is less common, if only for the reason that it is more difficult for communities to do. It takes time and careful consideration to define appropriate conditions for a particular use. In fact, if it is possible to attach specific conditions to a particular use, I believe it is preferable not to use the discretionary review procedure of the special use technique, but rather to define the use as a "limited use" permitted by right in the district, but subject to performance standards that are spelled out in the zoning ordinance.[9]

The employment of special use permits as a tool for implementing a growth management strategy is a purpose that raises serious questions when there is no authorization for growth management in the first place. Obviously, the special use, if employed in this fashion, can, in effect, be turned into an antigrowth tool. I discuss this technique in more detail later.[10]

The fourth purpose identified in the ASPO report is an unabashed acknowledgment that the special use technique, if deliberately kept vague in its standards, can be used to exact amenities and other benefits from the developer. The U.S. Supreme Court's decision in the *Dolan* case now makes that a perilous course for communities to pursue.[11]

---

[9] This approach was taken in the zoning ordinance that was adopted by the City Council of Houston, Texas, in the spring of 1993. The council's action was subsequently overturned by referendum in November 1993.

[10] *See* Ch. 3, Secs. 3.09[6] and 3.11[2], *infra.*

[11] *See* discussion of *Dolan* case in Ch. 1, Sec. 1.09, *supra.*

## § 3.04 Administrative Decision-Making Procedure

As intended by the drafters of the Standard State Zoning Enabling Act, the special exception or special use procedure was intended to be an "administrative" procedure. The final decision maker in most communities is either the planning commission or the zoning board. However, sometimes the local legislative body, i.e. the city council or the board of trustees, is the final decision maker. The majority of courts hold that regardless of who the decision maker is, the decision itself is administrative rather than legislative.[12]

The minority view is that when the local legislative body reserves to itself in the zoning ordinance the power to approve special uses, its decisions are legislative.[13] According to this minority view, when the local legislative body reserves to itself the granting of special exceptions or special uses, it need not set forth specific standards for the exercise of its discretion, provided it does not act capriciously.[14] However, if the decision is deemed "legislative," then it enjoys a presumption of validity that is difficult to overcome. Consequently, the potential for abuse of discretion is considerably greater when the local legislative body makes the final decision on a special use application.

## § 3.05 Decision-Making Authority Reserved by the Legislative Body

Because the Standard State Zoning Enabling Act provides that the governing body "may" authorize the

---

[12] *See, e.g.,* Powers v. Common Council of City of Danbury, 154 Conn. 156, 222 A.2d 337 (1966); Lemir Realty Corp. v. Larkin, 11 N.Y.2d 20, 226 N.Y.S.2d 374, 181 N.E.2d 407 (1962); Smith v. County of Los Angeles, 211 Cal. App. 3d 188, 259 Cal. Rptr. 231 (2d Dist. 1989).

[13] City of Richmond v. Randall, 215 Va. 506, 211 S.E.2d 56 (1975); Chesterfield Civic Ass'n v. Board of Zoning Appeals of Chesterfield County, 215 Va. 399, 209 S.E.2d 925 (1974).

[14] Cummings v. Town Bd. of North Castle, 62 N.Y.2d 833, 477 N.Y.S.2d 607, 466 N.E.2d 147 (1984).

board of adjustment to grant a special exception, some local legislative bodies retain this function for themselves. If the legislative body has retained for itself the power to grant special exceptions or special use permits, there are cases that hold that the local legislative body need not prescribe express standards or guidelines to control its discretion, because it is presumed to act in a lawful or constitutional manner.[15] This presumption of validity, of course, essentially immunizes the local legislative body from judicial review. Not all judges agree with that view. In an emphatic dissent to such a holding by the Illinois Supreme Court,[16] Justice Klingbiel, joined by Justice House, stated:

> It is not part of the legislative function to grant permits, make special exceptions, or decide particular cases. Such activities are not legislative but administrative, quasi-judicial, or judicial in character. To place them in the hands of legislative bodies, whose acts as such are not judicially reviewable, is to open the door completely to arbitrary government. I need not dwell at length on the obvious opportunity this affords for special privilege, for the granting of favors to political friends or financial benefactors, for the withholding of permits from those not in the good graces of the authorities, and so on. The rule is familiar enough that courts may not inquire into the motives or reasons on which the legislative body acted. (citation omitted)
>
> * * *
>
> Legislative bodies are not equipped, except in a very broad and general way, to ascertain factual questions which depend upon evidence or individual circumstances. Their function is not to grant permits but to say what facts and conditions should warrant the granting of permits. (citation omitted)

---

[15] Kotrich v. Du Page County, 19 Ill. 2d 181, 166 N.E.2d 601 (1960); Gino's of Maryland, Inc. v. City of Baltimore, 250 Md. 621, 244 A.2d 218 (1968).

[16] *See* Kotrich v. Du Page County, 19 Ill. 2d 181, 166 N.E.2d 601 (1960).

\* \* \*

> It is the nature of the proceeding, not the identity of the body assuming to act in the matter, which should determine the necessity for standards. Otherwise basic constitutional protections can readily be circumvented by the simple expedient of placing quasi-judicial functions in a legislative body.[17]

Since the U.S. Supreme Court's decision in *Dolan*, I think it can be argued that the mere fact that the local legislative body retains the right to decide special exceptions or special uses does not, by definition, make its decisions legislative. The Court's obvious impatience with the imposition of conditions or exactions that do not satisfy its "essential nexus" and "rough proportionality" tests suggests that particularly where *ad hoc* conditions are attached to a special use approval, the Court would subject a local legislative body's special use decision to the more rigorous "adjudicative" requirements for the exercise of discretion, namely, specific findings of fact to support the conditions imposed. In other words, regardless of whether the local legislative body articulates specific standards in advance, if its special use permit decision places *ad hoc* conditions upon the applicant and is challenged under *Dolan*, a court could decide to subject that decision to the more rigorous analysis required of adjudicative decisions. To echo Justice Klingbiel, it is the nature of the proceeding, not the identity of the decision-making body, that should determine what standards are applied.

---

[17] Ward v. Village of Skokie, 26 Ill. 2d 415, 186 N.E.2d 529, 533–34 (1962). In 1967, and again in 1969, the Illinois Municipal Code relating to special uses was amended to incorporate the views expressed by Justices Klingbiel and House, by requiring a public hearing before a designated commission or committee, based upon standards set out in the ordinance authorizing special uses, and requiring findings of fact. *See also*, Geneva Residential Ass'n, Ltd. v. City of Geneva, 77 Ill. App. 3d 744, 34 Ill. Dec. 177, 397 N.E.2d 849 (2d Dist. 1979).

## § 3.06   Burden of Proof

To the extent that a special use decision will be characterized as an "administrative" decision, the *Dolan* decision has changed the rules of the game with respect to burden of proof when conditions amounting to exactions are imposed through that decision-making process. Now, the local government's burden of proof must satisfy the "essential nexus" part of the constitutional test and include sufficient specificity to satisfy the "rough proportionality" part of the test.[18]

## § 3.07   Extent of Discretion to Deny Special Use

Because a special use is typically listed in the zoning ordinance, there is an immediate tension in the ordinance between the expectation that the special use is deemed appropriate in the particular zoning district, subject to conditions, and the possibility that in a particular instance, the special use may not be appropriate because of the particular location in which it is proposed. The basic rule is that if the applicant satisfies all of the criteria in the zoning ordinance for the grant of a special use, a denial will be considered arbitrary in the absence of evidence that the special use will cause substantial detriment to the surrounding community.[19] Even where the local legislative body retains the right to approve special uses, at least some courts have found that lack of a record evidencing the facts and reasons for the local legislative

---

[18] Dolan v. City of Tigard, 512 U.S. 374, 114 S. Ct. 2309, 129 L. Ed. 2d 304, 38 Env't. Rep. Cas. (BNA) 1769, 24 Envtl. L. Rep. 21083 (1994).

[19] Value Oil Co. v. Town of Irvington, 152 N.J. Super. 354, 377 A.2d 1225 (Law Div. 1977), judgment aff'd, 164 N.J. Super. 419, 396 A.2d 1149 (App. Div. 1978), certification denied, 79 N.J. 501, 401 A.2d 256 (1979); Robert Lee Realty Co. v. Village of Spring Valley, 61 N.Y.2d 892, 474 N.Y.S.2d 475, 462 N.E.2d 1193 (1984).

body's determination is a prima facie showing of arbitrariness.[20]

Demonstrating to the satisfaction of the decision making body that a proposed use truly satisfies all of the criteria set out in an ordinance for a conditional use can be difficult, if not impossible, particularly when the touchstone is "compatibility" with the surrounding area. A Little Rock, Arkansas case[21] illustrates this difficulty. The Little Rock Code delegates to the Planning Commission the authority to approve or disapprove conditional use permits "[a]fter detailed review of [the use's] compatibility with the area. . . ." The applicant in that case sought conditional use approval for 19 manufactured homes in an R-2 single family zoning district.

The conditional use provisions of the Little Rock Code contain both general standards and eight specific standards for the placement of a manufactured home in the R-2 zone. One of the general standards is that the "proposed use is compatible with and will not adversely affect other property in the area where it is proposed to be located." Another general standard allows conditional uses "provided they do not have objectionable characteristics, and provided further that they otherwise conform to the provisions of this chapter." Of the eight specific standards for conditional use permits for manufactured homes, six are explicit in defining dimensional and structural elements (e.g., roof pitch, foundation) and parking requirements that must be satisfied. The other two address "compatibility" concerns, namely, use of exterior wall finish "so as to be compatible with the neighborhood" and building orientation, so as to be "compatible with the placement of adjacent structures."[22]

The planning staff recommended approval of the conditional use permit, finding that the applicant had met all

---

[20] See, e.g., Zylka v. City of Crystal, 283 Minn. 192, 167 N.W.2d 45 (1969); Holasek v. Village of Medina, 303 Minn. 240, 226 N.W.2d 900 (1975).

[21] Rolling Pines Ltd. Partnership v. City of Little Rock, 73 Ark. App. 97, 40 S.W.3d 828 (2001).

[22] Id. at 831.

eight specific standards. But the commission, "after hearing opposition from subdivision owners," denied the application. The applicant reduced the number of manufactured homes from 19 to 5 and reapplied for the conditional use permit. Again staff recommended approval; again the commission denied, reiterating its rationale from the first denial: Manufactured homes did not meet the standard of compatibility and that the applicant had failed to show that the placement of manufactured homes would not have an adverse effect on the neighborhood.[23]

Normally, when a municipality writes specific approval standards for uses classified as conditional uses under a zoning ordinance, those become the principal focus for the conditional use decision, and are intended to guide the decision making body in making its determination under the general conditional use standards that typically are also made applicable to all conditional use applications. In this case, the applicant, not unreasonably, thought that by satisfying the eight specific standards, it was satisfying the "compatibility" criterion under the general standards in the Code for conditional uses. As noted above, two of these standards explicitly addressed compatibility in terms of exterior finish and building orientation. Yet the commission denied the application, and both the trial court and appeals court affirmed.

The court's conclusions relied heavily on the fact that the eight specific standards in the Little Rock Code are defined as "minimum siting standards." According to the court, the use of the term "minimum" means that the commission could "consider matters over and above those eight requirements in assessing a conditional use."[24] But this reasoning is troubling. In a discretionary review context, the reference to "minimum standards" does not mean that the decision making body in determining to *deny* a conditional use application can consider "matters over and above" the scope of considerations set out in the eight

---

[23]*Id.*
[24]*Id.* at 833.

specific standards designed to assure "compatibility" of the use with the surrounding area. Rather, the reference to "minimum" in the context of conditional use regulations is properly intended to give the decision maker the discretion to impose more stringent conditions of the same type as those listed in order to assure that the proposed use will be compatible with surrounding uses both in character and operations.

In this case, the court noted that the commission had determined that the "aggregate placement of manufactured homes was not compatible with the character of the existing neighborhood." What is the existing character? The court explained: "[O]ne that is well-established and consists of modest, well-kept homes where all but one are brick and frame structures." The concern, according to the court, was the "long-term quality of manufactured homes" and their "effect. . . on property values."[25] Presumably, these concerns relate to the "general" standard that a conditional use should not "adversely affect other property in the area. . . ." The applicant apparently never provided a requested "impact study" that might have answered the property value question-a strategic mistake.

But the real issue appears to be that to the extent that the "character" of homes in the R-2 district is defined as one of "modest, well-kept brick-and-frame houses," manufactured homes, in the view of the commission and the opposing subdivision owners, inherently, just didn't fit in and should never have been listed as a conditional use in the R-2 district. Based on the conditional use regulations in the Code and the specific standards for manufactured homes, the applicant had a reasonable expectation that demonstrated compliance with the specific standards would secure an approval. Unfortunately, the court's decision, based upon its expansive interpretation of the meaning of "minimum" standards gives local decision making

---

[25]*Id.* at 834.

bodies a justification for exceeding the proper scope of discretion in making conditional use decisions.

## ALL ABOUT TOWN

"TEASING, MR. FENWICK? THE PLANNING BOARD NEVER TEASES!"

### § 3.08 Findings of Fact Required

The fact-finding requirement in special use decisions is a procedural safeguard that introduces discipline to the exercise of discretion by the zoning board and helps to guard against *ad hoc* decisions. The reason the fact-finding step functions as a safeguard is that, in a subsequent challenge to a denial of the use, the zoning board cannot credibly present reasons for denial that were not articulated or evidenced from the initial decision.[26] Equally important, where the local legislative body makes the final decision upon receipt of recommendations from the board, the

---

[26] Metro 500, Inc. v. City of Brooklyn Park, 297 Minn. 294, 211 N.W.2d 358 (1973).

legislative body cannot then proceed to make new findings of fact separate from the record made before the board.[27]

## § 3.09   Approval Standards

The most typical standards for approving special uses are:

(1)   That the use is in harmony with the intent and purpose of the zoning ordinance;

(2)   That the use is consistent with the comprehensive plan;

(3)   That the proposed use will not diminish surrounding property values;

(4)   That the proposed use is a matter of public need or convenience;

(5)   That the proposed use will not overburden municipal services;

(6)   That the proposed use will not cause traffic, parking, population density, or environmental problems; and

(7)   That the proposed use will not adversely affect the health, safety, and welfare of the community.

These standards are discussed separately below.

### [1]   Harmony with the Intent and Purpose of the Zoning Ordinance

Because the zoning ordinance lists the use as a special use, the finding and level of proof with respect to this standard is minimal. Presumably there can be no substantial impairment of the intent of the zoning plan and ordinance if there has been a prior legislative determination that the particular use belongs in a particular zoning district,

---

[27] *See* Verona, Inc. v. Mayor and Council of Borough of West Caldwell, 49 N.J. 274, 229 A.2d 651 (1967).

subject to conditions.[28] However, even where a special use may be listed in the zoning ordinance, the developer must be sure that the zoning board or planning commission pays attention to the purposes of the zoning ordinance and good zoning practices and makes appropriate findings. In one instance in Virginia, for example, the court invalidated a special use permit for a ten-story apartment building for elderly and handicapped persons because the board based this decision on the conclusion that the broad standards of public and municipal general welfare would be met under the zoning ordinance without considering the fact that the project would violate specific building and zoning regulations, including density, height, parking, and setback restrictions. For this reason, the court held that the ordinance under which the board had acted was defective and invalid because it did not require the board to consider the special permit in light of the zoning policy and objectives of the municipality.[29]

### [2]  Consistency with the Comprehensive Plan

Since a special use is authorized in a particular zone by the zoning ordinance, and the zoning ordinance is supposed to implement the comprehensive plan, a required finding that the special use is, in fact, consistent with the comprehensive plan should not be difficult to make. But, in reality, the zoning ordinance and the comprehensive plan are not always in sync, and this criterion is sometimes used to deny a special use where the use is perceived as inconsistent with the pattern of development contemplated by the comprehensive plan[30] or some other objective of the

---

[28] Tullo v. Millburn Tp., Essex County, 54 N.J. Super. 483, 149 A.2d 620 (App. Div. 1959).

[29] Cole v. City Council of City of Waynesboro, 218 Va. 827, 241 S.E.2d 765 (1978).

[30] International Villages, Inc. of America v. Board of County Com'rs of Jefferson County, 224 Kan. 654, 585 P.2d 999 (1978).

comprehensive plan.[31] In cases where a proposed special use will have a negative impact upon provision of municipal services, some courts have found that the proposed use will detrimentally impact the public's health, safety, and welfare, and therefore is inconsistent with the overall concept of the comprehensive plan.[32] Other cases hold that another consideration in determining consistency between the proposed special use and the comprehensive plan is whether the proposed use is "consistent with good zoning practices." For example, in one Virginia case, the court overturned the board's grant of a special use permit to construct a ten-story apartment building for the handicapped and elderly because, despite the desirability of the project from the standpoint of the public welfare, the board had failed to adequately consider the fact that the project would violate certain zoning and building restrictions, and therefore was inconsistent with the zoning policy of the city.[33] This result could have been avoided if the applicant had not tried to use the special permit process to circumvent the applicable zoning restrictions. Instead, the project should have been accompanied by a zoning amendment proposal so as to make zoning policy conform to the purpose and land use characteristics of this type of development.

### [3] Detrimental Impact on Surrounding Property Values

This criterion, by itself, can lead to justified denial of a special use application where the proposed use will nega-

---

[31] *See, e.g.,* Hubbard Broadcasting, Inc. v. City of Afton, 323 N.W.2d 757 (Minn. 1982) (denial of special use permit for commercial satellite station in area intended under comprehensive plan to be preserved as a rural area).

[32] *See, e.g.,* Josephs v. Town Bd. of Town of Clarkstown, 24 Misc. 2d 366, 198 N.Y.S.2d 695 (Sup 1960).

[33] *See, e.g.,* Cole v. City Council of City of Waynesboro, 218 Va. 827, 241 S.E.2d 765 (1978).

tively impact surrounding property values.[34] On its face, however, this standard would appear to be inconsistent with the findings of inherent compatibility of the use with surrounding properties that is made by the legislative body in establishing the conditional use in a zoning district.[35] In fact, there are some limitations to the general rule. A denial cannot be based on this ground if the effect of the proposed use is less detrimental than uses already existing in the area by right.[36] In addition, if there is a special need for the proposed use, notwithstanding its negative impact, the denial may not be justified.[37]

### [4] Public Need

JEFF STAHLER. Reprinted by permission of Newspaper Enterprise Association, Inc.

---

[34] Mason v. Zoning Bd. of Appeals of Town of Clifton Park, 72 A.D.2d 889, 422 N.Y.S.2d 166 (3d Dep't 1979); LaSalle Nat. Bank v. Lake County, 27 Ill. App. 3d 10, 325 N.E.2d 105 (2d Dist. 1975).

[35] *See, e.g.,* North Shore Steak House, Inc. v. Board of Appeals of Incorporated Village of Thomaston, 30 N.Y.2d 238, 331 N.Y.S.2d 645, 282 N.E.2d 606 (1972).

[36] Gallagher v. Zoning Bd. of Review of City of Pawtucket, 95 R.I. 225, 186 A.2d 325 (1962); Long Island Lighting Co. v. Griffin, 272 A.D. 551, 74 N.Y.S.2d 348 (2d Dep't 1947).

[37] Appeal of Gage, 402 Pa. 244, 167 A.2d 292 (1961).

This standard has the potential for considerable abuse if the zoning board interprets it to require a positive showing of need or convenience. What the phrase "reasonably necessary" for the convenience of the community really means is that it is "practical," or "reasonably convenient,"[38] given the location of the proposed use.[39] A New Jersey court explained why public need or convenience should not be interpreted broadly to defeat a special use application:

> [A]ppellants claim that the section sets up a standard of reasonable necessity for the convenience of the community. . . . The argument misconstrues both the intent and requirement of the section. *It does not have to be established on each application that the particular use involved is reasonably necessary to the community or its convenience. Such would go beyond the function and power of zoning and invade the social and economic fields.* The whole purpose of the section, as set forth in the initial recital, is that the listed uses, public or private, are recognized by the governing body as such as are or may be necessary and desirable for the convenience and well-being of a well-rounded community and should be permitted, but the special zoning problems arising in connection with them involve individual consideration and permission with respect to their particular location. *It is the location, and not the use, to which reference is intended in the body of the section when the standard of reasonable necessity for the convenience of the community is prescribed.*[40]

In fact, it is generally held that the lack of public necessity for a proposed special use is not a sufficient ground to

---

[38] Fisher v. Pilcher, 341 A.2d 713 (Del. Super. Ct. 1975).

[39] Tullo v. Millburn Tp., Essex County, 54 N.J. Super. 483, 149 A.2d 620, 627 (App. Div. 1959).

[40] *Id.* at 627. (Emphasis added.)

justify denial of a permit.[41] In a New Jersey case, the court stated that to allow the absence of public necessity to defeat a special use approval:

> [W]ould not constitute the appropriate discretionary weighing of zoning harms against community benefits from the facility at that location, but an administrative veto of a perfectly legitimate and socially useful facility not hurtful to the community in any zoning sense at all, as found by the body charged with the facts for determination.[42]

Drawing by Ed Fisher © 1989 The New Yorker Magazine, Inc.

## [5] Regulation of Competition

If the special use is used as a means to restrict the number of special permits based on the number of similar uses existing in the zoning district, most courts will find this to be an arbitrary and unreasonable use of the special use procedure.[43] However, where it can be shown that there will be a cumulative impact from permitting ad di-

---

[41] Pioneer Trust and Sav. Bank v. McHenry County, 41 Ill. 2d 77, 241 N.E.2d 454 (1968); Texaco, Inc. v. Board of Adjustment of Millburn Tp., 73 N.J. Super. 313, 179 A.2d 768 (App. Div. 1962).

[42] *Texaco*, 179 A.2d at 774.

[43] West Whiteland Tp. v. Sun Oil Co., 12 Pa. Commw. 159, 316 A.2d 92 (1974); Metro 500, Inc. v. City of Brooklyn Park, 297 Minn. 294, 211 N.W.2d 358 (1973); *See generally* Mandelker, "Control of Competition as a Proper Purpose in Zoning," 14 Zoning Digest 1 (1962).

tional special uses of the same type, resulting in traffic or other negative impacts, a court may uphold the denial of a special use.[44] The issue in most "cumulative effect" cases is the geographical radius in which the cumulative effect is ascertained. If the geographical radius within which the special use is being judged is too large, the decision denying the special use is more likely to be found arbitrary and capricious.[45]

## [6] Traffic and Other Impact Considerations

Although a standard addressing traffic impact is a reasonable one in light of the range of potential impacts of a special use, the *Dolan* case as well as the general principles governing administrative decision making indicate that more than a generalized statement is needed to support the conclusion that a proposed special use will negatively impact the traffic and parking. Mere increase in traffic at the site of a proposed use is not a valid basis to deny a special use.[46] Of course, with respect to parking, if the special use cannot satisfy the parking space requirements, the use request may be denied.[47]

A recent Kentucky case[48] signals a warning to communities that may seek to rely on special uses and development "impact" analysis almost to the exclusion of traditional zoning districts. In 1984, Hardin County, Kentucky, adopted a "Development Guidance System"—a planning and zoning ordinance that departed from the traditional system of establishing separate zoning districts for particular types of uses, some permitted as of right and others by special use. Instead, the ordinance designated all the

---

[44] Blair v. Board of Adjustment of Borough of Hatboro, 403 Pa. 105, 169 A.2d 49 (1961).

[45] *See West Whiteland Tp. v. Sun Oil Co., 12 Pa. Commw. 159, 316 A.2d 92 (1974).*

[46] Toohey v. Kilday, 415 A.2d 732 (R.I. 1980). *See* discussion of *Dolan* case in Ch. 1, Sec. 1.09, *supra*.

[47] Howland v. Board of Appeals of Plymouth, 13 Mass. App. Ct. 520, 434 N.E.2d 1286 (1982); Vasilopoulos v. Zoning Bd. of Appeals, 34 Ill. App. 3d 480, 340 N.E.2d 19 (1st Dist. 1975).

[48] Hardin County v. Jost, 897 S.W.2d 592 (Ky. Ct. App. 1995).

unincorporated portions of the county as one zone and defined three categories of uses for it. Agricultural and single-family residential uses were defined as "uses by right." Any uses with negative impacts on water supplies, public health, or historic sites were termed "prohibited uses." All other uses were categorized as "conditional uses." In order for an application that fell within the "conditional uses" category to be approved, the application first had to receive a satisfactory score on a point system ("growth guidance assessment"). If the "conditional use" received a satisfactory score, it then was subjected to a "compatibility assessment," an informal meeting between the applicant, planning commission staff, and surrounding property owners. If the informal meeting produced no consensus on the application, the planning commission held a public meeting to decide whether to approve the application.

This system was challenged by the operator of an animal refuge center whose conditional use application was denied. The Kentucky Court of Appeals affirmed the trial court's invalidation of the entire Hardin County zoning ordinance, finding the fatal flaw to be the ordinance's reliance on conditional uses under a scheme that deliberately avoided predetermining that a conditional use was compatible with any particular location—"zoning without planning"[49] —and failed to indicate the basis upon which a conditional use would be permitted or denied. Consequently, said the court, the Development Guidance System left "land use to the subjective whim and caprice of the zoning authority."[50] For these reasons, the court held that the zoning scheme did not substantially relate to the state's zoning enabling act.

### [7] Public Health, Safety, and Welfare

Because of its breadth, this standard can be utilized only as a complement to the other more specific standards.

---

[49] *Id.* at 596.
[50] *Id.* at 597.

It cannot be used as a substitute for the standards.[51] In addition, the term "welfare" in this context refers to the community as a whole, not just the immediate neighborhood.[52] To satisfy this standard, the applicant must show that the proposed special use will not be detrimental to the health, safety, or welfare of the community.[53]

### § 3.10 Conditions Imposed upon Special Use Permits

The types of conditions that may be imposed pursuant to a grant of a special use permit are of three general types: (1) conditions upon the operation of the use; (2) conditions designed to address potential incompatibility between the new use and adjacent uses; and (3) site design conditions intended to improve the layout of the use on the site and the effect of that layout upon adjacent uses. Typically, the zoning board is authorized to impose such "additional conditions" as it deems appropriate under the circumstances when granting a special use application. This clause in zoning ordinances can give rise to abuses of discretion, particularly where there are inadequate standards to guide the exercise of discretion. It is especially problematic when the local legislative body has reserved the final decision to itself, since courts have held that no standard need be included in the ordinance to govern the legislative body's exercise of discretion.[54]

---

[51] Powers v. Common Council of City of Danbury, 154 Conn. 156, 222 A.2d 337 (1966).

[52] Preston v. Zoning Bd. of Review of City of Cranston, 92 R.I. 463, 169 A.2d 908 (1961); Fisher v. Pilcher, 341 A.2d 713 (Del. Super. Ct. 1975).

[53] See Rockville Fuel & Feed Co. v. Board of Appeals of City of Gaithersburg, 257 Md. 183, 262 A.2d 499 (1970); Lee v. Zoning Bd. of Appeals of Town of Bethlehem, 122 A.D.2d 423, 505 N.Y.S.2d 235 (3d Dep't 1986).

[54] T & R Associates, Inc. v. City of Amarillo, 688 S.W.2d 622 (Tex. App. Amarillo 1985), writ refused n.r.e., (May 15, 1985); South Woodbury Taxpayers Ass'n, Inc. v. American Institute of Physics, Inc., 104 Misc. 2d 254, 428 N.Y.S.2d 158 (Sup 1980).

The abuse of discretion by a local legislative body when imposing conditions on special permits frequently occurs when a development that requires a special permit is proposed at a busy intersection. Typically, because of projected growth in the community, it can be argued that the anticipated increase in traffic volume from the community's growth will necessitate the installation of a traffic signal at the intersection at some point in the future. However, the city engineer may decide that the proposed development will itself cause additional traffic and that circumstance requires the installation of the traffic signal now. If the city council then conditions approval of the special permit for the development on the developer providing the funds to pay for the full cost of the traffic signal, that *ad hoc* condition can be challenged as a taking under the *Nollan/Dolan* standards for testing the constitutional validity of discretionary exactions.[55]

Reprinted from Planning, copyright 1989 by the American Planning Association.

Requiring the developer to shoulder the entire cost of the traffic signal may satisfy the "essential nexus"

---

[55] *See* discussion of these U.S. Supreme Court cases in Chapter 1, sec. 1.08.

(substantially advance the legitimate state interest) test, but probably fails the "rough proportionality" test. However, because the general growth of the community also generates the need for a traffic signal at the intersection, the city council is overreaching by imposing the entire cost of the signal on a development that will contribute only partially to the traffic requiring the new signal. Under these circumstances, the city would have difficulty defending its decision against a taking claim.

If the zoning board determines that the proposed special use satisfies the criteria in the ordinance and imposes conditions that relate to the use of the land, the special use may not then be made subject to any time limitation.[56]

### § 3.11   Practice Tips

#### [1]   Do Not Overuse the Special Use Technique

One of the surest ways for local governments to create the potential for abuse of discretion is through overreliance upon the use of the special use technique as a substitute for clear standards in the zoning ordinance. Standards and preconditions to the grant of a special use permit can be established in the zoning ordinance up front. If such standards and conditions are not indicated, local officials have complete discretion. If, in fact, it is possible to define specific conditions for a particular use, it is preferable not to use the discretionary special use review procedure. Rather, the use should be defined as a "limited use" permitted by right in the district, subject to performance standards that are spelled out in the zoning ordinance.

#### [2]   Do Not Use the Special Use Permit as a Substitute for a Growth Management Strategy

Growth management programs are intended to provide control over the rate of growth and the provision of neces-

---

[56] *See* Appeal of Farrell & Desautels, Inc. 383 A.2d 619 (Vt. 1978).

sary public facilities. Such programs usually impose timing, phasing, and quota controls. However, because the
Standard State Zoning Enabling Act did not authorize
these types of land use controls, attempts by local governments to implement growth management regulations
without express statutory authorization raise serious
problems. In particular, when the special use permit is
used as a "wait-and-see" technique to address growth,
without express growth management policies authorized
by state law, the special use permit can, in effect, be
turned into an antigrowth tool. Local governments should
avoid making this mistake.

### [3] Do Not Use the Special Use Permit to Achieve Unspecified Objectives

Municipal attorneys frequently advise their municipal
clients to keep standards and conditions for certain types
of land use approvals deliberately vague. In this way, the
municipality can extract a larger number of amenities
during the negotiation process in exchange for the
approval. The U.S. Supreme Court's decision in *Dolan*
raises serious questions about the continued efficacy of
that practice. Local governments should endeavor to be
clear regarding the standards and conditions they wish to
attach to special use permits in order to ensure that their
decision satisfies the "essential nexus" and the "rough
proportionality" parts of the constitutional test for any
exactions that may be imposed through the special use
permit process. The special use permit situation should be
distinguished from a private-public project in which public
funding or land is contributed. In such circumstances, the
local government is in a stronger negotiating position.
However, even in these circumstances, it is preferable to
define policies and design criteria up front as a condition
for public investment rather than leave such important
considerations to open-ended negotiations.

### [4]  Make Adequate Findings of Fact

The *Dolan* decision has changed the rules of the game with respect to burden of proof when conditions amounting to exactions are imposed through the special use permit process. It is imperative that the local government make findings of fact as part of its decision-making process. This fact-finding step functions as a safeguard for both the local government and the developer in that it imposes discipline on the exercise of discretion and helps to guard against *ad hoc* decisions.

### [5]  Make Sure the Local Government Makes Appropriate Findings to Support Its Decision

It is sometimes tempting for a developer's counsel to allow the local government to be sloppy in its procedures and fail to make appropriate findings, so long as the decision is favorable. However, doing so is a mistake. Because there can always be a subsequent challenge to a special use approval, the developer's attorney should make sure that the record is as strong as possible and contains the appropriate findings of fact and conclusions. So long as a court can find credible reasons for the approval, or evidence from the record, the approval is likely to be upheld.

### [6]  Prepare Analysis or Studies to the Extent Necessary to Address the Issue of Compatibility

Special use regulations frequently include a standard requiring that a proposed special use be "compatible with surrounding uses." The term "compatibility" can encompass a wide range of considerations, including not only type of use and operations, but also architectural elements such as building scale, mass and materials and, unfortunately, degree of neighborhood opposition to the proposed use. Without an adopted plan that describes the types of uses in an area and identifies those elements of building scale, mass and materials that are considered important to the community, the "compatibility" standard is too vague to give sufficient guidance to the decision maker.

If compatibility cannot be defined with reference to an adopted plan for an area, then a developer with a significant investment at stake should take the initiative in preparing a study that analyzes the extent to which an area has use and building characteristics that are relevant to the "compatibility" determination, and assesses the impact that the proposed special use will have upon the surrounding area. By taking this initiative, the developer can limit the nature and scope of "compatibility" review to more objective factors, and reduce the potential for the decision maker to treat opposition from neighboring property owners as the principal measure of "compatibility".

# CHAPTER 4

# The Floating Zone

## Scope of Chapter

## § 4.01 Introduction

[A] persuasive case can be made to show that the floating zone technique is more apt to guard against discrimination and irrationality than is reliance on traditional small parcel reclassifications even if subjected to judicial review.
—I. Michael Heyman in *The New Zoning: Legal, Administrative, and Economic Concepts and Techniques*

The "floating zone" offers opportunities for creative approaches to land use development involving special land use considerations that can be defined by more discrete geographical areas. Because this technique requires a rezoning decision, often based on standards that allow for

159

a larger dose of discretion than in the typical rezoning, it also has the potential to be used by local zoning officials "as leverage in order to negotiate, impose, coerce and compel concessions and conditions on the developer."[1] The same potential for abuse also exists, of course, with other techniques, such as conditional zoning.[2] However, if the floating zone is properly established in the text of the zoning ordinance, the developer at least has the benefit of knowing up front that most, if not all, of the conditions must be satisfied in order to have the zone applied to a particular parcel.

## § 4.02   Definition

A floating zone is no different from a Euclidean or conventional zone except that it is not designated on the zoning map. A Connecticut court defined the floating zone this way:

> A floating zone is a special detailed use district of undetermined location in which the proposed kind, size and form of structures must be preapproved. It is legislatively predeemed compatible with the area in which it eventually locates its specified standards on that and the particular application is not reasonable. . . . It differs from the traditional "Euclidean" zone in that it has no defined boundaries and is said to "float" over the entire area where it may eventually be established. (Citations omitted.)[3]

Obviously, a "floating zone" eventually "overlays" upon a geographical area. In that sense, it can also be called an overlay zone and, in fact, some people refer to floating

---

[1] Snyder v. Board of County Com'rs of Brevard County, 595 So. 2d 65, 73 (Fla. Dist. Ct. App. 5th Dist. 1991), jurisdiction accepted, 605 So. 2d 1262 (Fla. 1992) and decision quashed, 627 So. 2d 469 (Fla. 1993).

[2] *See* discussion of conditional zoning in Ch. 7, *infra.*

[3] Homart Development Co. v. Planning and Zoning Com'n of Town of Watertown, 26 Conn. App. 212, 600 A.2d 13, 14 (1991), citing Sheridan v. Planning Bd. of City of Stamford, 159 Conn. 1, 266 A.2d 396 (1969).

zones as "overlay zones." However, there is a difference. Once the floating zone has been designated on the zoning map, it replaces whatever existing Euclidean zone may be on the map. On the other hand, an overlay zone is meant merely to "overlay" on top of the existing Euclidean zone and, in effect, coexist with that underlying zone by either supplementing and/or overriding certain standards in the underlying zoning district.[4] In this sense, the overlay zone also has a narrower purpose: to focus upon a particular geographical area because of the area's environmental, historical, or other qualities deemed important by the local government.[5]

## § 4.03 Purpose

Apart from the general advantage that the floating zone gives in terms of flexibility, the more specific purpose of the floating zone is more akin to a special use permit in that it enables a community to permit specific uses, subject to conditions, without having to prelist those special uses within a particular mapped zoning district. By not specify-

---

[4] The term *overlay zoning* "derived its name from being drawn on tracing, mylar, or other translucent paper which was then placed or 'layed over' the official zoning map." Callies, D. & Freilich, R., *Cases and Materials on Land Use* 80 (1986).

[5] *See*, for example, Franchise Developers, Inc. v. City of Cincinnati, 30 Ohio St. 3d 28, 505 N.E.2d 966 (1987) (upholding the constitutionality of the city's use of an environmental quality-urban design district overlay to preserve and revitalize certain neighborhoods. The overlay district restricted franchise businesses to those that were primarily pedestrian-oriented). *But see* Jachimek v. Superior Court In and For County of Maricopa, 169 Ariz. 317, 819 P.2d 487 (1991) (holding that the creation of an "Inebriate" Overlay District in a commercial portion of the city, and requiring use permits for uses otherwise permitted by right in other commercial districts, violated the "uniformity" requirement and also was not authorized under the Arizona zoning enabling act). *See also* Cox v. Department of Revenue, 12 Or. Tax 535, 1993 WL 523361 (1993) (holding that valuation of a vacant lot subject to the stringent regulation of the city's Environmental Protection overlay zone should not be assessed as if it could be developed, but rather must take into consideration the market response to the uncertainty created by the restriction).

ing the district location of these "special uses" in advance, the floating zone can literally "float" until a developer makes an application to have the zone applied to a particular geographical area. This regulatory approach can be advantageous to both the local government and the developer, particularly for such uses as shopping centers and multifamily and elderly housing. For example, the following Neighborhood Shopping District in Knoxville, Tennessee, was designed as a floating zone:

---

**KNOXVILLE, TENNESSEE
FLOATING ZONE LEGISLATION**

**Article IV, Section SC-1**

An application for development of a shopping center shall follow a two-step procedure for (1) the proper rezoning of land and (2) review and approval of development plans.

(1) An application of rezoning for a neighborhood shopping center shall include the following in addition to the requirements set forth in Article VII, Section 6, of this ordinance.

   a. The developer shall submit a summary report of his economic analysis or other evidence illustrating the need for a shopping center in the proposed area.

   b. The developer shall submit a general land use map of the surrounding neighborhood showing the relationship between the proposed shopping center and the traffic arteries, public transportation, neighborhood land uses, available community services (sewer, water, etc.), general draining patterns and topographic features.

   c. The developer shall furnish a sketch site plan of the proposed shopping center showing tentative building size, shape and location, general parking lot arrangement, access to public streets and patterns of ingress and egress.[6]

---

Included in this floating zone ordinance is a list of permitted uses and standards for minimum and maximum area of the parcel, yards, maximum lot coverage, height limits, off-street parking, loading and screening, and

---

[6] Knoxville, Tennessee Zoning Ordinance (1971).

landscaping. One of the unusual features of this type of floating zone is the requirement that the developer provide a market analysis. Such a requirement is becoming more frequent in connection with large commercial developments, whether proposed as plan developments or under the concept of a floating zone. The market analysis requirement, in effect, gives more weight to the concept of need than would ordinarily be given in determining compatibility of adjacent uses.

Unlike a special use or conditional use permit, which in many jurisdictions must be granted if the applicant can demonstrate compliance with the conditions listed in the ordinance,[7] the floating zone requires a zoning amendment.[8] Because it is a discretionary legislative action, the new zone need not be approved. In this context, evidence of need becomes an important consideration in determining whether to apply the floating zone to a particular geographical area, especially when the adjacent uses are residential.

Another specialized use for which the floating zone can be used appropriately is housing, particularly elderly housing or affordable housing. Because the floating zone is used for a single use, it has been attacked as an attempt to circumvent the uniformity requirement which requires that all regulations be uniform for all classes or kinds of buildings throughout each zoning district. It is argued that by mandating the single use within the floating zone, such a zone violates the uniformity requirement.[9] However, courts have held that the uniformity provision is not

---

[7] Lurie v. Planning and Zoning Commission of Town of Westport, 160 Conn. 295, 305, 278 A.2d 799, 49 A.L.R.3d 476 (1971); Hanson v. Glastonbury Town Council, 1994 WL 197608 at 3 (Conn. Super. Ct. 1994).

[8] Heithaus v. Planning and Zoning Com'n of Town of Greenwich, 26 Conn. L. Rptr. 486, 2000 WL 327411 (Conn. Super. Ct. 2000).

[9] Blitz v. Town of New Castle, 94 A.D.2d 92, 463 N.Y.S.2d 832 (2d Dep't 1983).

violated so long as the floating zone is employed as part of the community's comprehensive plan.[10]

The argument is also made that a floating zone constitutes illegal "spot zoning." For example, in one New York case, town residents challenged a zoning ordinance that established a floating zone for a senior-citizen housing development. The court found that the petitioners had not established that the purpose behind the floating zone was to benefit the owners of the proposed location for the senior-citizen housing. Rather, it appeared to be for the benefit of the community by providing low-cost senior-citizen housing under the town's comprehensive plan.[11]

---

[10] *Id.*

[11] Beyer v. Burns, 150 Misc. 2d 10, 567 N.Y.S.2d 599, 601 (Sup 1991). Of course, a debate over whether a floating zone helps to further the objectives of a comprehensive plan may obscure a much more fundamental debate over land use policy and development in a community. In an article entitled "On New York Developmentalk," in *The New York Times*, Philip J. Hess, then counsel to the New York City Planning Commission, cut through the rhetoric of advocates and opponents of development in the city, and offered a revealing explanation of "what some of the most popular tag lines in the debate really mean. . . ." The following are two examples from his "handy guide":

* * *

*Example 5.* When a developer says, "What is needed is more comprehensive planning," he usually means, "A proper comprehensive plan would have permitted what I wanted to do on this site on an as-of-right basis."

*Example 6.* When a neighborhood group says, "What is needed is more comprehensive planning," it usually means, "A moratorium should be imposed on all development until the conclusion of a zoning study lasting long enough to discourage all developer interest in the area."

* * *

Source: Hess, Philip J., "On New York Developmentalk," *The New York Times*, Sec. 4, Col. 1, p. 19, 1987.

## The Treadwells

"THE POOR NEEDN'T ALWAYS BE WITH US, TREADWELL... IT'S BASICALLY A MATTER OF ZONING."

In jurisdictions where the floating zone is accepted, it may also be possible to incorporate elements of development agreements, such as covenants between the applicant and the local government that are agreed to as part of the amendment process that applies the floating zone. This approach may insulate the development agreement aspects from being characterized as contract zoning.[12]

---

[12] *See, e.g.*, Montgomery County v. Greater Colesville Citizens Ass'n, Inc., 70 Md. App. 374, 521 A.2d 770 (1987).

## § 4.04 Floating Zone—Legality

The first and most often cited case supporting the legality of the concept of floating zones involved the Village of Tarrytown, New York.[13] The village had adopted a new zoning district for garden apartments, provided the tract was a minimum of ten acres. The zoning district included detailed site and density standards. Typical of the floating zone concept, the boundaries of the zone were to be established by amendment to the zoning map on a case-by-case basis. After a floating zone had been approved for a garden-apartment site, a neighboring landowner challenged both the map amendment and the text adopted as part of the floating zone district.

The court found nothing wrong with the floating zone procedure, holding that the village could decide on "the choice of methods" to amend the ordinance, and a procedure that triggered a map amendment upon application of a landowner was not invalid. In addition, because the floating zone applied to the entire village and was not designed to benefit a particular landowner, the court held that the village had not divested its "power to regulate future zoning." Whether or not to map a floating zone remained within the discretion of the planning board and the governing body. The court noted that the floating zone enabled the development of the property to meet the housing needs of the community in furtherance of the general welfare of the entire community.[14] Some courts have followed this same reasoning in upholding the floating zone

---

[13] Rodgers v. Village of Tarrytown, 302 N.Y. 115, 96 N.E.2d 731 (1951).

[14] *Id.*

concept.[15] Other courts, in states such as Washington, have not sanctioned the floating zone concept.[16]

## § 4.05 Floating Zone—Procedural Posture

Some courts view the floating zone as more analogous to "administrative" decision making rather than legislative policy making.[17] However, regardless of how the floating zone is characterized, it can only be given effect by means of a zoning map amendment. Until the floating zone "lands" through use of the zoning amendment procedure, it is a zoning district in text form only, without specific application. Because the floating zone is in a state of procedural limbo until an applicant requests a zone change in order to apply the zone to a particular parcel, the mere creation of the zone does not adversely affect any other property owner's legally protected interest. If there is no real possibility of such adverse effect, an objecting property owner cannot appeal the creation of the floating zone, claiming "aggrievement."[18] In many states "aggrievement"

---

[15] *See, e.g.,* Sheridan v. Planning Bd. of City of Stamford, 159 Conn. 1, 266 A.2d 396 (1969); Pleasant Valley Neighborhood Ass'n v. Planning and Zoning Com'n of Town of South Windsor, 15 Conn. App. 110, 543 A.2d 296 (1988); Huff v. Board· of Zoning Appeals of Baltimore County, 214 Md. 48, 133 A.2d 83 (1957); Bellemeade Co. v. Priddle, 503 S.W.2d 734 (Ky. 1973); Treme v. St. Louis County, 609 S.W.2d 706 (Mo. Ct. App. E.D. 1980).

[16] Lutz v. City of Longview, 83 Wash. 2d 566, 520 P.2d 1374 (1974); *See also* Cheney v. Village 2 at New Hope, Inc., 429 Pa. 626, 241 A.2d 81 (1968).

[17] Snyder v. Board of County Com'rs of Brevard County, 595 So. 2d 65, 73 (Fla. Dist. Ct. App. 5th Dist. 1991), jurisdiction accepted, 605 So. 2d 1262 (Fla. 1992) and decision quashed, 627 So. 2d 469 (Fla. 1993), applying the reasoning in Fasano v. Board of County Com'rs of Washington County, 264 Or. 574, 507 P.2d 23 (1973) (holding that rezoning of thirty-two acres was administrative or quasi-judicial in nature because the action did not involve the formulation of a general policy applicable to a large portion of the public, but rather the application of a general policy to specific parties and interests).

[18] Paucatuck Eastern Pequot Indians of Connecticut v. Connecticut Indian Affairs Council, 18 Conn. App. 4, 555 A.2d 1003 (1989). The word *aggrievement* is a technical legal term used in the "appeals" provi-

is presumed as a matter of law if the objecting property owner is located within a statutorily prescribed radius of the applicant's property. This is known as "statutory aggrievement." If the objecting property owner is located outside the statutorily prescribed distance, there still may be a factual basis to allege aggrievement. However, in the case of a floating zone, there can be no aggrievement, statutory or factual, until the zone is actually "mapped" onto a particular parcel.[19]

## § 4.06  Floating Zone—Compliance with Conditions

Although the floating zone may be more akin to a special use permit, the developer should not assume that if requirements establishing the floating zone are met that the local government is bound to grant the application for a zone change. At least in those jurisdictions that treat the zone change as a legislative act, the courts defer to the local legislative body's discretion to approve or deny a requested zone change.[20]

On the other hand, when the local legislative body does decide to approve a floating zone, and impose conditions as part of its approval, the developer may be in for a rude surprise at the extent to which "guidelines" can become hard-edged conditions for approval. Such a case occurred

---

sions of many zoning enabling statutes and in other statutes such as the Bankruptcy Code. Black's Law Dictionary defines the word "aggrieved" as a "substantial grievance, a denial of some personal, pecuniary or property right. . . ," and an aggrieved" is "[o]ne whose legal right is invaded by an act complained of. . . . " Black's Law Dictionary (St. Paul, Minn.: West Publishing Co., 1990) (6th ed.), p. 65.

[19] Nick v. Planning & Zoning Com'n of Town of East Hampton, 6 Conn. App. 110, 503 A.2d 620 (1986).

[20] Homart Development Co. v. Planning and Zoning Com'n of Town of Watertown, 26 Conn. App. 212, 600 A.2d 13, 15 (1991). Because the special use is also discretionary, the courts in some jurisdictions also hold that compliance with the special use standards of the zoning ordinance does not make issuance of a permit mandatory. *See, e.g.*, LaSalle Nat. Bank v. Lake County, 27 Ill. App. 3d 10, 325 N.E.2d 105, 111 (2d Dist. 1975).

in Prince George's County, Maryland.[21] By authorization of the state legislature, the Prince George's District Council was given the authority to adopt a General Plan to regulate development in a portion of the county known as the Maryland Washington Regional District. In accordance with the new legislation and the General Plan, the District Council adopted a new zoning approval scheme called the Comprehensive Design Zone (CDZ) process as an alternative to conventional zoning approval. The new CDZ process marries flexibility with rigidity, allowing flexiblity with respect to scope of permissible uses and intensity of use, but rigidly applying conditions to developers' proposals. The process involves three stages of approval: (1) Basic Plan; (2) Comprehensive Design Plan (CDP); and (3) Specific Design Plan (SDP). These regulations are implemented by the Prince George's County Planning Board (Planning Board) of the Maryland-National Capital Park and Planning Commission (M-NCPPC).

A developer proposed to develop a 196-acre tract with 357 attached townhouses and 119 detached single-family houses. The entire tract was zoned R-S (Residential-Suburban), one of the Comprehensive Design Zones established under the new zoning scheme—a "floating zone" classification. After receiving Basic Plan approval for the entire tract, the developer sought and obtained Comprehensive Design Plan (CDP) approval for approximately 82 acres. Under the CDP regulations, the CDP proposal must include a "description of design principles" for the units to be constructed. So the developer's proposal included the following section entitled "Architecture," which stated in part:

—Material selection will provide for development that is distinctive and reflects high-quality design.

—Materials which should be encouraged are the fol-

---

[21] Coscan Washington, Inc. v. Maryland-National Capital Park and Planning Com'n, 87 Md. App. 602, 590 A.2d 1080 (1991).

lowing: wood, stone, brick, stucco and other comparable selections.[22]

In approving the developer's CDP proposal, however, the
Planning Board went one step further, revising the
developer's design guidelines to read:

> The choice and mix of materials on the facades of
> buildings will provide an attractive living environ-
> ment. Materials which will be encouraged include
> wood, stone, brick, and stucco. Aluminum and vinyl
> siding will be discouraged.[23]

Then, at the suggestion of a member of the Urban Design
Section of the Maryland-National Capital Park and Planning Commission (M-NCPPC), the Planning Board inserted an additional proviso that approval of the SDP be
conditioned upon 60 percent of the units being constructed
of brick, wood, stone, or stucco.

The developer appealed the imposition of this 60 percent
condition, alleging that the Planning Board lacked authority under both the County zoning code and the General
Plan to impose that condition, and that the condition was
an impermissible exercise of the police power—zoning for
aesthetics only.[24] The Maryland court concluded that the
Planning Board did have the requisite authority, but one
statement by the court is perhaps the most instructive.
The court said:

> Appellant chose to pursue the CDZ approval process
> instead of conventional zoning. As noted previously,
> the CDZ process involves certain trade-offs. The ap-
> plicant receives more liberal zoning classifications in
> exchange for the applicant's agreement to certain
> conditions. One such condition is that the SDP
> [Specific Design Plan] will conform to the CDP
> [Comprehensive Design Plan]. Prince George's County
> Code § 27–528(a). Appellant, at the CDP stage, agreed

---

[22] *Id.* at 1084.
[23] *Id.*
[24] *Id.* at 1085.

that brick, stone, wood and stucco should be encouraged. [Court footnote: In fact, appellant suggested this condition in its CDP proposal]. While aesthetics may have been a partial basis for this guideline, appellant agreed to it.[25]

Certainly, as the court notes, the developer suggested the types of materials to be encouraged. However, under the three-step review process, the developer's design principles were gradually reduced to a rigid "60 percent" rule for types of building materials—an arbitrary percentage under the circumstances, and, in my view, an example of abuse of discretion.[26] Unfortunately, in this case, the developer unwittingly may have invited the result.

## § 4.07 Floating Zone—Reverter Provision

Frequently, the floating zone ordinance will contain a "sunset" provision which provides that the property will revert to its original zoning classification if a building permit is not applied for and actual construction commences in a specific period of time following the rezoning. Although this type of reverter provision is not viewed favorably by the courts in many jurisdictions,[27] some courts have upheld such a reverter provision when utilized in conjunction with the floating zone.[28] In one New York case in which the court did uphold the reverter provision, the court found persuasive the following argument from the town:

> In the past, the Town Board had granted zoning changes for Planned Residence Districts which had

---

[25] Id. at 1088.

[26] See Ch. 8, infra, for discussion of abuse of discretion in the context of aesthetic regulation and design review.

[27] See additional discussion of reverter clauses in Ch. 7, Sec. 7.05[2], infra.

[28] See Beyer v. Burns, 150 Misc. 2d 10, 567 N.Y.S.2d 599, 601 (Sup 1991) (floating zone reverter provision requiring construction to be commenced within two years of rezoning upheld).

remained on the map for years but were never built. As the years passed, the neighborhoods and character of the communities surrounding them changed so that the initial project approval was no longer appropriate for the area. It was only then, that the developers sought to pursue such project. To avoid this zoning dilemma, the Town Board determined to place a time restriction for the commencement of the project.[29]

## § 4.08    Practice Tips

### [1]    Define Adequate Standards to Support the Floating Zone

It is in the interests of both the local government and the developer to have the floating zone defined in the text of the zoning ordinance with adequate performance standards. If adequate standards have been established as part of the floating zone, then at the time the discretionary amendment anchoring the zone is adopted, the zone can withstand the potential charge that it is invalid "spot zoning."

### [2]    Tie the Floating Zone to the Comprehensive Plan

One way to fortify the use of the floating zone is to include in the comprehensive plan a policy statement that identifies the floating zone as a method of policy implementation. For example, if the community wishes to have a regional shopping center, its policy statement in the comprehensive plan could state certain basic planning objectives relative to parcel size and proximity to a transportation corridor and recommend use of a floating zone to establish performance standards consistent with this policy. The developer, after reviewing the parameters of this comprehensive plan policy on regional shopping centers, can select the most appropriate site, consult the

---

[29] *Id.*

development standards in the floating zone, and request a zoning amendment to anchor the zone to the site.

### [3] Do Not Overuse Floating Zone

Just as heavy reliance upon the special use technique can make a local government vulnerable to the charge that the zoning regulations are too discretionary and lack clear standards, extensive use of the floating zone in a regulatory scheme will invite a charge that the community's regulation is *ad hoc* and violates the comprehensive zoning requirement. This potential challenge can be avoided if the floating zone is reserved to achieve carefully defined community objectives.

# CHAPTER 5

# Site Plan Review

## Scope of Chapter

## § 5.01 Introduction

> [D]espite the petitioner's repeated and costly concessions made in attempts to gain final [site plan] approval, the planning board consistently withheld approval. It appears that the proposed development, five stores with two residential apartments above, is a permitted use in the downtown zoning district. . . . The reason given by the planning board for its refusal of approval, i.e., added traffic congestion, is simply not supported by the traffic accessibility study in the record.
>
> —*Bongiorno v. Planning Board*, 533 N.Y.S.2d 631, 632
> (App. Div. 1988)

Costly concessions made in a futile quest for site plan approval is the experience of many developers who

175

stumble just short of the building permit stage. This unfortunate circumstance is attributable to the fact that as a regulatory device, site plan review is neither fish nor foul; that is, it is neither a zoning nor a subdivision process,[1] and it often suffers from abuses of discretion for lack of proper standards and procedures. As one planner observed with candor: "Site plan review used to be a pretty cut-and-dried affair. This is how you lay out a neighborhood, or a commercial district, or an industrial area. No more. Today, fixed standards have all but disappeared, which means a lot more discretion for the reviewers."[2] Not surprisingly, this circumstance causes much apprehension in the development community.

Site plan review frequently becomes the last means by which local governments attempt to evaluate a proposed development in terms of its possible impacts upon the surrounding community—a misuse of this device. As a relatively new regulatory device, only a handful of states have enacted enabling legislation. In states that have not enacted such legislation, communities have either relied upon their home-rule authority or argued that the authority for exercising site plan review can be implied from their general zoning powers.

## § 5.02 Definition of Site Plan Review

Simply described, a site plan "shows the proposed design and layout of the improvements to be placed on a parcel."[3] Compare the following definitions of site plan review found in New Jersey and Washington:

---

[1] Subdivision regulations address the division of a parcel into multiple lots. Site plan review concerns the details of the activity on a specific lot. Similar to subdivision regulations, site plan review addresses issues pertaining to design and public infrastructure, but only in the context of a specific lot.

[2] Pollock, "The Red Penciler's Guide to Site Plan Review," *Planning* at 22 (April 1991).

[3] Moriarty v. Planning Bd. of Village of Sloatsburg, 119 A.D.2d 188, 506 N.Y.S.2d 184, 186 (2d Dep't 1986).

**DEFINITIONS OF SITE PLAN REVIEW
IN STATE STATUTES
New Jersey**

A plan of an existing lot or plot or a subdivided lot on which is shown topography, location of all existing and proposed buildings, structures, drainage facilities, roads, rights-of-way, easements, parking areas, together with any other information required by and at a scale specified by a site plan review and approval resolution adopted by the board of chosen freeholders pursuant to this act. N.J. Stat. § 13:17–3 (s) (1993)

**Washington**

A drawing to a scale specified by local ordinance which: (a) Identifies and shows the areas and locations of all streets, roads, improvements, utilities, open spaces, and any other matters specified by local regulations; (b) contains inscriptions or attachments setting forth such appropriate limitations and conditions for the use of the land as are established by the local government body having authority to approve the site plan; and (c) contains provisions making any development be in conformity with the site plan. Rev. Code Wash. (ARCW) § 58.17.020 (7) (1994)

The purpose of requiring this type of plan is to enable the reviewing body to review (1) the quantity, quality, utility, size, and type of a project's proposed open space and landscaping improvements; (2) the ability of a project's traffic circulation system to provide for the convenient and safe internal and external movement of vehicles and pedestrians; (3) the type and location of parking facilities; (4) the quantity, quality, utility, and type of a project's required community facilities; and (5) the location and adequacy of a project's provision for drainage and utilities.

In other words, site plan review is directed at the site details of a development. Site plan review should not address off-site conditions except to the extent that an *on-site* condition (e.g., ingress/egress) affects off-site conditions (e.g., traffic). Unfortunately, some states and many local ordinances define the purpose of site plan review more broadly, making the process a ready candidate for abuse of discretion. For example, a New York State publication states that site plan review enables a planning board to review a proposal's physical, social, and economic effects on the community.[4] What do the site details of a development have to do with social and economic effects? The following section addresses this and other fundamental legal issues relevant to site plan review.

## § 5.03 Proper Scope of Review

Before considering the basis or authority for local governments to exercise site plan review, it is important to continue with the question of what are proper subjects for review under site plan review. The fact that state legislatures and municipalities may enact statutes and ordinances that allow site plan review to reach issues of concern that go beyond the proper scope of site plan review does not justify such practice. There are some wrongly decided cases involving site plan review.

### [1] Avoiding Redetermination of Issues Previously Decided

In one Connecticut case,[5] for example, the zoning commission denied the applicant's application for site plan approval of a retail shopping mall located in a B-3 (designed business development) zone. The zoning commission based its denial on the following reasons:

> (1) No proof of need for the proposed use was established by the applicant; (2) a shopping mall of the scope proposed with its related traffic activity and after-dark operation would be most harmful to the

---

[4] Site Development Plan Review, N.Y. Dep't of State, Local Government Technical Series at 3 (1984).

[5] Goldberg v. Zoning Commission of Town of Simsbury, 173 Conn. 23, 376 A.2d 385 (1977).

> residential character of the neighborhood; and (3) because of the inherent nature of the location and operation of the proposed development, the commission was unable to establish any safeguards to protect adjacent property or the neighborhood from the detrimental effect of a shopping center.[6]

Because there was testimony to the effect that there was no need for the shopping mall at the proposed location, that the projected additional traffic would add to the overburdened existing road and adversely impact a nearby school facility, and that the site plan had no sufficient safeguards to protect the area from the detrimental effects of the shopping mall, the appellate court upheld the trial court's determination that the commission's reasons were reasonably supported by the record.

What does proof of "need" have to do with the review of site details? That's what the applicant wanted to know, along with why the other reasons given by the commission were pertinent to this type of review. The appellate court appeared to agree that demonstrated need was not pertinent to the site plan review, but found the other two reasons sufficient to uphold the commission's denial.

The dissenting judge got it right, however, pointing out that the B-3 zone had been created in the nature of a special use district. Therefore, the real issue was whether the zoning commission, having determined at the time it rezoned the property to B-3 that the location was suitable for a shopping center and no traffic hazard existed, could now redetermine these issues at the site plan approval stage. As the dissenting judge observed, the commission's first two reasons, no proof of need and adverse traffic impacts, are appropriate in considering a zone change. But they are not relevant to site plan review. Moreover, to the extent site plan review takes into account traffic issues, it should be limited to "the details of traffic management: number of parking spaces, placement of entrances

---

[6] *Id.* at 387.

and exits, and traffic circulation within the site."[7] The third reason, the commission's "inability to establish any safeguards to protect adjacent property or the neighborhood from the detrimental effect of a shopping center," was more revealing of the commission's inadequacy than the applicant's. As the dissenting judge noted, the commission did not disapprove the site plan merely because the safeguards proposed by the developer were inadequate, but because the commission itself could not come up with any adequate safeguards. Said the dissenting judge: "Once the commission has changed the zone it cannot disapprove a site plan for a permitted use because it does not know what to do."[8]

### [2]  Limited Discretion to Deny Site Plan Approval

The desire of planning boards and commissions to revisit and redetermine issues through site plan review that were previously decided raises the larger issue of the extent of authority that is delegated by ordinance to the decision-making body, whether it is the planning commission or the legislative body itself. The simple answer is that most courts regard the site plan review step as akin to a building permit. If the requirements are met, the decision-making body has no discretion to deny site plan approval. In other words, the site plan review and approval process are *ministerial*—the application must be approved if it meets the requirements of the ordinance.

Unfortunately, the temptation to use the process to reexamine basic zoning decisions previously made is often

---

[7] *Id.* at 390.

[8] *Id.* at 391. The Connecticut General Assembly subsequently passed Public Acts 1978, No. 78-104, amending General Statutes § 8-3 (g) to provide that site plan could be modified or denied only if they failed to comply with requirements already set forth in the zoning regulations. The Connecticut Supreme Court concluded that by so narrowing the scope of the commission's inquiry, the statutory amendment effectively overruled its holding in Goldberg v. Zoning Commission of Town of Simsbury, 173 Conn. 23, 376 A.2d 385 (1977). *See* TLC Development, Inc. v. Planning and Zoning Com'n of Town of Branford, 215 Conn. 527, 577 A.2d 288, 290 n.2 (1990).

irresistible. This temptation frequently occurs when the use itself raises a concern. For example, a planning and zoning commission which belatedly decides that a retail complex that meets all of the site plan requirements of the ordinance is a "poor use of the site" and should be denied site plan approval is exceeding its authority.[9] The temptation to revisit prior decisions is particularly powerful if the site plan review requirements are vague.

In a New Jersey case,[10] the applicant applied for preliminary and final site plan approval for a convenience store. The C-1 zoning district's stated purpose was "to permit the delivery of *low traffic generating* retail and professional services which directly benefit the residents of the surrounding neighborhood." The "purpose" paragraph also stated that the type of activity that may be conducted in the district must be based upon "traffic, site planning and land use considerations."[11] Even though the proposed convenience store was a permitted use, the planning board denied site plan approval because it concluded that the convenience store would generate excessive traffic. It appears that witnesses had testified that the convenience store would be a "medium" as opposed to a "low" traffic generator. The planning board asserted that the "low traffic generating" language in the ordinance effectively classified neighborhood retail stores as conditional uses, ignoring the fact that conditional uses were specifically listed in the ordinance. The court properly overturned the denial and mandated that the site plan be approved, stating:

> The lack of definite standards in this ordinance compels the conclusion that it does not comply with the requirements established in the Municipal Land Use Law for delegation of conditional use approval to a planning board. . . . The undefined requirement that uses be 'low traffic generating' effectively allowed

---

[9] Kosinski v. Lawlor, 177 Conn. 420, 418 A.2d 66, 68 (1979).

[10] PRB Enterprises, Inc. v. South Brunswick Planning Bd., 105 N.J. 1, 518 A.2d 1099 (1987).

[11] *Id.* at 1100.

the Board to grant or deny approval based on its
subjective evaluation of a use's impact on traffic
congestion in the . . . neighborhood.[12]

The court's conclusion that an "undefined requirement"
invited the board to engage in a "subjective evaluation" of
traffic impact may remind the reader of the dialogue between the developer's attorney and the traffic commissioner whose commission had no standards to guide its
analysis—only "our experience, from living in the village,
our common sense as drivers, and not necessarily the
opinions of a 'hired gun' " [the professional traffic
engineer].[13] To be sure, personal experience and common
sense are essential to exercising proper judgment, but
they cannot substitute for adequate standards and professional analysis. All four ingredients must be present when
the administrative body deliberates in order for its decision to be well reasoned and fair to the applicant.

### [3]   Public Health, Safety, and Welfare

The advancement of the public "health, safety, and
welfare" is found in the recitals and list of standards of
virtually every police power enactment. Indeed, the courts
traditionally have been comforted by this phrase when
clothing land use regulations with the presumption of
validity. However, the courts have been less willing to allow local governments to use the public health, safety, and
welfare concern to justify site plan disapproval. The reason is obvious: Site plan review is a *ministerial* decision
that follows from the applicant's demonstrated compliance
with specific standards. The public health, safety, and
welfare standard is a broad standard that demands the
exercise of discretion. For this reason, the courts will usually rule that it is arbitrary and capricious to deny site
plan approval on grounds of public health, safety, and

---

[12] *Id.* at 1103.
[13] *See* Ch. 1, Sec. 1.04[3], *supra.*

welfare.[14] The only qualification to this general rule is that the general health, safety, and welfare factors may be considered insofar as they affect matters expressly within the decision-making body's scope of review. In other words, if traffic congestion on the street from which customers of a proposed development would enter is an explicit consideration under site plan review, the body could address the health, safety, and welfare factors from that perspective.[15]

## [4] Off-Site Considerations

As I emphasized in the introduction to this chapter, site plan review is directed at the site details of a development. It should not address off-site conditions except to the extent that on-site conditions affect off-site conditions. Courts have agreed with this circumscribed view of site plan review.[16] However, other courts, usually relying upon the health, safety, and welfare rationale, have ruled that off-site considerations are within the scope of site plan review.[17] Typically, these off-site considerations include traffic impact, adequacy of water supply for fire protection, and drainage, lighting, and aesthetic impacts on surrounding properties or neighborhoods.

### [a] Off-Site Traffic Impacts

Retail carryout food establishments—fast-food restaurants, bakeries, etc.—consistently trigger traffic concerns.

---

[14] Apache Associates v. Planning Bd. of Village of Nyack, 131 A.D.2d 666, 517 N.Y.S.2d 28 (2d Dep't 1987).

[15] Bongiorno v. Planning Bd. of Incorporated Village of Bellport, 143 A.D.2d 967, 533 N.Y.S.2d 631, 632 (2d Dep't 1988). *But compare* Holmes v. Planning Bd. of Town of New Castle, 78 A.D.2d 1, 433 N.Y.S.2d 587 (2d Dep't 1980).

[16] *See, e.g.,* Moriarty v. Planning Bd. of Village of Sloatsburg, 119 A.D.2d 188, 506 N.Y.S.2d 184, 186 (2d Dep't 1986); Lionel's Appliance Center, Inc. v. Citta, 156 N.J. Super. 257, 383 A.2d 773 (Law Div. 1978).

[17] *See, e.g.,* Grossman v. Planning Bd. of Town of Colonie, 126 A.D.2d 887, 510 N.Y.S.2d 929 (3d Dep't 1987); Eastern New York Properties, Inc. v. Cavaliere, 142 A.D.2d 644, 530 N.Y.S.2d 842 (2d Dep't 1988).

The concern is appropriate, but at the site plan review stage? Arguably not. One of the better explanations I have seen as to why site plan review should not address this issue is in a New Jersey state court decision.[18] The court was asked to review a denial of site plan approval for a Dunkin' Donuts shop that was based solely on the anticipated detrimental impact of the proposed use on traffic congestion and safety. In fact, the New Jersey site plan review statute authorized the planning board to consider off-site traffic flow and safety in reviewing proposals for vehicular ingress to and egress from a site, and to condition site plan approval upon contribution to needed off-site improvements.[19] But the court held that the board had no authority to deny site plan approval because of off-site traffic conditions because:

> [T]he authority to prohibit or limit uses generating traffic into already congested streets or streets with a high rate of accidents is an exercise of the zoning power vested in the municipal governing body.[20]

Just the opposite view was expressed by a New York court which found it proper to consider traffic congestion during the site plan review process because "[i]t is beyond question in this State that traffic congestion is related to the public health, safety and welfare."[21] The New York court also relied on the town's code, which required evaluation of whether "pedestrian and vehicular access, traffic circulation and the general layout of the site is properly planned with regard to the safety of cars and pedestrians using the site, *as well as those on neighboring properties*

---

[18] Dunkin' Donuts of New Jersey, Inc. v. North Brunswick Tp. Planning Bd., 193 N.J. Super. 513, 475 A.2d 71 (App. Div. 1984).

[19] N.J. Gen. Stat. Ann. §§ 40:55D-7, 41(b); 40:55D-42.

[20] *Dunkin' Donuts of New Jersey*, at 73, citing Lionel's Appliance Center, Inc. v. Citta, 156 N.J. Super. 257, 383 A.2d 773 (Law Div. 1978).

[21] Holmes v. Planning Bd. of Town of New Castle, 78 A.D.2d 1, 433 N.Y.S.2d 587, 595 (2d Dep't 1980).

*and streets.*"[22] The danger of utilizing site plan review to address off-site traffic concerns, as highlighted in the preceding sentence, from the town's code is illustrated by a Massachusetts case involving a similar off-site traffic impact standard requiring "adequate provision for the convenience of vehicular and pedestrian movement within the site *and in relation to adjacent streets, property and improvements.*"[23] In this instance, the applicant sought site plan approval for two four-story office buildings—a use permitted by right in the zoning district. Because the board of appeals had not been "reasonably assured" that the proposed site plan had adequately addressed this standard, the board rejected the site plan. Before the court, the board argued that, in this case, the site plan approval process was "analogous to an application for a special permit."[24] In other words, the board argued that it had the right to exercise the discretion usually accorded a decision maker in deciding a special use permit, even though the use was permitted as of right! I suggest that because traffic impacts "on neighboring properties and streets" are the subject *only* of special use permit reviews, an attempt to address off-site traffic impacts will invariably invite an abuse of discretion as occurred and was overturned by the court in the Massachusetts case.[25]

### [b]  Adequacy of Fire Protection Facilities

Certainly fire protection is a public health, safety, and welfare concern. So, if water pressure from the fire hydrant nearest to a proposed development is insufficient because of the distance, wouldn't it seem reasonable to deny site plan approval on the general public health, safety, and welfare standard? A New York court said no

---

[22] *Id.*

[23] Prudential Ins. Co. of America v. Board of Appeals of Westwood, 23 Mass. App. Ct. 278, 502 N.E.2d 137, 139 n.2 (1986).

[24] *Id.* at 139.

[25] For a discussion of this type of abuse of discretion, *see* Ch. 1, Sec. 1.04, *supra.*

and it was right. The site plan was not denied "not because of any perceived design deficiencies, but because of the lack of nearby public water for fire protection purposes, a factor unmentioned in the State enabling statute or . . . the zoning ordinance."[26] Rather, the question of fire protection is solely for consideration by the building or fire inspector at the time of building permit application. In response to the fact that enabling legislation authorizes the planning board to review "such other elements as may reasonably be related to the health, safety and general welfare," the court made a very perceptive statement:

> [T]here is something redundant about the use of general welfare language in police power legislation because such power must always be granted and exercised for the protection of health, safety or, at least, the general welfare.
>
> * * *
>
> [C]onstruction of the health, safety and general welfare provision in the instant enabling legislation [citation omitted] is limited by its relation to the specific factors a planning board may consider with respect to site plan review. The provision does not constitute a grant of the entire police power of the State nor even of the entire power to regulate land use. . . .[27]

In other words, the appropriateness of considering adequacy of fire protection for the site was defined by the statute itself. The planning board exceeded its delegated powers by trying to expand its authority using the general public health, safety, and welfare standard.

---

[26] Moriarty v. Planning Bd. of Village of Sloatsburg, 119 A.D.2d 188, 506 N.Y.S.2d 184, 187 (2d Dep't 1986).
[27] *Id.* at 191.

## § 5.04  Legal Authority for Site Plan Review

### [1]  Express Statutory Authority

Connecticut, Michigan, New Jersey, New York, and Rhode Island have statutes that expressly authorize the use of site plan review.[28] Appeal from a denial of site plan approval is presented to an administrative body, such as the zoning board of review,[29] or to state court.[30] If specific statutory authority exists, a municipality or planning board may not apply a broader review than is granted in the enabling legislation.[31] Also, for site plan review to be valid in a state that has adopted enabling legislation, the local government must comply with the statutory requirements for exercising site plan review at the local level.[32]

### [2]  Implied Authority

In states that have not expressly authorized site plan review, local governments have either derived their authority from home-rule powers or implied it from the general delegation of zoning power.[33]

## § 5.05  Can Conditions Be Imposed?

Because most site plan enabling statutes do not specifically authorize the site plan review bodies to impose condi-

---

[28] *See* Connecticut: Conn. Gen. Stat. Ann. § 8-3(g); Michigan: townships M.C.L. § 125.584d; New Jersey: N.J. Gen. Stat. Ann. § 40:55D-67; New York: N.Y. Town Law § 274-a; N.Y. Village Law § 7-725; N.Y. Gen. City Law § 30-a; Rhode Island: R.I. Gen. Stat. Ann. § 45–24–49.

[29] *See, e.g.,* R.I. Gen. Stat. Ann. § 45–24–64.

[30] *See, e.g.,* N.Y. Gen. City Law § 30-a.

[31] Johnston v. Town of Exeter, 121 N.H. 938, 436 A.2d 1147 (1981); Chiplin Enterprises, Inc. v. City of Lebanon, 120 N.H. 124, 411 A.2d 1130 (1980).

[32] Eddy Plaza Associates v. City of Concord, 122 N.H. 416, 445 A.2d 1106 (1982).

[33] *See, e.g.,* Wesley Investment Co. v. County of Alameda, 151 Cal. App. 3d 672, 198 Cal. Rptr. 872, 874 (1st Dist. 1984) (home-rule authority); Y. D. Dugout, Inc. v. Board of Appeals of Canton, 357 Mass. 25, 255 N.E.2d 732 (1970) (general zoning power).

tions through the site plan review process, planning boards and other reviewing agencies venture into potential abuses of discretion when they do so, particularly if the use is permitted by right. When such a practice has been challenged, the courts usually examine whether the conditions are on-site or off-site. If the conditions are on-site and reasonably related to the factors that the planning board is authorized to consider, the courts have generally said that such conditions are valid.[34] In addition, if site plan review is required as part of a conditional use or planned unit development approval, then there is an even greater likelihood that a court will uphold the imposition of conditions recommended through the site plan review process, since the principal approval process (conditional use or planned unit development) usually authorizes the imposition of conditions.

Because of the U.S. Supreme Court's decisions in the *Nollan* and *Dolan* cases, the required connection ("nexus") between the condition imposed and the adverse impact or problem that a proposed development is supposedly the cause of, must be clearly demonstrable.[35]

## § 5.06   Procedural Requirements

Site plan review procedures can be critical to the outcome of a developer's project. If the developer's project is located in one of the states that has authorized site plan review by statute, he or she should be aware that the procedures will be spelled out and that they are generally similar. However, in states without statutorily established procedures, the procedural steps can vary considerably.

### [1]   Key Statutory Procedural Provision

Perhaps the most important procedural provision found in the site plan review statutes of some states, such as

---

[34] Lionel's Appliance Center, Inc. v. Citta, 156 N.J. Super. 257, 383 A.2d 773 (Law Div. 1978); Charter Tp. of Harrison v. Calisi, 121 Mich. App. 777, 329 N.W.2d 488 (1982).
[35] *See* discussion of these two cases in Ch. 1, *supra.*

Connecticut and New Jersey, and many zoning statutes whose procedures apply to site plan review, is the "deemed approved" provision. This provision provides that approval of a site plan is *presumed* unless a decision to deny or modify the site plan is made within a fixed number of days after the site plan has been filed.[36] In New York, failure by the planning board to act within the established time limits does not mandate an approval. Rather, the applicant must then go through a special proceeding that forces the planning board to make a decision.[37]

### [2] Other Procedural Requirements

In addition to any specific procedures that site plan review statutes prescribe, these statutes may also require that procedures be established by local ordinance. For example, the Michigan statute requires local governments to adopt "procedures and requirements for the submission and approval of site plans" in their zoning ordinances.[38] Similarly, the New Hampshire statute requires that when a local planning board exercises site plan review, the municipality must adopt regulations that include notice and hearing requirements.[39]

Because a planning board or municipal body charged with site plan review acts in an administrative capacity, it

---

[36] Conn. Gen. Stat. §§ 8-3(g), 8–7d(b); N.J. Gen. Stat. Ann. § 40:55D-46(c). For cases upholding time limits for site plan review decisions under zoning statutes, *see* Burcam Corp. v. Planning Bd. of Medford Tp., 168 N.J. Super. 508, 403 A.2d 921 (App. Div. 1979); SSM Associates Ltd. Partnership v. Plan and Zoning Com'n of Town of Fairfield, 211 Conn. 331, 559 A.2d 196 (1989). But see Center Shops of East Granby, Inc. v. Planning and Zoning Com'n of Town of East Granby, 253 Conn. 183, 757 A.2d 1052, 1058 (2000) (clarifying that "where a special permit application must necessarily include a site plan, that fact, by itself, does not trigger automatic approval of either the special permit or its accompanying site plan, pursuant to §§ 8-3(g) and 8-7d, when the commission does not meet the time limits set forth by § 8-3c (b).").

[37] N.Y. Village Law § 7-725(2); N.Y. Town Law § 274-a(2); N.Y. Gen. City Law § 30-a(2).

[38] *See* Mich. Compiled Laws § 125.286e.

[39] *See* N.H. Rev. Stat. Ann. § 36:19-a.

must comply with constitutional standards of procedural due process. This means that it must review and evaluate the specific site plan evidence without bringing in information or considerations outside the proper scope of review, and must afford the applicant and any objectors a fair hearing.[40]

## § 5.07 Principles for Drafting a Site Plan Review/Approval Process

Because it is tempting for communities to make site plan review the catchall process for development review, it is very important to address certain issues up front before drafting the actual provisions.

### [1] Purpose

I have already expressed my view that, as practiced by many communities, site plan review is used to accomplish objectives that go well beyond the proper purpose of the site plan review. That purpose, properly conceived, is to address the details of a specific site, not to examine a project's potential impacts upon the surrounding community. If the community intends that site plan review be advisory only, not binding upon the developer, then the expanded purpose I mentioned may be of little consequence. However, if the community decides that site plan review will be a required approval step, it should define the purpose of the review carefully, consistent with purposes authorized by state legislation authorizing site plan review or, if no statute, then the judicial decisions that have addressed the purpose of site plan review.

### [2] Scope of Applicability

If the community has settled on the purpose of its site plan review process, it is important next to decide exactly

---

[40] Geiger v. Levco Route 46 Assocs., Ltd., 437 A.2d 336 (N.J. 1981).

what array of uses will be subject to this type of review, and if it will be used for those uses whether or not they are subject to discretionary approval processes such as conditional use and special exception approvals.

### [a]   Uses Subject to Site Plan Review

Admittedly, site plan review is a means to ensure review of nonresidential developments and multifamily developments which typically fall outside the subdivision review process. But certainly it does not follow that all nonresidential (commercial, retail, and industrial) uses should be subjected to site plan review. Whether or not there is staff capacity to properly and efficiently process site plan review applications for all nonresidential uses, the community should ask itself whether such a broad utilization of the review process is really necessary. The more important considerations should be size and complexity of development. For example, site plan review may be limited to commercial developments above a certain number of square feet or above a certain floor area ratio (FAR), multifamily developments above a certain number of units, and industrial developments above a certain size or FAR.[41]

### [b]   By Right and/or Special Permit Approvals

A briefing paper prepared by the Pioneer Valley Planning Commission in Massachusetts states that site plan approval "is essentially a Special Permit granting process." As a result of this process, "any comments or recommendations subject to the permit granting criteria of the Board must be implemented and complied with by the developer."[42] However, in Massachusetts there is no

---

[41] *Floor area ratio (FAR)* is the gross floor area of all buildings or structures on a lot divided by the total lot area.

[42] "Using Site Plan Review/Approval Effectively," Growth Management Briefing Paper #6, Pioneer Valley Planning Commission, June 1988.

legislation specifically authorizing site plan review. Massachusetts courts have sanctioned the use of site plan review,[43] but they have not authorized the use of the site plan review process to convert a by-right use to a use requiring a special use permit. Nevertheless, as the briefing paper indicates, communities in Massachusetts apparently are instructed to administer the site plan approval process in the same manner as a special permit review process. The result is clearly an invitation to abuse of discretion. It is preferable for all concerned, and legally defensible, for the community to clearly distinguish between the application of site plan review/approval to by-right uses and to uses requiring discretionary approval. For example, a site plan review ordinance might provide as follows:

> **Site Plan Approval Required.** Site plan approval is required in connection with the following use approvals and development projects permitted in the applicable zoning district:
>
> (a)  Any use requiring special use approval;
>
> (b)  Any use involving planned development approval;
>
> (c)  A multifamily project in excess of ____ ( ) units;
>
> (d)  A commercial retail center in excess of ____ sq. ft.;
>
> (e)  An industrial development whose FAR exceeds ____ and abuts a residential zoning district.

This language clarifies that there are uses permitted by right which are not subject to site plan approval unless they exceed a certain use intensity threshold, and further distinguishes between these by-right uses and those that are subject to discretionary approvals, such as special use approval or planned development approval.

---

[43] *See, e.g.,* Y. D. Dugout, Inc. v. Board of Appeals of Canton, 357 Mass. 25, 255 N.E.2d 732 (1970).

### [3]  Decision Maker

The planning board, or planning commission, is typically made the decision maker by statute or local ordinance. If the process is advisory only, then a site plan review committee (SPRC) may also be appropriate. However, if a local community lacks the staff or planning board expertise necessary to conduct site plan review competently, then it should either retain the services of a professional to assist in the review or postpone the use of site plan review until such expertise is available.

### [4]  Site Plan Informational Requirements

The information required on the site plan as part of the site plan application should be adequate but not excessive. It should be sufficient to allow the reviewer to determine the layout of structures, parking, circulation patterns (both pedestrian and vehicular), utilities (on-site and public), stormwater runoff, and landscaping. Plans should be at a scale of at least 1"=50'. The plan should show the following:

---

**SITE PLAN INFORMATIONAL REQUIREMENTS**

- The zoning classification, zoning district boundaries and present use of the property.
- A vicinity map with north point, scale and date, indicating the zoning classifications and current uses of properties within two hundred fifty feet (250') of the property.
- The boundaries of the property, all existing property lines, setback lines, existing streets, buildings, water courses, water ways or lakes, wetlands, and other existing physical features in or adjoining the project.
- Topographic survey, showing the elevation of streets, alleys, buildings, structures, water courses and their names. Additionally:
  - Significant topographical or physical features of the site, including existing trees.
  - The elevation of the curb (if existing or proposed) in front of each lot.

---

---

**SITE PLAN INFORMATIONAL REQUIREMENTS (cont'd)**

- Elevations of the top of bank and toe of slope, slope ratio of fill, and limits of fill, including access.

- The location and size of sanitary and storm sewers, water, gas, telephone, electric and other utility lines, culverts and other underground structures in or affecting the project, including existing and proposed facilities and easements for these facilities.

- The location, dimensions and character of construction of proposed streets, alleys, loading areas (including numbers of parking and loading spaces), outdoor lighting systems, storm drainage and sanitary facilities, sidewalks, curbs and gutters and all curb cuts.

- The location of all proposed buildings and structures, accessory and principal, showing the number of stories and height, dwelling type, if applicable, major excavations and the total square footage of the floor area by proposed use.

- The location, height, type and material of all fences and walls.

- The location, character, size, height and orientation of proposed signs, as proposed to be erected.

- The proposed nature and manner of grading of the site, including proposed treatment of slopes in excess of ten percent (10) to prevent soil erosion and excessive runoff.

- The location of dumpsters or other outdoor trash receptacles.

- The location and dimensions of proposed recreation areas, open spaces and other required amenities and improvements.

- A tabulation of the total number of acres in the project and the percentage and acreage thereof proposed to be allocated to off-street parking, open space, parks, and other reservations.

- A tabulation of the total number of dwelling units in the project and the overall project density in dwelling units per gross acre (for residential projects).

- The proposed and required off-street parking and loading areas, including parking and access for the handicapped, as specified in the state building code.

---

It is important that the zoning administrator, or designated administrative staff person, has the authority to waive any of the above-listed requirements upon making a determination that such requirements are unnecessary due to the scope and nature of the proposed development. The following is a basic illustration and explanation of the essential components of a site plan that was prepared to assist commissioners in addressing site plan applications. *(See Illustration No. 1 below and accompanying explanation.)*[44] Following this illustration is another example of a site plan for a residential development which illustrates existing site features (property boundaries, existing walls, etc.), topography, soils, wetland boundaries, spot elevations, existing vegetation, and the proposed development, including building layout, utilities, driveways, and proposed landscaping. *(See Illustration No. 2.)*

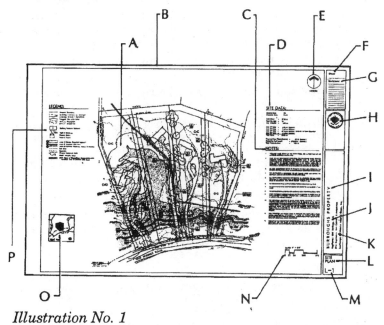

*Illustration No. 1*

---

[44] Reprinted from Keane Callahan, et al. *An Inland Wetland Commissioner's Guide to Site Plan Review* at 16–19, Connecticut Department of Environmental Protection, 1992.

## SITE PLAN COMPONENTS

A. **Development Plan:** The crux of the site plan. It is the graphic representation of the proposed project and its relationship to the existing conditions of the site.

B. **Drawing Border:** A line drawn around the edge of the drawing which frames the drawing area and allows for binding several sheets along the left edge.

C. **Notes:** Information about specific aspects of the plans—for instance, the name of the drawing, name of the surveyor, information about phasing and wetland field markings, etc.

D. **Site Data:** A chart indicating wetland acreage, wetland soil types, zoning district and compliance with specific zoning requirements, such as minimum lot size, yard requirements, building coverage, parking specifications, etc.

E. **North Arrow:** An arrow that indicates the direction of north as related to the site plan.

F. **Submission Date:** The "original" date on the drawings at the time of submission.

G. **Revision Dates:** Dates of site plan revisions, along with a brief explanation about the nature of the revision.

H. **Professional Seal:** The stamp or seal of the professional whose work is represented on the plans. Seals are generally required as an indication that the plans were prepared by a licensed professional. A signature over the seal is usually required as well.

I. **Project Title:** The name of the project.

J. **Owner/Developer:** The name of the owner or developer of the project. The developer often does not own the land, but may have an option to purchase or some other agreement with the owner whereby the land may be jointly developed.

K. **Professional Consultants:** A list of the various professional consultants who prepared the site plan. These might include a soil scientist, biologist, architect, landscape architect, engineer, attorney, etc.

L. **Drawing Title:** The title of a particular sheet in the set of plans.

---

## SITE PLAN COMPONENTS (cont'd)

**M.**     **Drawing Number:** A simple alpha-numeric system of organizing drawings. For instance, the site-related drawings might be set up as follows: L-1 Site Preparation, L-2 Site Layout, L-3 Site Grading, L-4 Site Planting, L-5 Site Details.

**N.**     **Graphic/Written Scale:** A graphic or written representation of the mathematical relationship between the size of the drawing and the actual site. For example, 1" on the drawing may represent 20'. Note: the written scale may be inaccurate if the plan has been enlarged or reduced by photocopy. However, the graphic scale will always be accurate.

**O.**     **Location Map:** A simple map showing the location of the project site in relation to major town roads and abutting properties.

**P.**     **Legend:** Sets forth the various symbols and line types used to denote boundaries, setbacks, and existing and proposed features. A legend should be part of any plan because it will help tremendously in "reading" a site plan that may contain a number of overlapping layers of information. *(See example opposite this page.)*

---

## SITE PLAN LEGEND

| EXISTING | | PROPOSED |
|---|---|---|
| S 09° 44'-66" W | PROPERTY LINE | SAME |
| 15' SIDE YARD | SETBACK LINE | SAME |
| 20' R.O.W. | R.O.W./EASEMENT | SAME |
| ⊕ | BENCH MARK | N/A |
| O | TEST PIT | N/A |
| N/A | POTABLE WELL | ● |
| N/A | SEPTIC SYSTEM | |
| | INTERMITTENT WATERCOURSES | N/A |
| WETLANDS | WETLANDS | N/A |
| | STREAM | N/A |
| | STONE WALL | |
| 98 | CONTOUR LINE | 98 |
| ——— 98 ——— | SAN. SEWER | ——— 98 ——— |
| ——— 4 ——— | STORM SEWER | ——— 4 ——— |
| ——— E ——— | ELECTRIC LINE | ——— E ——— |
| ——— W ——— | WATER LINE | ——— W ——— |
| Ω | HYDRANT | |
| ⊖ | UTILITY POLE | ⊕ |
| ⊘ | MANHOLE | ◐ |
| ⊠ | CATCH BASIN | ◣ |
| N/A | FLARED END | |
| N/A | SPLASH PAD | |
| N/A | SILT FENCING | |
| | TREES AND SHRUBS | |
| | EDGE OF WOODS | |

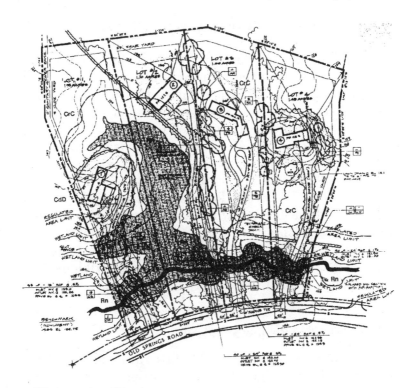

*Illustration No. 2*

### [5] Standards—General Considerations

Site plan review and approval processes can be flexible, or rigid, depending primarily upon the type of standards used. If the technical knowledge and expertise of staff are limited, then fixed standards—those that prescribe specifically what must be satisfied—are easier to administer. From the developer's perspective, however, reasonably designed performance standards are preferable. Performance standards specify an outcome, but give the applicant/developer the flexibility to satisfy the standard through a variety of different means. For example, in the case of stormwater runoff, a fixed standard might prescribe that a retention basin be constructed. By contrast, a performance standard might state that the rate of storm-

199

water runoff after the development may not exceed the rate prior to runoff for a 25-year storm. This type of standard would allow the developer to select among a number of options to ensure the required outcome. For example, instead of using a retention basin, the developer might elect to reduce the amount of impervious surface in the development or create a vegetated buffer.

If the site plan review process is advisory only, standards may seem less important. However, as we have seen, it is these "advisory" recommendations which, when followed, can be disastrous for the applicant because there are no standards against which to measure the reasonableness of the "recommendations." The next section presents a summary and comment on the most typical categories of standards found in site plan review provisions from jurisdictions around the country.

## § 5.08    Site Plan Review Standards

Site plan review standards fall into approximately eleven general categories. Communities approach these categories of concern in a variety of ways. However, certain basic points deserve mentioning.

### [1]    Parking

The principal concern of staff site plan reviewers should be that surface parking lots will be located and designed to provide safe and efficient vehicular and pedestrian circulation within the site. The appropriateness of going beyond that concern should depend upon the type of use. For example, it is not unusual to see a site plan review standard that states that surface parking should be designed to "minimize the visual impact of cars." To accomplish this objective, a further guideline should be added stating that parking lots will be located toward the rear or sides of structures. However, the success of large box users and multiple movie-screen theater complexes, for example, may very well depend upon patrons being able to park conveniently in front of the store or theater. It simply may not be commercially practical to locate parking at the rear or sides of the principal structures. Instead, in order to soften the visual impact of parking located in the front of the principal buildings without blocking the visual location of the parking fields, the parking islands within the parking areas and the parking perimeter can be landscaped.

Also, particularly for commercial uses, the site plan reviewer should be prepared to listen to the commercial user's evaluation of the amount of parking needed. Frequently, the number of parking spaces required for a particular type of commercial use may be excessive. Provided the applicant can demonstrate the adequacy of the proposed number of parking spaces, the objective should be, where possible, to limit the amount of impervious surface area on the site.

### [2] Loading

Loading areas should be located so as to minimize conflicts with vehicles and pedestrians. This means that, to the extent possible, they should be separated from parking areas. Loading docks should be located in relation to service roads and away from major streets and public view.

### [3] Circulation

The key concerns regarding circulation should be that vehicular and pedestrian circulation on a site will be safe, efficient, and convenient for drivers and pedestrians. This means that entrance driveways should provide for adequate stacking of traffic. Traffic counts should determine whether deceleration lanes are necessary. Parking areas should be designed to discourage their use as through-access drives. Directional signage should be simple and legible so as to facilitate safe driving. Depending upon the type of use or combination of uses, a pedestrian circulation plan, separate from vehicular circulation, may be appropriate. However, in certain cases, encouraging pedestrian activity where the use is predominantly oriented to motor vehicles may not enhance safety. Of course, barrier-free pathways to accommodate the handicapped must be provided. In the case of mixed use (commercial/residential) projects, the circulation should be designed to offer occupants of the residential component convenient access to the commercial component. Also, access to the commercial portion should be designed so as to discourage patrons from cutting through the residential portion of the site.

## [4]  Lighting

The lighting plan should be reviewed primarily to ensure that on-site exterior lighting will illuminate sufficiently to provide safe nighttime activity without intruding unnecessarily onto adjacent properties, particularly residential areas. This means that the illumination should be focused on vehicle driveways, pedestrian pathways, building entrances, and property addresses. Light fixtures should be consistent with the building scale and use of the site. This element of site plan design is frequently addressed through performance standards that give the developer a number of alternatives.

## [5]  Grading

Grading should take into account the existing topography and other natural resources on the site. In other words, if there are reasonable alternatives, efforts should be made to preserve the site's natural landforms. Slopes and berms that will be visible from public areas should be designed to appear as naturalistic forms. Where feasible, the design and location of drainage devices should be integrated with the grading plan in order to minimize adverse visual impacts.

## [6]  Landscaping

Insofar as practicable, the existing landscape should be preserved, minimizing tree and vegetation removal. Landscaping should be used on the site to visually screen storage areas, machinery, service areas, truck-loading areas, utility buildings, and structures; enhance architectural features; block noise generated by intense-use areas; generally shade and cool the area; and direct wind movements.

## [7]  Buffers

Buffering should be used to provide a logical transition to the existing or permitted uses on adjacent areas, recognizing that the scale of proposed structures for a site cannot always be compatible with those of adjacent uses because of the nature of the use permitted on the site. In those instances, the scale of such structures can be made more compatible with those of adjacent uses through the use of buffering elements.

## [8]  Open Space

Open space on the site should be designed to relate to the natural characteristics of the site so as to complement and, where possible, enhance their scenic and functional qualities.

## [9]  Utilities

The proposed development must have adequate water supply and sewage disposal systems. Water lines must be of a sufficient size to provide adequate flow for fire hydrants. The development must also be provided with adequate access to gas and electricity where applicable. The lines must be constructed to meet the technical standards established by the appropriate utility company.

## [10]   Stormwater and Drainage

The site development plan should demonstrate that adequate measures have been taken to prevent pollution of surface or groundwater, to minimize erosion and sedimentation, to prevent changes in groundwater levels and increased rates of runoff, and to minimize potential for flooding. The design of drainage should maximize groundwater recharge and not increase the rate of runoff at the boundaries of the site. In particular, parking areas and driveways should be sufficiently drained so as to prevent ponding.

## § 5.09   Practice Tips

### [1]   Do Not Attempt to Implement Zoning Through Site Plan Review

As emphasized in the beginning of this chapter, site plan review is not zoning and should not be used to address issues within the scope of zoning regulations. It should not be used to require changes to uses permitted by right under the zoning ordinance, or to alter fixed dimensional standards controlling height, size, setbacks, etc.

### [2]   Consider Carefully Whether to Incorporate Site Plan Review in the Zoning Ordinance

There is the danger that site plan review can be used to go beyond its ministerial function and expand discretionary review of standards that are fixed by the zoning ordinance or subject to alteration only through other established procedures (e.g., variance or planned development). Therefore, it is often preferable to make site plan review a free-standing ordinance. That means, however, that the separate site plan review ordinance must have separate administrative provisions, definitions, standards, and appeal provisions that must be consistent with zoning and other ordinance provisions. Because the necessary consistency between separate ordinances can sometimes be difficult, some communities may prefer to integrate the site plan review process with zoning. Care must then be taken to define clearly the limited scope of items subject to site plan review, and to ensure that its ministerial decision-making level is not tied to other decision-making steps that involve discretion.

### [3] Staff Must Be Competent to Do Site Plan Review

A community that decides to implement site plan review must make sure that it has or hires competent staff to do the job properly. At first, it may be wiser to retain the services of a consultant to establish internal procedures, train staff, and perform the first reviews until the process works properly.

# CHAPTER 6

# Planned Unit Developments

## Scope of Chapter

## § 6.01  Introduction

How the planned unit development is viewed depends on who does the viewing: The architect talks about cluster housing when he says PUD—cluster housing and the *preservation* of natural features. . . . The developer considers the higher density when he talks about PUDs. . . . The municipality sees the amenities furnished at the developer's expense, higher assessed value, and, finally, the preservation of a considerable

> portion of the land . . . and, thus available to absorb
> storm water and provide recreation.
>
> —Shepard D. Robinson in
> *Land Use Guide for Builders,*
> *Developers and Planners (1977)*

By departing from the assumptions and requirements of traditional zoning practice, the planned unit development does, indeed, provide a framework of opportunity through which both government and the private sector can derive site-specific land use and development design solutions. It was originally conceived as an innovative land use regulatory technique for projects in which the primary land use was residential. However, planned unit developments have broad application to any type or mix of land uses, whether residential, commercial, or industrial. This chapter explains the essential features of the PUD, defines the threshold legal issues that must be addressed when utilizing a PUD, and addresses the practical issues from the perspectives of both the developer and the government.

## § 6.02 Purposes of Planned Unit Development

Not every state statute that authorizes the use of the planned unit development device necessarily explains the purposes of this device. Those that do are relatively sparse in their explanation. For example, the New Jersey statute merely states that the PUD is a means to incorporate "the best features of design and relate the type, design and layout to residential, commercial, and industrial and recreational development to the particular site."[1] By contrast, the purpose statement in the Nebraska statute is an example of PUD enabling legislation that provides a more useful explanation of the purposes of planned unit developments:

> The purpose of [a planned unit development] ordinance shall be to permit flexibility in the regulation of land development, to encourage innovation in land use and variety in design, layout, and type of struc-

---

[1] N.J. Stat. § 40–27–4 (1993).

tures constructed, to achieve economy and efficiency in the use of land, natural resources, energy, and the provision of public services and utilities, to encourage the preservation and provision of useful open space, and to provide improved housing, employment, or shopping opportunities particularly suited to the needs of an area.[2]

Whether or not aided by the more comprehensive statement of purpose found in a statute such as Nebraska's, it is not surprising that communities have adopted local ordinances establishing PUD approval processes to achieve a wide range of stated purposes.

The purpose statements of local PUD ordinances reflect a wide range of objectives. The following are "purpose" statements from a sampling of ordinances around the country:

(1)   To provide flexibility in architectural design, placement, and clustering of buildings; use of open areas and outdoor living areas; provision of circulation facilities and parking; and related site and design considerations;

(2)   To encourage the conservation of natural features;

(3)   To provide for efficient use of public services and improvements;

(4)   To encourage and preserve opportunities for energy-efficient development;

(5)   To promote attractive and functional business environments, which are compatible with surrounding development, in nonresidential zones;

(6)   To promote an attractive and safe living environment in residential zones;[3]

---

[2] R.R.S. Neb. § 19–4401 (1994).
[3] Portland, Oregon PUD ordinance (Ch. 33.269).

(7)   To promote the use of land in a socially and economically desirable manner;[4]

(8)   To use for development in areas which include steep slopes in such a manner to achieve minimum disturbance of the natural terrain and vegetation[5]

(9)   To facilitate use of the most advantageous construction techniques in the development of land for residential and other secondary uses;

(10)  To encourage the provision of dwellings within the means of families of low and moderate income[6]

(11)  To accommodate preferred high-density land uses which could produce detrimental effects on neighboring properties if not strictly controlled as to location and design;

(12)  To ensure high standards in the layout, design, and construction of commercial developments[7]

(13)  To provide an opportunity and incentive to the developer to achieve excellence in physical, social, and economic planning.[8]

Viewed from economic and practical standpoints, it is apparent that some of these purpose statements, particularly those that include social planning objectives, cannot realistically be achieved through a PUD, let alone zoning. Such objectives raise community expectations of what can be achieved through the PUD that are not supported by the economic realities of the real estate market.

---

[4] Novi, Minnesota PUD ordinance (Art. 27 of Municipal Code).

[5] San Diego, California PUD ordinance (Sec. 101.0900).

[6] Fairfax County, Virginia PDH Planned Development Housing Regulations (Sec. 6–101).

[7] Fairfax County, Virginia PDC Planned Development Commercial District Regulations (Sec. 6–201).

[8] Fairfax County, Virginia PRC Planned Residential Community District Regulations (Sec. 6–301).

## § 6.03  Statutory Definitions of Planned Unit Development

The essential purpose of planned unit developments—to encourage innovation in design and construction through flexibility—determines, to a certain extent, the way in which this development technique is defined. But it is interesting to compare the definitions used in different jurisdictions. The most noteworthy of these definitions, as found in state statutes, are set out in the chart on the next page.

---

### DEFINITIONS OF PLANNED UNIT DEVELOPMENT IN STATE STATUTES

#### Colorado

An area of land, controlled by one or more landowners, to be developed under unified control or unified plan of development for a number of dwelling units, commercial, educational, recreational, or industrial uses, or any combination of the foregoing, the plan for which does not correspond in lot size, bulk, or type of use, density, lot coverage, open space, or other restriction to the existing land use regulations.

#### Idaho

An area of land in which a variety of residential, commercial, industrial, and other land uses are provided for under single ownership or control. Planned unit development ordinances may include, but are not limited to, requirements for minimum area, permitted uses, ownership, common open space, utilities, density, arrangements of land uses on a site, and permit processing. Planned unit developments may be permitted under processing for special use permits as defined in this chapter. Permits for planned unit developments may be granted following the notice and hearing procedures provided in section 67–6512, Idaho Code.

---

**DEFINITIONS OF PLANNED UNIT
DEVELOPMENT IN STATE STATUTES (cont'd)**

### Massachusetts

A mixed use development on a plot of land containing a minimum of the lesser of sixty thousand square feet or five times the minimum lot size of the zoning district, but of such larger size as an ordinance or bylaw may specify, in which a mixture or residential, open space, commercial, industrial or other uses and a variety of building types are determined to be sufficiently advantageous to render it appropriate to grant special permission to depart from the normal requirements of the district to the extent authorized by the ordinance or bylaw. Such open space, if any, may be situated to promote and protect maximum solar access within the development.

### Maryland

A development comprised of a combination of land uses or varying intensities of the same land use in accordance with an integrated plan that provides flexibility in land use design approved by the local jurisdiction with at least 20% of the land permanently dedicated to open space. Zoning approvals for a planned unit development may require the approval of a schematic or other development plan at the time of zoning.

### Montana

A land development project consisting of residential clusters, industrial parks, shopping centers, or office building parks that comprise a planned mixture of land uses built in a prearranged relationship to each other and having open space and community facilities in common ownership or use.

### Nebraska

Any development of a parcel of land or an aggregation of contiguous parcels of land to be developed as a single project which proposes density transfers, density increases, and mixing of land uses, or any combination thereof, based upon the application of site planning criteria.

### Nevada

An area of land controlled by a landowner, which is to be developed as a single entity for one or more planned unit residential developments, one or more public, quasi-public, commercial or industrial areas, or both.

> **DEFINITIONS OF PLANNED UNIT
> DEVELOPMENT IN STATE STATUTES (cont'd)**
>
> **New Jersey**
> An area with a specified minimum contiguous acreage of 10 acres
> or more to be developed as a single entity according to a plan,
> containing one or more residential clusters or planned unit resi-
> dential developments and one or more public, quasi-public, com-
> mercial or industrial areas in such ranges of ratios of nonresiden-
> tial uses to residential uses as shall be specified in the zoning
> ordinance.

## § 6.04    Constitutionality of Technique

The planned unit development technique has been challenged on general constitutional grounds, and on statutory
grounds, where there is no enabling statute that expressly
authorizes the technique. The most apparent statutory
authority problem that the PUD presents is that it permits
flexibility in the mix of uses and location of density within
the unified development. It has been argued that this flexible approach to the combination of uses or transfer of
density within the development site or PUD district is not
authorized under the Standard State Zoning Enabling Act
or the state zoning enabling acts of most states. These
acts typically include the requirement that each zoning
district contain *uniform* zoning regulations for each class
or kind of building, from which it has been inferred that
each zoning district must be limited to a single use
category.

However, the real concern behind this *uniformity requirement* in most zoning enabling statutes was that the
zoning regulations should impact, equally and impartially,
owners whose land is similarly situated. The concern was
not to prevent different regulations from being applied in
the same zoning district to owners who choose to develop
their property under differing circumstances.

For this reason, courts have not interpreted the uniformity requirement to prohibit the essential features of the

PUD. For example, one court rejected a uniformity objection to a PUD ordinance that allowed for clustering of the density on the site, stating that the PUD ordinance "accomplishes uniformity because the option is open to all developers."[9] Even though this option was not expressly stated in the state zoning enabling statute, the court concluded that the PUD ordinance "reasonably advance[d] the purposes of the state zoning legislative purposes, namely, to secure open spaces, prevent overcrowding and undue concentration and to promote the general welfare."[10]

---

[9] Chrinko v. South Brunswick Tp. Planning Bd., 77 N.J. Super. 594, 187 A.2d 221, 225 (Law Div. 1963).
[10] *Id.*

**THE FAR SIDE**          By GARY LARSON

**Prairie dog developers**

Although the PUD is intended to be flexible, the standards governing such aspects of the development as permitted land uses, densities, access, circulation, and site design must be sufficiently definite to avoid violating the nondelegation doctrine or creating the void for vagueness problems discussed in Chapter 1.[11] If the PUD ordinance contains standards that guide the exercise of discretion and allow for meaningful judicial review, the courts will

---

[11] *See* Ch. 1, Sec. 1.04[2], *supra.*

uphold it.[12] One court in upholding a PUD ordinance explained these concerns as follows:

> [T]he same flexibility which is the primary virtue of a PUD ordinance also results in a loss of certainty and a concomitant concern with the misuse or abuse of discretionary authority. Consequently, courts have generally required that standards be incorporated into a planned unit development ordinance in order to protect against arbitrary site action in violation of the right to due process of law. . . . Such a requirement, properly applied, does not undercut a desirable degree of flexibility, but serves to ensure that a City Council's enhanced discretion under a planned unit development ordinance will be guided by proper considerations, and that a benchmark for measuring the Council's action will be available in case of subsequent judicial review. We conclude that a planned unit development ordinance must contain sufficient standards to serve these twin goals.[13]

What if the city council reserves for itself the authority to approve or disapprove PUDs and does not delegate that authority to an independent administrative body? In a Florida case,[14] the court, although recognizing the legislative prerogative of a city council in matters of zoning policy, held nevertheless that there must be sufficient standards to guide the city council's exercise of discretion. The challenged PUD ordinance contained the following provision:

---

[12] Tri-State Generation & Transmission Co. v. City of Thornton, 647 P.2d 670 (Colo. 1982); Zanin v. Iacono, 198 N.J. Super. 490, 487 A.2d 780 (Law Div. 1984); Appeal of Moreland, 1972 OK 87, 497 P.2d 1287 (Okla. 1972). *But see* Harnett v. Board of Zoning, Subdivision and Building Appeals, 350 F. Supp. 1159 (D.V.I. 1972); City of Miami v. Save Brickell Ave., Inc., 426 So. 2d 1100 (Fla. Dist. Ct. App. 3d Dist. 1983).

[13] Tri-State Generation and Transmission Co. v. City of Thornton, 647 P.2d 670, 678 (Colo. 1982).

[14] City of Miami v. Save Brickell Ave., Inc., 426 So. 2d 1100 (Fla. Dist. Ct. App. 3d Dist. 1983).

(3) USES, DENSITY, OPEN SPACE AND FLOOR
AREA RATIO AND OTHER REGULATIONS

Within a Planned Area Development, any principal
and accessory use, density, open space and floor area
ratio and other regulations is [sic] permitted which is
already permitted in the existing zoning district or
districts *or PAD Districts as may be determined by the
City Commission pursuant to a PAD application*, in
which such Planned Area Development is located. The
distribution of these permitted principal and accessory uses, density, open space and floor area ratio,
and other regulations or deviations therefrom, *shall
not be affected by existing zoning regulations, but shall
be subject to the approval of the City Commission.*
Deviations from the permitted principal and accessory uses, density, open space and floor area ratio and
other regulations may be granted upon approval of a
PAD Conditional Use Application by the City
Commission. Criteria to be considered by the City
Commission for approval of deviations as described
above *may include but are not limited to:* . . . .[15]

Because the criteria listed in the PUD ordinance were
permissive and not mandatory ("may include but are not
limited to"), and because the wording of the ordinance allowed the City Commission to completely disregard the
listed criteria and use other criteria or none at all, the
court held that the PUD ordinance lacked sufficient standards for guidance and control of the Miami City
Commission. It therefore held that the ordinance was "an
unpermitted, arbitrary and unfettered delegation of
authority to itself."[16]

## § 6.05   Effect of PUD on Comprehensive Plan

Because of its flexibility as a land use approval mechanism, the PUD may create a conflict with the formal land
use and intensity designations of a comprehensive land
use plan. The extent to which such a conflict is fatal

---

[15] *Id.* at 1104–05. (Emphasis in opinion.)
[16] *Id.*

depends upon whether the comprehensive plan in the particular jurisdiction is considered advisory only, or whether state legislation mandates that local zoning regulations be consistent with the comprehensive plan. In those states in which the comprehensive plan is advisory only, the courts have rejected arguments that approval of a PUD was invalid because it was inconsistent with the comprehensive plan or amounted to spot zoning.[17] In states where the consistency requirement is mandated, the validity of a PUD that is inconsistent with an adopted comprehensive plan has been adjudicated only recently.[18]

However, the zoning enabling legislation of most states speaks of zoning "in accordance with a comprehensive plan." Therefore, it is important to note some earlier cases involving use of the PUD as a "floating zone"[19] where the courts have found a proposed PUD to be inconsistent with the comprehensive *zoning* plan. For example, in one Pennsylvania case,[20] a township amended its general zoning ordinance to provide for a floating industrial zoning district, the provisions of which required that any proposed development be constructed on a minimum of twenty-five acres pursuant to an overall plan, including a single architectural scheme, common landscaping, parking, and other requirements. Because the court found that the floating zone was not adopted "in accordance with a comprehensive plan" and its provisions appeared to give the town-

---

[17] Moore v. City of Boulder, 29 Colo. App. 248, 484 P.2d 134 (1971); Town of North Hempstead v. Village of North Hills, 38 N.Y.2d 334, 379 N.Y.S.2d 792, 342 N.E.2d 566, 80 A.L.R.3d 87 (1975); Cheney v. Village 2 at New Hope, Inc., 429 Pa. 626, 241 A.2d 81 (1968); Wiggers v. Skagit County, 23 Wash. App. 207, 596 P.2d 1345 (Div. 1 1979).

[18] *See, e.g.,* Bridger Canyon Property Owners' Ass'n, Inc. v. Planning and Zoning Com'n for Bridger Canyon Zoning Dist. and 360 Ranch Corp., 270 Mont. 160, 890 P.2d 1268 (1995), reh'g denied, (Mar. 30, 1995) (holding conditionally approved PUD development to be inconsistent with the General Plan, which is part of the adopted Bridger Canyon Development Pattern). *See also* Mont. Code Ann. § 76–1-605 and §§ 76–2-101 through 76–2-112.

[19] The floating zone technique is defined and discussed in Ch. 4, *supra.*

[20] Eves v. Zoning Bd. of Adjustment of Lower Gwynedd Tp., 401 Pa. 211, 164 A.2d 7 (1960).

ship supervisors the right to exercise discretion in a way not provided in the state's zoning enabling legislation for townships, the court found this new PUD-type zoning scheme objectionable.[21] The Pennsylvania Supreme Court has since reversed this position.[22]

However, in this earlier decision, the court added several "secondary" reasons why it found the zoning scheme invalid. These reasons, while seeming parochial in light of modern zoning practice, are noteworthy for two reasons. To the extent that such a floating PUD is proposed in states with no more than zoning enabling legislation based on the original Standard State Zoning Enabling Act and where the local government, such as a township, is not endowed with significant zoning powers, these arguments may still arise. The court stated:

> [The zoning scheme] would produce situations in which the personal predilections of the supervisors or the affluence or political power of the applicant would have a greater part in determining rezoning applications than the suitability of the land for a particular use from an overall community point of view. Further, while it may not be readily apparent with a minimum acreage requirement of 25 acres, "flexible selective zoning" carries evils akin to "spot zoning," for in theory it allows piecemeal placement of relatively small acreage areas in differently zoned districts. Finally, because of the absence of a simultaneous delineation of the boundaries of the new "F-1" district, no notice of the true nature of his vicinity or its limitations is afforded the property owner or the prospective property owner. . . . [T]he zoning ordinance and its accompanying zoning maps should nevertheless at any given time reflect the current planned use of the community's land so as to afford as much notice as possible.[23]

---

[21] *Id.* at 10–11.

[22] *See* Cheney v. Village 2 at New Hope, Inc., 429 Pa. 626, 241 A.2d 81 (1968).

[23] *Eves*, 164 A.2d at 11.

Because more limitations can be imposed on development through the floating zone technique more analogous to a special exception, some courts have utilized this rationale to uphold the implementation of a PUD through the floating zone technique.[24] These courts conclude that because the PUD involves project-wide planning considerations, if the proposed density is consistent with the density in the comprehensive plan for the area, it can be approved despite the fact that the PUD will allow uses not identified in the comprehensive plan.[25]

## § 6.06  Proper Delegation of Authority to Approve PUDs

The proper delegation of PUD approval authority is a critical concern of both the developer and the local government. As a general rule, where planned unit development regulations require a *rezoning* to a PUD district—a "legislative" act in most jurisdictions—a PUD rezoning approval requires action by the city council or other local legislative body. Some communities provide that the local legislative body first establish the PUD district by legislative action, leaving the approval of the details of the PUD development to an administrative body such as the planning commission. This approach was upheld under the typical state zoning enabling act in a Pennsylvania case,[26] where the PUD regulations sufficiently spell out the development standards. In that case, the borough council rezoned a tract to a planned development district under an ordinance that specified permissible uses, maximum densities and heights, and minimum distances between buildings, but delegated to the plan-

---

[24] *See* Ch. 4, Sec. 4.03, *supra.*

[25] Sheridan v. Planning Bd. of City of Stamford, 159 Conn. 1, 266 A.2d 396 (1969); Moore v. City of Boulder, 29 Colo. App. 248, 484 P.2d 134 (1971); Beall v. Montgomery County Council, 240 Md. 77, 212 A.2d 751 (1965).

[26] Cheney v. Village 2 at New Hope, Inc., 429 Pa. 626, 241 A.2d 81 (1968).

ning commission the authority to approve the details of the development. The court upheld this delegation of decision-making authority under the rationale that the flexibility inherent in the PUD process dictates that the planning commission or a similar administrative body is best equipped to review the details of a development plan.[27] The court's reasoning is persuasive:

> There is no doubt that it would be statutorily permissible for the council itself to pass a PUD ordinance and simultaneous zoning map amendment so specific that no details would be left for any administrator. . . . But what would be the practical effect of such an ordinance? One of the most attractive features of Planned Unit Development is its flexibility; the chance for the builder and the municipality to sit down together and tailor a development to meet the specific needs of the community and the requirements of the land on which it is to be built. But all this would be lost if the Legislature let the planning cement set before any developer could happen upon the scene to scratch his own initials in that cement.[28]

Of course, if the planning commission or other administrative body is delegated the authority to approve the actual district, then the courts have invalidated the PUD ordinance because that is an improper delegation of the local government's legislative authority under the zoning enabling act.[29]

On the other hand, the PUD could be defined as a type of conditional use or special use. Then there is the more difficult question of whether, as a special or conditional use, the PUD can be approved by an administrative body. The answer to this question depends in large part upon the law of each state jurisdiction and whether, by statute or judicial decisions, the special or conditional use is deemed a legislative decision. Generally, if the PUD

---

[27] *Id.* at 88.
[28] *Id.* at 87.
[29] Lutz v. City of Longview, 83 Wash. 2d 566, 520 P.2d 1374 (1974).

conditional use is characterized statutorily or judicially as a "rezoning" rather than the execution of an existing zoning law, the conditional use will require adoption by the local legislative body.

Even if PUD approval authority is delegated by the local legislative body to itself, it does not necessarily mean that a court will conclude that the PUD approval process is legislative. That characterization depends upon the extent of change made in the zoning regulations. For example, in one Ohio case,[30] utilizing PUD floating zone provisions, a developer submitted a development plan proposing multifamily and commercial uses in a single-family zone. The board of county commissioner's approval of the plan was subsequently subjected to a referendum which, under state law, provides voters with the opportunity to reject any amendment to the zoning code adopted by the local legislative body. The court employed a "nature of the action" test to decide whether the board's action was legislative or administrative, explaining that creation of law is legislative action, while execution of preexisting law is administrative action. It held that the board's action was the "functional equivalent" of a legislative action because the board's action altered the zoning classification of a significant section of the township. Therefore, the referendum was appropriate.[31]

## § 6.07 Validity of Mandatory PUD Districts

Can a local government *impose* a PUD on a parcel of land? There are few cases on this issue. At least one court, however, has invalidated such an attempt. There, a county initiated a rezoning to a PUD and established in the process a detailed site plan showing uses, buildings, and densities. The court held that planned unit development is

---

[30] Peachtree Development Co. v. Paul, 67 Ohio St. 2d 345, 21 Ohio Op. 3d 217, 423 N.E.2d 1087 (1981).

[31] *Id. See also* Todd Mart, Inc. v. Town Bd. of Town of Webster, 49 A.D.2d 12, 370 N.Y.S.2d 683 (4th Dep't 1975).

a voluntary procedure designed to provide flexibility not possible under the traditional zoning district, but it cannot be imposed on an owner who may want to rezone.[32]

## § 6.08 Proper Procedural Steps and Considerations

Obviously it is in the interests of both the developer and the local government to ensure that no significant procedural mistakes are made in the approval process. Deficiencies that have invalidated the approval of a planned unit development include lack of proper notice,[33] lack of sufficient findings by the legislative body or local planning officials,[34] or where the specific procedure for authorizing the type of PUD project is not authorized under the zoning ordinance.[35] However, concern by the local government that the market may be too weak to support a proposed PUD cannot be the basis for imposing a condition that a developer demonstrate that a sufficient market exists for the type, size and character of the PUD development. One court has held such proof of market-sufficiency to be an invalid requirement, unrelated to the general welfare.[36] A municipality that has this concern will manage to address it indirectly, if not directly, during the review process, and the developer should be prepared to respond to the issue.

After a PUD is approved, additional procedural steps may be imposed on the developer by the local government to ensure that the project is completed and approved in a timely manner.

---

[32] Porpoise Point Partnership v. St. Johns County, 532 So. 2d 727 (Fla. Dist. Ct. App. 5th Dist. 1988).

[33] Barrie v. Kitsap County, 84 Wash. 2d 579, 527 P.2d 1377 (1974). *See also* "Report of Subcommittee of the American Bar Association Committee on Public Regulation of Land Use, Planned Unit Developments and Floating Zones," 7 Real Prop. Prob. & Trust J. 1, 63 (1972).

[34] Lund v. City of Tumwater, 2 Wash. App. 750, 472 P.2d 550 (Div. 2 1970).

[35] Millbrae Ass'n for Residential Survival v. City of Millbrae, 262 Cal. App. 2d 222, 69 Cal. Rptr. 251 (1st Dist. 1968).

[36] Soble Const. Co. v. Zoning Hearing Bd. of Borough of East Stroudsburg, 16 Pa. Commw. 599, 329 A.2d 912 (1974).

## § 6.09  Specter of Contract Zoning

The inherent give and take of the PUD process raises the specter of contract zoning, which is discussed in detail in Chapter 7.[37] Most courts, however, have upheld the PUD process in the face of contract zoning challenges.[38] An Illinois court explained it as follows:

> Since the overall aims of . . . [PUD] zoning cannot be accomplished without negotiations and because conferences are indeed mandated by the regulatory ordinance, the conduct of the . . . county cannot be read as contributing to contract zoning.[39]

Of relevance to this type of negotiation process, it is important for both local government officials and the developer to consider potential conflicts of interest and to act to avoid them before commencing the PUD approval process. A conflict of interest by a planning official could cause a PUD approval to be held invalid.[40]

---

[37] *See* Ch.7, Sec. 7.03, *infra.*
[38] *See* Scrutton v. Sacramento County, 275 Cal. App. 2d 412, 79 Cal. Rptr. 872 (3d Dist. 1969).
[39] Rutland Environmental Protection Ass'n v. Kane County, 31 Ill. App. 3d 82, 334 N.E.2d 215, 219 (2d Dist. 1975).
[40] *See* Dover Tp. Homeowners & Tenants Ass'n v. Dover Tp., 114 N.J. Super. 270, 276 A.2d 156 (App. Div. 1971). *But see* Webster Associates v. Town of Webster, 59 N.Y.2d 220, 464 N.Y.S.2d 431, 451 N.E.2d 189 (1983).

SPACIOUS SKIES

PURPLE MOUNTAIN MAJESTIES

MALLS, MOTELS & FAST FOOD

GAS   MOTEL   HOT DOGS   BURGER QUICK

AMBER WAVES OF GRAIN

Reprinted with permission of Henry R. Martin © 1995.

## § 6.10   Process-Based PUD Versus Standards-Based PUD

A threshold consideration for a local government wishing to adopt a PUD ordinance is the extent to which the PUD regulations should be driven by the development standards in the base zoning districts or contain separate standards. If the objective of the PUD regulations is primarily to provide a means to apply existing standards with flexibility, then the PUD regulations are more *process*-oriented, leaving to the decision maker, usually the legislative body, the discretion to modify the applicable base zoning district regulations on a case-by-case basis. But there is an inherent danger in this approach. The decision maker, without clear rules for when and to what extent to modify the base district standards, may arrive at decisions guided by no particular criteria and may produce inconsistencies between projects that undermine the credibility of the process. The alternative, namely, placing most of the standards in the PUD ordinance, can avoid the potential pitfalls of a process-only PUD ordinance. However, care must be taken in the drafting of standards to provide sufficient flexibility in the application of those standards to ensure that the PUD ordinance itself does not function, in effect, as a rigid, base zoning district. Also, if the PUD standards do not address a certain aspect or feature of development, it is important to provide a "default" provision that references the base zoning district standards for features not addressed specifically in the PUD regulations. In the case of residential PUDs, adopted after the base zoning districts were established, it may be advisable to substitute the PUD standards for the base zoning districts, since the PUD standards may best reflect current zoning policy and market expectations for residential subdivisions.

## § 6.11 Approval of PUD as Zoning District or as Conditional Use

The decision whether to implement the PUD either as a new zoning district in the form of an "overlay" district or a separate base zoning district, or as a type of conditional use, depends upon such considerations as whether the local community wishes to limit the PUD to relatively large minimum-size parcels, and whether the particular state jurisdiction characterizes conditional use approvals as legislative in nature, requiring a final decision by the local legislative body. If the PUD is to be limited to large parcels of a certain minimum size, it is more appropriate to utilize an overlay district concept to reflect the PUD boundaries on the zoning map. If parcel size is not a consideration, then whether the district approach or conditional use approach is preferable depends in large part upon whether the local legislative body prefers to retain final decision-making authority on PUDs or to delegate it to an administrative body such as the planning commission. If PUD approvals can be delegated under state law to the administrative body, then the administrative body's decision will require certain procedural steps, including findings of fact, which is a more rigorous process. If PUD approval is kept at the legislative level and designed to be a true legislative decision, it can potentially give the community more flexibility to review and approve PUDs.

## § 6.12   Regional Planned Unit Development

By virtue of their size, large tracts of land can be well suited for treatment as a planned unit development. There is no provision in PUD enabling legislation that would prevent development of such large tracts of land as a PUD. Nevertheless, in recent years, often at the developer's initiative, specific ordinances authorizing the concept of a "regional" planned unit development, or RPUD, have been adopted in some communities. These RPUD ordinances allow for a broad range of uses on large tracts of land over an extended time horizon, recognizing that uncertainties in the real estate market as to the ultimate development of uses on large tracts require a flexible approach. For example, one Illinois community adopted the following statement of purposes and objectives for its RPUD ordinance:

> The purpose of the regional planned unit development is to encourage and allow more creative, flexible and imaginative design for land developments than is possible under the more conventional zoning regulations. The regional planned unit development also provides for more efficient use of the land and thus results in more economical land development consistent with the preservation of natural site qualities, better urban amenities, and a higher quality project, all in general conformity with the goals and planning objectives of the Comprehensive Plan of the Village existing as of the date of approval of the

227

conceptual land use plan by the Village Board of Trustees.

Regional planned unit developments are permitted only for large tracts of land having unique site characteristics for which it is possible to determine, at the time of application, a broad range of possible uses. Even though uncertainties surrounding the development of uses on the site and on adjacent properties and the anticipated duration of development may make it difficult to determine the specific location of application, the procedures and standards set forth herein are intended to afford the corporate authorities an opportunity to review each proposed conceptual RPUD zoning lot's preliminary and final plan to assure that it meets or promotes the following criteria and objectives: [Text Omitted]

The regional planned unit development is intended to provide for projects each of which may incorporate a single type or a variety of related uses which are planned and developed as a unit. Such development may consist of conventionally subdivided lots to be sold, unsubdivided single ownership, separate condominium ownership of structures, or other ownership methods, and shall provide for development by means of RPUD zoning lot, preliminary and/or final development plans which establish the location and extent of the uses within the regional planned unit development in keeping with the purpose of the conceptual plan.

A regional planned unit development may depart from strict conformance with the required density, dimension, area, height, bulk, use and other regulations for the standard zoning districts and other provisions of this Article and the other codes and other ordinances of the Village to the extent specified in the documents authorizing the regional planned unit development or to the extent specified in any ordinance or resolution

approving a conceptual, RPUD zoning lot, preliminary or final plan.[41]

The key concept utilized in the RPUD ordinance is the
"Conceptual Plan" which "allows for approval of an overall
land use concept without the necessity of anticipating
long-range markets or preparing precise plans for un-
known quantities of development."[42] This type of plan
enables an owner of a portion of the RPUD to obtain approval from the village of a conceptual site plan, called a
"RPUD zoning lot plan," so long as the lot plan is consistent with the conceptual plan for the RPUD. Following its
approval, the RPUD zoning lot plan may be developed in
phases, with submittal of preliminary and final plans. But
there is still considerable flexibility at this lot plan level.
The village ordinance provides:

> An approved RPUD zoning lot plan shall constitute
> an expression of an applicant's intentions with re-
> spect to the development of the RPUD zoning lot. Such
> plan, however, shall not be binding upon the ap-
> plicant, the owners of the RPUD zoning lot or the
> RPUD zoning lot itself insofar as the use of land,
> layout of buildings, construction of streets or roads, or
> other matters depicted on the RPUD zoning lot are
> concerned. It is anticipated that an RPUD zoning lot
> plan will be revised and updated from time to time as
> the owners of the RPUD zoning lot determine with
> greater certainty the anticipated use and develop-
> ment of the various portions of the RPUD zoning lot.
> From time to time, the boundaries of an RPUD zon-
> ing lot may be changed, and an RPUD zoning lot may
> be increased or decreased in size, provided that: a) at
> no time shall the RPUD zoning lot consist of less than
> five (5) acres; b) at all times the developments
> constructed or to be constructed on the RPUD zoning
> lot, when taken as a whole, shall conform to the bulk
> regulations applicable to the regional planned unit

---

[41] Ch. 14, Art. A, Sec. 9–14A-1 of the Village of Woodridge, Illinois
Zoning Ordinance.
[42] *Id.* Sec. 9–14A-3B.

development (except to the extent that departures therefrom are authorized by the Village Board in the course of the RPUD zoning lot plan approval process or otherwise); and c) the general nature of the development originally anticipated to be constructed on the RPUD zoning lot is not being changed.[43]

Regional planned unit developments are authorized in the residential, office, research, and light industrial zoning districts as a special use.

## § 6.13  Essential Provisions of a PUD Ordinance

This section outlines essential provisions of a PUD ordinance and explains the rationale for including these provisions.

### [1]  Purpose Statement

It is important that the PUD ordinance include its own statement of purposes, consistent with the general purposes of the zoning ordinance. Although courts give little substantive weight to the "purpose" section of any ordinance, to the extent that greater discretionary authority is authorized to modify the standards of base zoning districts to achieve the purposes of a planned unit development, a tailored set of purpose statements will be to the benefit of both the government and the developer in supporting the design and intensity of the development that is approved.

### [2]  Zoning Districts and Uses Allowed

The PUD ordinance should define exactly in what zoning districts the PUD is allowed or, alternatively, those districts in which it is excluded. As for uses allowed in a PUD, the PUD ordinance should allow the same range of

---

[43] *Id.* Sec. 19–14A-3C.

permitted and conditional uses as allowed in the base zoning districts. This is consistent with one of the objectives of planned unit development regulations: to provide for a mixture of uses. The following are examples of alternative language provisions that could be used, depending upon whether the PUD is implemented as a conditional use or as a zoning district map amendment:

> A PUD may include all of the uses which are allowed in the applicable base zoning district by right or as a conditional use. *(Alternative No. 1)*

> *OR*

> Any permitted or conditional use authorized by this Zoning Ordinance may be included in an approved PUD district, consistent with the General Plan land use designation(s). *(Alternative No. 2)*

In communities that treat the PUD as a special type of conditional use and utilize a separate review procedure (e.g., preliminary and final development steps) for PUD approval, a frequent question is how to review and approve proposed uses for the PUD that are specifically classified as "conditional uses" in the zoning ordinance and that are proposed to be included in the PUD. In other words, what is the procedure for reviewing a specific conditional use when the conditional use is proposed at the time the PUD is approved or, alternatively, *after* the PUD has already been approved? If the specific conditional use is proposed at the time of the PUD application, it would seem unnecessarily redundant to review that use separately under the conditional use procedure, which typically requires a new public hearing. The reason is that if the PUD itself is a conditional use, the standards addressed under the PUD provisions are essentially the same as for a non-PUD conditional use, and may, in fact, require compliance with additional standards.

Similarly, it can be argued that once the PUD review and approval process is completed, that approval means that the potential impact of the PUD on the surrounding neighborhood has been addressed and the range of conditional uses that are permissible in the zoning district within which the PUD site is located should be permissible within the PUD. If a specific conditional use is then proposed to be added to the PUD site, it should require site plan review, but not a new, separate review and approval under the standard conditional use procedures. However, not all communities concur with this last point. For example, Salt Lake City has the following zoning provision, which is explicit about what happens when the specific conditional use is proposed as part of the PUD application and when it is proposed later:

> CONDITIONAL USE APPROVALS AND PLANNED DEVELOPMENTS. When a development is proposed as a planned development pursuant to the procedures in Section 27–14 and also includes an application for conditional use approval, the Planning Commission shall decide the planned development application and the conditional use application together. In the event that a new conditional use is proposed after a planned development has been approved pursuant to Section 27–13, the proposed conditional use shall be reviewed and approved, approved with conditions or disapproved under the standards set forth in Section 27–8 [Conditional Use Standards].[44]

In communities that define the PUD as a new district, requiring a zoning map amendment, the approach to the review and approval of conditional uses can be different. For example, the zoning ordinance of a Michigan township authorizes the establishment of a Planned Unit Development (PUD) District. A preliminary development plan must be submitted as part of the application to rezone the PUD district. The regulations then provide that subject to the procedures for review and approval of a development plan for the PUD district, the "permitted uses" include "[a]ny use as listed as either a permitted use *or a special use* in the B-1 Convenience Business District, B-2 General

_____

[44] Salt Lake City Code of Ordinances, Title 21A, Sec. 27–14.

Business District or the SC-1 Shopping Center District."[45] In effect, the special uses become uses permitted by right within the PUD district, so long as they are approved as part of the procedures for submittal and approval of a development plan for the PUD district.

### [3] Development Standards—Minimum Area and Density

### [a] Minimum Area

Generally, the advantages of a PUD, particularly the design flexibility it allows, are difficult to realize on a site less than one acre. However, there are instances when, because of specific site conditions, the ability to modify standards can make a proposed development economically viable. If a community decides to establish no minimum size for a PUD, it should have a means to reject a PUD proposal that is proposed as a means to achieve what otherwise would be appropriate through a variance procedure.[46] The following are some typical provisions:

> The minimum area of a PUD or PPD district shall be
> _____ ( ) contiguous acres. The city council may approve a PUD that contains less than _____ acres, but at least _____ ( ) acres, upon a finding that special site characteristics exist and the proposed land uses justify development of the property as a PUD. *(Alternative No. 1)*
>
> OR
>
> There are no minimum or maximum size limitations required for a PUD. *(Alternative No. 2)*

### [b] Residential Density

In jurisdictions that require zoning consistency with a comprehensive plan, or in communities that have elected

---

[45] Township of Fruitport, Michigan Zoning Ordinance, Ordinance No. 638, Sec. 16.187. (Emphasis added.)

[46] *See* discussion of zoning variances in Ch. 2, *supra*.

to require consistency with an adopted comprehensive plan, Alternative No. 1 below is most appropriate and would encompass the provisions of Alternative No. 2, which is appropriate in jurisdictions that do not have or impose a comprehensive plan requirement.

> The total number of dwelling units in a PUD shall not exceed the maximum number permitted by the general plan for the total area allocated to residential use. Dwelling units may be placed without regard to residential zoning district boundaries. *(Alternative No. 1)*
>
> *OR*
>
> If the PUD is located in more than one residential zoning district, the total number of units allowed in the PUD shall be calculated by adding up the number of units allowed by each zoning district, and dwelling units may be placed without regard to the residential zoning district boundaries. *(Alternative No. 2)*

### [c]  Nonresidential Density

A community must decide whether increased density will encourage the use of planned unit development for certain areas that would benefit from more careful review and appropriate modifications in applicable standards. That is a matter of zoning policy. The alternative provisions below reflect two zoning policy choices.

> The density allowed for a PUD established in a nonresidential district or districts shall be calculated by totaling the floor area ratios (FARs) allowed in each district. However, the FAR may be allocated throughout the PUD without regard to zoning district boundaries, unless specifically restricted by an overlay zone or other provisions of the zoning ordinance. *(Alternative No. 1)*
>
> *OR*
>
> The density allowed for a PUD established in a nonresidential district or districts may exceed the

total density allowed in the applicable zoning districts, in exchange for those public amenities defined in Section ____. (*Alternative No. 2*)

### [4] Development Standards—Height

Again, it is a question of zoning policy whether it should be possible to exceed base zoning district heights through a PUD. For nonresidential districts, it is appropriate in most cases to allow for an increase in height, subject to standards established through either a specific area plan or in exchange for provision of defined public amenities.

> *Residential District Height Provision:* The maximum height of buildings in a residential PUD shall be the maximum height permitted in the base zoning district. If the PUD is located in more than one residential zoning district, the maximum height allowed in the PUD shall not exceed the maximum height of the [most/least] restrictive district.

> *Nonresidential District Height Provision:* The maximum height of buildings in a nonresidential PUD shall be the height limit of the base zoning district, subject to such modification as may be approved by the [approval authority] pursuant to an approved development plan.

### [5] Development Standards—Open Space

There are a number of alternative ways to draft this particular development standard. As discussed in Section 6.02[4], the open space provision must be carefully considered in light of design objectives and recent case law.

### [6] Authority to Modify Regulations

The following provisions, when utilized in combination with the specific development standards discussed above,

235

allow for the balancing of flexibility with established standards:

> *Authority to Modify Regulations:* The [legislative body] shall have the authority in approving any planned unit development to change, alter, modify or waive any provisions of the zoning ordinance as they apply to the proposed planned unit development in order to achieve the purposes set forth in Section ____.

> *Limitation:* No change, alteration, modification or waiver authorized by Section ____ shall authorize a change in the uses permitted in any district or a modification with respect to any zoning district standard made specifically applicable to planned unit developments, unless such district regulations expressly authorize such a change, alteration, modification or waiver.

### [7]  Development Plan Approval Steps

The development plan approval process typically requires two, or three, approval steps: (1) a concept plan; (2) a preliminary development plan; or (3) a final development plan. The size of the local community, extent of development occurring, and the preferences of the development community are all factors that may determine whether a two- or three-step approval process works best. The concept plan step is the foundation of a three-step process and may be required or made optional.

### [8]  Procedures for Review and Approval

Most PUD ordinances either mandate or suggest that the applicant attend a *preapplication conference* prior to submitting a planned unit development application for approval. At the preapplication conference, the applicant typically meets with the planning staff, the zoning administrator, the chairman of the planning commission and, in some jurisdictions, the member of the city council in whose district the proposed planned unit development is located. The purpose of the conference is to enable the applicant to present the concept of the proposed planned unit development, and to discuss the procedures and standards for planned unit development approval. The preapplication conference is intended to facilitate the filing and consideration of a complete application.

The developer may be asked to provide certain information for the preapplication conference, such as (1) a site plan, (2) a plat of survey, (3) proposed elevations, (4) a narrative summary of proposal, and (5) a description of adjacent land uses and neighborhood characteristics. Following the conference, staff should be available to assist the developer in preparing any suggested modifications to the site plan that were discussed during the conference, and to assist the developer in the application procedure for the planned unit development. It is in the interests of both the developer and the planning staff to keep minutes of the preapplication conference. The PUD ordinance may provide that any representation made by any city official during the conference is not binding upon the City with respect to the application that the developer subsequently submits. But the basic understandings reflected in the minutes are important to guide the subsequent application process.

After the developer submits the formal PUD application, the zoning administrator should notify the developer of any deficiencies and/or modifications necessary to perfect the application. If a community wants to encourage the use of the PUD procedure, it should provide in its ordinance that all reviews of PUD applications will be given priority review.

Once the zoning administrator has determined that the PUD application is complete, a public hearing should be noticed and held by the planning commission on the application. The ordinance should provide that the commission make its recommendation to the legislative body within a reasonable number of days, unless an extension is requested by the developer. The legislative body, following its own hearing either approves, approves with conditions, or disapproves the planned unit development.

The structure of the application and review process may parallel either that of a zoning amendment, if the PUD results in a district zoning amendment, or that of a conditional use, if the PUD is treated as a special type of conditional use. From the developer's perspective, the potential uncertainties associated with the PUD process must be offset by flexibility toward design and efficient review procedures. If these attributes cannot be made part of the PUD process, the PUD process will fail to attract developers.

### [9] Adjustments to the Development Plan

Depending upon the size of a community and sophistication of its planning staff, the legislative body may wish to control the extent of any adjustment permitted after a planned unit development is approved. The following are provisions governing adjustments that are frequently included in PUD ordinances:

> *General Provision:* No alteration or amendment shall be made in the construction, development or use without a new application under the provisions of this ordinance; provided, however, that minor alterations may be made subject to written approval of the zoning administrator; and provided further, that the date for completion may be extended by the Plan Commission for good cause.

> *Minor Adjustments:* During build-out of the planned unit development, the Zoning Administrator may authorize minor adjustments to the approved Development Plan, when such adjustments appear necessary in light of technical or engineering considerations. Such minor adjustments shall be limited to the following:

> (1) Altering the location of any one structure or group of structures by not more than one-fourth of the distance shown on the approved Development Plan between such structure or structures, and any other structure or any vehicular circula-

tion element or any boundary of the site, whichever is less.

(2)  Altering the location of any circulation element by not more than one-fourth (1/4) of the distance shown on the approved Development Plan between such circulation element and any structure, whichever is less.

(3)  Altering the location of any open space by not more than twenty percent (20%).

(4)  Altering any final grade by not more than twenty percent (20%) of the originally planned grade.

(5)  Altering the types of landscaping elements and their arrangement within the required landscaping buffer area.

Such minor adjustments shall be consistent with the intent and purpose of the Ordinance and the Development Plan as approved pursuant to this Section, and shall be the minimum necessary to overcome the particular difficulty and shall not be approved if such adjustments would result in a violation of any standard or requirement of this Ordinance.

*Major Adjustments:* Any adjustment to the approved Development Plan not authorized as a minor adjustment above, shall be considered to be a major adjustment. The Plan Commission following notice to all property owners whose properties are located within two hundred fifty (250) feet of the planned unit development, may approve an application for a major adjustment to the Development Plan not requiring a modification of written conditions of approval or recorded easements upon finding that any changes in the plan as approved will be in substantial conformity with such Development Plan. If the Commission determines that a major adjustment is not in substantial conformity with the Final Development Plan as approved, then the Commission shall review the request in accordance with the procedures for approving a Preliminary Development Plan.

The foregoing "adjustment" provisions, from the local government's perspective, have the advantage of defining the specific range of discretion allowed by the zoning administrator. However, from the developer's perspective, two problems exist with the provisions. First, the language does not require the zoning administrator to make adjustments if the proposed adjustments satisfy the standards for minor adjustments. The local government should not hesitate to change the "Minor Adjustment" provision to read that the "Zoning Administrator *shall* authorize minor adjustments" since the extent of adjustments is defined and, if necessary for technical or engineering considerations, it only invites an abuse of discretion if the zoning administrator can hide behind the permissive "may."

The second problem from the developer's perspective is that everything not defined as a minor adjustment is, by definition, a major adjustment. Usually, if the local government carefully thinks through the essential categories or thresholds of what should be considered a "major" adjustment, there is no need for the type of catchall approach reflected in the sample provision. An alternative to this approach is to use the catchall phrase approach, in reverse, as follows:

*Major Changes:* Changes to a PUD zoning lot, preliminary or final plan involving increases in density, building height, the intensity of land use, or floor area ratios or which reduce proposed open space by more than ten percent (10%) or which change designated land uses may be approved only by submission of a new PUD zoning lot, preliminary or final plan and supporting data following the procedures.

*Minor Changes:* Minor changes to an approved PUD zoning lot, preliminary or final plan shall be any change not defined above as a major change. Minor changes to an approved PUD zoning lot, preliminary or final plan shall be subject to the prior approval of the Zoning Administrator.

The success of both of these "catchall" aproaches to PUD adjustments depends upon the competency and practical judgment of the staff that administers the PUD ordinance.

### [10] Amendments—Notice

Frequently overlooked in drafting PUD ordinances, particularly those that authorize the technique for use on large parcels, is the importance of being able to amend a *portion* of an approved PUD without having to give notice to all property owners within a radius of the entire PUD. This drafting failure can work to the detriment of both the local government and the developer by potentially triggering opposition to the amendment from property owners who are not in direct proximity to the PUD amendment area. Therefore, unless prohibited by state enabling legislation or case law, the PUD ordinance should include a provision that provides for more limited notice in the case of an amendment to only a portion of a PUD. The following type of provision should be included:

> In the event an application for a major change or a minor change to a conceptual plan is submitted to the corporate authorities for only a portion of the lands described by a conceptual plan, the notices which are to be published, sent or posted pursuant to the notice provisions of this ordinance shall be based upon the legal descriptions of the lands described by such application.

Both the developer's counsel and the local government's counsel should confirm the viability of this type of provision under their state law.

### § 6.14 Practice Tips

#### [1] Clearly State the Public Objectives of the PUD in the Ordinance

There is tremendous potential for the planned unit development to promote quality developments that reflect variety and public amenities. However, if the public objectives of the PUD are not articulated carefully in the ordinance, the purpose of flexibility is lost and the PUD mechanism can be perceived by the public as a concession to the developer rather than a means by which both the public and the private developer can achieve their respective objectives.

### [2] The PUD Must Have Good Design Standards

The PUD will not be perceived as a form of flexibility that leads to lower design standards if the standards themselves are clearly articulated in the PUD ordinance and are drafted by competent professionals.

### [3] The Community Must Have Adequate Skills and Resources to Utilize the PUD Successfully

It is a mistake for a community to utilize the PUD as a principal approval mechanism in its regulatory scheme if it does not have adequate staff skills and resources to administer the provisions. If the local government has competent professional design reviewers, the relaxation of rigid requirements can produce a better rather than a worse product. Similarly, these competent design reviewers on the government's side must be met by competent design professionals on the developer's side. Only if both the local government and the developer utilize competent design professionals can the PUD process work effectively.

### [4] Retain Certain Specific Standards in the PUD Ordinance in Order to Limit Administrative Discretion

One of the public objectives of a planned unit development, particularly when applied to a large-scale project, is to ensure that it relates appropriately to its surroundings. This objective can be achieved in significant respects if standards as to density or intensity of use are retained in the PUD provisions so that the focus of the PUD development plan review is the design of the overall project. Of course, adjustments in density or intensity of use can be provided for through the PUD provisions, but it is usually better for both the municipality and the developer if the extent of additional permissible density or intensity of use is defined up front.

**CHAPTER 7**

# Contract/Conditional Zoning and Development Agreements

## Scope of Chapter

## § 7.01   Introduction

Most recently, there has been brought before the courts the most ingenious technique of all: "contract zoning." Unlike the variance, the special permit, or the floating zone, contract zoning does not require

245

> the municipality to preannounce in its ordinance any
> of its intentions, however equivocal.
> —**Richard Babcock in** *The Zoning Game*

As observed in its infancy by Richard Babcock in the 1960s, "contract zoning" was a "ploy" by which local governments flaunted the standard zoning enabling act requirement that a community divide itself into districts and specify the rules of the game in advance. Unlike other less traditional techniques, such as the special permit or the floating zone whose ordinance provisions acknowledge that there is no certainty in their application, contract zoning, he suggested, subjects the developer to the whim of the particular local legislature regardless of what the zoning text says.[1]

In the years since Babcock's observation, the concept of "contract zoning" has become intertwined with another concept—"conditional zoning." Both terms refer to rezoning decisions that in one way or another are tied to explicit or implicit government/private party agreements. Those courts that hold a jaundiced view of such arrangements (and there still are many) tend to use the term "contract zoning" as an epithet for an illegal act—the local government's contracting away of its police power. Those courts that use the term "conditional zoning" use it to describe rezoning decisions in which there is no express promise from the government to rezone. The distinction that is made between these two terms has become sharper as both local governments and developers have found that such arrangements can help to achieve their respective public and private objectives for land development. The distinction has been further clarified as the courts have refined their analysis of these arrangements.

Developers' need for entitlement certainty in the face of antigrowth sentiment and the local government's need to finance infrastructure without help from traditional state

---

[1] Babcock, Richard F., *The Zoning Game* at 9, University of Wisconsin Press, 1966.

and federal funding sources[2] have impelled some state legislatures to authorize the most formal of these government-developer arrangements—the development agreement, a logical extension of contract zoning. But first we address the distinction between contract zoning and conditional zoning.

"LEON, YOU KNOW THAT'S AGAINST THE ZONING LAW."

Reprinted by permission of Inman News Features.

## § 7.02 Difference Between Contract Zoning and Conditional Zoning

As some courts have concluded, a meaningful distinction can be made between contract zoning and conditional zoning. The extent of judicial grasp of this distinction usually determines the extent of judicial acceptance or rejection of the particular government-developer arrangement.

---

[2] Delaney, "Development Agreements: The Road from Prohibition to 'Let's Make a Deal,'" 25 The Urb. Law. 49 (Winter 1993).

"Contract zoning," broadly defined, is when a local government either promises to zone the landowner's property to a requested classification or, without formally agreeing to zone the property, actually zones the property to that classification, after the landowner voluntarily imposes restrictions on his land. As I've just described it, the first situation is in the form of a *bilateral* contract; the second is in the form of a *unilateral* contract. If it is a bilateral contract, it means that each party has made reciprocal promises in which the government promises to zone property in a certain manner in return for some promise from the landowner. By contrast, a unilateral contract is the promise by only one of the contracting parties—usually the landowner. No reciprocal promise is made from the other party—usually the government. There is only action, namely, rezoning or some other land use approval.

After a series of early cases in which "unilateral" contract zoning and "bilateral" contract zoning, as described above, were lumped together and condemned as illegal "contract" zoning, some courts began to distinguish between government-landowner arrangements that could be described as bilateral, from those that were unilateral, using the term "conditional zoning" to describe and justify unilateral contract zoning.[3]

In the following discussion of the debate over contract zoning, I use the term "contract" zoning to include both unilateral and bilateral forms of contract zoning, and to identify where the particular arrangement—bilateral or unilateral—affects the strength of the arguments over validity. At this stage of the discussion, this is appropriate for two reasons. First, it is worth acknowledging that even in the case of unilateral contract zoning, the landowner's unilateral offer to self-impose restrictions is a significant incentive for local government action.[4] Second, the fact that the label "unilateral" may fit the particular circum-

---

[3] Church v. Town of Islip, 8 N.Y.2d 254, 203 N.Y.S.2d 866, 168 N.E.2d 680, 683 (1960).

[4] *See* Wegner, "Moving Toward the Bargaining Table: Contract Zoning, Development Agreements, and the Theoretical Foundations of

stances does not prevent the conclusion that, as a matter of contract law, the arrangement is still a contract; it is not a "promise," but rather the government's act of rezoning or some other land use approval that arguably constitutes the consideration.[5]

---

Government Land Use Deals," 65 N.C. L. Rev. 976, 979 n.122 (1987), citing Scrutton v. Sacramento County, 275 Cal. App. 2d 412, 79 Cal. Rptr. 872 (3d Dist. 1969).

[5] *See* Corbin, Arthur L., *Corbin on Contracts* § 21 (1963). It has been argued, with some validity, I think, that this type of unilateral zoning involves no exchange of consideration, so long as the agreed upon conditions "reasonably approximate those that might otherwise be legitimately imposed under the police power." Wegner, "Moving Toward the Bargaining Table: Contract Zoning, Development Agreements, and the Theoretical Foundations of Government Land Use Deals," 65 N.C. L. Rev. 976, 981 (1987). Wegner argues:

> Such agreements . . . are adopted within the context of legislation that uses only, or primarily, regulatory language. Local governments entering into such arrangements cannot be presumed to intend to cede away regulatory authority; and private parties lack the power to elect independently to alter the character of their relationship with the government in question by deciding to enter into a cooperative agreement rather than to insist on the involuntary imposition of equivalent controls. [Citation omitted] Nor do private parties have reason for contrary expectations. Concurrence in particularized land use controls is induced by regulatory authority that can and will be exercised in the event of nonconcurrence, not by independent government promises.

> *Id.*, citing Arkenberg v. City of Topeka, 197 Kan. 731, 421 P.2d 213, 218 (1966) (agreement to convey right of way did not render rezoning invalid as contract zoning when governing body reasonably could have required right of way as a prerequisite to rezoning).

> However, under unusual factual circumstances, a local government's refusal to act upon a rezoning petition may give rise to a theory of contract. In an Illinois case, River Park, Inc. v. City of Highland Park, 281 Ill. App. 3d 154, 217 Ill. Dec. 410, 667 N.E.2d 499 (2d Dist. 1996) (overruled on other grounds by, Village of Bloomingdale v. CDG Enterprises, Inc., 196 Ill. 2d 484, 256 Ill. Dec. 848, 752 N.E.2d 1090 (2001)), the appellate court held that the plaintiff had stated a valid cause of action for breach of implied contract when the defendant municipality refused to consider its zoning petitions in good faith. The highly fact-specific circumstances concerned the municipality's

## § 7.03   Contract Zoning—The Debate over Validity

The debate surrounding contract zoning concerns both the validity of the concept itself (Is it inherently flawed?), and how it is applied to a particular fact situation.

### [1]   Is Contract Zoning Inherently Invalid?

Courts that view contract zoning as inherently flawed make two per se arguments against contract zoning: It constitutes a "bargaining away" of the police power, and it falls outside the powers expressly authorized by state statute.

The "bargaining away" argument is based on the general rule that local governments, as political subdivisions of the state, have been delegated the power to legislate. Therefore, they do not have the power to make contracts that control or limit their present or future ability to exercise that legislative power.[6] Because in most states the act of zoning (a police power function) is regarded as a legislative act, some courts, in earlier decisions, concluded that contract zoning (rezoning) is automatically illegal because it constitutes a bargaining away of the local government's police power.[7] These same courts also conclude that contract zoning is *ultra vires*; that is,

---

knowledge that the developer's financing required approval of the final plat within one year or the lender would foreclose on the property. Unbeknownst to the developer, the city was also attempting to purchase a portion of the property. The plaintiffs' complaint alleged that the city had deliberately delayed the processing of two zoning amendment petitions in order to force its property into foreclosure and then to purchase the portion of the property. The court allowed the plaintiffs to go forward on Count II of their complaint based on breach of an implied contract.

[6] *See generally* McQuillin, *The Law of Municipal Corporations* § 29.07 (Callaghan, 3d ed., 1971).

[7] *See, e.g.,* Hartnett v. Austin, 93 So. 2d 86 (Fla. 1956); V. F. Zahodiakin Engineering Corp. v. Zoning Bd. of Adjustment of City of Summit, 8 N.J. 386, 86 A.2d 127 (1952); Baylis v. City of Baltimore, 219 Md. 164, 148 A.2d 429 (1959).

because it is not expressly authorized by state legislation, contract zoning is outside the scope of zoning authority delegated to local governments. Except for some,[8] many of these courts have since shifted away from these "bargaining away" and *ultra vires* theories and approved the concept of conditional zoning discussed below.[9] In fact, some state legislatures have taken the step of expressly authorizing contract zoning.[10]

I think this judicial trend away from finding contract zoning inherently flawed on police power and statutory grounds is salutary; it is far more useful to look at the timing, structure, and outcome of an actual contractual relationship between the local government and the developer or landowner.

### [2] Is Contract Zoning Invalid as Applied?

The application of contract zoning to address specific situations usually raises three potential issues: (1) Is it done in accordance with statutorily prescribed notice and hearing procedures? (2) Does it violate the uniformity requirement in zoning? (3) Does it amount to "spot zoning"? The answers to these questions are not always clear.

### [a] Notice and Hearing Requirements

The argument based on a failure to comply with statutorily prescribed procedures for adopting zoning amendments overlaps with the *ultra vires* argument, since both arguments concern the manner in which the author-

---

[8] Hartman v. Buckson, 467 A.2d 694 (Del. Ch. 1983).

[9] *See, e.g.,* Broward County v. Griffey, 366 So. 2d 869 (Fla. Dist. Ct. App. 4th Dist. 1979); Cross v. Hall County, 238 Ga. 709, 235 S.E.2d 379 (1977); Church v. Town of Islip, 8 N.Y.2d 254, 203 N.Y.S.2d 866, 168 N.E.2d 680 (1960); Nicholson v. Tourtellotte, 110 R.I. 411, 293 A.2d 909, 70 A.L.R.3d 118 (1972); Konkel v. Common Council, City of Delafield, 68 Wis. 2d 574, 229 N.W.2d 606 (1975).

[10] *See, e.g.,* Ariz. Rev. Stat. Ann. SS ll-832; Idaho Code § 67-6511A; Md. Code Ann., Art. 66B, § 4.01(b); R.I. Gen. Laws. § 45-24-53(H); Va. Code Ann. § 15.1-491.1 through 15.1-491.6.

ity to exercise the zoning power must be implemented. But, in reality, this issue arises primarily in the context of specific fact situations, where notice and public hearing requirements have been ignored or misused. One court described the basic problem this way:

> A contract in which a municipality promises to zone property in the specified manner is illegal because, in making such a promise, a municipality grants the power of the zoning authority to zone the property according to prescribed legislative procedures. Our statutes require notice and a public hearing prior to passage, amendment, supplement, or repeal of any zoning regulation. [citation omitted] The statutes also grant the citizens and parties in interest the opportunity to be heard at the hearing. [citation omitted] By making a promise to zone before a zoning hearing occurs, a municipality denigrates the statutory process because it purports to commit itself to certain acts and before listening to the public's comments on that action. Enforcement of such a promise allows the municipality to circumvent established statutory requirements to the possible detriment of affected landowners and the community as a whole.[11]

The problem is due process; the failure to provide proper notice and a hearing to affected property owners will cause a court to invalidate the rezoning.[12] But because the conditions imposed on the landowner/developer through the rezoning are usually more restrictive than those in the zoning ordinance itself and designed to benefit neighboring property owners, courts will not invalidate the entire ordinance merely because of a technical deficiency in the notice preceding the hearing.[13]

---

[11] Dacy v. Village of Ruidoso, 114 N.M. 699, 845 P.2d 793, 797 (1992).

[12] *See, e.g.,* Pyramid Corp. v. DeSoto County Bd. of Sup'rs, 366 F. Supp. 1299 (N.D. Miss. 1973).

[13] Albright v. Town of Manlius, 28 N.Y.2d 108, 320 N.Y.S.2d 50, 268 N.E.2d 785 (1971), reargument denied, 29 N.Y.2d 649, 324 N.Y.S.2d 1031, 273 N.E.2d 320 (1971) and reargument denied, 29 N.Y.2d 649, 324 N.Y.S.2d 1031, 273 N.E.2d 320 (1971).

Put differently, if the rezoning and related conditions are accomplished through the normal public adoption procedures, the potential due process issue does not arise. It is this public regulatory process that, for one leading land use commentator, is the key to contract zoning:

> [M]y objection to contract zoning depends on the answer to the question whether you can rezone a property and, coincidentally, limit its development to the design plans that the developer has presented, as a public regulatory matter, not as a private contract matter. If you cannot, then my objection to contract zoning is simply that you ought not to be permitted to do by contract what you are not permitted to do by public regulation. If you can rezone and limit that rezoning to specific plans, and I have consistently argued that you can, then contract zoning is still bad because it is preferable to impose such limitations by public regulation then by private agreement.[14]

### [b]   Uniformity Problem

Does contract zoning, which rezones a specific parcel based upon an individualized agreement as to use and other conditions, violate the *uniformity* rule that requires that the regulations for each class or kind of buildings within a use district must be uniform? Yes, technically. As one court said:

> [Contract zoning] subjects some land within a district or classification to restrictions that are not applicable to other land within the same district or classification and thus tends to create unique mini-districts not provided for in the general zoning ordinance.[15]

But what about other flexibility mechanisms that allow the imposition and relaxation of restrictions otherwise applicable within a zoning district? The court acknowledged:

---

[14] Krasnowiecki, "Abolish Zoning," 31 Syracuse L. Rev. 719, 738–39 (1981).

[15] Rodriguez v. Prince George's County, 79 Md. App. 537, 558 A.2d 742, 749–50 (1989).

To some extent, of course, dis-uniformity may be achieved in other ways—through variances, special exceptions, and, increasingly through floating or general development zones, such as the E-I-A zone at issue here, and the site plan review process that governs development in those zones. But in terms of *use* restriction, those appear to be the only methods authorized; permitted uses cannot be excluded by contract with the zoning authority as part of the basic rezoning.[16]

In other words, the real problem with respect to the uniformity rule is not the ability by contract to vary or make more stringent the applicable development standards—something achieved already by conditions imposed through variances, conditional uses, and planned developments—but rather the exclusion of certain *uses* that would otherwise be permitted by right in the zoning district. Why does that circumstance necessarily violate the uniformity rule?

An early Connecticut decision interpreted the rule under the Connecticut zoning enabling act to distinguish between uniformity of regulations of buildings and structures and uniformity based on land use.[17] It was only after that decision that the uniformity provision under the Connecticut statute was amended to read: "All such regulations shall be uniform for each class or kind of building structures or *use of land* through each district, but the regulations in one district may differ from those in another district. . . ." (emphasis added).[18]

The zoning enabling acts of most states do not contain this explicit reference to "use of land." In my view, the *exclusion* of certain uses by means of contract zoning does not violate the intent of the uniformity provision. Moreover, other than the argument based on the broad prohibitory effect of the uniformity provision, I have seen no

---

[16] *Id.*

[17] Pecora v. Zoning Commission of Town of Trumbull, 145 Conn. 435, 144 A.2d 48 (1958).

[18] Conn. Gen. Stat. Ann. § 8-2 (1977).

credible argument why it is detrimental to the public interest or the landowner's interest to limit, upon rezoning, the range of uses permissible under the zoning district. So long as the agreement is to limit, not expand, the types of uses permissible in the zone, such an agreement furthers the original premise of zoning—to segregate incompatible uses by eliminating the possibility of certain uses that could be judged less compatible with other uses both within and adjacent to the new zoning district. If the landowner enters into such an agreement unilaterally, who suffers?

Certainly no legal impediment exists for a landowner entering into private covenants with adjacent property owners to address perceived negative impacts of a proposed development in order to lessen their opposition to the development proposal. That is a right of ownership, the risks of which the owner bears in the marketplace. Provided the contract zoning "agreement" is recorded, as it should be, a future buyer is on notice as to the use restrictions and can either decline to purchase or discount the offering price. So long as the standards for zone changes are adhered to and the purpose of the contract zoning is to lessen the potential for negative impacts upon surrounding property by imposition of conditions on the proposed use under the rezoned parcel and/or an exclusion of certain high-impact uses, the public benefits.[19]

A more flexible view of the uniformity rule is reflected in a Nebraska case[20] where the court endorsed the following statement from a Maryland court:

> [T]he purpose of the provision was mainly a political rather than a legal one, i.e., to give notice to property owners that there shall be no improper discriminations. [Citations omitted.] . . . The uniformity requirement does not prohibit classification

---

[19] The more practical reason why contract zoning may be problematic is that where there is a proliferation of a large number of zoning agreements, zoning enforcement can become very complicated. *See* Mandelker, *Land Use Law*, 3d ed. at 288, Charlottesville, Va.: Michie, 1993.

[20] Giger v. City of Omaha, 232 Neb. 676, 442 N.W.2d 182 (1989).

within a district, so long as it is reasonable and based upon the public policy to be served.[21]

The real touchstone for assessing the validity of contract zoning should be whether the reason for the zone change or the agreement was for the primary or sole benefit of the landowner or developer. The Washington Supreme Court suggested the following balancing test in deciding contract zoning proposals:

> We hold the better rule to be that, before deciding to amend a zoning ordinance, the city must weigh the benefits which will flow to the public generally against the detriment, if any, to the adjacent property owners or to the public which may result therefrom.[22]

Some courts condemn contract zoning for the additional reason that the landowner's or developer's promise provides improper motivation for the rezoning. This reasoning is not persuasive. Private interests pervade every zoning matter. It seems disingenuous to condemn a method of zoning because it benefits private interests in some way.

The more important consideration, particularly with unilateral contract zoning, or conditional zoning, is the extent to which the conditions imposed unilaterally by the landowner improve upon the protection already afforded to surrounding land uses through the zoning district scheme. Economists refer to this effect as avoiding or minimizing the "negative externalities" of a proposed land use. The term "negative externalities" is the economist's jargon for describing the effect of an action, i.e., the development project, which produces a cost (noise, pollution, traffic, etc.) that is not taken into account by the developer, and therefore is borne by other landowners and

---

[21] *Id.* at 194, citing Montgomery County v. Woodward & Lothrop, Inc., 280 Md. 686, 376 A.2d 483, 501 (1977).

[22] State ex rel. Myhre v. City of Spokane, 70 Wash. 2d 207, 422 P.2d 790, 796 (1967).

often the community as a whole.[23] Conditional zoning can be a means by which the developer unilaterally agrees to be subject to certain restrictions and/or performance standards intended to minimize the negative externalities of the development project. Obviously, in the real world, the developer has no incentive to unilaterally propose conditions on a rezoning unless the local government makes its desires known.

### [c] "Spot Zoning" Argument

It is ironic that sometimes a conditional zoning may actually save the rezoning from being characterized as illegal "spot zoning." Two cases illustrate this saving effect. In a North Carolina case,[24] based on conditions attached to the approval of the landowner's rezoning request and identifiable benefits to the community, the court upheld the county's rezoning from agricultural to conditional use manufacturing. The landowner sought the rezoning in order to store and sell agricultural chemicals on his property. The court found that the rezoning, with all of its attendant restrictions and conditions, actually represented minimal change in the allowable use of the property. The prior agricultural use classification allowed the landowner to carry out all of his current operation, except for the storage and sale of agricultural chemicals. For example, the landowner's storage and sale of grain was a permitted use under the prior classification and could legally continue irrespective of any zoning change. Moreover, the conditions accompanying the disputed rezoning restricted the landowner to one additional activity that he could not carry out without the rezoning to the conditional use classification—the storage and sale of agricultural chemicals and nothing more. By virtue of the condition imposed, the

---

[23] *See* Kneese, Ayres, and D'Arge, *Economics and the Environment: A Materials Balance Approach* at 2–4, Johns Hopkins Press, 1970; Ellickson, "Alternatives to Zoning: Covenants, Nuisance Rules and Fines as Land Use Controls," 40 U. Chi. L. Rev. 681, 728–31 (1973).

[24] Chrismon v. Guilford County, 322 N.C. 611, 370 S.E.2d 579 (1988).

court concluded that the rezoning was not the sort of drastic change from surrounding uses that would constitute illegal spot zoning.

In another case, this one in Texas,[25] the city of Pharr relied on its imposition of various development conditions to justify its approval of a request to rezone a ten-acre subdivision tract from a single-family to a multifamily residential area. The tract was situated in a largely undeveloped farming area, with a nearby cluster of single-family homes. The city expected to protect and, in fact, enhance the value of single-family homes in the vicinity of the rezoned tract by imposing a conditional permit requirement which would compel the city to complete a prior analysis of the subdivision design before development. Most of the traffic from the rezoned tract would be directed away from existing homes and the subdivision would have its own internal streets and off-street parking. The evidence also showed that the number of potential structures would not substantially increase (fifty family units compared with forty-four under existing zoning).[26] Thus, the impact upon the surrounding area would be slight and even beneficial.

The court concluded that the ordinance was not spot zoning, noting that the ten-acre tract was located in an undeveloped farming area and that large areas of rural land were located to the east, south, and southeast—the direction in which the town must grow. Said the court: "To hold that the undeveloped land cannot be used for anything other than single-family residences (R-1) would mean, for all practical purposes, that there can be no more multiple housing in Pharr within its present city limits, since there is almost no presently undeveloped area which is available for R-3 housing."[27] The court reasoned that because the size of the tract was large enough for planning as "a self-contained orderly development which can in advance provide for the direction and the flow of traffic

---

[25] City of Pharr v. Tippitt, 616 S.W.2d 173 (Tex. 1981).
[26] Id. at 178.
[27] Id. at 178–89.

and assure a careful development of necessary public utilities," the development would not cause "that measure of disharmony" which results from a rezoning that permits a use which impacts lands or tracts that are already developed. In other words, said the court, "this is not an instance of an unplanned or piecemeal zoning of an isolated lot or small tract."[28]

## § 7.04 Conditional Zoning—Methods of Implementing

The increasing judicial acceptance of unilateral contract zoning, or conditional zoning, reflects the reality recognized by practitioners and seasoned commentators[29] : The majority of significant land use and development decisions occur through a government-developer bargaining process that results in the new zoning classification requested by the developer being limited or tailored more specifically to the proposed plan of development. In dealing with this reality of the land development process, the courts focus upon one or both of the following characteristics: (1) the rezoning accords the developer no greater rights as to use than would otherwise be possible under the new zoning district; but rather, it imposes restrictions designed to protect surrounding properties from potential negative impacts of the zone change[30] ; and (2) the local government has not restricted its police power because it has expressed only a willingness, not a promise, to rezone, in exchange for protective covenants.[31] What forms have been used to accomplish this conditioned zoning?

---

[28] *Id.*

[29] Krasnowiecki, "Abolish Zoning," 31 Syracuse L. Rev. 719, 737 (1981).

[30] Church v. Town of Islip, 8 N.Y.2d 254, 203 N.Y.S.2d 866, 168 N.E.2d 680 (1960).

[31] Sylvania Elec. Products, Inc. v. City of Newton, 344 Mass. 428, 183 N.E.2d 118 (1962); Scrutton v. Sacramento County, 275 Cal. App. 2d 412, 79 Cal. Rptr. 872 (3d Dist. 1969).

## [1]  Inclusion of Conditions in Rezoning Ordinance

In the early decisions invalidating conditional zoning, courts pointed to the fact that the conditions were inserted in the rezoning ordinance as evidence of a bilateral contract. The more recent court decisions do not view that as a flaw.[32] The rezoning ordinance usually will be structured so as to rezone the land first and then recite the conditions agreed to by the developer.[33] This would appear to avoid the appearance of a negotiated bilateral agreement. In Wisconsin, another approach has been to make the performance of conditions a prerequisite to the act of rezoning.[34] This allows the court to conclude that the rezoning is not effective immediately, but rather depends upon the prior performance.[35] A similar approach, sanctioned by the courts in the state of Washington, utilizes two separate documents: the zoning ordinance and a "concomitant agreement," which is signed at the same time as the adoption of the zoning amendment. In effect, however, the developer is asked to sign the concomitant agreement before the rezoning. It seems to me that these approaches are impractical since the developer's incentive to perform any conditions normally depends upon having the new zoning in place. This sequencing problem is solved if the agreement provisions are included in the zoning ordinance, as done in most jurisdictions that approve of conditional zoning.[36]

---

[32] *See, e.g.,* Sweetman v. Town of Cumberland, 117 R.I. 134, 364 A.2d 1277 (1976); City of Colorado Springs v. Smartt, 620 P.2d 1060 (Colo. 1980).

[33] Sweetman v. Town of Cumberland, 117 R.I. 134, 364 A.2d 1277 (1976); American Nat. Bank & Trust Co. of Chicago v. Village of Arlington Heights, 115 Ill. App. 3d 342, 71 Ill. Dec. 210, 450 N.E.2d 898 (1st Dist. 1983).

[34] Konkel v. Common Council, City of Delafield, 68 Wis. 2d 574, 229 N.W.2d 606 (1975).

[35] *Id.* at 608.

[36] *See, e.g.,* Goffinet v. Christian County, 65 Ill. 2d 40, 2 Ill. Dec. 275, 357 N.E.2d 442 (1976); King's Mill Homeowners Ass'n, Inc. v. City of Westminster, 192 Colo. 305, 557 P.2d 1186 (1976).

## [2]  Recording of Restrictive Covenants Prior to Rezoning

An alternative that local governments may think is more attractive than including the conditions in the zone change ordinance is to require the developer to execute and record a restrictive covenant against the land either prior to or contemporaneously with the adoption of the zoning ordinance. As used here, a restrictive covenant is essentially a private agreement between two parties expressed in the form of either a written agreement or a deed to land with provisions that impose limitations upon the use of the land. The right to enforce the provisions of a restrictive land covenant is usually based on the theory that the covenant "touches" and "concerns" the land so as to be said to "run with the land" and is enforceable against any subsequent owner of the land.[37] The right to enforce the covenant may also be based on a theory of equitable easement or servitude or of a third-party beneficiary to a contract. So long as such a covenant is enforceable, it would seem like an ideal legal instrument by which to accomplish the objectives of conditional zoning. But therein lie a number of difficulties. Generally, to be enforceable against the developer and the developer's successors in interest, the developer must do one of two things. The developer must either grant some property interest in the land or a portion of the land to the local government so that the benefits and burdens that run with the land also flow to the government, or the developer must covenant through a contract not involving transfer of land to the government, provided all the essentials of a contract are present.[38] Both methods present problems.[39]

The method of giving the local government the power to enforce a restrictive covenant is unlikely to be the

---

[37] *See generally* Stoeback, "Running Covenants: An Analytic Primer," Wash. L. Rev. 861 (1977).

[38] Bowes v. City of Chicago, 3 Ill. 2d 175, 120 N.E.2d 15 (1954). If the developer merely records a declaration of restrictions, those restrictions may not be enforceable against the developer's successor in interest because the declaration is viewed as only the original developer's

developer's method of choice, since it may require a modification in site design to accomplish and inject public ownership into a private land development, which a developer may instinctively dislike. However, if done properly, this method may be the simplest way to achieve both public and private objectives in the development of a parcel. The property interest transferred to the local government need not be the fee interest; it can be an easement.

One way to structure the transfer of a fee interest to the government is to use an option to purchase agreement for a specific piece or strip of property made subject to a restrictive covenant. This property is part of the larger parcel for which the rezoning is being requested. The restrictive covenant is included in a proposed deed which is attached to an option to purchase agreement with the government. During the term of the option, the government has the power to acquire the property, giving it the power to enforce the covenant. In one case, the option agreement ran for thirty years. The ordinance rezoning the entire parcel also authorized the mayor to accept the option agreement, which the developer executed. The option agreement with the attached form of deed was then recorded with a certified copy of the zoning amendment

---

declaration of intent to restrict. *See* MacEliven, "Land Use Control Through Covenants," 13 Hastings L.J. 310, 316 (1962).

[39] The state of Idaho solved this problem by enacting a statute that enables the governing board to "require or permit as a condition of rezoning that an owner or developer make a written commitment concerning the use or development of the subject parcel." The statute also states that by permitting or requiring a commitment, the governing board "does not obligate itself to recommend or adopt the proposed zoning ordinance." This "commitment" must be recorded in the office of the county recorder and is binding upon the owner and any subsequent person acquiring an interest in the parcel. Only the governing board can modify or terminate the "commitment." The statute also provides that even if the "commitment" is unrecorded, it still binds the owner of the parcel. An unrecorded "commitment" is also binding upon subsequent owners or persons acquiring an interest in the parcel, if they have "actual notice" of the "commitment." Idaho Code § 67-6511A. *See also* discussion of development agreements statutes in Secs. 7.06 and 7.07, *infra*.

ordinance containing the mayor's approval. In its review of a challenge to this arrangement, the court acknowledged that the developer's offer of the option agreement was an inducement for the approval of the zone change, and vice versa, but that this conduct by the mayor and aldermen was "proper activity, precedent to the exercise of the zoning power, not the exercise thereof."[40]

## § 7.05   Conditional Zoning—Noncompliance

Assuming, for the moment, that conditional zoning is an accepted public-private arrangement in a particular jurisdiction, what if there is noncompliance by either the government or the developer under the terms of the conditional zoning? What are the remedies? The reported cases involving contract and conditional zoning typically do not address this issue with any clarity, in part because the courts frequently do not get past the threshold legality of the particular arrangement, holding that if it is illegal, it is unenforceable, and traditional remedies such as damages, specific performance, and injunctive relief are not available to the private party.[41] For some guidance, particularly under circumstances where the government fails to comply with a *valid* public-private arrangement, we must look to the general constitutional and contract law principles applicable to the government's performance of its contractual obligations.

### [1]   Noncompliance by the Government

If the government fails to comply with the expectations that the developer has by virtue of the conditional zoning

---

[40] Sylvania Elec. Products, Inc. v. City of Newton, 344 Mass. 428, 183 N.E.2d 118, 121/N123 (1962).

[41] Dacy v. Village of Ruidoso, 114 N.M. 699, 845 P.2d 793, 798 (1992) ("The trial court was correct in stating that damages are unavailable as relief to a party to an illegal contract. *See Restatement (Second) of Contracts* § 346(1) (1979). . . . Additionally, neither specific performance nor an injunction will be granted to a party to an illegal contract. See id. § 365 . . . .").

arrangement, the developer is faced with some difficult choices. There are some basic principles that govern the extent to which the government can be held liable for breach of contractual-type obligations. The first of these involves the so-called "reserved powers" doctrine of the Contract Clause of the United States Constitution.[42] The Contract Clause states that "No State shall . . . pass any . . . Law impairing the Obligations of Contracts." This clause was included in the Constitution to ensure that the government exercises its police power for a truly legitimate public purpose rather than for the benefit of private interests.[43] The "reserved powers" doctrine refers, in constitutional terms, to that old epithet for contract zoning—the "bargaining away" of the police power.

As this doctrine was articulated by the U.S. Supreme Court in an 1880 case,[44] a state cannot contract away its right to exercise its fundamentally inalienable police power.[45] This doctrine was subsequently applied by the U.S. Supreme Court to local governments in land use matters. For example, the Court upheld a city's right to require a railroad to alter road grades despite the fact that the requirement was inconsistent with prior ordinances and agreements involving bridge construction. The court reasoned that determining street standards was an inherently public function, and therefore the city could not relinquish its jurisdiction over streets without express legislative authorization.[46] This early case law and subsequent U.S. Supreme Court decisions recognized that government can legitimately impair *private* contracts

---

[42] U.S. Const., Art. I, § 10 cl. 1.

[43] Energy Reserves Group, Inc. v. Kansas Power and Light Co., 459 U.S. 400, 412, 103 S. Ct. 697, 74 L. Ed. 2d 569, 50 Pub. Util. Rep. 4th (PUR) 489 (1983).

[44] Stone v. State of Mississippi, 101 U.S. 814, 1 Ky. L. Rptr. 146, 25 L. Ed. 1079 (1879).

[45] *Id.* at 817–18.

[46] Wabash R. Co. v. City of Defiance, 167 U.S. 88, 94, 17 S. Ct. 748, 42 L. Ed. 87 (1897).

when necessary in the exercise of its police power.[47] Therefore, implicit in all private contracts is a condition that the state may exercise its police power as necessary in the public interest.[48] But the Court has also indicated that there are limits to the extent to which the police power condition can justify government noncompliance—most notably whether such noncompliance is justified by a public purpose and "reasonable and necessary" because of changed circumstances.[49]

In the event of government noncompliance with a valid *public-private* contract, the remedies to the private party depend upon the nature of the governmental noncompliance. A court will assess whether the government intended a simple breach of contract or intended to repudiate its contractual obligations outright. If only a breach is involved, the court will consider awarding traditional compensatory relief in the form of damages.[50] If government noncompliance can be characterized as a repudiation and a resulting impairment of its contractual obligations, then the question is whether the impairment was justified. If it was justified for reasons of public safety, then the private party is out of luck—no damages, declaratory relief, or injunctive relief is available. However, if the government cannot present justification that satisfies the

---

[47] *See, e.g.,* Atlantic Coast Line R. Co. v. City of Goldsboro, 232 U.S. 548, 34 S. Ct. 364, 58 L. Ed. 721 (1914); Manigault v. Springs, 199 U.S. 473, 26 S. Ct. 127, 50 L. Ed. 274 (1905).

[48] *See, e.g.,* Keystone Bituminous Coal Ass'n v. DeBenedictis, 480 U.S. 470, 107 S. Ct. 1232, 94 L. Ed. 2d 472, 25 Env't. Rep. Cas. (BNA) 1649, 17 Envtl. L. Rep. 20440 (1987); Home Bldg. & Loan Ass'n v. Blaisdell, 290 U.S. 398, 345, 54 S. Ct. 231, 78 L. Ed. 413, 88 A.L.R. 1481 (1934).

[49] U. S. Trust Co. of New York v. New Jersey, 431 U.S. 1, 13–14, 97 S. Ct. 1505, 52 L. Ed. 2d 92 (1977), reh'g denied, 431 U.S. 975, 97 S. Ct. 2942, 53 L. Ed. 2d 1073 (1977); City of El Paso v. Simmons, 379 U.S. 497, 515–16, 85 S. Ct. 577, 13 L. Ed. 2d 446 (1965), reh'g denied, 380 U.S. 926, 85 S. Ct. 879, 13 L. Ed. 2d 813 (1965).

[50] *See, e.g.,* Hays v. Port of Seattle, 251 U.S. 233, 40 S. Ct. 125, 64 L. Ed. 243 (1920) (private contractor had action for damages under breach of contract theory where state abandonment of waterway excavation did not constitute a repudiation leading to an impairment of contractual obligations).

"reasonable and necessary" test described above, the developer may prevail in an action for specific performance which, if successful, will force the government to perform its obligations under the terms of the agreement.[51]

## [2] Noncompliance by the Developer

If conditional zoning is valid in the particular jurisdiction and the rezoning is tied to an express agreement, then, in the event of developer noncompliance, the government will have available to it the traditional contract remedies discussed above. If, instead, the rezoning is conditioned upon the developer-owner of the land recording restrictive covenants, their later enforceability, as discussed above, will depend upon whether the government is also a benefited property owner by virtue of having been deeded a property interest in land benefited by the restrictive covenant, or whether the covenant includes a specific provision giving the government the power of enforcement.

Another remedy governments sometimes attempt to use to address developer noncompliance with conditions is the inclusion of a provision in the rezoning ordinance called a "reverter clause." This provision provides that in the event the developer fails to perform the conditions, or perform them within a specified period of time, the zoning automatically "reverts" to its original classification. In those states that characterize the zoning amendment as a "legislative" act, the courts have invalidated these clauses because they accomplish the reversion back to the original zoning without complying with the formal procedural

---

[51] *See* U. S. Trust Co. of New York v. New Jersey, 431 U.S. 1, 32, 97 S. Ct. 1505, 52 L. Ed. 2d 92 (1977), reh'g denied, 431 U.S. 975, 97 S. Ct. 2942, 53 L. Ed. 2d 1073 (1977) and discussion of the decision in Note, "Takings Law and the Contract Clause: A Takings Law Approach to Legislative Modifications of Public Contracts," 36 Stan. L. Rev. 1447 (1984) (The decision "mandates that government comply with the exact terms of public contract; grants public contract holders a constitutional right to specific performance; . . . . The [Contract Clause] does not authorize courts to award damages in lieu of requiring the state to adhere to the original terms of the contract.").

requirements for legislative acts—normally a published notice and a public hearing.[52] Only in certain instances, where the court has been persuaded that the zoning approval is analogous to a special exception or conditional use, for which time limits are considered valid, has a reverter-type clause been upheld.[53]

## § 7.06 Development Agreement—An Antidote for the Vesting Problem

Predictability in the development process is always of paramount concern to a developer, but particularly when a development project requires local approvals beyond the rezoning stage—conditional use, planned development, variance, subdivision, site plan review, stormwater management—and reviews and approvals from federal, state, and regional governmental bodies and agencies with jurisdiction over wetlands, endangered species, archeological sites, and traffic impacts. The developer's need for predictability rises precipitously with the size and complexity of the project and the number of planned phases. Therefore, the developer's objective is to secure the necessary "entitlements" that allow the project to become "vested" so that it has the right to proceed through to construction.[54]

### [1] Vested Rights and Estoppel

"Vested rights" and "equitable estoppel"—in theory, distinct doctrines—are used interchangeably by the courts

---

[52] D'Angelo v. DiBernardo, 106 Misc. 2d 735, 435 N.Y.S.2d 206 (Sup 1980), judgment aff'd, 79 A.D.2d 1092, 436 N.Y.S.2d 1021 (4th Dep't 1981); Spiker v. City of Lakewood, 198 Colo. 528, 603 P.2d 130 (1979); Scrutton v. Sacramento County, 275 Cal. App. 2d 412, 79 Cal. Rptr. 872 (3d Dist. 1969); Andres v. Village of Flossmoor, 15 Ill. App. 3d 655, 304 N.E.2d 700 (1st Dist. 1973); Bucholz v. City of Omaha, 174 Neb. 862, 120 N.W.2d 270 (1963).

[53] See, e.g., Hopengarten v. Board of Appeals of Lincoln, 17 Mass. App. Ct. 1006, 459 N.E.2d 1271 (1984).

[54] See Blaesser, "Negotiating Entitlements," in *Urban Land* (December 1991).

to address factual circumstances in which landowners seek protection from subsequent changes in regulations.[55] The *vested rights* doctrine is constitutionally based, giving constitutional protection to property rights acquired by the landowner.[56] *Equitable estoppel* is derived from the legal principle of equity or fairness. When applied to government and the development process, equitable estoppel means that the government should be prevented from enacting new zoning or other land use regulations after giving certain land use approvals and project approvals if the developer has made substantial expenditures in good faith reliance upon those approvals. The rules for *when* that estoppel arises and *when* the developer's right to complete the project are "vested."[57]

### [2] Vesting of Entitlements

Like many new words that have made their way into our vocabulary, the use of the term *"entitlement,"*[58] with its connotation of certainty, appears to have gained currency first in California, where the court-made vesting rules produced the opposite of certainty in the development process and extreme frustration in the development community.

The unfairness of the California court-made rules on vesting was exemplified by one decision, in particular,

---

[55] Allen v. City and County of Honolulu, 58 Haw. 432, 571 P.2d 328 (1977).

[56] The vested rights doctrine does not necessarily apply to increases in taxes or the subsequent imposition of impact fees on developers. *See, e.g.,* City of Key West v. R.L.J.S. Corp., 537 So. 2d 641 (Fla. Dist. Ct. App. 3d Dist. 1989).

[57] *See generally* Mandelker, D.R., *Land Use Law,* 3d ed., §§ 6.12–6.21, Charlottesville, Va.: Michie, 1993.

[58] Black's Law Dictionary defines *entitlement* as the "[r]ight to benefits, income or property which may not be abridged without due process." Black's Law Dictionary (St. Paul, Minn.: West Publishing Co., 1990) (6th ed.), p. 532.

involving a 5,000-acre phased planned unit development.[59] The developer had obtained PUD and subdivision approval and expended close to $3 million in planning and site improvements, including the conveyance of parkland to the county at less than market value. The developer had not yet received a building permit for a 74-acre parcel intended for multiple-family use when it was advised that it would have to obtain a permit from the newly created California Coastal Zone Commission before its development could proceed. When the developer sued, arguing that it had a vested right to develop the 74-acre parcel without obtaining the Coastal Zone Commission permit, the court pointed to the absence of a building permit and reiterated the rule that a vested right to complete construction requires evidence that substantial work was performed and substantial liabilities were incurred in good faith reliance upon a permit.[60] In other words, without the permit, the developer had nothing.

Enter the development agreement as the California legislature's attempt to remedy the harshness of this late vesting rule. The legislation expressly authorizes local governments and developers to enter into a development agreement, a *bilateral* contract, and directs local governments to establish procedures and requirements for the process of adopting development agreements.[61] The California statute was the first in the nation. In a 1991 decision, the California Supreme Court succinctly described the nature of the legislation:

> [D]evelopment agreements (§§ 65864–65869.5) between a developer and a local government limit the power of that government to apply newly enacted ordinances to ongoing developments. Unless otherwise provided in the agreement, the rules, regulations, and official policies governing permitted uses, density,

---

[59] Avco Community Developers, Inc. v. South Coast Regional Com., 17 Cal. 3d 785, 132 Cal. Rptr. 386, 553 P.2d 546 (1976).

[60] *Id.* at 389.

[61] Cal. Gov't Code §§ 65864–65899 (West 1983 & Supp. 1993).

design, improvements, and construction are those in effect when the agreement is executed. (§ 65866).[62]

In other words, the California development agreement law authorizes agreements that "freeze" or "lock in" the applicable use regulations, rules, and policies in effect at the point of agreement. This is particularly important for the developer of a large, long-term project that may need a series of discretionary approvals over time. The California legislation allows the developer to complete such a project despite intervening changes in the local regulations.[63]

Unlike conditional zoning that flirts with contract theory by displaying some, but not all, aspects of a contract, the development agreement is a deliberate effort by these state legislatures to create a binding contract between the local government and the developer. This authorization by statute certainly avoids the *ultra vires* problem discussed in Section 7.03. Such enabling legislation may still be objected to on the "bargaining away" of the police power theory, particularly because of the authority given to "freeze" regulations in effect at the time of project approval. But that argument is not persuasive for two reasons. First, state legislation authorizing development agreements and local government ordinances approving development agreements are police power acts. Second, the local government does not surrender its police power to the confines of the development agreement since it still reserves the right to enact regulations that do not conflict with the development agreement.[64]

---

[62] City of West Hollywood v. Beverly Towers, Inc., 52 Cal. 3d 1184, 1193 n.6, 278 Cal. Rptr. 375, 805 P.2d 329 (1991), reh'g denied, (Apr. 25, 1991).

[63] *Id.*

[64] *See* Curtin, "Protecting Developers' Permits to Build: Development Agreement Practice in California and Other States," 18 *Zoning and Planning Law Report* 11 at 88–89 (December 1995). See also Santa Margarita Area Residents Together v. San Luis Obispo County, 84 Cal. App. 4th 221, 100 Cal. Rptr. 2d 740 (2d Dist. 2000) (upholding denial of petition for a writ of mandate to set aside development agreement.)

## § 7.07   Development Agreement—Common Statutory Purposes

In addition to California, twelve other states have adopted either development agreement statutes or statutes that "vest," for a period of time, the developer's right to proceed with an approved project under existing rules and regulations. These states are Arizona, Colorado, Florida, Hawaii, Idaho, Louisiana, Maryland, Minnesota, Nevada, Oregon, South Carolina, and Washington.[65] The complete text of each state's statute is included at the end of this chapter (*see* Section 7.14).

There are three essential purposes of the development agreement statutes: (1) to "freeze" land use rules, regulations, and policies in effect at a particular point in time; (2) to confer on the developer a vested right to proceed with an approved project; and (3) to provide a means to ensure that infrastructure needed to support the development will be in place at the point of development.

### [1]   Regulatory "Freeze"

Almost all of the development agreement statutes contain the all-important "lock-in" provision similar to California's; this provision provides that rules and regulations applicable to the development project are those in effect when the agreement is adopted. But the statutes of some of these states also provide exceptions to the regulatory "freeze" language. For example, Florida and South Carolina have very similar provisions allowing subsequently adopted laws to be applied to a development. South Carolina's statute states:

---

[65] Ariz. Rev. Stat. Ann. § 9-500.05; Cal. Gov't Code §§ 65864 - 65869.5; Colo. Rev. Stat. §§ 24-68-101 - 24-68-106; Fla. Stat. §§ 163.3220 - 163.3242; Haw. Rev. Stat. §§ 46-121 - 46-132; Idaho Code § 67-6511A; La. Rev. Stat. Ann. §§ 33:4780.21 - 33:4780.33; Md. Ann. Code., Art. 66B, §§ 1.00 and 13.01; Minn. Stat. § 462.358, Subd. 3C; Nev. Rev. Stat. §§ 278.0201 - 278.0207; Ore. Rev. Stat. §§ 94.504 - 94.528; Wash. Rev. Code §§ 36.70B.170 - 36.70B.210.

### § 6-31-80 Law in effect at time of agreement governs development; exceptions.

(A) Subject to the provisions of Section 6-31-140 and unless otherwise provided by the development agreement, the laws applicable to development of the property subject to a development agreement, are those in force at the time of execution of the agreement.

(B) Subject to the provisions of Section 6-31-140, a local government may apply subsequently adopted laws to a development that is subject to a development agreement only if the local government has held a public hearing and determined:

(1) the laws are not in conflict with the laws governing the development agreement and do not prevent the development set forth in the development agreement;

(2) they are essential to the public health, safety, or welfare and the laws expressly state that they apply to a development that is subject to a development agreement;

(3) the laws are specifically anticipated and provided for in the development agreement;

(4) the local government demonstrates that substantial changes have occurred in pertinent conditions existing at the time of approval of the development agreement which changes, if not addressed by the local government, would pose a serious threat to the public health, safety, or welfare; or

(5) the development agreement is based on substantially and materially inaccurate information supplied by the developer.

(C) This section does not abrogate any rights preserved by Section 6-31-140 herein or that may vest pursuant to common law or otherwise in the absence of a development agreement.

There are two differences between the South Carolina and the Florida "exceptions" provisions that could prove significant to a developer. First, in defining what applies to the development agreement, the Florida statute refers to "laws and policies," not just "laws," as does the South Carolina statute. It is perhaps not immediately clear how a "policy" can impact an approved development agreement unless it is put into some regulatory form. However, because of the heavy emphasis in Florida upon planning policies and the requirement of consistency between state-mandated local plans and development ordinances, planning policies adopted subsequent to the approval of a development agreement could have a significant impact upon the viability of a development agreement.

The second distinction is in the language used in each statute's statement that subsequently adopted laws (and policies) do not prevent the development under the development agreement. Both statutes require that subsequently adopted laws (and policies) neither conflict with those governing the development agreement, nor prevent the development. However, the Florida statute's specific language is that the laws and policies "do not prevent the land uses, intensities, or densities in the development agreement."[66] South Carolina's statute merely states that the laws "do not prevent the development set forth in the development agreement." Which phrase affords the developer the most protection? Does the South Carolina statute's language mean that subsequently adopted laws may not prevent the development set forth in the development agreement *in all significant respects*? The potential danger in this language is that key aspects, such as the intensity of use and the design of the development, could be seriously compromised by the application of subsequently adopted laws. So long as the local government can argue that the development "set forth in the development agreement" can still go forward, the statutory language does not give the developer a very clear basis to argue that the development, as the developer conceived it, has been prevented by application of the new

---

[66] Fla. Stat. § 163.3233(2)(a).

laws. Because of the vagueness of this language in the South Carolina statute, the developer's attorney should carefully draft in the development agreement what is meant by the statutory reference to "the development."[67] By comparison, the Florida statute's comparable phrase states that the laws and policies "do not prevent development of the *land uses, intensities,* or *densities* in the development agreement." Although this language is narrower than the South Carolina statute's language, it is very specific where it counts most to the developer, namely, use and intensity or density of development.

Other states' development agreement statutes are not as detailed as Florida's and South Carolina's in defining the exception to the regulatory "freeze" rule. Hawaii, for example, defines the necessity of imposing subsequently adopted laws in terms of preventing a condition "perilous to the residents' health or safety."[68] Washington's statute requires the development agreement to "reserve authority to impose new or different regulations to the extent required by a serious threat to public health and safety."[69] California merely provides that new rules, regulations, and policies may be applied "which do not conflict with those rules, regulations, and policies applicable to the property. . . ."[70]

## [2] Vested Right to Proceed

When the California legislature enacted the development agreement statute, one of its findings was that:

> Assurance to the applicant for a development project that upon approval of the project, the applicant may proceed with the project in accordance with existing

---

[67] This is particularly important since the definition of "development" in the South Carolina development agreement statute is very generic. *See* Code of Laws of South Carolina, Ch. 31, § 6-31-20.

[68] Haw. Stat. § 46–127.

[69] Wash. Rev. Code § 36.70B.170.(4).

[70] Cal. Gov't Code § 65866.

policies, rules and regulations, and subject to conditions of approval, will strengthen the public planning process, encourage private participation in comprehensive planning, and reduce the economic costs of development.

The Hawaii statute states:

> The purpose of this [development agreements statute] is to provide a means by which an individual may be assured at a specific point in time that having met or having agreed to meet all of the terms and conditions of the development agreement, the individual's rights to develop a property in a certain manner shall be vested.

The language in the Hawaii statute makes a distinction between the "freezing" of rules and regulations applicable to a development project, and the developer's acquiring a "vested right" to proceed with the development. This distinction is important.

The Hawaii statute, for example, makes it clear that the "right" to develop property in a certain manner, unaffected by subsequent regulation, becomes "vested" only at the point that the developer either has "met, or . . . agreed to meet all of the terms and conditions of the development agreement. . . ."[71] The statute enacted by Colorado, entitled "Vested Property Rights," is another example of this distinction. Although it is not a full-blown development agreements statute, it enables property owners to obtain a "vested property right" in connection with any "site development plan," a term defined to include almost all land use approval designations used by local governments.[72] The Colorado statute defines "vested prop-

---

[71] Haw. Stat. Sec. 46–121.

[72] A "site development plan" is defined as "planned unit development plan, a subdivision plat, a specially planned area, a planned building group, a general submission plan, a preliminary or general development plan, a conditional or special use plan, a development agreement, or any other land use approval designation as may be utilized by a local government." Colo. Rev. Stat. § 24-68-102(4).

erty right" as: "[T]he right to undertake and complete the development and use of property under the terms and conditions of a site specific development plan."[73] In this statute as well, exactly when the vested property right is acquired depends upon the local government's definition of the type of approval and terms that are sufficient to vest the right. The statute states:

> What constitutes a site specific development plan under this article that would trigger a vested property right shall be finally determined by the local government either pursuant to ordinance or regulation or upon an agreement entered into by the local government and the landowner, and the document that triggers such vesting shall be so identified at the time of its approval.[74]

It is important, therefore, for the developer to remember that the "vesting" of property rights under most of the development agreements statutes is very much dependent upon a process—a process that begins with the execution of the development agreement and ends when the developer can demonstrate compliance with all the terms and conditions of the development agreement. This is why the Hawaii statute, for example, states that development agreements "will encourage the vesting of property rights by protecting such rights from the effect of subsequently enacted . . . legislation."[75] In other words, the development agreement "freezes" the regulations applicable to the project, and the developer must, in turn, begin to meet the agreed-upon terms and conditions of the development agreement that ensure his right to proceed with the development. Monitoring provisions in most development agreements statutes provide for the termination of the

---

[73] Colo. Rev. Stat. § 24-68-102(5).

[74] Colo. Rev. Stat. § 24-68-102(4).

[75] Haw. Rev. Stat. § 46-121. The same language is found in the South Carolina development agreements statute. *See* S.C. Code Ch. 31, § 6-31-10.

development agreement if the developer fails to satisfy the terms or conditions of the agreement.[76]

### [3]  Necessary Infrastructure Improvements

Developers are always concerned that the public facilities and services needed to support their developments will be in place upon project completion. Local governments also understand that the lack of public facilities, such as streets, sewerage, transportation, drinking water, school, and utility facilities, can seriously impede development and lead to the overburdening of existing facilities and services. The development agreement is a means to ensure that public facilities and services will be available, or constructed in time, to sustain the development once built, and that adequate public or private financing for the improvements is available. Not surprisingly, local governments look to the developer either to construct or finance public improvements in exchange for conferring a vested right to develop. The development agreements statutes of Hawaii and South Carolina each contain the same provision which states:

> Public benefits derived from development agreements may include, but are not limited to, affordable housing, design standards, and on- and off-site infrastructure and other improvements. Such benefits may be negotiated for in return for the vesting of development rights for a specific period.[77]

In contrast to the above provision, Arizona's development agreements statute does not link negotiation of infrastructure improvements to vesting of development rights, but merely provides that the development agreement may be used to address the requirements and financing for public infrastructure and subsequent reimbursements over

---

[76] *See, e.g.,* Cal. Gov't Code § 65865.1. The development agreements statutes are set forth in full in Sec. 7.14, *infra.*

[77] Haw. Stat. § 46-121; S.C. Stat. § 6-31-10(B)4.

time.[78] Although the Arizona statute is not explicit regarding the negotiation of infrastructure improvements in exchange for the vesting of development rights, the statute provides the same opportunity as the other statutes for negotiating the terms for vesting development rights.

*"Someday, all this will be infrastructure."*

**Drawing by W. Miller © 1988 The New Yorker Magazine, Inc.**

Given this basic purpose in development agreements of ensuring the timely availability of public facilities, it is important that the development agreement not be used by local governments as a means for raising general revenue in the face of revenue-raising and -spending limitations. Use of a state-sanctioned public-private contractual mechanism for that purpose is another form of abuse of discretion that goes beyond the individual and affects the public interest. As some commentators have explained in the wake of the U.S. Supreme Court's decision in the *Nollan* case:

> [S]elling land use regulations in order to have owners of private property provide public services subverts

---

[78] Ariz. Rev. Stat. § 9-500.05.F.1.(g).

the rule of law because it lets elected officials avoid accountability for their decisions. The evil of funding public works through "amenities" rather than by raising taxes is that the cost is hidden from citizens—who at least in theory have the right to decide whether to accept or reject the burden of maintaining a significant addition to the infrastructure.[79]

Although the Court's decision in *Nollan,* and its later decision in *Dolan,* suggests that this type of abuse against the public interest is less likely, it appears that at least some courts have concluded that the development agreement makes the local government immune to the "essential nexus" test required by *Nollan* (*see* discussion in Section 7.12).

### § 7.08 Development Agreement—Key Provisions

All of the statutes authorizing development agreements contain some common requirements and conditions with which the local government must comply when entering into a development agreement with a private landowner or developer. The developer's or landowner's attorney should consult the specific statute before proceeding with negotiations. However, those negotiations are likely to include discussion of the following key provisions of the development agreement which are prescribed in the state enabling legislation:

---

[79] Tufo, P. and Schreibman, B., "High Court Limits Zoning Deals," *Legal Times*, March 28, 1988, S26, S28.

279

---

### Development Agreement—Key Provisions

1. Parties to the Agreement.
2. Duration of the Agreement.
3. Definition of Development Approvals Required.
4. Amendments to the Agreement.
5. Developer's Vested Rights.
6. Developer's Obligations.
7. Fees, Assessments and Other Charges.
8. Assignment of the Agreement.
9. Compliance Review and Remedies for Default.

---

Even though the content of a development agreement is generally prescribed in the state statute and/or the local ordinance, the actual terms of the agreement must be negotiated. The nature and scope of that negotiation will depend upon the type and size of the proposed project and the respective needs and objectives of the municipality and developer. At the bargaining table, each will seek to condition its commitments on the guaranteed performance of the other. To be successful, the agreement must provide sufficient flexibility and a procedure for modifying the agreement in the likely event that changing economic and market conditions significantly affect the project. The following discussion addresses the negotiation of some of these key provisions.

### [1] Parties to the Agreement

The developer and the local government are the two obvious and important parties to the agreement. The local government may seek to include all other private parties with a legal interest in the property, including secured lenders, easement holders, and ground lessees. Before agreeing to such an expansion of the parties to the agreement, the developer should carefully consider whether inclusion of all legally interested parties will unnecessarily hinder the developer's flexibility under the agreement. On the government side, limited authorization in the statute generally will preclude other governmental bodies, such as federal and state agencies, coastal commissions, and local sanitation, water, and fire districts, from being parties to the agreement.

### [2] Duration of the Agreement

The development agreement must specify the duration of the agreement. Some state statutes limit the term of the agreement to a specific term, in which case the developer has little say about the duration. In that circumstance, particularly if the statutorily prescribed term is relatively short, it is in the interest of both the developer and the local government to include a provision providing that if any of the terms of the agreement are challenged in court, then, to the extent permitted by law, the time period during which the litigation is pending may not be included in calculating the statutorily prescribed time period for the agreement. If the term of the development agreement is negotiable, the developer will certainly want the longest possible term to assure completion of the project. The developer should negotiate a provision that allows for extensions, including "automatic" extensions of the time period. The best strategy here is for the developer to make a reasonable estimate of the time needed to complete the project and then add one more increment of time to allow for contingencies.

### [3] Definition of Development Approvals Required

It is important that the agreement indicate up front that the developer has the right to develop the property and to implement the project in accordance with a specific list of approvals described in relation to the comprehensive plan (if it exists), the zoning ordinance, and a concept or preliminary plan. These can be collectively defined in the agreement as the "Approvals." It is also important that the agreement provide that the developer may make applications for other land use approvals, entitlements, and permits necessary or desirable in connection with the development of the property and construction of the project. These approvals can be defined as "Subsequent Approvals" and defined, for example, to include, without limitation, amendment of the development agreement, design review, annexations, special use permits, preliminary and final subdivision plans, grading permits, building permits, lot line adjustments, sewer and water connection permits, certificates of occupancy, and any amendments to, or repealing of, any of the foregoing. The duration of these various approvals should also be defined. The best approach is to define that as the longer of (1) the term of the agreement, and (2) the term provided with respect to the applicable Approval or Subsequent Approval. These two defined terms, "Approvals" and "Subsequent Approvals," can also be used to help define what laws, rules, and regulations are applicable to the property during the life of the project.

### [4] Amendments to the Agreement

Amendments to the agreement generally cannot be made without the same formal public hearing and adoption of ordinance procedures used to approve the development agreement. Obviously, an amendment subsequent to the original approval of the development agreement can be time-consuming and costly for both sides. The best approach, therefore, is to provide in the agreement for certain "minor" changes that require no formal amendment procedures. A typical provision for that purpose, which takes into account the "approvals" and "subsequent approvals" concepts discussed above, would be:

> Any amendment to this Agreement or to the Approvals or the Subsequent Approvals which does not relate to the term of this Agreement, permitted uses, density or intensity of use, or conditions, terms, restrictions and requirements relating to subsequent discretion-

ary actions, monetary contributions by Developer, or any conditions or covenants relating to the Project or the Property shall be deemed a "minor amendment" to this Agreement and may be approved by the City without notice and a public hearing.

By defining as "minor" everything but certain specific items, the local government and the developer provide for the necessary flexibility without having to define in advance all possible changes that should be considered "minor."

### [5] Developer's Vested Rights

Even though the statute authorizing development agreements will state that, except as otherwise provided in the agreement, the project will be subject only to the land use regulations in effect at the time of adoption of the agreement, the developer will want an explicit provision in the agreement that "locks in" the existing regulations. The provision can be as simple as the following: "Developer shall have the vested right to develop the property and construct the project subject to this agreement and the Applicable Law (a defined term)." The municipality will want to spell out the developer's rights and make applicable subsequent regulatory changes not in conflict with existing approvals. It can be useful to expressly identify in the agreement all the regulations governing the development and compile them in a separate binder for ongoing reference.

### [6] Developer's Obligations

The local government will seek affirmative obligations from the developer, such as the obligations to (1) proceed with the development; (2) cooperate with the municipality in implementing public financing mechanisms; (3) make dedications; or (4) provide for public facilities. The developer should try to limit its affirmative obligations and provide instead that its rights to develop are conditioned on meeting certain planning and financing requirements. In other words, the developer's affirmative obligation should be referenced to specific planning and financing documents, making compliance a condition for exercising its rights under the agreement.

### [7]  Fees, Assessments, Contributions, and Other Charges

The developer should try to freeze applicable fees, assessments, contributions, and any other charges at levels in effect at the time of adoption of the development agreement. Usually the parties can agree that the local government will not increase or impose development fees unless uniformly imposed on all development projects in the jurisdiction. Perhaps the most critical negotiation will involve how to address fees and assessments related to the financing of the developer's future infrastructure obligations. The solution can take many forms, depending upon the nature of the development and how the parties weigh the project's infrastructure needs against its benefits to the community. To the extent that development fees will be imposed on the developer, a good approach is to agree on a financing plan based on the developer's reasonable cost estimates. Once the applicable fees, assessments, and other charges have been negotiated, it is important for the developer to include a provision that clearly limits additional charges. The following is one example:

> No fees, donations or contributions of any type or description whatsoever other than those specifically set forth in this Agreement shall be due and payable to the City as a result of the development of the property or the project, and developer, nor any successors, assigns, grantees, transferees, lessees or licensees of developer, shall be liable for the payment of any such fees, donations or contributions.

### [8]   Assignment and Transfer of Rights and Obligations

The developer will want to negotiate a provision for assignment or transfers of rights and obligations in connection with sale or transfer of ownership. The local government will want the right to approve any assignments or transfers—something the developer should be reluctant to give. The local government may also seek to limit transfers and assignments to certain kinds of assignees based on financial resources, experience, and other factors. However, it is frequently the case, particularly in commercial development, that the developer who is most capable of stepping into the shoes of the original developer may not necessarily have the depth of financial resources that the city believes desirable. The flexibility desired by both may be best achieved by providing for a "process" that ensures sufficient communication before any assignment is made. For example, the development agreement might provide as follows:

> In the event that developer proposes to assign this agreement, the city shall receive written notice thereof and shall have ten (10) working days to review and comment on the proposed assignment. The developer agrees to give all reasonable consideration to city's comments but shall retain the right to assign this agreement without city approval.

The developer should also negotiate a relatively short time period for when the transfer or assignment will take effect.

### [9]   Compliance Review and Remedies for Default

Most development agreements statutes provide for periodic review of the developer's good faith compliance with the terms of the agreement. It is important for the local government and the developer to negotiate the manner in which the review is to be conducted because lack of compliance may be grounds to terminate or amend the agreement. Because all parties will rely on the agreement to their mutual benefit, the right to terminate the agreement should be subject to a procedure for resolving and curing any default. Termination should be the last resort for resolving a dispute arising under the agreement. Both parties should seek to limit remedies to equitable relief or termination, and preclude demands for monetary damages.

## § 7.09 Development Agreement Challenge—Initiative and Referendum

Many states, by statute, state constitution, or local charter, allow citizen challenges to local government action through initiative and referendum. The United States Supreme Court has sanctioned this method of citizen challenge by holding in an Ohio rezoning case involving a charter-mandated referendum that the referendum provision was authorized by the state constitution, which reserved legislative power in the people. According to the Court, this meant that the referendum on the rezoning, a legislative act, was valid despite the fact that there were no substantive standards to guide the people in their decision. As legislators need not have standards when enacting legislation, the people need not have standards to guide them when acting in their reserved legislative capacity.[80]

The California statute declares that the development agreement is a legislative action subject to referendum.[81] Apparently it was thought that subjecting development agreements to referendum would provide a means to correct abuse by lame duck city councils. Nevertheless, in my view, this "legislative" characterization of development agreements is unfortunate because the development agree-

---

[80] City of Eastlake v. Forest City Enterprises, Inc., 426 U.S. 668, 96 S. Ct. 2358, 49 L. Ed. 2d 132 (1976).

[81] Only where a rezoning was characterized as administrative because it was accomplished pursuant to a settlement agreement was it held not to be subject to referendum. *See* Southwest Diversified, Inc. v. City of Brisbane, 229 Cal. App. 3d 1548, 280 Cal. Rptr. 869 (1st Dist. 1991).

ment is intended to address a specific parcel, or combination of parcels, and provide for an agreed-upon package of permitted uses, exactions, and other related requirements subject to a time frame during which regulations will remain unchanged for the project. By being subject to rescission by referendum, the very certainty and stability intended through this approach to the vesting problem is undercut.[82] In Hawaii, the development agreement statute expressly declares that adoption of a development is an adjudicatory action, and therefore, is not subject to referendum.[83]

## § 7.10  Development Agreement—Government Noncompliance

The basic rules discussed in the context of conditional zoning also have application to development agreements when the government fails or refuses to perform its agreed-upon obligations.

### [1]  Public Health and Safety Purpose

The government may refuse to perform its contractual obligations when the exercise of the police power is necessary in the public interest to ensure public health and safety.[84] This rule could apply even in instances where, for example, a developer had acquired infrastructure capacity

---

[82] The California development agreement statute limits the opportunity for repeal by referendum to thirty days after the local government's adoption of the ordinance approving the agreement. Cal. Gov't Code § 65867.5.

[83] Haw. Rev. Stat. §§ 46-121 - 46-132 (Michie 1988). See also Callies, "How Development Agreements Work in Hawaii," in Development Agreements: Practice, Policy and Prospects, Douglas R. Porter and Lindell L. Marsh eds., Urban Land Inst., 1989.

[84] See, e.g., Keystone Bituminous Coal Ass'n v. DeBenedictis, 480 U.S. 470, 107 S. Ct. 1232, 94 L. Ed. 2d 472, 25 Env't. Rep. Cas. (BNA) 1649, 17 Envtl. L. Rep. 20440 (1987); Home Bldg. & Loan Ass'n v. Blaisdell, 290 U.S. 398, 345, 54 S. Ct. 231, 78 L. Ed. 413, 88 A.L.R. 1481 (1934).

through the development agreement, but the development itself was subsequently determined to threaten health and safety, for example, because of sewage overflow. If in response to this perceived health danger, the government refused to issue a building permit, its action would likely be upheld.[85] The developer, however, may still have a valid claim for damages.

### [2] No "Public Health or Safety" Purpose

If the government cannot point to an essential police power purpose for its refusal to perform, then the inquiry is whether it can demonstrate that its inaction substantially advances a legitimate state interest.[86] According to the U.S. Supreme Court, the test is whether an "essential nexus" exists between the government action and the substantial advancement of a legitimate state interest. Having presumably determined in the first instance that a proposed development falls within the general health, safety, and welfare parameters of land use, and underscored that finding in the development agreement, a local government is unlikely to persuade a court that refusal to issue a building permit or give other approvals identified in the agreement satisfies the essential nexus test or any equitable standard.

In fact, if there is any indication in the sparse case law on development agreements, it is that a court will focus on the equitable factors in a development agreement. In one Maryland case, for example, the city, by ordinance, gave developers who donated a portion of their developable land

---

[85] *Keystone*, 480 U.S. at 492 n.22; Goldblatt v. Town of Hempstead, N. Y., 369 U.S. 590, 593–94, 82 S. Ct. 987, 8 L. Ed. 2d 130 (1962); Mugler v. Kansas, 123 U.S. 623, 8 S. Ct. 273, 31 L. Ed. 205 (1887). *See also* Delaney, "Development Agreements: The Road from Prohibition to 'Let's Make a Deal!'" 25 Urb. Law. 61 (Winter 1993).

[86] Nollan v. California Coastal Com'n, 483 U.S. 825, 107 S. Ct. 3141, 97 L. Ed. 2d 677, 26 Env't. Rep. Cas. (BNA) 1073, 17 Envtl. L. Rep. 20918 (1987); Dolan v. City of Tigard, 512 U.S. 374, 114 S. Ct. 2309, 129 L. Ed. 2d 304, 38 Env't. Rep. Cas. (BNA) 1769, 24 Envtl. L. Rep. 21083 (1994).

to the city an offsetting increase in density on the remainder of their tracts. A developer did just that, transferring land to the city for road purposes. Subsequent to the transfer, the city comprehensively rezoned the area and denied the developer's application to develop at the full density allowed by the offsetting provision in the ordinance. The Maryland Court of Appeals held for the developer, not on a vested rights theory, but rather on the basis that the developer had acquired "vested contractual rights," which estopped the city from denying the developer the right to proceed with the development.[87]

## § 7.11 Developer Agreement—Developer Noncompliance

If the developer reneges on its obligations under the development agreement while still seeking the benefits of the agreement, then the government normally has the power, under the development agreement and by virtue of its permitting ordinances, to withhold development approvals until the developer performs. In addition, or in combination with its regulatory powers, the government would have contractual remedies—damages, injunction, and specific performance. However, if changes in the particular development market or the economy lead the developer to conclude that the benefits contracted for are no longer desirable or available, can the government force the developer to proceed with the development? In one New Jersey case,[88] after a developer abandoned the project, a township sued for specific performance of a development agreement that had been approved in conjunction with site plan approval and the grant of a variance for the project. The court refused to grant specific performance, reasoning that the improvements required as a condition of the development agreement were subject to an implied

---

[87] Mayor and City Council of Baltimore v. Crane, 277 Md. 198, 352 A.2d 786, 790 (1976).

[88] River Vale Planning Bd. v. E & R Office Interiors, Inc., 241 N.J. Super. 391, 575 A.2d 55 (App. Div. 1990).

or constructive condition that the improvements were required only if the developer went forward with the project.

Many development agreement statutes require that the developer have a legal or equitable interest in the property to which the development agreement applies. What happens if the developer fails to obtain or retain control of all, or a portion of, the property subject to the agreement? A California case involving a development agreement for a proposed landfill provides some helpful reasoning on this issue.[89] The development agreement had been approved by the county as part of the county's approval of an environmental impact report (EIR) prepared for the landfill, even though the developer's interest in the property was contingent upon a pending land exchange. The association, as part of its challenge to certification of the EIR, argued that, under the property control provision of the California Development Agreements Statute, the developer must have a current legal or equitable interest in the property before it could enter into the development agreement.

The trial court noted that the agreement did not actually become effective until the developer acquired the fee interest in the property. The court also noted that the developer already had a legal interest in the bulk of the adjacent land that would be developed. Applying common sense to the circumstances, the court construed the California statute liberally to allow the agreement to stand. The court explained that, generally, the proper test for statutory compliance is "substantial compliance." To hold otherwise under the circumstances would hamstring public agencies' efforts to work with private entities to develop housing and other public facilities.

A court would also conclude that substantial compliance is the appropriate test for statutory compliance in circumstances where, in the face of difficult market conditions,

---

[89] National Parks & Conservation Assn. v. County of Riverside, 42 Cal. App. 4th 1505, 50 Cal. Rptr. 2d 339 (4th Dist. 1996).

the developer loses legal or equitable control of a portion of the property, but is otherwise prepared to continue to perform on the property still subject to the development agreement.

## § 7.12 Development Agreement and Takings Claims

If a condition imposed by local government through an executed development agreement is excessive and does not satisfy the "rough proportionality" test recently articulated by the U.S. Supreme Court,[90] is it enforceable against a subsequent taking claim by the developer? The few existing cases that shed light on this issue suggest that the developer gets the short end of the argument.

A general rule followed in California and other states is that a developer cannot challenge conditions imposed in conjunction with a land use permit if the developer specifically agrees to the conditions or fails to challenge the validity and accepts the benefits of the permit.[91] Obviously, a developer who receives the benefits of the bargain, even if he claims he entered into it under duress, will not find a court sympathetic to the taking argument. For example, in a Maryland case, the developer made a "duress" argument, but the court found that because the agreement had been initiated by the developer and was "an informed business decision" that benefited both the government and the developer, no taking occurred.[92]

A more recent decision from the U.S. Court of Appeals for the Ninth Circuit is consistent with the outcome in the

---

[90] Dolan v. City of Tigard, 512 U.S. 374, 114 S. Ct. 2309, 129 L. Ed. 2d 304, 38 Env't. Rep. Cas. (BNA) 1769, 24 Envtl. L. Rep. 21083 (1994).

[91] *See* County of Imperial v. McDougal, 19 Cal. 3d 505, 138 Cal. Rptr. 472, 564 P.2d 14 (1977), application denied, 434 U.S. 899, 98 S. Ct. 294, 54 L. Ed. 2d 187 (1977); Rossco Holdings Inc. v. State of California, 212 Cal. App. 3d 642, 260 Cal. Rptr. 736 (2d Dist. 1989).

[92] Meredith v. Talbot County, 80 Md. App. 174, 560 A.2d 599, 604 (1989).

Maryland case.[93] The case involved a condominium project that became subject to new mitigation rules by the Tahoe Regional Planning Agency (TRPA) after the developer had commenced its project. The project was not the subject of a development agreement, but after the developer sought an injunction against the new mitigation rules, the parties entered into a settlement agreement. The settlement agreement required the developer to perform off-site as well as on-site mitigation in exchange for permission to construct 185 of 203 proposed units. Despite agreeing to commence the off-site mitigation measures upon completion of the fiftieth unit, the developer sought to have the agreement declared void on the ground that the off-site measures did not satisfy the "essential nexus" test articulated by the U.S. Supreme Court.[94] The trial court agreed that the off-site mitigation measures lacked the proper nexus, but the appellate court disagreed, holding: "[A] contractual promise which operates to restrict a property owner's use of land cannot result in a 'taking' because the promise is entered into voluntarily, in good faith and is supported by consideration."[95] Although the case can be distinguished as pertaining only to settlement agreements, developers can expect that local governments will cite the case and the court's reasoning as applicable to development agreements.[96]

---

[93] *See* Leroy Land Development v. Tahoe Regional Planning Agency, 939 F.2d 696, 21 Envtl. L. Rep. 21376 (9th Cir. 1991).

[94] Nollan v. California Coastal Com'n, 483 U.S. 825, 107 S. Ct. 3141, 97 L. Ed. 2d 677, 26 Env't. Rep. Cas. (BNA) 1073, 17 Envtl. L. Rep. 20918 (1987).

[95] *Id.*

[96] *See* Curtin, "Protecting Developers' Permits to Build: Development Agreement Practice in California and Other States," 18 *Zoning and Planning Law Report* 91 (December 1995). For the view that the rough proportionality and essential nexus tests should apply to development agreements, *see* Starritt & Mcclannahan, "Land-Use Planning and Takings: The Viability of Conditional Exactions to Conserve Open Space in the Rocky Mountain," 30 *Land & Water L. Rev.* 415 (1995); *see also* Crew, "Development Agreements After Nollan v. California Coastal Commission, 483 U.S. 825 (1987)," 22 *Urb. Law.* 23 (1990).

## § 7.13 Practice Tips

### [1] Understand the Local Government's Goals and Objectives

A developer who does not know what the local government wants out of a project that it is prepared to authorize through conditional zoning or a development agreement can be blind-sided with demands or objectives late in the approval process. Therefore, the developer must always be cognizant of the public's goals and objectives relative to the project. These may involve, for example, the inclusion of specific uses in the project or historic preservation. In the case of a public-private venture in which the public partner participates in the income stream or uses some of the space, the goals may include the maximization of project revenues of the long-term maintenance of quality and setasides for particular groups in hiring, contracting, or leasing.

### [2] Be Aware of Which Communications Are Covered by the Sunshine Law

Much of a developer's communication with local government officials will be open to the public by virtue of the jurisdiction's *Sunshine Law*. These laws generally provide that all meetings of public bodies must be public, subject to certain exceptions. A public body usually is defined broadly, and a meeting under the Sunshine Law can be any gathering of some of its members held for the purposes of discussing public business. In the context of discussions aimed at achieving certain zoning entitlements or a development agreement, there may be the temptation to meet or lobby with more than one member of the city council or other public decision-making body. Even though such meetings or discussions are outside a formal public meeting, they may qualify as a meeting under the Sunshine Law. For the developer who does not appreciate the scope of "a meeting of a public body," it can be very embarrassing later.

### [3] Be Aware of Public Disclosure Requirements

The developer should also remember that every written communication to a public entity is the document that ultimately may be disseminated to interested third parties, the press, and the public at large if disclosure is requested under the state's *freedom of information requirements*. The developer should study carefully any state or local *conflict of interest laws* and avoid doing business with public officials who may be involved in the project, or with their family members or affiliates.

### [4] Seek to Provide for Concept Approval Under a Development Agreement

Concept approval can be one of the keys to a successful development. The developer should endeavor in the development agreement or, if necessary, by an amendment to the permitting ordinance, to provide that a project that has obtained concept approval need not go back to the legislative body for approval. In this way, the preliminary development plan, final plan, and final engineering drawings are reviewed at the *staff* level. The developer avoids having to go through the city council or village board at a late stage when legislative discretion to make radical alterations can be costly. Flexibility must be built into concept approval, as in the following language:

> This [concept approval] procedure allows for the approval of an overall concept without the necessity of prejudging long-range markets and preparing precise plans for unknown quantities and allows the Developer to complete long-range commitments knowing that a viable and acceptable project has been approved.

This language is similar to that used in the regional planned unit development (RPUD) ordinance discussed in Chapter 6.[97]

### [5] Provide for Building Envelope Approvals in the Development Agreement

Once the developer and local government have agreed upon the project's density, the concept of building envelope[98] approvals can free the developer to build within the envelope and whatever building configuration or locations are needed to make the project work, without having to go back for additional approvals.

### [6] Utilize Performance Standards

Where possible, performance standards should be used to identify minimum requirements or maximum limits on the effects or characteristics of a project. Performance standards may address such aspects of bulk,[99] impervious surface,[100] traffic, parking, noise, landscaping, and open space. These standards can be incorporated into the development agreement or made part of an approved plan of development. Properly drafted, performance standards tied to stages of development approvals can narrow the scope of discretion to exercise by the public body during the approval process, thus giving the developer the predictability needed to manage the project successfully from a financial standpoint.

---

[97] *See* Ch. 6, Sec. 6.12, *supra.*

[98] The term *building envelope* is used here to refer to the three-dimensional space, usually defined by maximum height and yard setback requirements, within which a structure may be built on a lot or parcel.

[99] The term *bulk* refers to the size of a building or structure in relation to the lot. Typical provisions in zoning ordinances that control bulk are standards for maximum height, building coverage, floor area ratio (FAR), and yard setbacks.

[100] *Impervious surface* is usually defined as any material or structure, such as sidewalk and parking lot pavements and buildings that prevent absorption of stormwater into the ground.

### [7]    Pay Attention to the Timing of Public Involvement

At the public hearing, the developer must be responsive to the concerns that are expressed; however, once those concerns are addressed, the developer can legitimately take the position that further public involvement, through which significant changes to the project may be requested, should be foreclosed. Language in the development agreement should specifically address the scope of changes permissible after the developer has been responsive to concerns expressed at the public hearing.

### [8]    Provide for Consolidated Approvals or Lodge Approval at the Staff Level

To expedite the approval process, the developer should seek to consolidate approvals or lodge the approval authority at the staff level so that the project is not subject to further changes through discretionary reviews. In lieu of a concept approval approach, the developer can request that the city council meet as a "committee of the whole" to discuss the project. This procedure is usually authorized by statute and allows for special meetings to be called using general public notice rather than expensive and time-consuming individual property owner notices. This gives the developer the opportunity to build a council-wide consensus for the project concept, which is difficult if the review work is done by separate council committees. Once the council has reached the conceptual agreement, the project is less likely to encounter difficulties when it comes up for formal council approval.

### [9]    Draft Documents That Define Key Terms and Provide Provisions Against Subsequent Regulatory Changes

The developer's substantive and procedural strategies must be reflected in well-drafted documents that define key terms, provide provisions against subsequent regulatory changes, and, where possible, ensure that the developer can argue as strongly as possible that the local government is estopped from making unwarranted changes to the project late in the approval process.

### [10]   Define the Term "Substantial Change"

A developer does not want to be subject to the requirement of further approvals because the community perceives that a significant change has been made to the project, a change which the developer believes to be insubstantial. If substantial change can be objectified, it becomes more difficult for the project's critics to assert in vague terms that a given change is substantial.

### [11]   Define the Term "Substantial Conformity"

The developer does not want to leave the determination of "conformance" with plan requirements to the whim of the local government. The term "conformance" should be limited to "substantial" conformance in order to provide a reasonable basis from which to judge the sufficiency of the developer's performance. One definition of "substantial conformity" is as follows:

> The corporate authority shall not unreasonably withhold approval, nor shall it impose unreasonable restrictions or conditions thereon, with respect to any proposed development that is in substantial conformity with [reference specific exhibits] for which concept approval is being granted pursuant to this agreement.

### [12]   Create a Basis from Which to Argue That the Government Is "Estopped" from Making Subsequent Changes to the Project

The developer's approval strategy should include creating an estoppel, or a basis from which the developer can argue that a government is precluded (estopped) by its own acts from making a zoning change that affects the developer's property. For example, to establish the developer's ability to rely upon understandings contained in an approved concept plan, the developer should heavily "footnote" the plan, tying down specific understandings so that they cannot be challenged later as elements not contemplated by the concept plan.

**See full text of Development Agreement Statutes in Appendix.**

# CHAPTER 8

# Design Review

## Scope of Chapter

## § 8.01   Introduction

The Appearance Commission attempted to negotiate us down from what was acceptable per the code [10' x 10'], to a five foot wide sign. After much discussion, we finally agreed on an eight foot wide sign, which they approved. I asked them if we had any other choice in the matter, and they commented that our proposal could be tabled again until next month.

—Letter of shopping center developer to mayor of a village in suburban Illinois

> [A]s long as zoning codes favor low-density develop-
> ment over the creation of compact communities,
> developers will not be able to shake their reputation
> as land rapists, as they turn farm after farm into
> cookie-cutter sprawl. This is why one can buy a
> bumper sticker that reads: LEAVING TOWN? TAKE A
> DEVELOPER WITH YOU.
> —Andres Duany, Elizabeth Plater-Zyberk, Jeff Speck
> *The Suburban Nation: The Rise of Sprawl and the*
> *Decline of the American Dream*

Perhaps one of the most ubiquitous advisory bodies
found in local communities is the appearance committee.
The appearance committee, or commission, with its charge
to serve as the aesthetic watchdog for the community, has
become a fixture in many communities. Developers find it
easier to accommodate this body's requests than to challenge them.[1] The exasperated and resigned shopping
center developer whose letter of frustration to the village
mayor is quoted above is not alone in feeling that this
type of action by an advisory body is an abuse of discretionary authority at the local level.

With the aid of two U.S. Supreme Court decisions,[2]
courts generally have taken a more permissive attitude toward land use regulations that address "aesthetic"
concerns of a community. Although these two decisions
upheld the regulation of signs for aesthetic and traffic
safety reasons, the language from these cases helped move
many state courts toward the view that aesthetics alone is

---

[1] For the handful of cases involving challenges to such bodies, *see*
Wakelin v. Town of Yarmouth, 523 A.2d 575 (Me. 1987); Morristown
Road Associates v. Mayor and Common Council and Planning Bd. of
Borough of Bernardsville, 163 N.J. Super. 58, 394 A.2d 157 (Law Div.
1978). *See also* Poole and Kobert, "Architectural Appearance Review
Regulations and the First Amendment: The Constitutionally Infirm
'Excessive Difference' Test," 12 *Zoning and Planning Law Report* (Janu-
ary 1989).

[2] Metromedia, Inc. v. City of San Diego, 453 U.S. 490, 101 S. Ct.
2882, 69 L. Ed. 2d 800, 16 Env't. Rep. Cas. (BNA) 1057, 11 Envtl. L.
Rep. 20600 (1981); Members of City Council of City of Los Angeles v.
Taxpayers for Vincent, 466 U.S. 789, 104 S. Ct. 2118, 80 L. Ed. 2d 772
(1984).

a legitimate governmental purpose in land use regulation.[3] These state and federal court decisions also encouraged local governments to adopt regulations focusing on aesthetic impacts of "ugly" signs, loss of open space, and erosion of community "character." In these regulations, communities are increasingly adopting discretionary review approaches to design review issues ranging from fences in neighborhoods to office buildings in downtowns.

## § 8.02 Aesthetics in Land Use Regulation

The difficulty of using aesthetics as a principal basis for land use regulation is that the meaning of "aesthetics" is unclear to most people. Perhaps that is not surprising when we learn that the term itself is derived from a Greek word that means perception.[4] In fact, originally, the term "aesthetics" did not exclude the concept of ugliness. The 1970 edition of the Oxford English Dictionary defines "aesthetic" as criticism of taste as a science of philosophy. But it is the second definition that invokes the concept of beauty: "of or pertaining to the appreciation or criticism of the beautiful."[5]

Equating aesthetics with "beauty" in land use regulation has caused nothing but trouble for those trying to

---

[3] See, e.g., Donrey Communications Co., Inc. v. City of Fayetteville, 280 Ark. 408, 660 S.W.2d 900 (1983); Metromedia, Inc. v. City of San Diego, 26 Cal. 3d 848, 164 Cal. Rptr. 510, 610 P.2d 407, 14 Env't. Rep. Cas. (BNA) 1865, 10 Envtl. L. Rep. 20862 (1980), judgment rev'd on other grounds, 453 U.S. 490, 101 S. Ct. 2882, 69 L. Ed. 2d 800, 16 Env't. Rep. Cas. (BNA) 1057, 11 Envtl. L. Rep. 20600 (1981); City of Lake Wales v. Lamar Advertising Ass'n of Lakeland, Florida, 414 So. 2d 1030 (Fla. 1982); John Donnelly & Sons, Inc. v. Outdoor Advertising Bd., 369 Mass. 206, 339 N.E.2d 709, 8 Env't. Rep. Cas. (BNA) 1671, 6 Envtl. L. Rep. 20123 (1975); Cromwell v. Ferrier, 19 N.Y.2d 263, 279 N.Y.S.2d 22, 225 N.E.2d 749, 21 A.L.R.3d 1212 (1967), reargument denied, 19 N.Y.2d 862, 280 N.Y.S.2d 1025, 227 N.E.2d 408 (1967); State v. Jones, 305 N.C. 520, 290 S.E.2d 675 (1982); Oregon City v. Hartke, 240 Or. 35, 400 P.2d 255 (1965); State v. Smith, 618 S.W.2d 474 (Tenn. 1981); LaSalle Nat. Bank v. Lake County, 27 Ill. App. 3d 10, 325 N.E.2d 105, 110 (2d Dist. 1975).

[4] See generally Bates, W., Plato's View of Art, 32–62 (1972).

[5] 1 Oxford English Dictionary 147–48 (rev. 1970).

administer such regulations and the courts that have been asked to review such regulations. As one New Jersey court said: "The concept is admittedly a most difficult one to put into fair practice. Beauty and taste are almost impossible to legislate affirmatively on any very broad scale because they are generally such subjective and individual things, not easily susceptible of objective, non-arbitrary standards."[6] Long before, in 1925, the Ohio Supreme Court best articulated the subjectivity problem with this visual beauty concept of aesthetics:

> It is commendable and desirable, but not essential to the public need, that our aesthetic desires be gratified. Moreover, authorities in general agree as to the essentials of a public health program, while the public view as to what is necessary for aesthetic progress greatly varies. Certain Legislatures might consider that it was more important to cultivate a taste for jazz than for Beethoven, for poster than for Rembrandt, and for limericks than for Keats. Successive city councils might never agree as to what the public needs from an aesthetic standpoint, and this fact makes the aesthetic standard impractical as a standard for use restriction upon property. The world would be a continual seesaw if aesthetic considerations were permitted to govern the use of the police power. We are therefore remitted to the proposition that the police power is based upon public necessity, and that the public health morals, or safety, and not merely aesthetic interest, must be in danger in order to justify its use.[7]

Put another way, the judicial view was: Aesthetic judgments and standards are a matter of individual taste, which run the gamut. Therefore, they are too subjective to be applied in any way that is not arbitrary and capricious,

---

[6] Westfield Motor Sales Co. v. Town of Westfield, 129 N.J. Super. 528, 324 A.2d 113, 119 (Law Div. 1974).

[7] City of Youngstown v. Kahn Bros. Bldg. Co., 112 Ohio St. 654, 3 Ohio L. Abs. 332, 148 N.E. 842, 844, 43 A.L.R. 662 (1925).

a violation of the due process clause of the fourteenth amendment.[8]

Until the early 1950s, the judicial angst caused by the pursuit of beauty through land use restrictions led most courts to hold that the government could not zone "solely for aesthetics;" that is, to be valid, aesthetic-based regulations must also further other traditional, nonaesthetic police power purposes such as traffic, safety, and property values. Of course, this judicial approach could also be a stretch, requiring some fancy legal reasoning to sustain aesthetic measures. Then, in 1954, a U.S. Supreme Court decision appeared to embrace a "beauty for beauty's sake alone" rationale for the power of eminent domain. In upholding the District of Columbia's urban renewal program against the charge, among others, that it was aesthetically based, the Court said:

> The concept of the public welfare is broad and inclusive. The values it represents are spiritual as well as physical, aesthetic as well as monetary. It is within the power of the legislature to determine that the community should be beautiful as well as healthy, spacious as well as clean, well balanced as well as carefully patrolled.[9]

Although the Court's pronouncement was made with reference to the power of eminent domain, not police power, its broad definition of the public welfare was seized upon by advocates of aesthetic regulation to justify zoning

---

[8] *See, e.g.,* Appeal of Medinger, 377 Pa. 217, 104 A.2d 118 (1954); City of Passaic v. Paterson Bill Posting, Advertising & Sign Painting Co., 72 N.J.L. 285, 62 A. 267 (N.J. Ct. Err. & App. 1905). *See also* Agnor, "Beauty Begins a Comeback: Aesthetic Considerations in Zoning," J. Pub L. 260 (1962). *See also* Kosalka v. Town of Georgetown, 2000 ME 106, 752 A.2d 183 (Me. 2000) (invalidating provision of zoning ordinance allowing campgrounds as a conditional use in Limited Residential-Recreational Districts so long as they "conserve natural beauty" as constituting unconstitutional delegation of legislative authority and violation of due process clause. The "conserve natural beauty" condition was held to be an "unmeasurable quality, totally lacking in cognizable, quantitative standards.")

[9] Berman v. Parker, 348 U.S. 26, 33, 75 S. Ct. 98, 99 L. Ed. 27 (1954).

"solely for aesthetics." And, in fact, beginning in the 1960s, there has been a gradual judicial turnabout to the point that the majority of state courts now accept regulations based on aesthetics alone.[10]

Unfortunately, this judicial turnabout has not cured the problems created in the first place by equating aesthetics with visual beauty—the lack of intelligible standards to help safeguard private property rights and due process. The remainder of this chapter is devoted to addressing these problems and ways to safeguard against the inevitable invitations to abuse of discretion in the implementation of aesthetically based regulatory programs.

## § 8.03  Varying Objectives of Design Review

Despite the weaknesses of the visual beauty rationale for aesthetic regulation, cities and towns have pushed forward with discretionary review processes intended to preserve, enhance, and promote aspects of their built and natural environments that they consider to be "good design" or visually pleasing. These discretionary design review processes usually take three forms: urban design-review, appearance review, and architectural review. *Urban design review* is a term and review process more typically employed in largely built environments or cities, where the focus is the urban fabric—light, air, views, open space, and spatial and functional relationships within the city.

In a survey published on design review practice, the author used the following definition of design review:

---

[10] Representative cases may be found in Mandelker, D., *Land Use Law* § 11.05, Charlottesville, Va.: Michie, 1993.

Design Review refers to the process by which private and public development proposals receive independent scrutiny under the sponsorship of the local government unit, whether through informal or formalized processes. It is distinguished from traditional (Euclidean) zoning and subdivision controls, in that it deals with urban design, architecture, or visual impacts.[11]

Of the three terms used in this definition of design review—urban design, architecture, and visual impacts—"urban design" is perhaps the least understood. In one helpful explanation, the author describes urban design as:

> . . . the composition of architectural form and open space in a community context. The elements of a city's architecture are its buildings, urban landscape, and service infrastructure just as form, structure, and internal space are elements of a building. . . . Like architecture, urban design reflects considerations of

---

[11] Survey by Professor Brenda Case Lightner, cited in Scheer, Brenda Case and Preiser, Wolfgang F.E., eds., *Design Review: Challenging Urban Aesthetic Control,* Chapman & Hall, 1994.

function, economics, and efficiency as well as aesthetic and cultural qualities.[12]

Stated differently, from a city planning policy perspective, urban design is "designing cities without designing buildings."[13]

By contrast, *appearance review*—a suburban and small-town phenomenon—is directed more at preserving and enhancing a perceived community identity or "character" and emphasizes compatibility with existing architectural styles and visual harmony throughout the community through review of site plans, landscape plans, and signage. Architectural design, of course, is an important component of these community appearance review programs. The third form of discretionary design review, *architectural design review*, is the result of communities focusing primarily on architectural design. To do so, communities establish architectural review boards. The architectural design review conducted by these boards can have varying missions. For example, in some communities, you will find that the board's mission is to disapprove *excessive similarity* to any other existing or approved structure within a certain distance. A mission of otherboards is to avoid *excessive differences* between structures. And then there is the architectural review board whose mission is to prevent *inappropriate* design. To confound matters further, some communities adopt architectural review ordinances that simultaneously prohibit excessive similarity, excessive dissimilarity, and inappropriateness in building design! Richard Babcock was fond of calling these architectural review and appearance review bodies "pretty committees."[14] I discuss these communities further in the following section.

---

[12] Tseng-yu Lai, R., *Law in Urban Design and Planning* at 1, New York: Van Nostrand Reinhold Co., 1988.

[13] Barnett, J., *An Introduction to Urban Design* at 55, New York: Harper & Row, 1982.

[14] *See, e.g.,* Blaesser and Weinstein, eds., *Land Use and the Constitution* at 25–26, Chicago, Ill.: Planners Press, 1989.

*"Great design, but, when the time comes, a bitch to implode."*

Drawings by Moller © The New Yorker Magazine, Inc.

## § 8.04   Legal Problems with Design Review

The general view held by most commentators is that the majority of courts have accepted the proposition that land use regulation can be justified on aesthetics alone if there are adequate standards and those standards are appropriately applied.[15] But those are big "ifs." Problems arise because of the limitations inherent in zoning enabling legislation—the difficulty of fashioning meaningful standards when aesthetics are equated with visual beauty—and because communities try to reach too far

---

[15] *See, e.g.,* 1 Young, K., *Anderson's American Law of Zoning* §§ 7.13-.25 (1996); 1 Rathkopf, A., *The Law of Zoning and Planning* § 14.01 (1975 & Supp. 1996); 1 Williams, N., *American Land Planning Law* § 11.02 (1974 & Supp. 1995); Bufford, "Beyond the Eye of the Beholder: A New Majority of Jurisdictions Authorize Aesthetic Regulation," 48 UMKC L. Rev. 125 (1980).

through aesthetics-based regulations. We now turn to these problems.

### [1]   Lack of Enabling Authority for Design Review

The fact that land use regulations for "aesthetics only" purposes is now viewed by most state courts as a proper exercise of police power does not mean that local governments in every state are free to fashion aesthetics-based design review programs. The right of local communities to exercise police power for zoning and other land use purposes is derived from the state. This right is based on "Dillon's rule," namely, that local governments have no inherent powers but are limited to those powers granted by the state constitution or legislature.[16] Absent a state constitutional or statutory grant of additional "home-rule" authority, which gives local governments broader powers of self-government, courts have construed Dillon's rule to require strict adherence to the scope of land use regulation and procedures established by the state.

This means that unless a community has this "home-rule" status which gives it broader land use regulatory powers, the extent and manner of permissable aesthetic regulation are limited by the provisions in the state zoning enabling legislation.

---

[16] *Dillon's* rule is used to construe statutes that delegate authority to local government:

> [A] municipal corporation possesses and can exercise the following powers and no others: First, those granted in express words; second, those necessarily implied or necessarily incident to the powers expressly granted; third, those absolutely essential to the declared objects and purposes of the corporation—not simply convenient, but indispensable.
> . . .

Merriam v. Moody's Ex'rs, 25 Iowa 163, 170, 1868 WL 253 (1868).

### [2] Improper Delegation of Power to Impose Design Review

Local legislative bodies may not delegate their legislative or policy-making power to administrative boards, commissions, or committees. In other words, if legislative power is improperly delegated to an administrative body, no amount of due process can cure the problem. In design review ordinances or appearance codes, it is not uncommon to find that the city council has delegated policy-making authority to a design review administrative body. When a developer challenges such an improper delegation of authority, the argument is usually cast in terms of vague standards that allow the administrative body to do whatever it wants. But the real problem is the act of improperly delegating in the first place, which, unfortunately, the courts frequently discuss as a vagueness problem, ignoring the true origin of the problem—improper delegation of policy-making authority.

Reprinted by permission of Phil Frank/San Francisco Chronicle

### [3] Vague, Meaningless Standards

In Chapter 1, I briefly describe how vague, regulatory language can invite abuses of discretion by decision-making bodies. Lack of clarity or certainty in the language of regulation violates the void for vagueness doctrine which is derived from the constitutional right to notice under the due process clause of the Fourteenth Amendment. The purpose of this due process right is to limit the arbitrary implementation of the law by decision makers. The following are some examples of these types of problems.

### [a] Failure to Use Commonly Understood Terms

A common failing in design review regulations is the use of terms that do not give meaningful guidance to those who are expected to implement and comply with the regulations, such as the public officials, the applicants, and the design professionals who frequently are appointed to serve on design review bodies or hired to assist applicants. There are two types of common failings. First, the words used may not be sufficiently "technical" so as to be understood by design professionals. Second, the words may not have any settled meaning based on usage and custom—what the courts call "common-law" meaning. For example, the building design requirements of the City of Issaquah, Washington, stated that the evaluation of a proposed building project would be based on "quality of its design and relationship to the natural setting of the valley and surrounding mountains." The project's windows, doors, eaves, and parapets should be of "appropriate proportions" and seldom "bright" or "brilliant"; its mechanical equipment should be screened from public view; its exterior lighting should be "harmonious" with the building design, and "monotony should be avoided." The project should also be "interesting."[17] Buildings and structures should be made "compatible" with adjacent buildings having "conflicting architectural styles" by use of "screens and site breaks, or other suitable methods and materials. Harmony in texture, lines and masses [is] encouraged."[18]

In 1989, the City's Development Commission denied the development application of a property owner whose property was located on Gilman Boulevard, the City's "signature street." Among the reasons given by the Commission was the owner's failure to be "sufficiently responsive" to the Commission's concerns relating to compliance with these building design requirements.[19] The property owner challenged these requirements as unconstitutionally vague. The court agreed with the property owner, noting that while the code was clear about such aspects as screening of mechanical equipment, "there is nothing in the code from which an applicant can determine whether his or her project is going to be seen by the Development Commission as 'interesting' versus 'monotonous' and as 'harmonious' with the valley and the mountains."[20]

The case also illustrates how, with only vague standards to work with, public officials are emboldened to rely upon their subjective feelings in applying the standards to a specific project. Note the presumptuous nature of the Commissioners' comments as quoted by the court from the minutes of the Commission's hearings:

---

[17] Issaquah Municipal Code (IMC) 16.16.060 (D) (1)–(6).

[18] Issaquah Municipal Code (IMC) 16.16.060 (B) (1)–(3).

[19] Anderson v. City of Issaquah, 70 Wash. App. 64, 851 P.2d 744 (Div. 1 1993).

[20] *Id.* at 751.

> Commissioner Nash suggested that Anderson "drive
> up and down Gilman and look at both good and bad
> examples of what has been done with flat facades."

* * *

Commissioner Steinwachs' observations from driving up
and down Gilman Boulevard were placed verbatim in the
minutes as follows:

> "I see certain design elements and techniques used in
> various combinations in various locations to achieve a
> visual effect that is sensitive to the unique character
> of our Signature Street. I see heavy use of brick, wood
> and tile. I see minimal use of stucco. I see colors that
> are mostly earth tones, avoiding extreme contrasts. I
> see various methods used to provide modulation in
> both horizontal and vertical lines, such as gables, bay
> windows, recesses in front faces, porches, rails, many
> vertical columns, and breaks in roof lines. I see long,
> sloping, conspicuous roofs with large overhangs. I see
> windows with panels above and below windows. I see
> no windows that extend down to floor level. This is
> the impression I have of Gilman Boulevard as it re-
> lates to building design."

* * *

> Commissioner Nash agreed with Commissioner
> Steinwachs, stating, "[T]here is a certain feeling you
> get when you drive along Gilman Boulevard, and this
> building does not give this same feeling."

* * *

> Commissioner Steinwachs wondered if the applicant
> had any option but to start "from scratch."[21]

The problem with these commissioners' observations, as
the court noted, is that the commissioners had no objective criteria or even guidelines to follow. The "statement"
that the City of Issaquah was apparently trying to make
on its "signature street" was not found anywhere in the

---

[21] *Id.* at 747–48.

code. Fortunately, during the owner's appeal to the City Council, one councilwoman, with unusual candor, acknowledged the subjective exercise engaged in by the Commission:

> [M]aybe we haven't done a good job in . . . communicating what kind of image we want. We all want an image. I bet you if I stated my image it would be certainly different from everyone of you here and everyone in the audience. . . . . [I]f we want a specific design, I agree with proponent's counsel, and that is that we come up with a specific district design. . . We don't have such a design requirement. So we all have to rely on some gut feel. And often times this gut feel gets us into trouble because it could be misinterpreted or misconstrued. . . .[22]

The councilwoman's statement illustrates another dimension of the due process problem. It is not only the property owner or applicant who is denied due process by being unable to determine the standards by which his or her project will be judged, but also the community and its officials who are charged with making those judgments. It can be argued that they, too, are denied due process of law because they are unable to review and approve standards as correctly representing their goals for design of new projects in their community.[23]

### [b]   Failure to Use Precise Language

Because the imposition of design review on development proposals impacts constitutional rights, design criteria, though inherently more focused upon the totality of a project,[24] must be responsive to the law's demand for language

---

[22] *Id.* at 752.

[23] Barry & Barry, Inc. v. State Dept. of Motor Vehicles, 81 Wash. 2d 155, 500 P.2d 540 (1972); Maranatha Min., Inc. v. Pierce County, 59 Wash. App. 795, 801 P.2d 985 (Div. 2 1990).

[24] Bross, "Taking Design Review Beyond the Beauty Part," 9 Envtl. L. 211, 226–27 (1979). ("[T]eachers of architecture 'respond to the 'Gestalt,' the perceived totality of the project being presented. . .

that is sufficiently precise for an applicant to ascertain what is being requested and to help the decision maker to arrive at fair, consistent decisions. Admittedly, this is a difficult task. Examples of imprecise language abound. For example, the following architectural review board criteria for signs in the Borough of Stone Harbor, New Jersey, ordinance were challenged on vagueness grounds. The court highlighted the offending terms:

> Signs that *demand* public attention rather than *invite* attention should be discouraged. Color should be selected to *harmonize* with the overall building color scheme to create a *mood* and reinforce symbolically the sign's primary communication message. . . . Care must be taken not to introduce *too many* colors into a sign. A restricted use of color will maintain a communication function of the sign and create a *visually pleasing* element as an integral part of the *texture* of the street. (Court's emphasis)[25]

Not surprisingly, the court found these criteria too vague, encouraging the imposition of subjective standards upon the applicant.[26]

But then, of course, there is always California, the pro-local government state, where vague standards are routinely upheld by the courts. An example is found in the recent case involving the City of Rolling Hills Estates and a challenge to its "neighborhood compatibility" ordinance, which governs new construction and modifications of existing structures in established neighborhoods.[27] The plaintiff, a homeowner, had received approval from the city for a house addition. But during construction, the neighbors

---

[T]here is considerable flexibility in the weighting of critical values applied. . . .' " quoting Wade, John W., *Architecture, Problems, and Purposes*, New York: John Wiley, 1977).

[25] Diller and Fisher Co., Inc. v. Architectural Review Bd. of Borough of Stone Harbor, 246 N.J. Super. 362, 587 A.2d 674, 678 (Law Div. 1990).

[26] *Id.* at 680.

[27] Briggs v. City of Rolling Hills Estates, 40 Cal. App. 4th 637, 47 Cal. Rptr. 2d 29 (2d Dist. 1995).

discovered and complained about a patio/deck structure that had not been approved as part of the addition. They claimed that the patio/deck created a "loss of privacy and created noise and light concerns." The city required the owner to stop all work and submit a new "neighborhood compatibility" application. As part of its approval of the new application, the planning commission required the owner to remove the patio/deck. He appealed to the city council, but to no avail, and then sued.

Before the trial court, the owner contended that the ordinance provisions upon which the neighbors had based their complaints was unconstitutionally vague on its face. Those provisions stated that building designs "shall respect the existing privacy of surrounding properties by maintaining an adequate amount of separation between proposed structure(s) and adjacent property lines. In addition, the design of balconies, decks and windows should also respect the existing privacy of surrounding properties."[28] Taking solace in another California court's upholding of a city's "view" ordinance, the court in this case made short shrift of the owners' argument: "Determining whether plaintiffs' particular project 'respected the existing privacy of surrounding properties' should be no more difficult than determining under the view ordinance whether a project adequately protects a view."[29] It is no wonder that California is often referred to as the "anything goes" state.

### [c]  Failure to Use Language That Has Practical Application

Sometimes language appears to have a commonly understood meaning, but when applied to actual circumstances, is still inadequate to give meaningful guidance.

---

[28] *Id.*
[29] *Id.*

For example, in one New Jersey case,[30] the court reviewed a design standard that required the building design to be "early American." The court did not really address whether "early American" was an adequately precise standard. Rather, when the court examined that standard in light of the actual physical development in the surrounding area, the court observed that there was no consistent character. Consequently, "early American" design could mean anything from log cabin or teepee to a Cape Cod or Dutch colonial style.

### [4]  The "Pretty Committee" Problem

The appearance committee, or "pretty committee," so ubiquitous in suburban communities deserves special attention because it embodies most of the problems we have described: reliance upon vague standards or guidelines; exercise of decision-making power beyond its official "advisory" role; and an excuse for exercising aesthetic controls independent of zoning.

### [a]  Vague Standards or Guidelines

The typical appearance committee's mission is to achieve "harmony" with existing structures in the community, with a few different twists, depending upon the particular community. For example, in one New Jersey case, the guidelines governing the committee's review prohibited "[e]xcessive similarity of appearance and the repetitiveness of features resulting in displeasing monotony of design. . . ."[31] Definitions of such critical terms as "harmonious" and "displeasing" almost defy definition. Perhaps that is why the ordinance containing this stan-

---

[30] Hankins v. Borough of Rockleigh, 55 N.J. Super. 132, 150 A.2d 63 (App. Div. 1959).
[31] Morristown Road Associates v. Mayor and Common Council and Planning Bd. of Borough of Bernardsville, 163 N.J. Super. 58, 394 A.2d 157, 159 (Law Div. 1978).

dard offered no definitions of these terms. Not surprisingly, the court concluded that this "harmony" standard "[did] not adequately circumscribe the process of administrative decision" and vested the committee "with too broad discretion," permitting "determinations based upon whim, caprice or subjective considerations."[32]

### [b] Exercise of Power Beyond an Official "Advisory" Role

When the local government characterizes its appearance committee as "advisory" only, it is difficult to address the extent to which specific standards must be established to guide the decisions of such a committee. In Chapter 1, I explain that there are recognized principles of administrative law that distinguish between decisions which are "declaratory" in nature and those which are "advisory" only. Advisory decisions generally are not reviewable and have no binding effect, except where estoppel[33] can be demonstrated. By contrast, declaratory decisions are binding upon applicants and are also appealable.

If the ordinance or resolution establishing the appearance committee does not clearly indicate the "advisory" role of the appearance committee, then problems arise. For example, in an Illinois case,[34] the particular ordinance stated that (1) if the committee determined that the building permit should be issued, then the village board had no authority in the matter; and (2) if the committee determined that the permit should be disapproved, then the building permit could not be issued unless expressly authorized by the village board on appeal. The court properly concluded that the committee's function under those procedures was not really advisory but mandatory, in effect giving the committee power without proper delegation of authority.

---

[32] *Id.* at 163.

[33] *See* definition and discussion of *estoppel* in Ch. 7, Sec. 7.06[1], *supra*.

[34] Pacesetter Homes, Inc. v. Village of Olympia Fields, 104 Ill. App. 2d 218, 244 N.E.2d 369, 372 (1st Dist. 1968).

## [c]  Application of Aesthetic Controls Independent of Zoning

Perhaps the most egregious problem with the appearance committee in most jurisdictions is that it has become the means for communities to impose aesthetic controls as a precondition to building permit approval. Lawyers like to call this a "condition precedent," which simply means that until that condition is satisfied, the developer should not even think of getting a building permit. Typical language in one appearance code reads:

> No building permit required under the ordinances of the City for all new construction, except accessory structures for single-family residences, and for all building alterations involving exterior design features of multifamily residential, commercial and institutional structures, and alterations affecting street elevations of single-family residences (except those limited to windows, doors, exterior cladding or roof covering), shall be issued except upon the granting of a certificate of approval indicating that the proposal is consistent with the Design Guidelines.

The tying of such broad aesthetic review authority to the issuance of building permits raises the question: Under what authority? Even though it is now clear from the majority of courts that aesthetics alone are a legitimate object of the police power, can aesthetic controls, without specific statutory authority, be imposed so broadly? The court in a New Jersey case articulated the problem this way:

> [D]efendants by the ordinance in question seek to aesthetically control construction in the municipality independently of the zoning law. The ordinance in effect imposes an additional condition precedent to the issuance of a permit. By that is meant that if a proposed use conforms to the zoning code, the additional burden is placed that it must conform to surroundings aesthetically. In effect, the ordinance places

aesthetic value first and creates an unjustifiable condition precedent to the issuance of a certificate.[35]

The court acknowledged the "irksome" problem of attempting to quantify the concept of aesthetics and establish standards, but concluded:

> One thing is clear. . . and that is, to the extent that zoning decisions are based upon aesthetics, these decisions are to be made by zoning and planning boards of this State pursuant to specific legislative authority and are not to be delegated absent said authority.[36]

It should be added that to the extent that zoning decisions are being made by architectural/building design "appearance" committees, particularly where these decisions affect homeowners' right to use their residentially zoned property, local communities should not ignore the "essential nexus" and "rough proportionality" tests articulated in *Nollan* and *Dolan*.[37]

### § 8.05 Is "Process" the Antidote for Subjectivity in Aesthetic Review?

The long-accepted argument has been that where there are subject matters that are not amenable to definite standards, local governments can compensate for that with process—that is, with review procedures and findings of fact. Richard Tustian, the former Executive Director of the Maryland National Park and Planning Commission,

---

[35] Diller and Fisher Co., Inc. v. Architectural Review Bd. of Borough of Stone Harbor, 246 N.J. Super. 362, 587 A.2d 674, 677 (Law Div. 1990), quoting Piscitelli v. Township Committee of Scotch Plains Tp., 103 N.J. Super. 589, 248 A.2d 274, 278 (Law Div. 1968).

[36] *Id.* at 680. *See also* Board of Sup'rs of James City County v. Rowe, 216 Va. 128, 216 S.E.2d 199 (1975).

[37] *See* discussion of these two cases and the constitutional tests in Ch. 1, Secs. 1.08 and 1.09, *supra*. *See also* Dennison, Mark S., *Zoning: Proof of Unreasonableness of Aesthetic Regulation* (American Jurisprudence: Proof of Facts 3d Series) New York: Lawyers Cooperative Publishing, 1995.

explained this preference for "procedure" over precise standards from the planner's perspective:

> The legal process deals with dimensions in time, a sequential process. The planning process deals with dimensions in space, which are structural and finite and concrete, and we're dealing with how to change those spatial things over time. You can set down specific criteria for time processes that endure. The U.S. Constitution sets down specific things that are procedural and they haven't been changed very much. But the physical environment is changing all the time and is supposed to be responsive to social pressures for such change—new building types, group homes, etc. And so to force the planning profession in the direction of requiring preset spatial criteria is to hamstring the ability of our society to marginally change the house it lives in. A rigid insistence upon preset quantitative criteria will prevent the holistic judgment that has to be made to blend all of these things together. I'm talking about an extreme, I recognize, but I'm arguing that we should keep the window open sufficiently to allow for change and discretion and rely more upon procedural due process.[38]

However, since before the U.S. Supreme Court's decision in *Dolan*, experts have noted the impatience of an increasing number of state courts with development review procedures based on subjective standards, and a growing movement toward more objective development standards.[39] The case involving the City of Issaquah, Washington, is a good example of a state court refusing to accept the city's argument that "process" cured the problems posed by the vagueness of its design review standards. It is worth quoting the court in full:

---

[38] Blaesser and Weinstein, eds., *Land Use and the Constitution* at 32, Chicago, Ill.: Planners Press, 1989.

[39] *See* symposium comments of Norman Williams, Orlando Delogu, Clyde Forrest, and Richard Babcock in Blaesser and Weinstein, eds., *Land Use and the Constitution* at 22–26, Chicago, Ill.: Planners Press, 1989.

Although the City argues that its code is not unconstitutionally vague, it primarily relies upon the procedural safeguards contained in the code. Because aesthetic considerations are subjective in concept, the City argues that they cannot be reduced to a formula or a number. The vagueness test does not require a statute to meet impossible standards of specificity [citation omitted].

As well illustrated by the appendices to the brief of amici curiae, aesthetic considerations are not impossible to define in a code or ordinance. Moreover, the procedural safeguards contained in the Issaquah Municipal Code [IMC] (providing for appeal to the city council and to the courts) do not cure the constitutional defects here apparent.

\* \* \*

Certainly, the IMC grants Anderson the right to appeal the adverse decision of the Development Commission. But just as IMC 16.16.060 provides no standards by which an applicant or the Development Commission or the City Council can determine whether a given building design passes muster under the code, it provides no ascertainable criteria by which a court can review a decision at issue, regardless of whether the court applies the arbitrary and capricious standard as the City argues is appropriate or the clearly erroneous standard as Anderson [the plaintiff] argues is appropriate. *Under either standard or review, the appellate process is to no avail where the statute at issue contains no ascertainable standards and where, as here, the Development Commission was not empowered to adopt clearly ascertainable standards of its own. The procedural safeguards provided here do not save the ordinance."*[40]

What the court is saying to this local government, and any other which is paying attention, is that if the standards used to make the decision in the first place are defective,

---

[40] Anderson v. City of Issaquah, 70 Wash. App. 64, 851 P.2d 744, 753 (Div. 1 1993). (Emphasis added.)

321

the appellate process will also falter because the standards at that level are not adequate to make up the deficiencies in the original standards. In other words, it is not enough to appendage an appeal process to a set of vague standards.

## § 8.06    Can Design Review Standards That Give Clear Guidance Be Written?

Certainly the mistake of equating aesthetics with beauty has made courts doubtful that the problem of amorphous language can be overcome. After all, as Louis Sullivan so aptly observed: "[A]rt will not live in a cage of words" because "there is a vast domain lying just beyond the reach of words" definable only "in terms of pictures, of states of feeling, of rhythm."[41] Sullivan's admonition notwithstanding, design professionals, including architects and landscape architects, will tell you that there is, in fact, sufficiently precise language in this field that can give meaningful guidance.

For example, in their brief as amici in the previously mentioned case in Issaquah, Washington, the Seattle Chapter of the American Institute of Architects, Washington Council of the American Institute of Architects, and the Washington Chapter of the American Society of Landscape Architects included provisions from the regulations of Bozeman, Montana, and the City of San Bernardino, California, as acceptable examples of design guidelines.[42]

In the examples on the following pages, each of these cities addresses the issue of scale and "boxy" buildings:

---

[41] Sullivan, Louis H., *Kindergarten Chats* at 139, 150 Wittenborn Art Books, 1968.

[42] *See* brief of Amici Curiae, the Seattle Chapter of the American Institute of Architects, the Washington Council of the American Institute of Architects, and the Washington Chapter of the American Society of Landscape Architects filed in Anderson v. City of Issaquah, 70 Wash. App. 64, 851 P.2d 744 (Div. 1 1993).

**City of Bozeman, Montana**
**Design Objectives Plan, Entryway Corridors**

Location:     All Corridors

Subject:      Building Design

Intent:       Soften otherwise harsh, boxy building forms and produce roof-
              lines that reflect the surrounding mountains and regional
              climate.

Guideline:    B.1.

              a.  Buildings should incorporate pitched roof forms with the
                  pitch between 6 inches of rise to 12 inches of horizontal
                  and 12 inches of rise to 12 inches of horizontal. The entire
                  building need not be covered with a pitched roof; the
                  entrance area may be emphasized in such a manner.

              b.  Alternatively, distinctively shaped roof forms, detailed
                  parapets, and exaggerated cornice lines can also be
                  proposed for consideration.

Illustration:

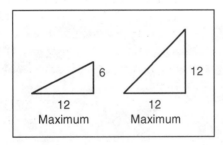

Example:

Location:     All Corridors

Subject:      Building Design

323

## § 8.06 / Discretionary Land Use Controls

Intent:    Encourage varied building massing to break down the scale of large buildings and complexes.

Guide-    B.2.
line:

Long, flat facades are strongly discouraged. Buildings over 100 feet in length should incorporate recesses, off-sets, angular forms or other features to provide a visually interesting shape. A single uninterrupted length of facade should not exceed 100 feet.

Illustra-
tion:

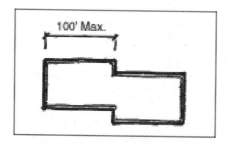

Example:

**San Bernardino, California Development Code**

9.    Architectural Design Guidelines

A.    Heights of structures should relate to adjacent open spaces to allow maximum sun and ventilation and protection from prevailing winds, enhance public views of surrounding mountains, and minimize obstruction of view from adjoining structures.

324

B.  Height and scale of new development should be compatible with that of surrounding development. New development height should "transition" from the height of adjacent development to the maximum height of the proposed structure.

C.  Large buildings which give the appearance of "box-like" structures are generally unattractive and detract from the overall scale of most buildings. There are several ways to reduce the appearance of large scale, bulky structures.

1.  Vary the planes of the exterior walls in depth and/or direction. Wall planes should not run in 1 continuous direction for more than 50 feet without an offset.

2.  Vary the height of the buildings so that it appears to be divided into distinct massing elements.

3.  Articulate the different parts of a building's facade by use of color, arrangement of facade elements, or a change in materials.

4.  Use landscaping and architectural detailing at the ground level to lessen the impact of an otherwise bulky building.

5.  Avoid blank walls at the ground floor levels. Utilize windows, trellises, wall articulation, arcades, change in materials, or other features.

6.  All structure elevations should be architecturally treated.

Awnings of the same form and location are repeated, with the signage on the awning's valance.

Varying roof planes, setbacks and articulated front facades add a pedestrian scale.

Example:

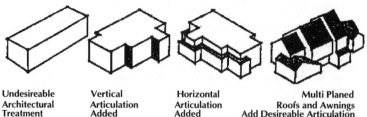

| Undesireable Architectural Treatment | Vertical Articulation Added | Horizontal Articulation Added | Multi Planed Roofs and Awnings Add Desireable Articulation |

D.  Scale, for purposes here, is the relationship between the size of the new structure and the size of adjoining permanent structures. It is also how the proposed building's size relates to the size of a human being (human scale). Large scale building elements will appear imposing if they are situated in a visual environment which is predominantly smaller in scale.

1.  Building scale can be reduced through the proper use of window patterns, structural bays, roof overhangs, siding, awnings, moldings, fixtures, and other details.

2.  The scale of buildings should be carefully related to adjacent pedestrian areas (i.e., plazas, courtyards) and other structures.

3.  Large dominating structures should be broken up by: 1) creating horizontal emphasis through the use of trim; 2) adding awnings, eaves, windows, or other architectural ornamentation; 3) use of combinations of complementary colors; and 4) landscape materials.

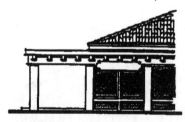

Storefront elements and pedestrian level details provide an intimate scale.

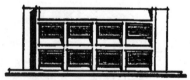

Form and Texture Shall be repeated in a manner to provide a sense of unity within a large mass.

Unfortunately, even these examples, when read carefully, raise vagueness problems. Of the two jurisdictions, Bozeman's guidelines are the clearest. But the vagueness in Bozeman's guidelines creates a significant loophole: The guideline for Building Design does not prevent the design of a *flat roof* building that has a pitched roof over the entranceway only—a phenomenon I'm sure many readers have seen. The solution would have been to refer to "boxy *flat roof* building forms" in the Intent statement. Otherwise, the language in the rest of the guideline is clear and easy to follow.

In contrast, the guidelines for San Bernardino use terms that raise one question after another as to meaning and intent. For example, the term "offset." Offset how far? Which direction? Is one inch acceptable? Is 200 feet acceptable? (If so, what is the use of the space in the "offset"—parking?) Another example is the verb to "vary" the height. How much variance is tolerable: Six inches? 100 feet? What is meant by "distinct massing elements"? Could these include large statues of people? What does "architecturally treated" mean? Other terms are equally vague: "other details," "carefully related," "broken up," etc.

In sum, the foregoing examples of design guidelines from Bozeman, Montana, and San Bernardino, California, suffer from their own deficiencies. The following drafting principles are offered as a way to avoid some of these problems.

### § 8.07 Principles for Drafting Design Review Standards and Guidelines

The local government must do better and develop meaningful standards in the first place. As evident from the examples given above, even the design professionals believe it can be done. And, as the *Issaquah* case demonstrates, a court will look to examples in other communities where it is being done properly in order to assess the adequacy of the standards it is being asked to evaluate. We turn now to some of the principles that can help the local government do a better job in defining design standards—assuming, of course, that it has been properly given the authority to do so!

327

## [1]  Preliminary Considerations

Before deciding to embark upon design review, a community should consider carefully whether it has the prerequisites for establishing a meaningful, effective, and legally defensible program. Unfortunately, the community that attempts to impose design controls is often the community that has no definable existing character, or any clear vision of what it wants to become, except that it wants to be more like the neighboring "upscale" community. The result of such an unprincipled effort is design review that is based upon vague and often contradictory standards and applied on an *ad hoc* basis, with inconsistent—and legally indefensible—results. The chart on the following page summarizes the basic steps and related considerations that the community should address.

| Preliminary Steps and Considerations |
|---|
| 1. Define Key Elements of Existing Character and/or Vision of What You Want to Become as a Community |
| 2. Define the Basic Characteristics of the Form and Organization of the Area and/or Community |
| 3. Determine Level of Control Desired |
|    a. Mandatory ("Must" or "Minimum Required") |
|    b. Desired ("Should") |
|    c. Permissive ("May") |
| 4. Choose Format/Structure |
|    a. Ordinance format (numbered and captioned subject areas) |
|    b. Manual format |
|    c. Use of graphics/photographs |
|    d. Combination |
| 5. Select Type of Review Process (Who implements the design review controls?) |
|    a. Staff |
|    b. Board/Commission |
|    c. Legislative Body |

## [a] Establish a Vision Supported with Plans and Studies

It is popular now to talk about the "visioning thing," that exercise by the community to create a vision of the direction in various areas, including land use and development, that it wishes to go, usually in relation to a fifteen- or twenty-year planning horizon. Sometimes the exercise can expose real fissures in the community and a fractured vision at best. But if done properly, the vision step can provide the foundation for preparing more in-depth, geographically based plans and studies—a necessary legal component—to justify the resulting design standards.

## [b] Define the Basic Characteristics of Community Form and Organization

This step addresses three basic questions: (1) the location of buildings in relation to the front property line and to adjacent buildings (i.e., build-to lines, setback lines); (2) land uses at the street level; and (3) locations of entrances, both pedestrian front doors and service.

The building location, in relation to the front property line and to adjacent buildings, addresses the basic formal and spatial characteristics of an urban area. It also addresses the idea of certain uses along the street; for example, in the idea of an offset, it leaves open the possibility of a parking lot at the street, which is far different from a row of shops or homes. It also deals with the question of building continuity along a street versus separation and discontinuity.

There are a number of questions with respect to land uses at the street level: Is a street to have pedestrian activity or not? Is it a shopping place, a residential place, etc.? With respect to locations of entrances, both pedestrian front doors and service: Where is the pedestrian activity to be located? Where are the back doors?

One community in Illinois had an interesting initial approach to the question of community form and organization. In the process of developing urban design

329

guidelines, the city of Park Ridge, at one point, prepared an "Urban Design Policy Framework" to help it relate the various characteristics within the community that reflected an overall community "image." The city's approach was based on the notion that its community could be organized spatially and visually into three areas: public space image, commercial image, and neighborhood image—creating an urban design policy framework. The next step was to establish objectives for each of these areas. The diagram below depicts this policy framework. Although the diagram is somewhat complicated and, ultimately, was not used in the guidelines as adopted by the city council, it reflects a thoughtful approach to the question of community form and organization.

## URBAN DESIGN POLICY

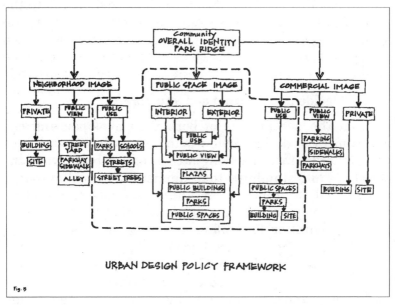

URBAN DESIGN POLICY FRAMEWORK

Fig. 5

Source: Raymond J. Green & Associates. City of Park Ridge, Illinois: Draft Urban Design Guidelines (1989), p. 9.

### [c] Determine the Level of Control That Will Be Exercised

The next step for the community is to decide what level of control it wishes to exercise through design review and whether state law (statutory or judicial decisions) authorizes that level of control. *Mandatory* ("must") *controls* are usually limited to these judicially accepted areas which have design implications, such as build-to lines, height, bulk, and setbacks. Whether the scope of mandatory aesthetic regulation may be broadened will depend upon whether the specific studies or plans have been done to support such requirements and the extent to which state law can be read to authorize such prescriptions. (*See* discussion in Sections 8.04 and 8.05, *supra.*) By contrast, *design guidelines* express the design outcomes that are desired ("should") but not mandatory. *Permissive* ("may") *controls* are the most relaxed form of guidelines. They

331

merely make a suggestion to the applicant, which the applicant may or may not decide to follow. Whether design considerations are mandatory, desirable, or permissive, certain drafting principles should be followed. These are discussed below.

### [d] Decide upon Format and Structure

From the perspective of both the developer and the government, if design review is to be imposed, it should be done by ordinance following a thorough debate about the objectives and standards to be applied. A design "manual," unless tied to an ordinance that establishes the actual standards, is a very dangerous document that can become an open invitation for staff or a commission to abuse their discretion. As for graphics and photos, you will note that the examples praised by the architects and landscape architects in the *Issaquah* case contained both graphics and photographs. Since these individuals are the design professionals who are usually retained by landowners and developers to address design requirements, their opinions should be given weight. At the same time, however, there are some principles that should guide the type and amount of graphic material to be included. These are discussed in Section 8.07.

### [e] Select the Type of Review Process

From my experience and observation, I have identified five basic models of design review processes. Some of these models are in fact in existence or about to be implemented in certain jurisdictions. Others, as will be discussed, represent ways in which the process could be structured depending upon the constraints and opportunities within a particular jurisdiction.

## Model No. 1

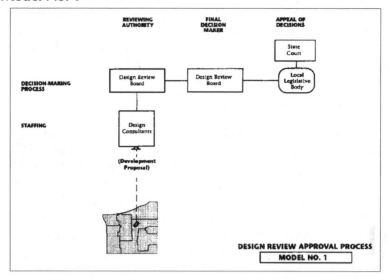

**DESIGN REVIEW APPROVAL PROCESS**
**MODEL NO. 1**

From the perspective of local government *and* the developer, Model No. 1 represents an ideal design review process. Why? Because the structure is based on state legislation that authorizes the establishment of a separate design review entity to implement design review plans and policies. The state legislation should also require that the local government take certain steps, including a careful planning study that identifies the critical design elements of a geographic area, followed by the adoption of clear standards and procedures to implement the plan.

## Model No. 2

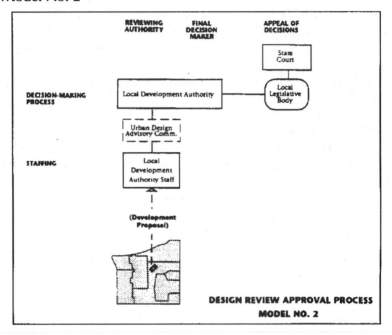

**DESIGN REVIEW APPROVAL PROCESS**
**MODEL NO. 2**

This model ties the objectives of design review to economic development policy by empowering a local development authority, enabled under state legislation, to carry out economic development policies as well as design review policies in order to further the overall economic viability of specific areas of a city, such as a downtown. This model can be found in Kentucky's legislation,[43] which authorizes the establishment of "overlay districts" to provide additional regulations for design standards and development in areas that have historical, architectural, natural, or cultural significance that is suitable for preservation or conservation. Under the legislation, the local legislative body is authorized to delegate the implementation of overlay district regulations to a department or agency of the city or to a nonprofit corporation established by the city. For example, the City of Louisville now utilizes an

---

[43] Kentucky Revised Statutes, Secs. 82.660–82.670.

overlay district as one means to implement design guidelines under its adopted downtown development plan. The responsibility for implementing the design guidelines overlay district was delegated to the Louisville Development Authority (LDA) by the board of aldermen. The state legislation also requires that an "advisory body" be established to assist the administrative body that administers the provisions of the overlay district ordinance.

Finally, the legislation provides that appeals of decisions by the administrative body may be taken first to the local legislative body, and then to the state court. While having the local legislative body listen to appeals is not always desirable, depending upon the political climate of the particular jurisdiction, it can prove to be a safety valve for resolving issues before they reach the litigation stage.

**Model No. 3**

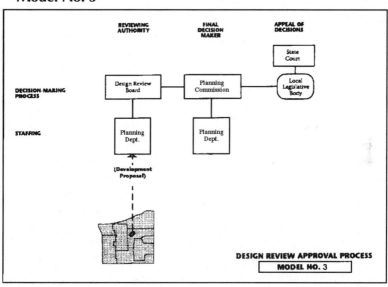

Model No. 3 is structured to reflect the situation that typically constrains jurisdictions that want to implement design review processes. If the state legislation recognizes aesthetics as a legitimate object of the police power, it is usually possible to establish a design review board to advise the body which in most jurisdictions is authorized by statute to make certain discretionary decisions—the planning commission. This structure has the advantage of limiting the design review board to an advisory role and, provided there are adequate standards, having the planning commission utilize either a conditional use mechanism or some other legally recognized mechanism through which to apply conditions that reflect certain aesthetic considerations. In addition, the appeal to the local legislative body is often desirable in this instance because, as in Model No. 2, it provides a safety valve through which disputes can be resolved administratively.

### Model No. 4

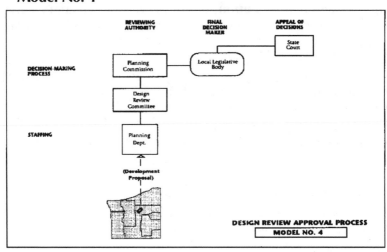

Model No. 4 reflects the reality that is prevalent in some jurisdictions, namely, that the planning commission has no authority to make final decisions on matters involving aesthetic considerations or even conditional uses. Under such circumstances, it is the local legislative body that acts as the final decision maker on most land use approvals. This model is typical of many villages and small cities.

## Model No. 5

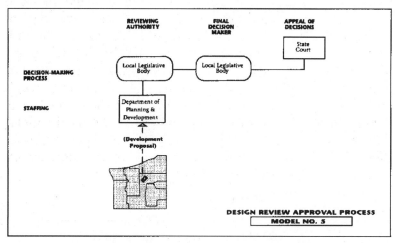

This last model has potential application in those circumstances, usually a downtown, where a city has retained control of certain parcels of land through urban renewal or other means. This model sets up the local legislative body as the final decision maker on development projects that may involve a public subsidy in one form or another. Usually because projects involving design review within a downtown involve significant sites—large structures with very visible benefits or detriments to the downtown—the local legislative body wants to be involved from the beginning. This model allows for that involvement, but its success depends upon how well staff can present the relevant issues on design review to the local legislators.

### [2] Drafting Principles

### [a] Detailed Not Visionary Language

Although it is important for a community to articulate the "vision" it has or desires for itself, the language of the standard or the guideline should *not* be visionary. If the community has done the requisite plans and studies for the geographical areas to which it wishes to apply design

337

review, it should be able to address specific subjects of design concern and develop related standards that are detailed and employ precise language. For example, a guideline stating that "signage should enhance the pedestrian experience" is not specific enough to be meaningfully applied and thus it creates a vagueness problem. Other examples of imprecise standards given by the design professionals are " 'desirable transition,' 'harmony in texture,' and 'compatible with adjacent buildings of conflicting architectural style.' "[44]

### [b] Avoid Overly Prescriptive Language

At the same time, the drafter must avoid being too design prescriptive. For example, simple pen-and-ink seating drawings for a plaza, coupled with a statement of how many linear feet of seating should be provided for each thirty square feet, convey the basic intent of seating without being too design prescriptive, stifling creative design responses. See "plaza perspective" and seating drawing on the following page.

### [c] Use Simple Hierarchy

In the examples from Bozeman, Montana, and San Bernardino, California, the specific standard or guideline was preceded by a statement of principle or intent. This hierarchy is particularly important with guidelines. First state the design principle and then the guidelines that implement that principle. This simple hierarchy provides

---

[44] Brief of Amici Curiae, the Seattle Chapter of the American Institute of Architects, the Washington Council of the American Institute of Architects, and the Washington Chapter of the American Society of Landscape Architects filed in Anderson v. City of Issaquah, 70 Wash. App. 64, 851 P.2d 744 (Div. 1 1993). For an example of very explicit zoning guidelines for architectural character, *see* the discussion of San Francisco's Downtown Plan in Lassar, Terry Jill, *Carrots & Sticks: New Zoning Downtown*, Washington, D.C.: ULI—The Urban Land Institute, 1989).

a foundation and rationale that is easily followed and aids the interpretation of how guidelines are to be applied.

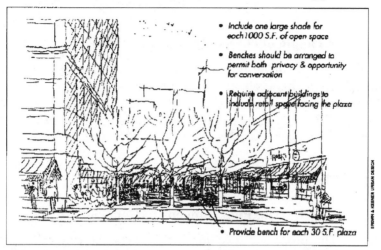

The location of seating is as important as its design, especially in its relationship to other seating, to buildings, and to pedestrian walkways.

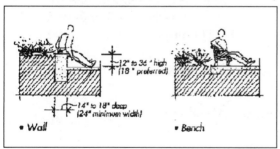

Seating can be of many types: walls, ledges, steps, benches, chairs. The only criterion is that they have comfortable seating dimensions.

### [d] Explain "Weight" to Be Given to Standard or Guideline

It is also important that if a series of standards or guidelines are articulated in an ordinance that the ordinance explain the *weight* or *effect* that should be attached to them. The courts have emphasized that this is necessary to provide sufficient guidance to the decision maker.[45]

## § 8.08   Example of Design Review Guidelines

At the risk of subjecting myself to the same criticism that I have directed at the efforts of some local governments, the following is offered as an example that reasonably fulfills the criteria outlined above. It is drawn from Hoboken, New Jersey.[46]

### [1]   The Vision

#### The Plan Concept in General

The proposed development extends the city to the water's edge by creating an urban neighborhood which echoes Hoboken's architectural character. This character is comprised of intimate residential streets, low-scale buildings and masonry materials. The proposed development will enhance these textures by juxtaposing them with the Hudson River waterfront and its spectacular views.

### [2]   Level of Control—Mandatory

#### Density/Bulk Controls

Urban complexity should be created through a variety of building heights, forms and styles. Streetwalls should be used extensively, on

---

[45] *See, e.g.,* Chandler v. Town of Pittsfield, 496 A.2d 1058 (Me. 1985); Pace Resources, Inc. v. Shrewsbury Tp. Planning Com'n, 89 Pa. Commw. 468, 492 A.2d 818 (1985); Sherman v. City of Colorado Springs Planning Com'n, 763 P.2d 292 (Colo. 1988).

[46] For their assistance in preparing and illustrating this example, as well as providing comments and suggestions on drafts of this chapter, I am indebted to Robert F. Brown, FAIA, and Mark R. Keener, AIA, principals of the Philadelphia Urban Design firm of Brown & Keener.

Marina Drive, First, Second, Third, and Fourth Streets. The bulk controls regulate the height of development and the configuration of the buildings on the parcels. These controls are described in more detail in the Building Design Standards.

The maximum height of buildings in the project will be no more than 125 feet, which is the height of the trees and lower buildings on Castle Point. This fixed height is compatible with the existing mid-rise residential buildings on Hudson Street, and with the (Baker) office building facing the Terminal Plaza. It also permits substantial new development, which will help realize the goal of adding significantly to the City's tax base.

## [3] Visual Character

### The Hoboken Block

In keeping with the rest of the City, where the typical "Hoboken Block" consists of a continuous row of buildings that surrounds the entire 200′ × 400′ block, these guidelines shall apply:

- Buildings must be located within 5′ of the street property lines.

- Retail, offices, residences, and/or building lobbies must be located along the entire lengths of the River Street and Sinatra Drive blocks.

- Retail, offices, residences and/or building lobbies must be located along at least two-thirds of the length of the east-west streets. Truck docks and parking entrances are permitted only in the remaining one-third. Because of this requirement, a service alley running north-south may be useful; in addition, building developments along the east-west streets must permit service access via north-south easements to developments located at the center of the blocks.

- More specifically, retail uses must be provided at

the corners (for at least 50′ in each direction) of the east-west streets and Sinatra Drive. These areas are especially suitable for restaurants, with outdoor dining on the sidewalk, and would be consistent with the corner stores and outdoor eating facilities that are so common throughout the rest of the City.

## [4]    Building Locations

### Hoboken Character

Because the design of new buildings in this area should be consistent with the appearance and detail characteristics of the older buildings of the City, these guidelines must apply:

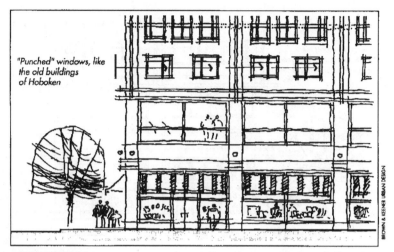

"Punched" windows, like the old buildings of Hoboken

BROWN & KEENER URBAN DESIGN

The openings in all facades (windows, doors, storefronts, etc.) must be on the "punched" type, and not in continuous vertical or horizontal strips; one result is that no allglass facades are permitted either. This design characteristic is consistent with the rowhouse facades of the City, and applies no matter how large (e.g., storefronts) or small (e.g., apartment windows) the opening.

343

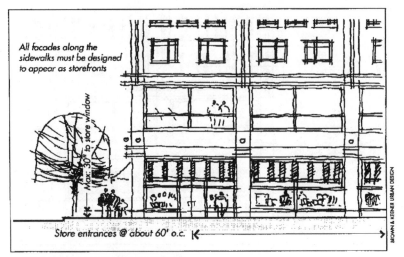

All facades along the sidewalks must be designed to appear as storefronts

Max. 30" to store window

Store entrances @ about 60' o.c.

MOWN & KEENER URBAN DESIGN

All facades along the sidewalks (except in those areas where service openings are permitted) must be designed to appear as storefronts, whether or not retail uses are located there. The storefront must include large clearglass, with sills no higher than 30" and with opportunities for entrances at lease every 60' (or about two normal older building widths).

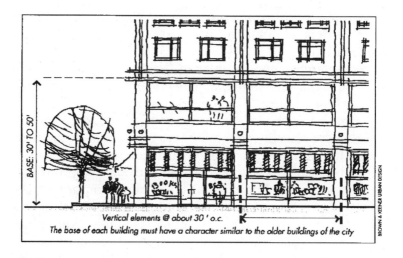

Vertical elements @ about 30 ' o.c.

*The base of each building must have a character similar to the older buildings of the city*

BROWN & KEENER URBAN DESIGN

The base of each building must be designed to have a character that feels as if it is similar to the older rowhouses and apartment buildings of the city—no matter the total height of the new building. The character is dominated by a rhythm of vertical elements, which typically are 25' to 30' apart (e.g., bay windows, columns, and piers), a height to a horizontal element (e.g., a cornice) that is 30' to 50' above the sidewalk, and many entrances located at the sidewalk.

I believe that the Hoboken design guidelines illustrate well the principles discussed above. I leave it to the reader to judge whether the guidelines satisfy the drafting principles articulated in this chapter.

## § 8.09  Design Review of Signs

Because signs are part of the urban fabric, they are a logical focus of regulations that address urban design. Along with architectural design controls, sign regulations are perhaps the most aesthetically based type of regulation. Typical sign regulations set out prescriptive or performance standards by zoning district or category of uses that address permitted (i) sign face area; (ii) height; (iii) number of signs; (iv) required setback and (v) illumination. Is a discretionary design review process on top of such regulations necessary? Some examples of design review applied to signs highlight some relevant considerations.

In reviewing some examples of the application of design review to signs, the same basic legal limitations discussed above are pertinent: (1) proper state enabling authority; (2) proper delegation of reviewing authority to an administrative body; and (3) adequacy (vagueness) of standards. Related to this third limitation concerning the adequacy of standards is the question of the constitutional appropriateness of standards. The regulation of signs implicates the separate First Amendment prohibition against the regulation of the *content* of speech. Only reasonable time, place and manner restrictions may be imposed on signs.[47] The purpose statements and related standards that accompany design review processes for signs sometimes ignore this fundamental constitutional limitation.

### [1]  Lack of Proper Enabling Authority

The New Jersey case involving the Borough of Stone Harbor, discussed in Section 8.04, highlights the problem created by lack of proper enabling authority for design review of signs.[48] In that case, the owners of commercial property sought to change the wording (logo and advertising language) on a sign facing their premises. They were told to apply to the architectural review board for approval pursuant to the Borough's ordinance. That ordinance bestowed upon the board "the authority to examine, review, approve or disapprove, because of location, quality and appropriateness of design, applications for permits for signs in the business and light industry districts."[49] After being denied permission by the architectural review board to change the lettering, the owners sued and argued that the

---

[47] Members of City Council of City of Los Angeles v. Taxpayers for Vincent, 466 U.S. 789, 104 S. Ct. 2118, 80 L. Ed. 2d 772 (1984).

[48] Diller and Fisher Co., Inc. v. Architectural Review Bd. of Borough of Stone Harbor, 246 N.J. Super. 362, 587 A.2d 674 (Law Div. 1990).

[49] *Id.* at 677.

board lacked statutory authority to exercise such aesthetic controls over its sign. After examining the New Jersey state zoning enabling legislation, the court agreed, stating:

> The question of aesthetics is both abstract and subjective. Attempts to quantify the concept and to establish standards will at best be irksome. One thing is clear, however, and that is, to the extent that zoning deicisions are based upon aesthetics, these decisions are to be made by zoning and planning boards of this State pursuant to specific legislative authority and are not to be delegated absent said authority.[50]

The court explained that clear statutory enabling authority and guidelines were particularly important where zoning ordinances have the potential to infringe upon freedom of speech considerations: "Government oversight of commercial expression can be expected to impose a chilling pall on the merchant and the marketplace. There is great wisdom in limiting these regulatory activities to those authorized by specific legislative edict."[51]

### [2] Improper Delegation of Review Authority to an Administrative Body

A case involving the City of Mobile, Alabama,[52] illustrates the failure to define adequate standards to guide decision making by an architectural review board—a violation of the nondelegation doctrine discussed at the beginning of this chapter. In 1988, the city adopted a revised sign ordinance which established a review process requiring approval of every sign within certain historical and nonhistoric geographical areas by the architectural review board if the sign satisfies the "criteria for issuance of a Certificate of Appropriateness." However, no criteria were set out in the sign ordinance nor were any guidelines

---

[50] *Id.* at 680.
[51] *Id.* at 681.
[52] City of Mobile v. Weinacker, 720 So. 2d 953 (Ala. Civ. App. 1998).

provided for determining whether a sign is "appropriate". Nevertheless, in 1994, the city ordered a shopping center owner located on a street corner in one of the nonhistoric areas to remove a sign found to be in violation of the new ordinance. After being denied a variance request, the owner brought suit challenging the constitutionality of the sign ordinance as impermissibly vague.

In defense of its sign removal order the city pointed to "sign design guidelines" that it had adopted in 1992. These guidelines utilized terms such as "modern materials," and "modern architectural design" but without defining them. For example, these terms were employed in the following guideline:

> The use of plastic, vinyl or similar materials is discouraged and will be approved only under the circumstances where the architecture of the building where the sign is to be located or if the surrounding buildings are of a modern architectural design and the building invorporates modern materials.[53]

Another guideline stated: "The use of neon will be considered in cases where the architecture of the building is compatible with neon." Faced with these vague and ambiguous terms and guidelines, the court held that the ordinance not only was impermissibly vague and ambiguous but also gave the architectural review board complete discretion to make decisions to grant or deny approval of signs on an ad hoc basis.[54]

### [3] Purposes and Standards of Design Review of Signs

Provisions for design review of signs reveal a wide range of purposes and standards, some of which are constitutionally suspect on their face because of their focus upon sign content. Others use purpose language that is not realistic or appropriate given the purpose of signage.

---

[53] *Id.* at 955.
[54] *Id.*.

## [a] Content Control

The City of Santa Clara, California, architectural committee's community design guidelines for signs state that the purpose of the guidelines is "to provide the community with a set of criteria which will establish the greatest degree of equity, effectiveness and sign quality." The criteria to achieve this purpose include "sign area, location, height, illumination, color, *content*, clarity and visibility." The guidelines define "sign clutter" as "excess in both number of signs and *content* of signs to the extent that it results in a deterioration in legibility of the sign and the attractive qualities of the street." Approval of new signs in Santa Clara requires consideration of "conditions of approval which will reduce existing sign clutter."[55] The design review procedures of the City of Walnut Creek, California, prohibit "signage which contains business slogans or advertising." Signs may only include "information describing the products sold or services provided."[56] The explicit reference to content control in these jurisdictions' design guidelines, although directed at "excessive" content, requires the reviewing body to engage in the constitutionally precarious task of choosing among items of content in order to reduce sign "clutter." Utilizing sign content as a means to address "clutter" is not a wise approach to design review of signs or signs regulations generally.

## [b] Sign Competition and Registered Service Marks

One of the standards in the City of Walnut Creek's design review procedures requires that all signs must be "architecturally integrated with their surroundings in terms of size, shape, color, texture, and lighting so that they are complementary to the overall design of the build-

---

[55] City of Santa Clara, California Architectural Committee Policies—Community Design Guidelines at 18–19.

[56] City of Walnut Creek, California Design Review Procedures (Updated Jan. 7, 1998) at 32.

ing and *are not in visual competition with other signs in the area.* If there is one fundamental aspect of signage, it is to be sufficiently competitive with other signs in the area so as to elicit customer attention. In addition to the vagueness of the phrase "not in visual competition," it reflects an objective that is not realistic in a market based economy where achieving market share is paramount to the success of a business.

The "not in visual competition" criterion is particularly inappropriate in light of recent case law involving signs and service marks under Section 1121(b) of the Lanham Act.[57] Section 1121(b)of the Act states in relevant part: "No state. . .or any political subdivision or agency thereof may require alteration of a registered mark. . .."[58] In a case of first impression in the U.S. Court of Appeals for the Ninth Circuit,[59] the court addressed the following question: Does section 1121(b) of the Lanham Act preempt a municipality's zoning authority to regulate signs for aesthetic purposes when those signs display registered service marks? In 1966, Video Update and Blockbuster Video, both national retail chains with registered service marks, leased space respectively in two separate shopping centers. Under the city's sign regulations, all exterior signs must conform to a shopping center's "sign package" which specifies, among other things, color, size, and location of signs. This package is created by the owner of the shopping center subject to review and approval by the Tempe Design Review Board. The sign package for the shopping center in which Video Update located required white letters on a turquoise background. The sign package for the shopping center in which Blockbuster Video located required blue, red, or yellow letters.

Video Update's registered service mark consists of the words "Video Update" in stylized red lettering, which is wider at the bottom and narrower at the top. Blockbuster

---

[57] 15 U.S.C. § 1121(b) (1994).
[58] *Id.*
[59] Blockbuster Videos, Inc. v. City of Tempe, 141 F.3d 1295, 46 U.S.P.Q.2d (BNA) 1437 (9th Cir. 1998).

Video has two registered service marks—a torn ticket with a blue background and yellow lettering, and a blue awning with the words "Blockbuster Video" in yellow block letters. When Video Update applied to the Tempe Design Review Board for approval to use red letters on two storefront signs, the Board allowed red letters on the sign facing the street, but required white letters for the sign inside the shopping center. For Blockbuster Video, the Board approved the torn ticket signs, but turned down the blue awning. Following unsuccessful appeals to the City Council, both companies sued. The federal district court upheld the companies' right to display their registered service marks against the city's argument that as an exercise of its police power, it must be able to alter a company's registered service mark in order to ensure compliance with aesthetic zoning.

On appeal, the Ninth Circuit held that a municipality may not enforce zoning regulations if those regulations require the alteration of a registered mark. It also held, however, that Section 1121(b) did not require municipalities to allow businesses to display their registered service marks; it only prohibits alteration of the mark. In other words, the city could have prohibited the display of registered service marks altogether. Under the facts of the case, the court's holding meant that the city could not require Video Update to change the red coloring of the lettering on the one sign in the shopping center, since that would "alter" Video Update's registered service mark. However, it could prevent Blockbuster Video from installing its blue awning service mark.[60]

### [c] "Compatibility" Standard

The standard that appears most frequently in sign regulations that utilize a design review process is

---

[60] *Id.* at 1298. But see Lisa's Party City, Inc. v. Town of Henrietta, 2 F. Supp. 2d 378, 46 U.S.P.Q.2d (BNA) 1718 (W.D.N.Y. 1998), aff'd, 185 F.3d 12, 51 U.S.P.Q.2d (BNA) 1523 (2d Cir. 1999).

compatibility. For example, the design review procedures of Walnut, California, discussed above, state: "New signs proposed by existing buildings shall provide a compatible appearance with the building signage of other tenants. With multiple signs on a single building, attempt to bring in a unifying element (such as size), even where no sign program exists."[61] The City of Santa Clara community design guidelines include "Design and Materials" criteria for signs which state: "Innovative design concepts are encouraged. Design shall be compatible with the project in style, scale, colors and materials and should utilize appropriate design elements of the building."[62]

In the architectural review context, the standard of "compatibility" became particularly important in the 1970s as a design standard for new structures in historic districts. As used in this context, the term "compatible" emphasized scale, mass, and materials more than the details of buildings. In the 1980s, the demand that new buildings be "compatible" with their historic surroundings gave way to a demand that new buildings be "contextual." Contextualism placed greater emphasis upon the details of buildings, borrowing, whether exact or not, shapes, detailing, and surface treatment from historic structures and styles, whether local or not.[63]

In the historic preservation context, the term "compatible," itself a vague term, can usually be applied in a reasonable manner because it is applied to a geographical area with defined historic building characteristics or

---

[61] City of Walnut Creek, California Design Review Procedures (Updated Jan. 7, 1998) at 29.

[62] City of Santa Clara, California Architectural Committee Policies—Community Design Guidelines at 21.

[63] *See* Ellen Beasley, "Reviewing New Design in Historic Districts," in Design Review: Challenging Urban Aesthetic Control, B. Scheer and W. Preiser, eds. Chapman & Hall: New York 1994, at 24–25.

styles. In other words, "compatibility" as a standard takes on more objective qualities in an historic district context. In a nonhistoric area, the "compatibility" standard does not retain the objective qualities to the same extent. Hence, it becomes more difficult to apply in design review of buildings, signs and other structures in areas—particularly automobile oriented urban and suburban areas—where the scale, mass and materials of structures are varied and cannot readily be reduced to a set of objective characteristics. In this nonhistoric context, the requirement of "compatibility" used in the design review of signs is usually too vague to give sufficient guidance to the reviewer. The only potential cure for this inadequacy is to define compatibility with reference to an adopted plan for a specific area that defines those elements of building scale, mass and materials that are deemed important to the community. If those elements cannot be meaningfully defined in a plan, then it is inappropriate to impose a compatibility standard upon the design review process for signs.

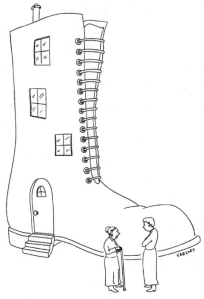

*"Once, I tried to change the laces, and the Landmarks Commission came down on me like a ton of bricks."*

## [4]  Appropriate Role for Design Review of Signs

Design review of signs can serve an important function in certain limited settings. It should not be used as a substitute for prescriptive or performance standards that address the basic elements of sign face area, height; number of signs; setback and illumination. As noted above, it can be most effective when applied in an historic district context where landmarks and identifiable architectural features have been consciously identified in a plan and aesthetic standards can be applied with some objectivity.

A second setting in which design review based upon review standards and guidelines can be effective is where the local regulations authorize developers or owners of large scale commercial developments (shopping centers, office parks etc) to propose sign plans that address size, placement and graphic formats of signs. Subject to the legal limitations imposed by the Lanham Act upon local regulation of registered service marks, design review can play a useful role in addressing "compatibility" in a specific, defined context, that gives guidance to businesses locating in such developments.

A third setting that can be appropriate for design review of signs is downtown districts or subdistricts that have been defined by an adopted downtown development plan that reflects the consensus of citizens, the business community and officials as to specific urban design criteria that should guide development and redevelopment in the downtown. In all three settings, the one constant is a specific geographical area defined either by historic structures, a common commercial purpose, or the traditional boundaries of an urban center. Without such conscious definition of place, the difficult task of aesthetic review of signs and other structures is nearly impossible to do with any meaningful consistency.

## § 8.10 Neo-Traditional Development and Design Codes

From a legal perspective, nothing could be less definite or certain than the New Urbanism[64] that is touted as the way to combat urban sprawl and return to a village tradition—the traditional neighborhood design (TND). Neo-traditionalists criticize the rigidity and complexity of traditional zoning and subdivision regulations, and what they believe those regulations have fostered—the suburban pattern of low density residential and commercial development extending outward from urban areas into rural areas.

*"We're glad you've moved here, even though we've been fighting increased population density."*

Reprinted by permission of William Hamilton, the Rockefeller Brothers Fund, and *The Use of Land: A Citizens' Policy Guide to Urban Growth* (1973).

---

[64] *See, e.g.*, Peter Katz, *The New Urbanism: Toward An Architecture of Community* (New York: McGraw Hill 1993); Andres Duany, Elizabeth Plater-Zyberk, and Jeff Speck, *Suburban Nation: The Rise of Sprawl and the Decline of the American Dream* (New York: North Point Press 2000). The term "New Urbanism" encompasses a variety of design theories, including Traditional Neighborhood Development, Neotraditional Development, Transit-Oriented Development, Pedestrian-Oriented Development and Communities of Place. *See generally* Robert Sitkowski, "The New Urbanism for Municipal Lawyers," Paper Presented to the International Municipal Lawyers Association (Washington, DC: Apr. 12, 1999).

Neo-traditionalists prefer instead to regulate through *design codes* that emphasize visual design archetypes rather than textual standards. The new urbanist view of our existing land use regulatory structure is not surprising since the land use "patterns" represented by neo-traditional villages, predate zoning in this country. The design of neo-traditional communities emphasizes compact, higher density, pedestrian friendly, mixed use communities, with single-family homes on small lots interspersed with multifamily townhouse and apartment developments. A "grid pattern" of streets is favored over cul-de-sacs in order to promote the village experience.

Neo-traditional "codes" emphasize flexibility over precision. Also, these codes are often imposed through private covenants, which must be accepted by homeowners upon purchase. As a development option, the neo-traditional development has clearly had an impact on the market place. However, when a local government tries to make these private codes "public" codes and "zone" for or mandate neo-traditional patterns of development, the void for vagueness problem and other due process concerns arise. In their *Lexicon of the New Urbanism*,[65] Duany Plater-Zyberk characterize an ordinance as the translation of a private code into legal language and the formal adoption of that code by a local government. It is not so simple and the New Urbanism design codes raise a number of the due process concerns described in Chapter 1 and at the beginning of this chapter. Here is a brief overview.

## [1] Void for Vagueness

Neo-traditional villages are supposed to be places of distinctive character—and whether a particular use is compatible in such a village context, or whether the village design is consistent with an ordinance that relies on visual aids and flexible standards are highly subjective determinations. The overt design emphasis and prescrip-

---

[65] Duany Plater-Zybert & Company, *The Lexicon of the New Urbanism* (Draft: Mar. 19,1 999) at M21.

tive nature of neo-traditional codes amounts to aesthetic regulation that most frequently fails the due process requirement for discrete and meaningful standards and therefore likely to violate the void for vagueness doctrine. As noted previously, the purpose of the doctrine is to place a limit upon arbitrary and discretionary action.[66] A developer must know or, in effect, have "notice" of what standards will apply. There must be consistency in the application of those standards from application to application, and a court must be able to evaluate the evidence with sufficient clarity to be able to judge whether or not the decision was arbitrary. Merely adding a special review process for neo-traditional design review is unlikely to cure this problem. If the standards used to make the decision in the first place are defective, the appellate process will also falter, because the standards at that level are not adequate to make up the deficiencies in the original standards. In other words, it is not enough to appendage an appeal process to a set of vague standards.[67]

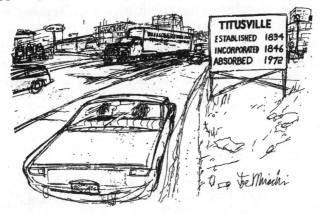

TITUSVILLE
ESTABLISHED 1834
INCORPORATED 1846
ABSORBED 1972

---

[66] Burien Bark Supply v. King County, 106 Wash. 2d 868, 725 P.2d 994, 996 (1986) (vagueness found) citing State v. White, 97 Wash. 2d 92, 640 P.2d 1061 (1982).

[67] See Anderson v. City of Issaquah, 70 Wash. App. 64, 851 P.2d 744 (Div. 1 1993) discussed at Section 8.04[2] supra.

## [2] Spot Zoning and Uniformity

The doctrine of "spot zoning" prohibits a local government from rezoning a parcel of land from a less intensive use classification to a more intensive use classification that is inconsistent with the surrounding uses.[68] The uniformity requirement found in most zoning enabling statutes requires that the regulations within each zoning district must be uniform, while regulations in the various zoning districts may differ from one another. The flexible design needed for a village may mean that a more intensive use should be inserted in the village — the equivalent of "spot" zoning. For example, it is generally recognized that local neighborhood commercial uses, such as hardware or ma & pa grocery stores found in many residential neighborhoods, although deemed nonconforming uses, are in fact compatible with the neighborhood. A zoning amendment by a local government in order to authorize such a neighborhood commercial use in a neo-traditional village, however, is questionable under the spot zoning doctrine. The uniformity requirement is also implicated by the distinct design of neo-traditional villages. The spot zoning and uniformity issues are not necessarily insurmountable if zoning enabling legislation is amended to authorize use flexibility to achieve neo-traditional village designs.

## § 8.11 Practice Tips

### [1] Community Must Be Clear About Its Values and Goals and Its Basic Characteristics of Community Form and Organization

The community must take the time to think through clearly and articulate the civic values and goals that it

---

[68] *See, e.g.,* Burkett v. City of Texarkana, 500 S.W.2d 242 (Tex. Civ. App. Texarkana 1973), writ refused n.r.e., (Jan. 23, 1974); Griswold v. City of Homer, 925 P.2d 1015 (Alaska 1996).

wishes to further through the combination of zoning and design standards or guidelines, and the basic characteristics of its community form and organization that must inform its design review process. Otherwise, design review will have no meaningful purpose and focus, inviting abuses of discretion. At an address to the Northeast Mayors' Institute on City Design, one professor noted:

> Most reputable developers are willing to work with a community if its design goals and objectives are clear. This is far preferable to fuzzy ideas and an uncertain process that begs developers to fall back on formulas. I have noticed that the cities that are good at telling developers what they can't do are typically the places where they most want to be.[69]

### [2] Use Illustrations and Specific Words to Explain Design Principles

The local government should use illustrations to support the text of the design standards or guidelines. The words used in the text should be very specific and easily understood by people outside the design professions. Where possible, photographs should be used to indicate desirable and undesirable conditions.

### [3] Community Should also Try to Understand the Objectives of the Developer

Once the objectives of the developer are understood, it should be easier to enter into a collaborative review and design process. If possible, the community should avoid getting into a situation where its acceptance or disapproval are the only options. The whole process should be made into a positive, working one. One technique is to assign one person to be a personal contact with the developer to help shepherd the entire design review process. The

---

[69] Dennis Frenchman, "Top Ten Secrets of Urban Design," DUSP@MIT.now p. 20 (Spring 2000).

developer, in turn, should fully explain the financial objectives of the project before the design is presented or complete, so that the community can understand the developer's limits as designs are reviewed.

The developer should fully explain the programmatic, design, and planning objectives of the project before presenting any complete design, again so the community has the opportunity to understand and therefore support the design when it is developed. In addition, the developer should select architects and design professionals who are comfortable and skilled in working in a design review process, and who seem to understand the objectives and values of the community where the building will be located.

### [4] Present Project Design in Terms of Public Values

The developer should first present the proposed building designs in terms of public values and of meeting the design guidelines' objectives. Then the developer can explain the project's design virtues and how they meet the developer's needs. In general, the developer should take an attitude of cooperation toward the community: If this place is worth building in, why not collaborate? Why create conflict when cooperation, in most cases, will reach the same objectives of the developer, with less time, money, and aggravation?

### [5] Design Proposals Should Be Previewed Before Formal Presentation

The developer should bring initial plan and site plan sketches to the design review committee before the design is completed. If possible, the developer should show design options to the committee. If members of the committee feel they are part of the design process, they will support the developer throughout the project. They will feel "ownership" of what is being done, and will not stand in the way of the developer's legitimate needs. For the reasons just given, the local government should encourage developers to meet with the review body prior to beginning or completing any designs.

### [6] Expedite the Decision-Making Process

The design review committee should be swift in making recommendations, refusals, and acceptances. The committee should not say, "We'll send you our response in writing," and then send the response several days later. If collaboration and cooperation are desired, the government must act promptly, since time is money to the developer and architect. Do not say, "our regular meetings are monthly, but this month we won't have quorum, so you must come next month." Also, be flexible and responsive when working with the developer's schedule. The government's objective is to have the developer's building meet the community's goals. Helping the developer to do that will make the process go smoothly and the developer will be responsive to the community's goals.

# Appendix
# Development Agreement Statutes

## Development Agreement Statutes

The states of Arizona, California, Colorado, Florida, Hawaii, Idaho, Louisiana, Maryland, Minnesota, Nevada, Oregon, South Carolina, Virginia, and Washington have adopted statutes authorizing development agreements statutes and/or providing for the "vesting" of property rights. The text of these states' statutes are set forth on the following pages.

### ARIZONA DEVELOPMENT AGREEMENTS STATUTE

#### § 9-500.05  Development Agreements; Public Safety; Definitions

A.  A municipality, by resolution or ordinance, may enter into development agreements relating to property in the municipality and to property located outside the incorporated area of the municipality. If the development agreement relates to property located outside the incorporated area of the municipality, the development agreement does not become operative unless annexation proceedings to annex the property to the municipality are completed within the period of time specified by the development agreement or any extension of such time.

B.  A development agreement shall be consistent with the municipality's general plan or specific plan, if any, as defined in § 9-461, applicable to the property on the date the development agreement is executed.

C.  A development agreement may be amended, or cancelled in whole or in part, by mutual consent of the parties to the development agreement or by their successors in interest or assigns.

D.   No later than ten days after a municipality enters into a development agreement, the municipality shall record a copy of the agreement with the county recorder of the county in which the property subject to the development agreement is located, and the recordation constitutes notice of the development agreement to all persons. The burdens of the development agreement are binding on, and the benefits of the development agreement inure to, the parties to the agreement and to all their successors in interest and assigns.

E.   Section 32-2181 does not apply to development agreements under this section.

F.   Notwithstanding any other law, a municipality may provide by resolution or ordinance for public safety purposes and with the written consent of an owner of property that has been granted a development agreement pursuant to this section, an owner of a protected development right pursuant to chapter 11 of this title or the owner of any other residential or commercial development subject to the supervision of a municipality pursuant to this title, for the application and enforcement of speed limits, vehicle weight restrictions or other safety measures on a private road that is located in any development in the municipality and that is open to and used by the public. A municipality may require payment from the property owner of the actual cost of signs for speed limits or other restrictions applicable on the private road, before their installation.

G.   In this section, unless the context otherwise requires:

1.   "Development agreement" means an agreement between a municipality and a community facilities district pursuant to § 48-709, subsection C, a landowner or any other person having an interest in real property that may specify or otherwise relate to any of the following:

(a) The duration of the development agreement.

(b) The permitted uses of property subject to the development agreement.

(c) The density and intensity of uses and the maximum height and size of proposed buildings within such property.

(d) Provisions for reservation or dedication of land for public purposes and provisions to protect environmentally sensitive lands.

(e) Provisions for preservation and restoration of historic structures.

(f) The phasing or time of construction or development on property subject to the development agreement.

(g) Conditions, terms, restrictions and requirements for public infrastructure and the financing of public infrastructure and subsequent reimbursements over time.

(h) Conditions, terms, restrictions and requirements for annexation of property by the municipality and the phasing or timing of annexation of property by the municipality.

(i) Conditions, terms, restrictions and requirements of deannexation of property from one municipality to another municipality and the phasing or timing of deannexation of property from one municipality to another municipality.

(j) Conditions, terms, restrictions and requirements relating to the governing body's intent to form a special taxing district pursuant to title 48.

(k) Any other matters relating to the development of the property.

2. "Governing body" means the body or board which by law is constituted as the legislative body of the municipality.

3. "Municipality" means an incorporated city or town.

## CALIFORNIA DEVELOPMENT AGREEMENTS STATUTE

### § 65864 Legislative findings and declarations

The Legislature finds and declares that:

(a) The lack of certainty in the approval of development projects can result in a waste of resources, escalate the cost of housing and other development to the consumer, and discourage investment in and commitment to comprehensive planning which would make maximum efficient utilization of resources at the least economic cost to the public.

(b) Assurance to the applicant for a development project that upon approval of the project, the applicant may proceed with the project in accordance with existing policies, rules and regulations, and subject to conditions of approval, will strengthen the public planning process, encourage private participation in comprehensive planning, and reduce the economic costs of development.

(c) The lack of public facilities, including, but not limited to, streets, sewerage, transportation, drinking water, school, and utility facilities, is a serious impediment to the development of new housing. Whenever possible, applicants and local governments may include provisions in agreements whereby applicants are reimbursed over time for financing public facilities.

### § 65865 Authorizations, procedures, and requirements; recovery of costs

(a) Any city, county, or city and county may enter into a development agreement with any person having a legal or equitable interest in real property for the development of the property as provided in this article.

(b) Any city may enter into a development agreement with any person having a legal or equitable interest in real property in unincorporated territory within that city's sphere of influence for the development of the property as provided in this article. However, the agreement shall not become operative unless annexation proceedings annexing the property to the city are completed within the period of time specified by the agreement. If the annexation is not completed within the time specified in the agreement or any extension of the agreement, the agreement is null and void.

(c)   Every city, county, or city and county shall, upon request of an applicant, by resolution or ordinance, establish procedures and requirements for the consideration of development agreements upon application by, or on behalf of, the property owner or other person having a legal or equitable interest in the property.

(d)   A city, county, or city and county may recover from applicants the direct costs associated with adopting a resolution or ordinance to establish procedures andrequirements for the consideration of development agreements.

### § 65865.1 Periodic review; termination or modification of agreement

Procedures established pursuant to Section 65865 shall include provisions requiring periodic review at least every 12 months, at which time the applicant, or successor in interest thereto, shall be required to demonstrate good faith compliance with the terms of the agreement. If, as a result of such periodic review, the local agency finds and determines, on the basis of substantial evidence, that the applicant or successor in interest thereto has not complied in good faith with terms or conditions of the agreement, the local agency may terminate or modify the agreement.

### § 65865.2 Contents

A development agreement shall specify the duration of the agreement, the permitted uses of the property, the density or intensity of use, the maximum height and size of proposed buildings, and provisions for reservation or dedication of land for public purposes. The development agreement may include conditions, terms, restrictions, and requirements for subsequent discretionary actions, provided that such conditions, terms, restrictions, and requirements for subsequent discretionary actions shall not prevent development of the land for the uses and to the density or intensity of development set forth in the agreement. The agreement may provide that construction shall be commenced within a specified time and that the project or any phase thereof be completed within a specified time.

The agreement may also include terms and conditions relating to applicant financing of necessary public facilities and subsequent reimbursement over time.

### § 65865.3 Newly incorporated city or annexed area; validity of development agreement entered into prior to incorporation or annexation; duration of validity; modification or suspension of agreement; application of section

(a) Except as otherwise provided in subdivisions (b) and (c), Section 65868, or Section 65869.5, notwithstanding any other law, if a newly incorporated city or newly annexed area comprises territory that was formerly unincorporated, any development agreement entered into by the county prior to the effective date of the incorporation or annexation shall remain valid for the duration of the agreement, or eight years from the effective date of the incorporation or annexation, whichever is earlier. The holder of the development agreement and the city may agree that the development agreement shall remain valid for more than eight years, provided that the longer period shall not exceed 15 years from the effective date of the incorporation or annexation. The holder of the development agreement and the city shall have the same rights and obligations with respect to each other as if the property had remained in the unincorporated territory of the county.

(b) The city may modify or suspend the provisions of the development agreement if the city determines that the failure of the city to do so would place the residents of the territory subject to the development agreement, or the residents of the city, or both, in a condition dangerous to their health or safety, or both.

(c) Except as otherwise provided in subdivision (d), this section applies to any development agreement which meets all of the following requirements:

   (1) The application for the agreement is submitted to the county prior to the date that the first signature was affixed to the petition for incorporation or annexation pursuant to Section 56704 or the adoption of the resolution pursuant to Section 56800, whichever occurs first.

   (2) The county enters into the agreement with the applicant prior to the date of the election on the question of incorporation or annexation, or, in the case of an annexation without an election pursuant to Section 57075, prior to the date that the conducting authority orders the annexation.

   (3) The annexation proposal is initiated by the city. If the annexation proposal is initiated by a petitioner other than the city, the development agreement is valid unless the city adopts written findings that implementation of the development agreement would create a condition injurious to the health, safety, or welfare of city residents.

(d) This section does not apply to any territory subject to a development agreement if that territory is incorporated and the effective date of the incorporation is prior to January 1, 1987.

### § 65865.4 Enforcement

Unless amended or canceled pursuant to Section 65868, or modified or suspended pursuant to Section 65869.5, and except as otherwise provided in subdivision (b) of Section 65865.3, a development agreement shall be enforceable by any party thereto notwithstanding any change in any applicable general or specific plan, zoning, subdivision, or building regulation adopted by the city, county, or city and county entering the agreement, which alters or amends the rules, regulations, or policies specified in Section 65866.

### § 65866 Rules, regulations and official policies

Unless otherwise provided by the development agreement, rules, regulations, and official policies governing permitted uses of the land, governing density, and governing design, improvement, and construction standards and specifications, applicable to development of the property subject to a development agreement, shall be those rules, regulations, and official policies in force at the time of execution of the agreement. A development agreement shall not prevent a city, county, or city and county, in subsequent actions applicable to the property, from applying new rules, regulations, and policies which do not conflict with those rules, regulations, and policies applicable to the property as set forth herein, nor shall a development agreement prevent a city, county, or city and county from denying or conditionally approving any subsequent development project application on the basis of such existing or new rules, regulations, and policies.

### § 65867 Public hearing; notice of intention to consider adoption

A public hearing on an application for a development agreement shall be held by the planning agency and by the legislative body. Notice of intention to consider adoption of a development agreement shall be given as provided in Section 65090 and 65091 in addition to any other notice required by law for other actions to be considered concurrently with the development agreement.

### § 65867.5 Approval by ordinance; referendum

A development agreement is a legislative act which shall be approved by ordinance and is subject to referendum. A development agreement shall not be approved unless the legislative body finds that the provisions of the agreement are consistent with the general plan and any applicable specific plan.

### § 65868 Amendment or cancellation; notice of intent

A development agreement may be amended, or canceled in

whole or in part, by mutual consent of the parties to the agreement or their successors in interest. Notice of intention to amend or cancel any portion of the agreement shall be given in the manner provided by Section 65867. An amendment to an agreement shall be subject to the provisions of Section 65867.5.

### § 65868.5 Recording copy of agreement; effect

No later than 10 days after a city, county, or city and county enters into a development agreement, the clerk of the legislative body shall record with the county recorder a copy of the agreement, which shall describe the land subject thereto. From and after the time of such recordation, the agreement shall impart such notice thereof to all persons as is afforded by the recording laws of this state. The burdens of the agreement shall be binding upon, and the benefits of the agreement shall inure to, all successors in interest to the parties to the agreement.

### § 65869 Local coastal programs

A development agreement shall not be applicable to any development project located in an area for which a local coastal program is required to be prepared and certified pursuant to the requirements of Division 20 (commencing with Section 30000) of the Public Resources Code, unless: (1) the required local coastal program has been certified as required by such provisions prior to the date on which the development agreement is entered into, or (2) in the event that the required local coastal program has not been certified, the California Coastal Commission approves such development agreement by formal commission action.

### § 65869.5 Modification or suspension to comply with state or federal laws or regulations

In the event that state or federal laws or regulations, enacted after a development agreement has been entered into, prevent or preclude compliance with one or more provisions of the development agreement, such provisions of the agreement shall be modified or suspended as may be necessary to comply with such state or federal laws or regulations.

### § 65460.10 Development agreement; density bonus

A city, county, or city and county may require a developer to enter into a development agreement pursuant to Article 2.5 (commencing with Section 65864) of Chapter 4 to implement a density bonus specified in the transit village plan pursuant to subdivision (g) of Section 65460.2.

## COLORADO VESTED PROPERTY RIGHTS STATUTE

### § 24-68-102 Definitions

As used in this article, unless the context otherwise requires:

(1) (1) "Application" means a substantially complete application for approval of a site specific development plan that has been submitted to a local government in compliance with applicable requirements established by the local government. For local governments that have provided for the review and approval of site specific development plans in multiple stages, "application" means the original application at the first stage in any process that may culminate in the ultimate approval of a site specific development plan.

(2) (1.5) "Landowner" means any owner of a legal or equitable interest in real property, and includes the heirs, successors, and assigns of such ownership interests.

(3) (2) "Local government" means any county, city and county, city, or town, whether statutory or home rule, acting through its governing body or any board, commission, or agency thereof having final approval authority over a site specific development plan, including without limitation any legally empowered urban renewal authority.

(4) (3) Property" means all real property subject to land use regulation by a local government.

(5) (4)(a) "Site specific development plan" means a plan that has been submitted to a local government by a landowner or such landowner's representative describing with reasonable certainty the type and

intensity of use for a specific parcel or parcels of property. Such plan may be in the form of, but need not be limited to, any of the following plans or approvals: A planned unit development plan, a subdivision plat, a specially planned area, a planned building group, a general submission plan, a preliminary or general development plan, a conditional or special use plan, a development agreement, or any other land use approval designation as may be utilized by a local government. What constitutes a site specific development plan under this article that would trigger a vested property right shall be finally determined by the local government either pursuant to ordinance or regulation or upon an agreement entered into by the local government and the landowner, and the document that triggers such vesting shall be so identified at the time of its approval.

(6)    (4)(b) "Site specific development plan" shall not include a variance, or a preliminary plan as defined in section 30-28-101 (6), C.R.S., or any of the following:

    (I)    A sketch plan as defined in section 30-28-101(8), C.R.S.;

    (II)   A final architectural plan;

    (III)  Public utility filings; or

    (IV)   Final construction drawings and related documents specifying materials and methods for construction of improvements.

(7)    (5) "Vested property right" means the right to undertake and complete the development and use of property under the terms and conditions of a site specific development plan.

## FLORIDA LAND DEVELOPMENT REGULATION STATUTE

### § 163.3223 Applicability

Any local government may, by ordinance, establish procedures and requirements, as provided in §§ 163.3220-163.3243, to consider and enter into a development agreement with any person having a legal or equitable interest in real property located within its jurisdiction.

## § 163.3225 Public hearings

(1) Before entering into, amending, or revoking a development agreement, a local government shall conduct at least two public hearings. At the option of the governing body, one of the public hearings may be held by the local planning agency.

(2) (a)Notice of intent to consider a development agreement shall be advertised approximately 7 days before each public hearing in a newspaper of general circulation and readership in the county where the local government is located. Notice of intent to consider a development agreement shall also be mailed to all affected property owners before the first public hearing. The day, time, and place at which the second public hearing will be held shall be announced at the first public hearing.

(b) The notice shall specify the location of the land subject to the development agreement, the development uses proposed on the property, the proposed population densities, and the proposed building intensities and height and shall specify a place where a copy of the proposed agreement can be obtained.

## § 163.3227 Requirements of a development agreement

(1) A development agreement shall include the following:

(a) A legal description of the land subject to the agreement, and the names of its legal and equitable owners;

(b) The duration of the agreement;

(c) The development uses permitted on the land, including population densities, and building intensities and height;

(d) A description of public facilities that will service the development, including who shall provide such facilities; the date any new facilities, if needed, will be constructed; and a schedule to assure public facilities are available concurrent with the impacts of the development;

(e) A description of any reservation or dedication of land for public purposes;

(f) A description of all local development permits approved or needed to be approved for the development of the land;

(g) A finding that the development permitted or proposed is consistent with the local government's comprehensive plan and land development regulations;

(h) A description of any conditions, terms, restrictions, or other requirements determined to be necessary by the local government for the public health, safety, or welfare of its citizens; and

(i) A statement indicating that the failure of the agreement to address a particular permit, condition, term, or restriction shall not relieve the developer of the necessity of complying with the law governing said permitting requirements, conditions, term, or restriction.

(2) A development agreement may provide that the entire development or any phase thereof be commenced or completed within a specific period of time.

### § 163.3229 Duration of a development agreement and relationship to local comprehensive plan

The duration of a development agreement shall not exceed 10 years. It may be extended by mutual consent of the governing body and the developer, subject to a public hearing in accordance with § 163.3225. No development agreement shall be effective or implemented by a local government unless the local government's comprehensive plan and plan amendments implementing or related to the agreement are found in compliance by the state land planning agency in accordance with § 163.3184, § 163.3187, or § 163.3189.

## § 163.3231 Consistency with the comprehensive plan and land development regulations

A development agreement and authorized development shall be consistent with the local government's comprehensive plan and land development regulations.

## § 163.3233 Local laws and policies governing a development agreement

(1)   The local government's laws and policies governing the development of the land at the time of the execution of the development agreement shall govern the development of the land for the duration of the development agreement.

(2)   A local government may apply subsequently adopted laws and policies to a development that is subject to a development agreement only if the local government has held a public hearing and determined:

    (a)   They are not in conflict with the laws and policies governing the development agreement and do not prevent development of the land uses, intensities, or densities in the development agreement;

    (b)   They are essential to the public health, safety, or welfare, and expressly state that they shall apply to a development that is subject to a development agreement;

    (c)   They are specifically anticipated and provided for in the development agreement;

    (d)   The local government demonstrates that substantial changes have occurred in pertinent conditions existing at the time of approval of the development agreement; or

    (e)   The development agreement is based on substantially inaccurate information supplied by the developer.

(3)   This section does not abrogate any rights that may vest pursuant to common law.

### § 163.3235  Periodic review of a development agreement

A local government shall review land subject to a development agreement at least once every 12 months to determine if there has been demonstrated good faith compliance with the terms of the development agreement. For each annual review conducted during years 6 through 10 of a development agreement, the review shall be incorporated into a written report which shall be submitted to the parties to the agreement and the state land planning agency. The state land planning agency shall adopt rules regarding the contents of the report, provided that the report shall be limited to the information sufficient to determine the extent to which the parties are proceeding in good faith to comply with the terms of the development agreement. If the local government finds, on the basis of substantial competent evidence, that there has been a failure to comply with the terms of the development agreement, the agreement may be revoked or modified by the local government.

### § 163.3237  Amendment or cancellation of a development agreement

A development agreement may be amended or canceled by mutual consent of the parties to the agreement or by their successors in interest.

### § 163.3239  Recording and effectiveness of a development agreement

Within 14 days after a local government enters into a development agreement, the local government shall record the agreement with the clerk of the circuit court in the county where the local government is located. A copy of the recorded development agreement shall be submitted to the state land planning agency within 14 days after the agreement is recorded. A development agreement shall not be effective until it is properly recorded in the public records of the county and until 30 days after having been received by the state land planning agency pursuant to this section. The burdens of the development agreement shall be binding upon, and the benefits of the agreement shall inure to, all successors in interest to the parties to the agreement.

### § 163.3241 Modification or revocation of a development agreement to comply with subsequently enacted state and federal law

If state or federal laws are enacted after the execution of a development agreement which are applicable to and preclude the parties' compliance with the terms of a development agreement, such agreement shall be modified or revoked as is necessary to comply with the relevant state or federal laws.

### § 163.3243 Enforcement

Any party, any aggrieved or adversely affected person as defined in § 163.3215(2), or the state land planning agency may file an action for injunctive relief in the circuit court where the local government is located to enforce the terms of a development agreement or to challenge compliance of the agreement with the provisions of §§ 163.3220–163.3243.

## HAWAII DEVELOPMENT AGREEMENTS STATUTE

### § 46-121 Findings and purpose.

The legislature finds that with land use laws taking on refinements that make the development of land complex time-consuming and requiring advance financial commitments, the development approval process involves the expenditure of considerable sums of money. Generally speaking, the larger the project contemplated, the greater the expenses and the more time involved in complying with the conditions precedent to filing for a building permit.

The lack of certainty in the development approval process can result in a waste of resources, escalate the cost of housing and other development to the consumer, and discourage investment in and commitment to comprehensive planning. Predictability would encourage maximum efficient utilization of resources at the least economic cost to the public.

Public benefits derived from development agreements may include, but are not limited to, affordable housing, design standards, and on- and off-site infrastructure and other improvements. Such benefits may be negotiated for in return for the vesting of development rights for a specific period.

Under appropriate circumstances, development agreements could strengthen the public planning process, encourage private and public participation in the comprehensive planning process, reduce the economic cost of development, allow for the orderly planning of public facilities and services and the allocation of cost. As an administrative act, development agreements will provide assurances to the applicant for a particular development project, that upon approval of the project, the applicant may proceed with the project in accordance with all applicable statutes, ordinances, resolutions, rules, and policies in existence at the time the development agreement is executed and that the project will not be restricted or prohibited by the county's subsequent enactment or adoption of laws, ordinances, resolutions, rules, or policies.

Development agreements will encourage the vesting of property rights by protecting such rights from the effect of subsequently enacted county legislation which may conflict with any term or provision of the development agreement or in any way hinder, restrict, or prevent the development of the project. Development agreements are intended to provide a reasonable certainty as to the lawful requirements that must be met in protecting vested property rights, while maintaining the authority and duty of government to enact and enforce laws which promote the public safety, health, and general welfare of the citizens of our State. The purpose of this part is to provide a means by which an individual may be assured at a specific point in time that having met or having agreed to meet all of the terms and conditions of the development agreement, the individual's rights to develop a property in a certain manner shall be vested.

### § 46-122 Definitions.

The following terms when used in this chapter shall have the following respective meanings:

"County executive agency" means any department, office, board, or commission of a county.

"County legislative body" means the city council or county council of a county.

"Person" means an individual, group, partnership, firm, association, corporation, trust, governmental agency, governmental official, administrative body, or tribunal or any form of business or legal entity.

"Principal" means a person who has entered into a development agreement pursuant to the procedures specified in this chapter, including a successor in interest.

### § 46-123 General authorization.

Any county by ordinance may authorize the executive branch of the county to enter into a development agreement with any person having a legal or equitable interest in real property, for the development of such property in accordance with this part, provided that such an ordinance shall:

(1) Establish procedures and requirements for the consideration of development agreements upon application by or on behalf of persons having a legal or equitable interest in the property, in accordance with this part;

(2) Designate a county executive agency to administer the agreements after such agreements become effective;

(3) Include provisions to require the designated agency to conduct a review of compliance with the terms and conditions of the development agreement, on a periodic basis as established by the development agreement; and

(4) Include provisions establishing reasonable time periods for the review and appeal of modifications of the development agreement.

### § 46-124 Negotiating development agreements.

The mayor or the designated agency appointed to administer development agreements may make such arrangements as may be necessary or proper to enter into development agreements, including negotiating and drafting individual development agreements, provided that the county has adopted an ordinance pursuant to section 46–123.

The final draft of each individual development agreement shall be presented to the county legislative body for approval or modification prior to execution. To be binding on the county, a development agreement must be approved by the county legislative body and executed by the mayor on behalf of the county. County legislative approval shall be by resolution adopted by a majority of the membership of the county legislative body.

### § 46-125 Periodic review; termination of agreement.

(a) If, as a result of a periodic review, the designated agency finds and determines that the principal has committed a material breach of the terms or conditions of the agreement, the designated agency shall serve notice in writing, within a reasonable time period after the periodic review, upon the principal setting forth with reasonable particularity the nature of the breach and the evidence supporting the finding and determination, and providing the principal a reasonable time period in which to cure such material breach.

(b) If the principal fails to cure the material breach within the time period given, then the county unilaterally may terminate or modify the agreement, provided that the designated agency has first given the principal the opportunity, (1) to rebut the finding and determination; or (2) to consent to amend the agreement to meet the concerns of the designated agency with respect to the finding and determination.

### § 46-126 Development agreement; provisions.

(a) A development agreement shall:

    (1) Describe the land subject to the development agreement;

    (2)   Specify the permitted uses of the property, the density or intensity of use, and the maximum height and size of proposed buildings;

    (3)   Provide, where appropriate, for reservation or dedication of land for public purposes as may be required or permitted pursuant to laws, ordinances, resolutions, rules, or policies in effect at the time of entering into the agreement; and

    (4)   Provide a termination date, provided that the parties shall not be precluded from extending the termination date by mutual agreement or from entering subsequent development agreements.

(b)    The development agreement may provide commencement dates and completion dates, provided that such dates as may be set forth in the agreement may be extended at the discretion of the county at the request of the principal upon good cause shown subject to subsection (a)(4).

(c)    The development agreement also may cover any other matter not inconsistent with this chapter, nor prohibited by law.

(d)    In addition to the county and principal, any federal, state, or local government agency or body may be included as a party to the development agreement. If more than one government body is made party to an agreement, the agreement shall specify which agency shall be responsible for the overall administration of the agreement.

### § 46-127 Enforceability; applicability.

(a)    Unless terminated pursuant to section 46-125 or unless canceled pursuant to section 46-130, a development agreement, amended development agreement, or modified development agreement once entered into, shall be enforceable by any party thereto, or their successors in interest, notwithstanding any subsequent change in any applicable law adopted by the county entering into such agreement, which alter or amend the laws, ordinances, resolutions, rules, or policies specified in this part.

(b) All laws, ordinances, resolutions, rules, and policies governing permitted uses of the land that is the subject of the development agreement, including but not limited to uses, density, design, height, size, and building specification of proposed buildings, construction standards and specifications, and water utilization requirements applicable to the development of the property subject to a development agreement, shall be those laws, ordinances, resolutions, rules, regulations, and policies made applicable and in force at the time of execution of the agreement, notwithstanding any subsequent change in any applicable law adopted by the county entering into such agreement, which alter or amend the laws, ordinances, resolutions, rules, or policies specified in this part and such subsequent change shall be void as applied to property subject to such agreement to the extent that it changes any law, ordinance, resolution, rule, or policy which any party to the agreement has agreed to maintain in force as written at the time of execution, provided that a development agreement shall not prevent a government body from requiring the principal from complying ·with laws, ordinances, resolutions, rules, and policies of general applicability enacted subsequent to the date of the development agreement if they could have been lawfully applied to the property which is the subject of the development agreement at the time of execution of the agreement if the government body finds it necessary to impose the requirements because a failure to do so would place the residents of the subdivision or of the immediate community, or both, in a condition perilous to the residents' health or safety, or both.

### § 46-128 Public hearing.

No development agreement shall be entered into unless a public hearing on the application therefor first shall have been held by the county legislative body.

### § 46-129 County general plan and development plans.

No development agreement shall be entered into unless

the county legislative body finds that the provisions of the proposed development agreement are consistent with the county's general plan and any applicable development plan, effective as of the effective date of the development agreement.

### § 46-130 Amendment or cancellation.

A development agreement may be amended or canceled, in whole or in part, by mutual consent of the parties to the agreement, or their successors in interest, provided that if the county determines that a proposed amendment would substantially alter the original development agreement, a public hearing on the amendment shall be held by the county legislative body before it consents to the proposed amendment.

### § 46-131 Administrative act.

Each development agreement shall be deemed an administrative act of the government body made party to the agreement.

### § 46-132 Filing or recordation.

The designated agency shall be responsible to file or record a copy of the development agreement or an amendment to such agreement in the office of the assistant registrar of the land court of the State of Hawaii or in the bureau of conveyances, or both, whichever is appropriate, within twenty days after the county enters into a development agreement or an amendment to such an agreement. The burdens of the agreement shall be binding upon, and the benefits of the agreement shall inure to, all successors in interest to the parties to the agreement.

## IDAHO DEVELOPMENT AGREEMENTS STATUTE

### § 67-6511A Development agreements.

Each governing board may, by ordinance adopted or amended in accordance with the notice and hearing provisions provided under section 67-6509, Idaho Code, require or permit as a condition of rezoning that an owner or developer make a written commitment concerning the use or development of the subject parcel. The governing board shall adopt ordinance provisions governing the creation, form, recording, modification, enforcement and termination of conditional commitments. Such commitments shall be recorded in the office of the county recorder and shall take effect upon the adoption of the amendment to the zoning ordinance. Unless modified or terminated by the governing board after a public hearing, a commitment is binding on the owner of the parcel, each subsequent owner, and each other person acquiring an interest in the parcel. A commitment is binding on the owner of the parcel even if it is unrecorded; however, an unrecorded commitment is binding on a subsequent owner or other person acquiring an interest in the parcel only if that subsequent owner or other person has actual notice of the commitment. A commitment may be modified only by the permission of the governing board after complying with the notice and hearing provisions of section 67-6509, Idaho Code. A commitment may be terminated, and the zoning designation upon which the use is based reversed, upon the failure of the requirements in the commitment after a reasonable time as determined by the governing board or upon the failure of the owner, each subsequent owner or each other person acquiring an interest in the parcel to comply with the conditions in the commitment and after complying with the notice and hearing provisions of section 67-6509, Idaho Code. By permitting or requiring commitments by ordinance, the governing board does not obligate itself to recommend or adopt the proposed zoning ordinance. A written commitment shall be deemed written consent to rezone upon the failure of conditions imposed by the commitment in accordance with the provisions of this section.

## LOUISIANA DEVELOPMENT AGREEMENTS STATUTE

### § 4780.21 Legislative findings and declarations

The Legislature of Louisiana finds and declares that:

(1)   The lack of certainty in the approval of development projects can result in a waste of resources, escalate the cost of housing and other development to the consumer, and discourage investment in and commit-

ment to comprehensive planning which would make maximum efficient utilization of resources at the least economic cost to the public.

(2) Assurance to the applicant for a development project that, upon approval of the project, the applicant may proceed with the project in accordance with existing policies, rules, and regulations, subject to conditions of approval, will strengthen the public planning process, encourage private participation in comprehensive planning, and reduce the economic costs of development.

(3) The lack of public facilities, including but not limited to streets, sewerage, transportation, drinking water, school, and utility facilities is a serious impediment to the development of new housing. Whenever possible, applicants and local governments may include provisions in development agreements whereby applicants are reimbursed over time for financing public facilities.

### § 4780.22 Authorizations, procedures, and requirements

A. Any parish or municipality may enter into a development agreement with any person having a legal or equitable interest in real property for the development of such property as provided in this Subpart.

B. Any parish or municipality may, upon request of an applicant, by resolution or ordinance, establish procedures and requirements for the consideration of development agreements upon application by or on behalf of the property owner or other person having a legal or equitable interest in the property.

### § 4780.23 Periodic review; termination or modification of agreement

Procedures established pursuant to R.S. 33:4780.22 shall include provisions requiring periodic review at least every twelve months, at which time the applicant or his successor in interest thereto shall be required to demonstrate good faith compliance with the terms of the agreement. If, as a result of such periodic review, the municipality or parish finds and determines, on the basis of substantial evidence, that the applicant or successor in interest thereto has not complied in good faith with terms or conditions of the agreement, the municipality or parish may terminate or modify the agreement.

### § 4780.24 Contents

A development agreement shall specify the duration of the agreement, the permitted uses of the property, the density or intensity of use, the maximum height and size of proposed buildings, and provisions for reservation or dedication of land for public purposes. The development agreement may include conditions, terms, restrictions, and requirements for subsequent discretionary actions, provided that such conditions, terms, restrictions, and requirements for subsequent discretionary actions shall not prevent development of the land for the uses and to the density or intensity of development set forth in the agreement. The agreement may provide that construction shall be commenced within a specified time and that the project or any phase thereof be completed within a specified time. The agreement may also include terms and conditions relating to financing of necessary public facilities by the applicant and subsequent reimbursement of the applicant over time.

### § 4780.25 Newly incorporated municipality; validity of development agreement entered into prior to incorporation; duration of validity; modification of agreement

A. Except as otherwise provided in R.S. 33:4780.30 and 4780.32, notwithstanding any other provision of law to the contrary, if a newly incorporated municipality comprises territory that was formerly unincorporated, any development agreement entered into by the parish prior to the effective date of the incorporation shall remain valid within the newly incorporated municipality for the duration of the agreement, or eight years from the effective date of the incorporation, whichever is earlier. The holder of the development agreement and the newly incorporated municipality may agree that the development agreement shall remain valid for more than eight years, provided that the longer period shall not exceed fifteen years from the effective date of the incorporation. The holder of the development agreement and the newly incorporated municipality shall have the same rights and obligations with respect to each other as if the property had remained in the unincorporated territory of the parish.

B.   The newly incorporated municipality may modify or suspend the provisions of the development agreement if the municipality determines that the failure of the municipality to do so would place the residents of the territory subject to the development agreement or the residents of the municipality, or both, in a condition dangerous to their health or safety, or both.

C.   Except as otherwise provided in Subsection D of this Section, this Section shall apply to any development agreement which meets both of the following requirements:

(1)   The application for the agreement is submitted to the parish prior to the date that the first signature was affixed to the petition for incorporation pursuant to R.S. 33:1.

(2)   The parish enters into the agreement with the applicant prior to the date of the special election on the question of incorporation conducted pursuant to R.S. 33:3.

D.   This Section shall not apply to any territory subject to a development agreement if that territory is incorporated and the effective date of the incorporation is prior to January 1, 1989.

### § 4780.26 Enforcement

Unless amended or cancelled pursuant to R.S. 33:4780.30 or modified or suspended pursuant to R.S. 33:4780.31 or 4780.25(B), a development agreement shall be enforceable by any party thereto notwithstanding any change in any applicable general or specific plan, zoning subdivision, or building regulation adopted by the municipality or parish entering the agreement which alters or amends the rules, regulations, or policies specified in R.S. 33:4780.27.

## § 4780.27 Rules, regulations, and official policies

Unless otherwise provided by the development agreement, the rules, regulations, and official policies governing permitted uses of the land, governing density, and governing design, improvement, and construction standards and specifications applicable to development of the property subject to a development agreement shall be those rules, regulations, and official policies in force at the time of execution of the agreement. A development agreement shall not prevent a municipality or parish, in subsequent actions applicable to the property, from applying new rules, regulations, and policies which do not conflict with those rules, regulations, and policies applicable to the property as set forth herein, nor shall a development agreement prevent a municipality or parish from denying or conditionally approving any subsequent development project application on the basis of such existing or new rules, regulations, and policies.

## § 4780.28 Public hearing; notice of intention to consider adoption

A public hearing on an application for a development agreement shall be held by the planning agency, if any, and by the governing authority of the municipality or parish. Notice of intention to consider adoption of a development agreement shall be published at least three times in the official journal of the municipality or parish and at least ten days shall elapse between the first publication and the date of the hearing.

## § 4780.29 Approval by ordinance

A development agreement shall be approved by ordinance of the governing authority of the parish or municipality.

## § 4780.30 Amendment or cancellation; notice of intent

A development agreement may be amended or cancelled in whole or in part by mutual consent of the parties to the agreement or their successors in interest. Notice of intention to amend or cancel any portion of the agreement shall be given in the manner provided by R.S. 33:4780.28. An amendment to an agreement shall be subject to the provisions of R.S. 33:4780.29.

## § 4780.31 Recording copy of agreement; effect

No later than ten days after a municipality or parish enters into a development agreement, the clerk of the municipal or parish governing authority shall record in the mortgage office of the parish a copy of the agreement, which shall describe the land subject thereto. From and after the time of such recordation, the agreement shall impart such notice thereof to all persons as is afforded by the recording laws of the state. The burdens of the agreement shall be binding upon and the benefits of the agreement shall inure to all successors in interest to the parties to the agreement.

## § 4780.32 Modification or suspension to comply with state or federal laws or regulations

In the event that state or federal laws or regulations, enacted after a development agreement has been entered into, prevent or preclude compliance with one or more provisions of the development agreement, such provisions of the agreement shall be modified or suspended as may be necessary to comply with such state or federal laws or regulations.

## § 4780.33 Restrictions on authority

Nothing in this Subpart shall be construed to authorize property use contrary to existing zoning classifications or to authorize the reclassification of such zones.

## MARYLAND DEVELOPMENT AGREEMENTS STATUTE[*]

### § 1.00 Definitions

(a) In this article the following words have the meanings

---

[*] This statute does not apply to Montgomery County or Prince George's County. Development agreements in these two counties are governed by a separate article in the Maryland State Code, Art. 28, Sec. 7-121.

indicated, except where the context clearly indicates otherwise.

(b)   "Adaptive reuse" means a change granted by a local legislative body, under § 4.05 of this article, to the use restrictions in a zoning classification, as those restrictions are applied to a particular improved property.

(c)   "Development" means any activity, other than normal agricultural activity, which materially affects the existing condition or use of any land or structure.

(d)   "Development rights and responsibilities agreement" means an agreement made between a governmental body of a jurisdiction and a person having a legal or equitable interest in real property for the purpose of establishing conditions under which development may proceed for a specified time.

(e)   (1) "Local executive" means the chief executive of a political subdivision.

    (2)   "Local executive" includes:

        (i)    A county executive;

        (ii)   A board of county commissioners;

        (iii)  An executive head; or

        (iv)   A mayor.

(f)   (1) "Local legislative body" means the elected body of a political subdivision.

    (2)   "Local legislative body" includes:

        (i)    A board of county commissioners;

        (ii)   A county council; or

        (iii)  A governing body of a municipal corporation.

(g)   "Local jurisdiction" means a county or municipal corporation and the territory within which its powers may be exercised.

(h)   (1) "Plan" means the policies, statements, goals, and

interrelated plans for private and public land use, transportation, and community facilities documented in texts and maps which constitute the guide for the area's future development.

    (2)   "Plan" includes a general plan, master plan, comprehensive plan, or community plan adopted in accordance with §§ 3.01 through 3.09 of this article.

(i)   "Regulation" means any rule of general applicability and future effect, including any map or plan.

(j)   "Sensitive areas" includes:

    (1)   Streams and their buffers;

    (2)   100-year flood plains;

    (3)   Habitats of threatened and endangered species;

    (4)   Steep slopes; and

    (2)   Other areas in need of special protection, as determined in the plan.

(k)   "Special exception" means a grant of a specific use that would not be appropriate generally or without restriction and shall be based upon a finding that certain conditions governing special exceptions as detailed in the zoning ordinance exist, that the use conforms to the plan and is compatible with the existing neighborhood.

(l)   (1) "Subdivision" means the division of a lot, tract, or parcel of land into two or more lots, plats, sites, or other divisions of land for the immediate or future purposes of selling the land or of building development.

    (2)   (i) "Subdivision" includes resubdivision.

          (ii)   As appropriate to the context, "subdivision" may include either the process of resubdividing or the land or territory resubdivided.

(m)   "Variance" means a modification only of density, bulk, or area requirements in the zoning ordinance that is:

(1)    Not contrary to the public interest; and

(2)    Specified by the local governing body in a zoning ordinance to avoid a literal enforcement of the ordinance that, because of conditions peculiar to the property and not any action taken by the applicant, would result in unnecessary hardship or practical difficulty.

## § 7.03  Article not applicable to chartered counties

(a)    If regulations adopted under this article require a greater width or size of yards, courts, or other open spaces, a lower height of building, a reduced number of stories, or a greater percentage of lot left unoccupied, or impose other higher standards than are required under any other statute, local ordinance, or regulations, the provisions of the regulations adopted under this article shall govern.

(b)    If the provisions of any other statute, local ordinance, or regulation require a greater width or size of yards, courts, or other open spaces, a lower height of building, a reduced number of stories, or a greater percentage of lot left unoccupied, or impose other higher standards than are required by the regulations adopted under this article, the provisions of the statute, local ordinance, or regulation shall govern.

(c)    (1) This subsection applies to the Maryland-Washington Regional District established under Chapter 992 of the Laws of Maryland of 1943, as amended.

(2)    Within the limits of the Maryland-Washington Regional District, in Montgomery and Prince George's counties where there is city and regional planning and zoning administered by local agencies, this article does not supplement Chapter 992 of the Laws of Maryland of 1943, as amended.

(3)    In the Maryland-Washington Regional District, the additional and supplemental powers vested by this article in a municipality or council may

not be considered vested in and may not be exercised by a county council acting as a district council under Chapter 992 of the Laws of Maryland of 1943, as amended.

(4) In the Maryland-Washington Regional District, the powers vested by this article in a planning commission or board of appeals may not be considered vested in and may not be exercised by the Maryland-National Capital Park and Planning Commission, the planning board, or the board of zoning appeals of the county affected.

(5) To the extent that the provisions of this article may be inconsistent with or contrary to the provisions of Chapter 992 of the Laws of Maryland of 1943, as amended, the provisions of this article do not apply within the Maryland-Washington Regional District.

(6) The provisions of this article do not affect the validity of Chapter 992 of the Laws of Maryland of 1943, as amended.

### § 13.01 Agreements

(a) (1) In this section the following words have the meanings indicated.

(2) "Agreement" means a development rights and responsibilities agreement.

(3) "Governing body" means the local legislative body, the local executive, or other elected governmental body that has zoning powers under this article.

(4) "Public principal" means the governmental entity of a local jurisdiction that has been granted the authority to enter agreements under subsection (b)(1) of this section.

(b) (1) Subject to subsections (c) through (l) of this section, the governing body of a local jurisdiction may:

(i) By ordinance, establish procedures and requirements for the consideration and execution of agreements; and

(ii) Delegate all or part of the authority established under the ordinance to a public principal within the jurisdiction of the governing body.

(2) The public principal may:

(i) Execute agreements for real property located within jurisdiction of the governing body with a person having a legal or equitable interest in the real property; and

(ii) Include a federal, State, or local government or unit as an additional party to the agreement.

(c) Before entering an agreement, a person having a legal or equitable interest in real property or the person's representative shall petition the public principal of the local jurisdiction in which the property is located.

(d) (1) After receiving a petition and before entering an agreement, the public principal shall conduct a public hearing.

(2) A public hearing that is required for approval of the development satisfies the public hearing requirements.

(e) The public principal of a local jurisdiction may not enter an agreement unless the planning commission of the local jurisdiction determines whether the proposed agreement is consistent with the plan of the local jurisdiction.

(f) (1) An agreement shall include:

(i) A legal description of the real property subject to the agreement;

(ii) The names of the persons having a legal or equitable interest in the real property subject to the agreement;

(iii) The duration of the agreement;

(iv) The permissible uses of the real property;

(v)    The density or intensity of use of the real property;

(vi)   The maximum height and size of structures to be located on the real property;

(vii)  A description of the permits required or already approved for the development of the real property;

(viii) A statement that the proposed development is consistent with the plan and development regulations of the local jurisdiction;

(ix)   A description of the conditions, terms, restrictions, or other requirements determined by the governing body of the local jurisdiction to be necessary to ensure the public health, safety, or welfare; and

(x)    To the extent applicable, provisions for the:

    1.   Dedication of a portion of the real property for public use;

    2.   Protection of sensitive areas;

    3.   Preservation and restoration of historic structures; and

    4.   Construction or financing of public facilities.

(2)   An agreement may:

(i)    Fix the time frame and terms for development and construction on the real property; and

(ii)   Provide for other matters consistent with this article.

(g)   An agreement shall be void 5 years after the day on which the parties execute the agreement unless:

(1)   Otherwise established under subsection (f)(1)(iii) or (2)(i) of this section; or

(2)   Extended by amendment under subsection (h) of this section.

(h) (1) Subject to paragraph (2) of this subsection and after a public hearing, the parties to an agreement may amend the agreement by mutual consent.

(2) Unless the planning commission of the local jurisdiction determines that the proposed amendment is consistent with the plan of the local jurisdiction, the parties may not amend an agreement.

(i) (1) The parties to an agreement may terminate the agreement by mutual consent.

(2) If the public principal or the governing body determines that suspension or termination is essential to ensure the public health, safety, or welfare, the public principal or its governing body may suspend or terminate an agreement after a public hearing.

(j) (1) Except as provided in paragraph (2) of this subsection, the laws, rules, regulations, and policies governing the use, density, or intensity of the real property subject to the agreement shall be the laws, rules, regulations, and policies in force at the time the parties execute the agreement.

(2) If the local jurisdiction determines that compliance with laws, rules, regulations, and policies enacted or adopted after the effective date of the agreement is essential to ensure the health, safety, or welfare of residents of all or part of the jurisdiction, an agreement may not prevent a local government from requiring a person to comply with those laws, rules, regulations, and policies.

(k) (1) An agreement that is not recorded in the land records office of the local jurisdiction within 20 days after the day on which the parties execute the agreement is void.

(2) The parties to an agreement and their successors in interest are bound to the agreement after the agreement is recorded.

(l) Unless the agreement is terminated under subsection

(i) of this section, the parties to an agreement or their successors in interest may enforce the agreement.

(m) This section does not require the adoption of an ordinance by a governing body or authorize a governing body to require a party to enter into an agreement.

## MINNESOTA VESTED RIGHTS STATUTE

### § 462.358 Procedure for plan effectuation; subdivision regulations

\* \* \*

**Subd. 3c Effect of subdivision approval.** For one year following preliminary approval and for two years following final approval, unless the subdivider and the municipality agree otherwise, no amendment to a comprehensive plan or official control shall apply to or affect the use, development density, lot size, lot layout, or dedication or platting required or permitted by the approved application. Thereafter, pursuant to its regulations, the municipality may extend the period by agreement with the subdivider and subject to all applicable performance conditions and requirements, or it may require submission of a new application unless substantial physical activity and investment has occurred in reasonable reliance on the approved application and the subdivider will suffer substantial financial damage as a consequence of a requirement to submit a new application. In connection with a subdivision involving planned and staged development, a municipality by resolution or agreement grants the rights referred to herein for such periods of time longer than two years which it determines to be reasonable and appropriate.

\* \* \*

## NEVADA DEVELOPMENT AGREEMENTS STATUTE

### § 278.0201 Agreement with governing body concerning development of land: Applicability of ordinances, resolutions and regulations adopted after agreement made; restrictions on subsequent action by governing body

1. In the manner prescribed by ordinance, a governing

body may, upon application of any person having a legal or equitable interest in land, enter into an agreement with that person concerning the development of that land. This agreement must describe the land which is the subject of the agreement and specify the duration of the agreement, the permitted uses of the land, the density or intensity of its use, the maximum height and size of the proposed buildings and any provisions for the dedication of any portion of the land for public use. The agreement may fix the period within which construction must commence and provide for an extension of that deadline.

2. Unless the agreement otherwise provides, the ordinances, resolutions or regulations applicable to that land and governing the permitted uses of that land, density and standards for design, improvements and construction are those in effect at the time the agreement is made.

3. This section does not prohibit the governing body from adopting new ordinances, resolutions or regulations applicable to that land which do not conflict with those ordinances, resolutions and regulations in effect at the time the agreement is made, except that any subsequent action by the governing body must not prevent the development of the land as set forth in the agreement. The governing body is not prohibited from denying or conditionally approving any other plan for development pursuant to any ordinance, resolution or regulation in effect at the time of that denial or approval.

4. The provisions of subsection 2 of NRS 278.315 and NRS 278.350 and 278.360 do not apply if an agreement entered into pursuant to this section contains provisions which are contrary to the respective sections.

### § 278.0205 Agreement with governing body concerning development of land: Amendment or cancellation; review of development by governing body; notice; approval of amendment; filing and recording of amendment

1.  The agreement for development of land may be amended or canceled, in whole or in part, by mutual consent of the parties to the agreement or their successors in interest, except that if the governing body determines, upon a review of the development of the land held at least once every 24 months, that the terms or conditions of the agreement are not being complied with, it may cancel or amend the agreement without the consent of the breaching party.

2.  Notice of intention to amend or cancel any portion of the agreement must be given by publication in a newspaper of general circulation in the applicable city or county. The governing body may approve any amendment to the agreement by ordinance if the amendment is consistent with the master plan. The original of the amendment must be filed for recording with the county recorder or the recorder of Carson City.

### § 278.0207 Agreement with governing body concerning development of land: Recording of certified copy of ordinance adopting agreement

A certified copy of any local ordinance adopting the agreement for the development of property and any amendments thereto must be recorded in the office of the county recorder or the recorder of Carson City.

## OREGON DEVELOPMENT AGREEMENTS STATUTE

### § 94.504 Development agreements; requirements; contents

(1)  A city or county may enter into a development agreement as provided in ORS § 94.504 to § 94.528 with any person having a legal or equitable interest in real property for the development of that property.

(2)  A development agreement shall specify:

(a)  The duration of the agreement, which may not exceed four years for a development of fewer than seven lots or seven years for a development of seven or more lots;

(b)  The permitted uses of the property;

(c)  The density or intensity of use;

(d)  The maximum height and size of proposed structures;

(e)  Provisions for reservation or dedication of land for public purposes;

(f)  A schedule of fees and charges;

(g)  A schedule and procedure for compliance review;

(h)  Responsibility for providing infrastructure and services;

(i)  The effect on the agreement when changes in regional policy or federal or state law or rules render compliance with the agreement impossible, unlawful or inconsistent with such laws, rules or policy;

(j)  Remedies available to the parties upon a breach of the agreement;

(k)  The extent to which the agreement is assignable; and

(l)  The effect on the applicability or implementation of the agreement when a city annexes all or part of the property subject to a development agreement.

(3)  A development agreement shall set forth all future discretionary approvals required for the development specified in the agreement and shall specify the conditions, terms, restrictions and requirements for those discretionary approvals.

(4)  A development agreement shall also provide that construction shall be commenced within a specified period of time and that the entire project or any phase of the project be completed by a specified time.

(5) A development agreement shall contain a provision that makes all city or county obligations to expend moneys under the development agreement contingent upon future appropriations as part of the local budget process. The development agreement shall further provide that nothing in the agreement requires a city or county to appropriate any such moneys.

(6) A development agreement must state the assumptions underlying the agreement that relate to the ability of the city or county to serve the development. The development agreement must also specify the procedures to be followed when there is a change in circumstances that affects compliance with the agreement.

### § 94.508 Approval by governing body; findings; adoption

(1) A development agreement shall not be approved by the governing body of a city or county unless the governing body finds that the agreement is consistent with local regulations then in place for the city or county.

(2) The governing body of a city or county shall approve a development agreement or amend a development agreement by adoption of an ordinance declaring approval or setting forth the amendments to the agreement. Notwithstanding ORS 197.015 (10)(b), the approval or amendment of a development agreement is a land use decision under ORS chapter 197.

### § 94.513 Procedures on consideration and approval

(1) A city or county may, by ordinance, establish procedures and requirements for the consideration of development agreements upon application by, or on behalf of, the owner of property on which development is sought or another person having a legal or equitable interest in that property.

(2) Approval of a development agreement requires compliance with local regulations and the approval of the city or county governing body after notice and hearing. The notice of the hearing shall, in addition

to any other requirements, state the time and place of the public hearing and contain a brief statement of the major terms of the proposed development agreement, including a description of the area within the city or county that will be affected by the proposed development agreement.

### § 94.518 Application of local government law and policies to agreement

Unless otherwise provided by the development agreement, the comprehensive plan, zoning ordinances and other rules and policies of the jurisdiction governing permitted uses of land, density and design applicable to the development of the property subject to a development agreement shall be the comprehensive plan and those ordinances, rules and policies of the jurisdiction in effect at the time of approval of the development agreement.

### § 94.522 Amendment or cancellation of agreement; enforceability

(1)   A development agreement may be amended or canceled by mutual consent of the parties to the agreement or their successors in interest. The governing body of a city or county shall amend or cancel a development agreement by adoption of an ordinance declaring cancellation of the agreement or setting forth the amendments to the agreement.

(2)   Until a development agreement is canceled under this section, the terms of the development agreement are enforceable by any party to the agreement.

### § 94.528 Recording

Not later than 10 days after the execution of a development agreement under ORS § 94.504 to § 94.528, the governing body of the city or county shall cause the development agreement to be presented for recording in the office of the county clerk of the county in which the property subject to the agreement is situated. In addition to other provisions required by ORS 94.504 to 94.528, the development agreement shall contain a legal description of the property subject to the agreement.

## SOUTH CAROLINA 1993 AGREEMENTS STATUTE

### § 6-31-10 Short title; legislative findings and intent; authorization for development agreements; provisions are supplemental to those extant

(A)   This chapter may be cited as the "South Carolina Local Government Development Agreement Act."

(B)   The General Assembly finds:

(1)   The lack of certainty in the approval of development can result in a waste of economic and land resources, can discourage sound capital improvement planning and financing, can cause the cost of housing and development to escalate, and can discourage commitment to comprehensive planning.

(2)   Assurance to a developer that upon receipt of its development permits it may proceed in accordance with existing laws and policies, subject to the conditions of a development agreement, strengthens the public planning process, encourages sound capital improvement planning and financing, assists in assuring there are adequate capital facilities for the development, encourages private participation in comprehensive planning, reduces the economic costs of development, allows for the orderly planning of public facilities and services, and allows for the equitable allocation of the cost of public services.

(3)   Because the development approval process involves the expenditure of considerable sums of money, predictability encourages the maximum efficient utilization of resources at the least economic cost to the public.

(4)   Public benefits derived from development agreements may include, but are not limited to, affordable housing, design standards, and on- and

off-site infrastructure and other improvements. These public benefits may be negotiated in return for the vesting of development rights for a specific period.

(5) Land planning and development involve review and action by multiple governmental agencies. The use of development agreements may facilitate the cooperation and coordination of the requirements and needs of the various governmental agencies having jurisdiction over land development.

(6) Development agreements will encourage the vesting of property rights by protecting such rights from the effect of subsequently enacted local legislation or from the effects of changing policies and procedures of local government agencies which may conflict with any term or provision of the development agreement or in any way hinder, restrict, or prevent the development of the project. Development agreements will provide a reasonable certainty as to the lawful requirements that must be met in protecting vested property rights, while maintaining the authority and duty of government to enforce laws and regulations which promote the public safety, health, and general welfare of the citizens of our State.

(C) It is the intent of the General Assembly to encourage a stronger commitment to comprehensive and capital facilities planning, ensure the provision of adequate public facilities for development, encourage the efficient use of resources, and reduce the economic cost of development.

(D) This intent is effected by authorizing the appropriate local governments and agencies to enter into development agreements with developers, subject to the procedures and requirements of this chapter.

(E) This chapter must be regarded as supplemental and additional to the powers conferred upon local governments and other government agencies by other laws and must not be regarded as in derogation of any powers existing on the effective date of this chapter.

## § 6-31-20 Definitions

As used in this chapter:

(1) "Comprehensive plan" means the master plan adopted pursuant to Sections 6-7-510, et seq., 5-23-490, et seq., or 4-27-600 and the official map adopted pursuant to Section 6-7-1210, et seq.

(2) "Developer" means a person, including a governmental agency or redevelopment authority created pursuant to the provisions of the Military Facilities Redevelopment Law, who intends to undertake any development and who has a legal or equitable interest in the property to be developed.

(3) "Development" means the planning for or carrying out of a building activity or mining operation, the making of a material change in the use or appearance of any structure or property, or the dividing of land into three or more parcels. "Development," as designated in a law or development permit, includes the planning for and all other activity customarily associated with it unless otherwise specified. When appropriate to the context, "development" refers to the planning for or the act of developing or to the result of development. Reference to a specific operation is not intended to mean that the operation or activity, when part of other operations or activities, is not development. Reference to particular operations is not intended to limit the generality of this item.

(4) "Development permit" includes a building permit, zoning permit, subdivision approval, rezoning certification, special exception, variance, or any other official action of local government having the effect of permitting the development of property.

(5) "Governing body" means the county council of a county, the city council of a municipality, the governing body of a consolidated political subdivision, or any

other chief governing body of a unit of local government, however designated.

(6) "Land development regulations" means ordinances and regulations enacted by the appropriate governing body for the regulation of any aspect of development and includes a local government zoning, rezoning, subdivision, building construction, or sign regulations or any other regulations controlling the development of property.

(7) "Laws" means all ordinances, resolutions, regulations, comprehensive plans, land development regulations, policies and rules adopted by a local government affecting the development of property and includes laws governing permitted uses of the property, governing density, and governing design, improvement, and construction standards and specifications, except as provided in Section 6-31-140(A).

(8) "Property" means all real property subject to land use regulation by a local government and includes the earth, water, and air, above, below, or on the surface, and includes any improvements or structures customarily regarded as a part of real property.

(9) "Local government" means any county, municipality, special district, or governmental entity of the State, county, municipality, or region established pursuant to law which exercises regulatory authority over, and grants development permits for land development or which provides public facilities.

(10) "Local planning commission" means any planning commission established pursuant to Sections 4-27-510, 5-23-410, or 6-7-320.

(11) "Person" means an individual, corporation, business or land trust, estate trust, partnership, association, two or more persons having a joint or common interest, state agency, or any legal entity.

(12) "Public facilities" means major capital improvements, including, but not limited to, transportation, sanitary sewer, solid waste, drainage, potable water, educa-

tional, parks and recreational, and health systems and facilities.

### § 6-31-30 Local governments authorized to enter into development agreements; approval of county or municipal governing body required

A local government may establish procedures and requirements, as provided in this chapter, to consider and enter into development agreements with developers. A development agreement must be approved by the governing body of a county or municipality by the adoption of an ordinance.

### § 6-31-40 Developed property must contain a certain number of acres of highland; permissible durations of agreements for differing amounts of highland content.

A local government may enter into a development agreement with a developer for the development of property as provided in this chapter provided the property contains twenty-five acres or more of highland. Development agreements involving property containing no more than two hundred fifty acres of highland shall be for a term not to exceed five years. Development agreements involving property containing one thousand acres or less of highland but more than two hundred fifty acres of highland shall be for a term not to exceed ten years. Development agreements involving property containing two thousand acres or less of highland but more than one thousand acres of highland shall be for a term not to exceed twenty years. Development agreements involving property containing more than two thousand acres and development agreements with a developer which is a redevelopment authority created pursuant to the provisions of the Military Facilities Redevelopment Law, regardless of the number of acres of property involved, may be for such term as the local government and developer shall elect.

### § 6-31-50 Public hearings; notice and publication

(a) Before entering into a development agreement, a local government shall conduct at least two public hearings. At the option of the governing body, the public hearing may be held by the local planning commission.

(b)

    (1)    Notice of intent to consider a development agreement must be advertised in a newspaper of general circulation in the county where the local government is located. If more than one hearing is to be held, the day, time, and place at which the second public hearing will be held must be announced at the first public hearing.

    (2)    The notice must specify the location of the property subject to the development agreement, the development uses proposed on the property, and must specify a place where a copy of the proposed development agreement can be obtained.

(c)    In the event that the development agreement provides that the local government shall provide certain public facilities, the development agreement shall provide that the delivery date of such public facilities will be tied to defined completion percentages or other defined performance standards to be met by the developer.

### § 6-31-60 What development agreement must provide; what it may provide; major modification requires public notice and hearing

(A)    A development agreement must include:

    (1)    a legal description of the property subject to the agreement and the names of its legal and equitable property owners;

    (2)    the duration of the agreement. However, the parties are not precluded from extending the termination date by mutual agreement or from entering into subsequent development agreements;

    (3)    the development uses permitted on the property, including population densities and building intensities and height;

(4)    a description of public facilities that will service the development, including who provides the facilities, the date any new public facilities, if needed, will be constructed, and a schedule to assure public facilities are available concurrent with the impacts of the development;

(5)    a description, where appropriate, of any reservation or dedication of land for public purposes and any provisions to protect environmentally sensitive property as may be required or permitted pursuant to laws in effect at the time of entering into the development agreement;

(6)    a description of all local development permits approved or needed to be approved for the development of the property together with a statement indicating that the failure of the agreement to address a particular permit, condition, term, or restriction does not relieve the developer of the necessity of complying with the law governing the permitting requirements, conditions, terms, or restrictions;

(7)    a finding that the development permitted or proposed is consistent with the local government's comprehensive plan and land development regulations;

(8)    a description of any conditions, terms, restrictions, or other requirements determined to be necessary by the local government for the public health, safety, or welfare of its citizens; and

(9)    a description, where appropriate, of any provisions for the preservation and restoration of historic structures.

(B)    A development agreement may provide that the entire development or any phase of it be commenced or completed within a specified period of time. The development agreement must provide a development schedule including commencement dates and interim completion dates at no greater than five year intervals; provided, however, the failure to meet a commencement or completion date shall not, in and of itself, constitute a material breach of the development agreement pursuant to Section 6-31-90, but must be judged based upon the totality of the circumstances. The development agreement may include other defined performance standards to be met by the developer. If the developer requests a modification in the dates as set forth in the agreement and is able to demonstrate and establish that there is good cause to modify those dates, those dates must be modified by the local government. A major modification of the agreement may occur only after public notice and a public hearing by the local government.

(C) If more than one local government is made party to an agreement, the agreement must specify which local government is responsible for the overall administration of the development agreement.

(D) The development agreement also may cover any other matter not inconsistent with this chapter not prohibited by law.

### § 6-31-70 Agreement and development must be consistent with local government comprehensive plan and land development regulations

A development agreement and authorized development must be consistent with the local government's comprehensive plan and land development regulations.

### § 6-31-80 Law in effect at time of agreement governs development; exceptions

(A) Subject to the provisions of Section 6-31-140 and unless otherwise provided by the development agreement, the laws applicable to development of the property subject to a development agreement, are those in force at the time of execution of the agreement.

(B) Subject to the provisions of Section 6-31-140, a local government may apply subsequently adopted laws to a development that is subject to a development agreement only if the local government has held a public hearing and determined:

(1) the laws are not in conflict with the laws governing the development agreement and do not prevent the development set forth in the development agreement;

(2) they are essential to the public health, safety, or welfare and the laws expressly state that they apply to a development that is subject to a development agreement;

(3) the laws are specifically anticipated and provided for in the development agreement;

(4) the local government demonstrates that substantial changes have occurred in pertinent conditions existing at the time of approval of the development agreement which changes, if not addressed by the local government, would pose a serious threat to the public health, safety, or welfare; or

(5) the development agreement is based on substantially and materially inaccurate information supplied by the developer.

(C) This section does not abrogate any rights preserved by Section 6-31-140 herein or that may vest pursuant to common law or otherwise in the absence of a development agreement.

### § 6-31-90 Periodic review to assess compliance with agreement; material breach by developer; notice of breach; cure of breach or modification or termination of agreement

(A) Procedures established pursuant to Section 6-31-40 must include a provision for requiring periodic review by the zoning administrator, or, if the local government has no zoning administrator, by an appropriate officer of the local government, at least every twelve months, at which time the developer must be required to demonstrate good faith compliance with the terms of the development agreement.

(B) If, as a result of a periodic review, the local government finds and determines that the developer has committed a material breach of the terms or conditions of the agreement, the local government shall serve notice in writing, within a reasonable time after the periodic review, upon the developer setting forth with reasonable particularity the nature of the breach and the evidence supporting the finding and determination, and providing the developer a reasonable time in which to cure the material breach.

(C) If the developer fails to cure the material breach within the time given, then the local government unilaterally may terminate or modify the development agreement, provided that the local government has first given the developer the opportunity:

(1) to rebut the finding and determination; or

(2) to consent to amend the development agreement to meet the concerns of the local government with respect to the findings and determinations.

### § 6-31-100 Amendment or cancellation of development agreement by mutual consent of parties or successors in interest

A development agreement may be amended or canceled by mutual consent of the parties to the agreement or by their successors in interest.

### § 6-31-110 Validity and duration of agreement entered into prior to incorporation or annexation of affected area; subsequent modification or suspension by municipality

(A) Except as otherwise provided in Section 6-31-130 and subject to the provisions of Section 6-31-140, if a newly incorporated municipality or newly annexed area comprises territory that was formerly unincorporated, any development agreement entered into by a local government before the effective date of the incorporation or annexation remains valid for the duration of the agreement, or eight years from the effective date of the incorporation or annexation, whichever is earlier. The parties to the development agreement and the municipality may agree that the development agreement remains valid for more than eight years, provided that the longer period may not exceed fifteen years from the effective date of the incorporation or annexation. The parties to the development agreement and the municipality have the same rights and obligations with respect to each other regarding matters addressed in the development agreement as if the property had remained in the unincorporated territory of the county.

(B)  After incorporation or annexation the municipality may modify or suspend the provisions of the development agreement if the municipality determines that the failure of the municipality to do so would place the residents of the territory subject to the development agreement, or the residents of the municipality, or both, in a condition dangerous to their health or safety, or both.

(C)  This section applies to any development agreement which meets all of the following:

(1)  the application for the development agreement is submitted to the local government operating within the unincorporated territory before the date that the first signature was affixed to the petition for incorporation or annexation or the adoption of an annexation resolution pursuant to Chapter 1 or 3 of Title 5; and

(2)  the local government operating within the unincorporated territory enters into the development agreement with the developer before the date of the election on the question of incorporation or annexation, or, in the case of an annexation, without an election before the date that the municipality orders the annexation.

### § 6-31-120 Developer to record agreement within fourteen days; burdens and benefits inure to successors in interest

Within fourteen days after a local government enters into a development agreement, the developer shall record the agreement with the register of mesne conveyance or clerk of court in the county where the property is located. The burdens of the development agreement are binding upon, and the benefits of the agreement shall inure to, all successors in interest to the parties to the agreement.

## § 6-31-130 Agreement to be modified or suspended to comply with later-enacted state or federal laws or regulations

In the event state or federal laws or regulations, enacted after a development agreement has been entered into, prevent or preclude compliance with one or more provisions of the development agreement, the provisions of the agreement must be modified or suspended as may be necessary to comply with the state or federal laws or regulations.

## § 6-31-140 Rights, duties, and privileges of gas and electricity suppliers, and of municipalities with respect to providing same, not affected; no extraterritorial powers

(A)    The provisions of this act are not intended nor may they be construed in any way to alter or amend in any way the rights, duties, and privileges of suppliers of electricity or natural gas or of municipalities with reference to the provision of electricity or gas service, including, but not limited to, the generation, transmission, distribution, or provision of electricity at wholesale, retail or in any other capacity.

(B)    This chapter is not intended to grant to local governments or agencies any authority over property lying beyond their corporate limits.

## § 6-31-145 Applicability to local government of constitutional and statutory procedures for approval of debt

In the event that any of the obligations of the local government in the development agreement constitute debt, the local government shall comply at the time of the obligation to incur such debt becomes enforceable against the local government with any applicable constitutional and statutory procedures for the approval of this debt.

## § 6-31-150 Invalidity of all or part of § 6-31-140 invalidates chapter

If Section 6-31-140 or any provision therein or the application of any provision therein is held invalid, the invalidity applies to this chapter in its entirety, to any and all provisions of the chapter, and the application of this chapter or any provision of this chapter, and to this end the provisions of Section 6-31-140 of this chapter are not severable.

## § 6-31-160 Agreement may not contravene or supersede building, housing, electrical, plumbing, or gas code; compliance with such code if subsequently enacted

Notwithstanding any other provision of law, a development agreement adopted pursuant to this chapter must comply with any building, housing, electrical, plumbing, and gas codes subsequently adopted by the governing body of a municipality or county as authorized by Chapter 9 of Title 6. Such development agreement may not include provisions which supersede or contravene the requirements of any building, housing, electrical, plumbing, and gas codes adopted by the governing body of a municipality or county.

## VIRGINIA DEVELOPMENT AGREEMENTS STATUTE

### § 15.2-2303.1 Development agreements in certain counties

A.  In order to promote the public health, safety and welfare and to encourage economic development consistent with careful planning, any county with a population between 10,300 and 11,000 according to the 1990 United States Census through which an interstate highway passes may include in its zoning ordinance provisions for the governing body to enter into binding development agreements with any persons owning legal or equitable interests in real property in the county if the property to be developed contains at least one thousand acres.

B.  Any such agreements shall be for the purpose of stimulating and facilitating economic growth in the county; shall not be inconsistent with the comprehensive plan at the time of the agreement's adoption, except as may have been authorized by existing zoning ordinances; and shall not authorize any use or condition inconsistent with the zoning ordinance or other ordinances in effect at the time the agreement is made, except as may be authorized by a variance, special exception or similar authorization. The agreement shall be authorized by ordinance, shall be for a term not to exceed fifteen years, and may be renewed by mutual agreement of the parties for successive terms of not more than ten years each. It may provide, among other things, for uses; the density or intensity of uses; the maximum height, size, setback and/or location of buildings; the number of parking spaces required; the location of streets and other public improvements; the measures required to control stormwater; the phasing or timing of construction or development; or any other land use matters. It may authorize the property owner to transfer to the county land, public improvements, money or anything of value to further the purposes of the agreement or other public purposes set forth in the county's comprehensive plan, but not as a condition to obtaining any permitted use or zoning. The development agreement shall not run with the land except to the extent provided therein, and the agreement may be amended or canceled in whole or in part by the mutual consent of the parties thereto or their successors in interest and assigns.

C.   If pursuant to the agreement, a property owner who is a party thereto and is not in breach thereof, (i) dedicates or is required to dedicate real property to the county, the Commonwealth or any other political subdivision or to the federal government or any agency thereof, (ii) makes or is required to make cash payments to the county, the Commonwealth or any other political subdivision or to the federal government or any agency thereof, or (iii) makes or is required to make public improvements for the county, the Commonwealth or any other political subdivision or for the federal government or any agency thereof, such dedication, payment or construction therefor shall vest the property owner's rights under the agreement. If a property owner's rights have vested, neither any amendment to the zoning map for the subject property nor any amendment to the text of the zoning ordinance with respect to the zoning district applicable to the property which eliminates or restricts, reduces, or modifies the use; the density or intensity of uses; the maximum height, size, setback or location of buildings; the number of parking spaces required; the location of streets and other public improvements; the measures required to control stormwater; the phasing or timing of construction or development; or any other land use or other matters provided for in such agreement shall be effective with respect to such property during the term of the agreement unless there has been a mistake, fraud or change in circumstances substantially affecting the public health, safety or welfare.

D. Nothing in this section shall be construed to preclude, limit or alter the vesting of rights in accordance with existing law; authorize the impairment of such rights; or invalidate any similar agreements entered into pursuant to existing law.

## WASHINGTON DEVELOPMENT AGREEMENTS STATUTE

### § 36.70B.170 Development agreements—Authorized

(1) A local government may enter into a development agreement with a person having ownership or control of real property within its jurisdiction. A city may enter into a development agreement for real property outside its boundaries as part of a proposed annexation or a service agreement. A development agreement must set forth the development standards and other provisions that shall apply to and govern and vest the development, use, and mitigation of the development of the real property for the duration specified in the agreement. A development agreement shall be consistent with applicable development regulations adopted by a local government planning under chapter 36.70A RCW.

(2) RCW 36.70B.170 through 36.70B.190 and section 501, chapter 347, Laws of 1995 do not affect the validity of a contract rezone, concomitant agreement, annexation agreement, or other agreement in existence on July 23, 1995, or adopted under separate authority, that

includes some or all of the development standards provided in subsection (3) of this section.

(3) For the purposes of this section, "development standards" includes, but is not limited to:

(a) Project elements such as permitted uses, residential densities, and nonresidential densities and intensities or building sizes;

(b) The amount and payment of impact fees imposed or agreed to in accordance with any applicable provisions of state law, any reimbursement provisions, other financial contributions by the property owner, inspection fees, or dedications;

(c) Mitigation measures, development conditions, and other requirements under chapter 43.21C RCW;

(d) Design standards such as maximum heights, setbacks, drainage and water quality requirements, landscaping, and other development features;

(e) Affordable housing;

(f) Parks and open space preservation;

(g) Phasing;

(h) Review procedures and standards for implementing decisions;

(i) A build-out or vesting period for applicable standards; and

(j) Any other appropriate development requirement or procedure.

(4) The execution of a development agreement is a proper exercise of county and city police power and contract authority. A development agreement may obligate a party to fund or provide services, infrastructure, or other facilities. A development agreement shall reserve authority to impose new or different regulations to the extent required by a serious threat to public health and safety.

## § 36.70B.180 Development agreements—Effect

Unless amended or terminated, a development agreement is enforceable during its term by a party to the agreement. A development agreement and the development standards in the agreement govern during the term of the agreement, or for all or that part of the build-out period specified in the agreement, and may not be subject to an amendment to a zoning ordinance or development standard or regulation or a new zoning ordinance or development standard or regulation adopted after the effective date of the agreement. A permit or approval issued by the county or city after the execution of the development agreement must be consistent with the development agreement.

## § 36.70B.190 Development agreements—Recording—Parties and successors bound

A development agreement shall be recorded with the real property records of the county in which the property is located. During the term of the development agreement, the agreement is binding on the parties and their successors, including a city that assumes jurisdiction through incorporation or annexation of the area covering the property covered by the development agreement.

## § 36.70B.200 Development agreements—Public hearing

A county or city shall only approve a development agreement by ordinance or resolution after a public hearing. The county or city legislative body or a planning commission, hearing examiner, or other body designated by the legislative body to conduct the public hearing may conduct the hearing. If the development agreement relates to a project permit application, the provisions of chapter 36.70C RCW shall apply to the appeal of the decision on the development agreement.

## § 36.70B.210 Development agreements—Authority to impose fees not extended

Nothing in RCW 36.70B.170 through 36.70.B.200 and section 501, chapter 347, Laws of 1995 is intended to authorize local governments to impose impact fees, inspection fees, or dedications or to require any other financial contributions or mitigation measures except as expressly authorized by other applicable provisions of state law.

---

# Table of Cases

References are to sections and footnotes.

References are to sections and footnotes.

**References are to sections and footnotes.**

Laurie v. Planning and Zoning Comm'n, 160 Conn. 295 (1971), **4.03, n7**

Lee v. Board of Adjustment, 37 S.E.2d 128 (N.C. 1946), **2.10, n50**

Lee v. Zoning Bd. of Appeals of Bethlehem, 505 N.Y.S.2d 235 (App. Div. 1986), **3.09, n46**

Lemir Realty Corp. v. Larkin, 181 N.E.2d 407 (N.Y. 1962), **3.04, n12**

Leroy Land Dev. v. Tahoe Regional Planning Agency, 939 F.2d 696 (9th Cir. 1991), **7.12, n92**

Lindell Co. v. Board of Permit Appeals, 144 P.2d 4 (Cal. 1943), **1.07, n57**

Lindquist, Appeal of, 73 A.2d 378 (Pa. 1950), **2.15, n73**

Lionel's Appliance Ctr., Inc. v. Citta, 383 A.2d 773 (N.J. Super Ct. Law Div. 1978), **5.03, ns16, 20; 5.05, n34**

Livingston v. Peterson, 228 N.W. 816 (N.D. 1930), **2.06, n12**

Long Island Lighting Co. v. Griffin, 74 N.Y.S.2d 348 (App. Div. 1947), *aff'd*, 297 N.Y. 897 (1947), **3.09, n29**

Loretto v. Teleprompter Manhattan CATV Corp., 458 U.S. 419 (1982), **1.08, ns65, 67, 68**

Louthan v. King County, 617 P.2d 977 (Wash. 1980), **1.07, n41**

Lucas v. South Carolina Coastal Council, 505 U.S. 1003, 112 S. Ct. 2886 (1992), **1.08, ns63, 64, 66, 67, 73-75**

Luger v. City of Burnsville, 295 N.W.2d 609 (Minn. 1980), **2.15, n75**

Lund v. City of Tumwater, 472 P.2d 550 (Wash. Ct. App. 1970), **6.08, n34**

Lutz v. City of Longview, 520 P.2d 1374 (Wash. 1974), **4.04, n15; 6.06, n29**

**M**

Manigault v. Springs, 199 U.S. 473 (1905), **7.05, n47**

Marantha Mining, Inc. v. Pierce Co., 802 P.2d 985 (Wash. Ct. App. 1990), **8.04, n23**

Marchi v. Scarborough, 511 A.2d 1071 (Me. 1986), **2.08, n37**

Marlowe v. Zoning Hearing Bd. of Haverford, 415 A.2d 946 (Pa. Commw. Ct. 1980), **2.09, n45**

Mason v. Zoning Bd. of Appeals, 422 N.Y.S.2d 166 (App. Div. 1979), **3.09, n27**

Mayor and City Council of Baltimore v. Crane, 352 A.2d 786 (Md. 1976), **7.10, n87**

McClurkan v. Board of Zoning Appeals, 565 S.W.2d 495 (Tenn. Ct. App. 1977), **2.11, n53**

Medinger, Appeal of, 104 A.2d 118 (Pa. 1954), **8.02, n8**

Members of City Council v. Taxpayers for Vincent, 466 U.S. 789 (1984), **8.01, n2; 8.09, n47**

Menges v. Jackson County Bd. of County Comm'rs, 606 P.2d 681 (Or. 1980), **1.07, n50; 1.11, n155**

Meredith v. Talbot County, 560 A.2d 599 (Md. 1989), **7.12, n91**

Merriam v. Moody's Executors, 25 Iowa 163 (1868), **8.04, n16**

New Burnham Prairie Homes, Inc. v. Village of Burnham, 910 F.2d 1474 (7th Cir. 1990), **1.11, n157**

New Castle Cty. Council v. BC Dev. Assocs., 567 A.2d 1271 (Del. 1989), **1.11, n156**

New York Life Insurance Co. v. Foley, 216 N.Y.S.2d 267 (N.Y. App. Div. 1961), **2.14, n71**

Nicholson v. Tourtelotte, 293 A.2d 909 (R.I. 1982), **7.03, n9**

Nick v. Planning & Zoning Comm'n of East Hampton, 503 A.2d 620 (Conn. App. Ct. 1986), **4.05, n18**

Nollan v. California Coastal Comm'n, 483 U.S. 825 (1987), **1.08, ns61, 69, 70-72; 1.09, ns78, 79; 7.10, n86; 7.12, ns93, 94**

North Hempstead v. Village of North Hills, 324 N.E.2d 566 (N.Y. 1975), **6.05, n17**

Northshore Steakhouse, Inc. v. Board of Appeals, 282 N.E.2d 606 (N.Y. 1972), **3.09, n28**

Nuckles v. Allen, 156 S.E.2d 633 (S.C. 1967), **2.09, n47**

Nunamaker v. Board of Zoning Appeals of Jerusalem Township, 443 N.E.2d 172 (Ohio 1982), **3.02, n5**

## O

Ogden v. Bellevue, 275 P.2d 899 (Wash. 1954), **1.10, n97**

O'Neill v. Philadelphia Zoning Bd. of Adjustment, 120 A.2d 901 (Pa. 1956), **2.12, n58**

Oregon City v. Hartke, 400 P.2d 255 (Or. 1965), **8.01, n3**

Osius v. City of St. Clair Shores, 75 N.W.2d 25 (Mich. 1956), **1.07, n43**

Otto v. Steinhilber, 24 N.E.2d 851 (N.Y. 1939), **2.07, ns15, 16, 29**

## P

Pace Resources, Inc. v. Shrewsbury Township Planning Comm'n, 492 A.2d 818 (Pa. 1985), **8.07, n45**

Pacesetter Homes, Inc. v. Village of Olympia Fields, 244 N.E.2d 369 (Ill. App. Ct. 1968), **1.04, ns18, 25, 26; 8.04, n34**

Packer v. Hornsby, 267 S.E.2d 140 (Va. 1980), **2.07, n18**

Parker v. Zoning Bd. of Review, 156 A.2d 210 (R.I. 1959), **2.15, n75**

Passaic, City of v. Paterson Bill Posting, Advertising & Sign Painting Co., 62 A. 267 (N.J. 1905), **8.02, n8**

Paucatuck Eastern Pequot Indians v. Indian Affairs Council, 555 A.2d 1003 (Conn. App. Ct. 1989), **4.05, n17**

Peachtree Dev. Co. v. Paul, 423 N.E.2d 1087 (Ohio 1981), **6.06, ns30, 31**

Pearl Inv. Co. v. City and County of San Francisco, No. 878-347, San Francisco Superior Court, **1.07, n58**

Pearl Inv. Co. v. City of San Francisco, 774 F.2d 1460 (9th Cir. 1985), *cert. denied*, 476 U.S. 1170 (1986), **1.07, n58**

Pearson v. City of Grand Blanc, 961 F.2d 1211 (6th Cir. 1991), **1.11, ns145, 147**

Triomphe Investors v. City of Norwood, 49 F.3d 198 (6th Cir. 1995), *cert. denied*, 116 S. Ct. 70 (1995), **1.11, ns124, 133**

Tripp v. Zoning Bd. of Review, 123 A.2d 144 (R.I. 1956), **2.10, n50**

Tri-State Generation & Transmission Co. v. City of Thornton, 647 P.2d 670 (Colo. 1982), **6.04, ns12, 13**

Tucker v. Township of May, 419 N.W.2d 836 (Minn. Ct. App. 1988), **2.09, n44**

Tullo v. Township of Millburn, 149 A.2d 620 (N.J. Super. Ct. 1959), **3.09, ns21, 32, 33**

Twigg v. Town of Kennebunk, 662 A.2d 914 (Me. 1995), **2.09, n44**

**U**

Union Nat'l Bank & Trust Co. v. Village of New Lenox, 505 N.E.2d 1 (Ill. App. 1987), **1.04, n13; 1.07, n56**

United States Trust Co. v. New Jersey, 431 U.S. 1 (1977), **7.05, ns49, 51**

**V**

Valleyview Civic Ass'n v. Zoning Bd. of Adjustment, 462, A.2d 637 (Pa. 1983), **2.07, ns20, 22**

Valley View Industrial Park v. City of Redmond, 733 P.2d 182 (Wash. 1987), **1.10, n103**

Value Oil Co. v. Town of Irvington, 377 A.2d 1225 (N.J. Super. Ct. Law Div. 1977), *aff'd*, 396 A.2d 1149 (N.J. Super. Ct. App. Div. 1978), **3.07, n17**

Vanguard Cellular Sys., Inc. v. Zoning Hearing Bd. of Smithfield Township, 568 A.2d 703 (Pa. Commw. Ct. 1989), **2.07, n34**

Vasilopoulos v. Zoning Bd. of Appeals, 340 N.E.2d 19 (Ill. 1975), **3.09, n40**

Vassallo v. Penn Row Ass'n, 429 A.2d 168 (Del. 1981), **2.07, n28**

Verona, Inc. v. Mayor & Council of West Caldwell, 229 A.2d 651 (N.J. 1967), **3.08, n20**

V.F. Zahodiakin Eng'g Corp. v. Zoning Bd. of Adjustment, 86 A.2d 127 (N.J. 1952), **7.03, n7**

Village of—see name of party

**W**

Wabash R.R. v. Defiance, 167 U.S. 88 (1897), **7.05, n46**

Wakelin v. Town of Yarmouth, 523 A.2d 575 (Me. 1987), **8.01, n1**

Walter v. Philadelphia Bd. of Adjustment, 263 A.2d 123 (Pa. 1970), **2.12, n61**

Walton v. Tracy Loan and Trust Co., 92 P.2d 724 (Utah 1939), **2.06, n12**

Waltz v. Town of Smithtown, 46 F.3d 162 (2d Cir. 1995), **1.11, n164**

Ward v. Village of Skokie, 186 N.E.2d 529 (Ill. 1962), **3.05, n17**

Warren, Town of v. Frost, 301 A.2d 572 (R.I. 1973), **2.13, n62**

Waterfront Estates Dev., Inc. v. City of Palos Hills, 597 N.E.2d 641 (Ill. App. 1992), **1.04, ns18, 30, 58**

Waterville Hotel Corp. v. Board of Zoning Appeals, 241 A.2d 50 (Me. 1968), **1.04, n8; 1.07, ns42, 43**

Webbs Fabulous Pharmacies v. Beckwith, 449 U.S. 155 (1980), **1.11, n142**

# Index

## K

**Krasnowiecki**
Generally, **1.03, 3.01, 7.03,
7.03[2][b], 7.04**

## L

**Land**
Variances running with the, **2.11**

**Landmarks**
Sign design review, compatibility with historic structures and styles, **8.09[3][c]**

**Landscaping**
Site plan review standards for, **5.08[6]**

**Language**
Legal problems with design review over vague, meaningless standards
Failure to use commonly understood terms, **8.04[3][a]**
Failure to use language that has practical application, **8.04[3][c]**
Failure to use precise language, **8.04[3][b]**
Practice tips on design review: illustrations and specific words explaining design principles, **8.11[2]**
Principles for drafting standards and guidelines for design review
Avoiding overly prescriptive language, **8.07[2][b]**
Detailed not visionary language, **8.07[2][a]**

**Lanham Act**
Sign design review, not in visual competition criterion, **8.09[3][b]**

**Legal authority**
*see* **Authority**

**Legal pronouncements**
Avoiding emphasis on, at hearing, variance practice tips, **2.16[9]**

**Legislative body**
Decision-making authority on special use permits reserved by, **3.05**
Limitation on legislative discretion, discretionary controls and, **1.10**
Substantive due process right, protection from arbitrary or capricious action by
Generally, **1.11[1]**
Clarification, issue needing, **1.11[4]**
Decisions
*see* **Decisions**
Definitions of arbitrary, varying courts', **1.11[3]**
Protected property interest, search for, **1.11[2]**
Undue legislative weight given to advisory recommendations, abuses of discretion and, **1.04[3]**

**Lighting**
Site plan review standards for, **5.08[4]**

**Limited discretion**
Under traditional zoning, **1.03**

**Loading**
Site plan review standards for, **5.08[2]**